Bottom Line's

Secret FOOD CURES

& Doctor-Approved Folk Remedies

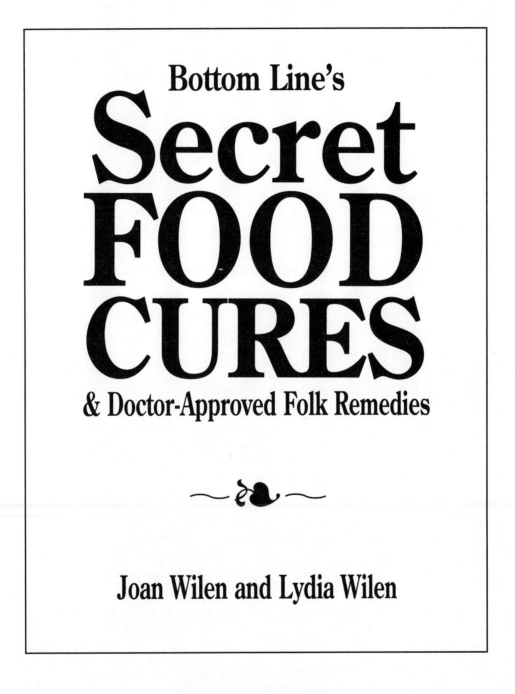

Joan Wilen and Lydia Wilen

Bottom Line Books

www.BottomLineSecrets.com

Bottom Line's Secret Food Cures & Doctor-Approved Folk Remedies
By Joan Wilen and Lydia Wilen

Adaptation © 2010 by Boardroom Inc.

Published by arrangement with Ballantine Books, an imprint of Random House Publishing Group, a division of Random House, Inc.

Remedies in this book adapted from:

Chicken Soup & Other Folk Remedies © 1984, 2000 by Joan Wilen and Lydia Wilen

More Chicken Soup & Other Folk Remedies © 1986, 2000 by Joan Wilen and Lydia Wilen

Deluxe, enhanced edition of *Bottom Line's Healing Remedies—Over 1,000 Astounding Ways to Heal Arthritis, Asthma, High Blood Pressure, Varicose Veins, Warts and More!*

10 9 8 7 6 5 4 3 2 1

ISBN 0–88723–605–7

Bottom Line Books® is a registered trademark of Boardroom® Inc.
281 Tresser Blvd., Stamford, CT 06901

Printed in the United States of America

Table of Contents

Acknowledgments x

A Word from the Authors xi

Introduction xii

Remedies for What Ails You A–Z (well, W)

Allergies and Hay Fever 3
   Allergy Relief.. 3
   Hay Fever Relief 4

Anemia 5
   Blood Fortifiers 5

Animal Encounters.................................. 6
   Animal Bites.. 6
   Insect Stings.. 6
   Other Stings 7
   Mosquito Bites 7
   Snakebites 8
   Spider Bites 9
   Tick Bites 9
   Skunk Spray 9

Arthritis.. 10
   Knowledge Is Power! 10
   Natural Remedies 10
   Topical Treatments for Relief............. 12

Asthma 16
   Worldly "Wisdom" 16
   Natural Remedies 17

Atherosclerosis 19
   Natural Remedies 19
   High Cholesterol Remedies 20

Back Pain... 23
   Healing Position................................... 23
   Natural Remedies 23
   Sciatica.. 24

Body Odor 25
   Dietary Remedies 25

Bruises and Skin Discoloration............ 27
   Bruises 27
   Brown Spots 28
   Dark Undereye Circles 28
   Black Eyes 28

Burns 29
   First-Degree Burns 30
   Second-Degree Burns.......................... 30
   Chemical and Acid Burns.................. 30
   Minor Burns 31

Carpal Tunnel Syndrome (CTS) 32
   Sleeping with CTS................................ 32
   Exercise for CTS Prevention.............. 32
   Herbs for CTS 33

Colds and Flu 35
   Hot Remedy for a Cold...................... 35
   Other Dietary Remedies 37
   Fight the Flu 40
   Fever Relievers 41
   Sore Throats 42
   Hoarseness/Laryngitis......................... 44
   Strep Throat 45
   Tonsillitis 45

Constipation.. 46
    Natural Remedies 46
Coughs 48
    Natural Remedies 48
    Types of Coughs 51
Depression and Stress 53
    Basic Solutions 53
    Dietary Remedies 53
    Other Mood Lifters 53
    Dietary Stress Relievers 54
    Nervous Tics 55
Diabetes 56
    Dietary Controls 56
Diarrhea 56
    Dietary Remedies 57
    Chronic Diarrhea 58
    Dysentery 59
Drinking Problems 59
    Dietary Remedies 59
    Sober Up 60
    Hangover Help 60
    Intoxication Prevention 62
Ear Problems 64
    Earaches 64
    Natural Remedies 64
    Ear Infections 65
    Ear Pressure 66
    Other Ear Problems 66
    Tinnitus (Ringing in the Ears) 67
    Hearing Loss 68
Emphysema 69
Eye Problems 69
    Bloodshot Eyes 69
    Cataracts 69
    Conjunctivitis (Pinkeye) 71
    Dry Eyes 71
    Eye Irritants 72
    Eye Inflammation 73
    Eye Puffiness 74
    Eyestrain/Tired Eyes 74
    Glaucoma 75
    Night Vision 76
    Sties 76
    Sun Blindness 77

    Eye Strengtheners 77
    Eyeglass Cleaners 79
    Eyewashes 79
Fainting 81
    Natural Remedies 81
Fatigue 81
    Natural Remedies 81
    Energy Boosters 82
Foot and Leg Problems 84
    Aching Feet 84
    Corns and Calluses 85
    Cold Feet 86
    Athlete's Foot 87
    Ingrown Toenails 87
    Pigeon Toes 88
    Cracked Heels 88
    Sweaty Feet 88
    Numb Toes 88
    Varicose Veins 88
    Natural Remedies 89
    Phlebitis 89
    Natural Remedies 90
    Weak Ankles 90
Frostbite/Frostnip 91
Gallbladder Problems 92
    Natural Remedies 92
Gout 92
    Best Remedy 92
    Other Remedies 93
Hair Problems 94
    Stopping Hair Loss/Promoting
        Hair Growth 94
    Natural Remedies 95
    Remedies for Bad-Hair Days 96
    Hair Revitalizers 97
    Green Hair 98
    "Natural" Hair Coloring 98
    Setting Lotions 100
    Helpful Hair Hints 100
Hand and Nail Problems 101
    Rough Hands 101
    Clammy Hands 102
    Fingernail Remedies 102

Headaches 103
   Natural Remedies 103
   Migraine Headaches 107
   Headache Prevention...Sort of........ 109
Heart Problems 109
   Heart Attack 109
   Heart Palpitations..................... 109
   Heart Helpers 110
Hemorrhoids 112
   Natural Remedies 113
   Hemorrhoid Prevention 114
Herpes 114
   Dietary Remedy 114
   Cold Sores and Fever Blisters 115
   Shingles 115
Hiccups 116
   Natural Remedies 116
Hypertension 118
   If Your Blood Pressure Is High... 119
   If Your Blood Pressure Is Low... 121
Indigestion 122
   Natural Remedies 122
   Indigestion Prevention 124
   Gas/Flatulence........................ 125
   Heartburn............................. 127
   Heartburn Prevention 128
   Stomach Cramps 128
Jet Lag 129
   Natural Remedies 129
Memory Problems 131
   Natural Remedies 131
Muscle Aches 133
   Charley Horse 133
   Neck Tension 133
   Stiff Neck 134
   Whiplash.............................. 134
   Leg Cramps 134
Nausea and Vomiting 137
   Natural Remedies 137
   Motion Sickness 138
   Seasickness............................ 139
Neuralgia 139
   Natural Remedies 140

Nosebleeds 140
   Natural Remedies 140
   Nosebleed Prevention................. 141
Rashes and Itchy Skin 142
   Eczema................................ 142
   Psoriasis 142
   Pruritis and Hives 143
   Genital Itching 144
   Rectal Itching......................... 144
   Heat Rash (Prickly Heat)............. 145
   Shaving Rash 145
   Ringworm 145
   Seborrhea 145
   Poison Ivy 146
Sexual Problems 148
   Natural Remedies 148
   Aphrodisiacs.......................... 150
Sinus Problems 152
   Natural Remedies 152
   Sinus Headaches...................... 153
Skin Problems 153
   Acne.................................. 153
   Acne Scars............................ 155
   Blackheads 155
   Dead Skin and Enlarged Pores......... 155
   Wounds and Sores 156
   Boils 156
   Dry Elbows and Knees 158
   Freckles............................... 158
   Cuts and Scrapes 158
   Scars.................................. 159
   Splinters 159
   Stretch Marks 159
   Wrinkles.............................. 160
Sleep Problems 161
   Insomnia 161
   Nightmares............................ 165
   Sleepwalking 166
   Snoring/Sleep Apnea 166
Smoking 167
   Stop Smoking...Seriously 167
   Natural Ways to Help You Quit 168

Sprains and Strains 171
    Treating Sprains 171
    Natural Remedies 171
Sunburn 172
    Soothing the Burn 173
    Sunburned Eyes and Eyelids 173
Tension and Anxiety 175
    Natural Remedies 175
    Stage Fright 177
Tooth and Mouth Problems 178
    Tooth Problems 178
    Preparing for Dental Work 180
    Tooth Extractions 180
    Gum Problems 181
    Cavity Prevention 182
    Halitosis (Bad Breath) 183
    Canker Sores 185
Ulcers 186
    Dietary Remedies 186
Urinary Problems 187
    Natural Remedies 187
    Bed-Wetting and Nighttime
        Urination 188
    Incontinence 189
    Kidney Problems 190
Warts 192
    Natural Remedies 192
    Plantar Warts 193
Weight Problems 193
    Weight Control Tips...................... 194
    Ancient Slimming Herbs................. 194
    Other Slimming Remedies.............. 196
    Healthy Snacks........................... 198
    Slowly, but Surely....................... 199
    Cellulite Eliminator...................... 200
    Rev Up Your Metabolism................ 200
    Holiday Challenges 201
    Determining Your Weight/Health
        Profile 202
    Body Mass Index Chart 203
Healing Remedies for Children.......... 207
    Safety First............................... 207
    Acne...................................... 207

Attention Deficit/Hyperactivity
    Disorder (ADHD) 208
Bed-Wetting 208
Chicken Pox................................ 209
Eye Irritants 209
Colds and Flu 209
Coughs...................................... 209
Croup 210
Diarrhea 210
Fever.. 211
Foreign Substance in the Nose 211
Head Lice 211
Indigestion, Colic and Gas 212
Picky Eaters 213
Rashes 213
Splinters.................................... 213
Teething 214
Tonsillitis 214
Healing Remedies for Men 217
    Prostate Enlargement 217
    Impotence (Erectile Dysfunction) ... 218
Healing Remedies for Women 225
    Bladder Control........................... 225
    Cystitis..................................... 225
    Lack of Desire 226
    Vaginitis (Vaginal Infections) 227
    Menstruation.............................. 227
    Pregnancy.................................. 230
    Menopause 231
Remedies for Natural Beauty............ 235
    Skin Care 235
    Basic Skin Care 235
    Firming Facial............................. 236
    Make Your Own Beauty Mask.......... 236
    Skin-Awakener Formula 236
    Skin Toner................................. 236
    Caring for Oily Skin..................... 237
    Caring for Dry Skin...................... 237
    Caring for Combination Skin 238
    Exfoliation Scrub 239
    Make Your Own Body Scrub............ 239
    Grooming................................... 239
    Enrich Your Night Cream................ 239

Magical Face Relaxer........................ 239
Double-Chin Prevention................... 239
Toweling Off 239
Chapped Lips 239
Pleasing Tweezing 240
Fingernail How-to 240
Matchbook Method 240
Polish Primer 240
Manicure Protection........................ 240
General Tips.................................... 240
Paint Remover for Skin 240
Pain-Free Bandage Remover 240
Mirror, Mirror in the Bathroom....... 240
Perfume Pick-Me-Up........................ 240

Remedies in a Class by Themselves .. 243
Kiss of Life...................................... 243
Exercise Your Lung Power............... 243
Yawn All the Way............................ 243
Confessions...Good for the
      Immune System........................ 244
Success Through Napping 244
Practice Preventive Medicine:
      Laugh!...................................... 244
Have a Good Cry............................. 244
Calcium Concern 245
Give Healing Orders........................ 245
The Ultimate Remedy...................... 245

Preparation Guide.............................. 249
Barley... 249
Coconut Milk.................................. 249
Eyewash 249
Garlic Juice 250
Ginger Tea...................................... 250
Herbal Bath 250
Herbal Tea 250
Onions 251
Pomanders 251
Potatoes 251
Poultices 252
Sauerkraut...................................... 252

Six Sensational Superfoods 257
Decisions, Decisions........................ 257

Expand Your Healthy Horizons 258
1. Bee Pollen 258
2. Flaxseed 262
3. Garlic 266
4. Ginger 270
5. Nuts 274
6. Yogurt.. 280

Amazing, Super-Duper
Facts and Advice 287
Think Positive, Live Longer 287
The Full Moon Boom 287
The "Rest" of the Story 287
Doctor's Fee 288
Fever: Friend or Foe?...................... 288
Freshen Up a Sickroom 288
Prescription Reading Made Easy 288
How to Take Pills...Really............... 288
Coming to Your Senses.................... 289
Dropper in a Pinch......................... 289
Do-It-Yourself Hot-Water
      Bottle and Ice Pack 289
A Fishy Story 289
Good Health, Italian-Style............... 290
Save Vitamins in the Microwave...... 290
Lettuce: Choose Dark Green 290
Moldy Food..................................... 290
Herb and Spice Storage 290
Remove Pesticides from
      Fruits and Vegetables 290
Sweet and Salty Substitutes 291
Working with Onions
      Tearlessly...Almost................... 291
Unhand Those Garlic and
      Onion Odors 291
Hold on to Your Pantyhose............. 291
Natural Insect Repellents 291
Natural Air Cleaners 292
Deodorizing Food Jars..................... 292
Salt Rub for Gas Odors................... 292
Stuffed Toys on Ice......................... 293
Cradling Baby................................. 293
Bathing Made Easy 293

Sources 297
    Herbal Products and More 297
    Gems, New-Age Products
        and Gifts 298
    Vitamins, Nutritional Supplements
        and More 298
    Natural Foods and More 299
    Bee Products and More 299
    Pet Food and Products 299
    Health-Related Products 300
    Health-Related Travel Products
        and More 300
    Wholesale/Retail Health
        Appliances 300
    Aromatherapy, Flower Essences
        and More 300
    Services 300

Health Resources 305
    Organizations, Associations and
        Journals 306
    Online-Only Resources 314
Recommended Reading List 319
    Body Power/Brain Power 319
    Food, Healthful Eating and
        Weight Programs 319
    Herbs 319
    Just for Men 319
    Just for Women 320
    Just for Pets 320
    New-Age and Age-Old (Mostly
        Alternative) Therapies 320
    Specific Health Challenges 320
    Vitamins and Other Supplements 320
Recipe Index 321
Index 323

Dedication

Bottom Line's Secret Food Cures &
Doctor-Approved Folk Remedies
is dedicated to the loving memory of our parents,
Lillian and Jack Wilen.

■

Acknowledgments

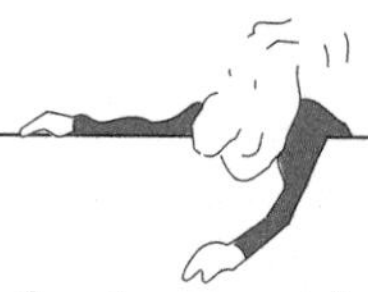

We give a **big thanks** to all the people who offered their loving support, good wishes and—of course—their wonderful healing remedies.

♦ Our **heartfelt thanks** to Ray C. Wunderlich, Jr., MD, PhD, who reviewed every remedy in this book, with your well-being in mind. Many of the "NOTE"s, "WARNING"s and "CAUTION"s found throughout these pages are a reflection of the good doctor's fastidious scrutiny. We feel blessed to know this healer, teacher and the only other person in our time zone who is awake if we call him with a question at 2:00 am.

♦ **Very special thanks** to Marty Edelston—the founder, publisher and resident genius of Boardroom Inc. and its Bottom Line Books division—for being so very special.

We're thrilled to be Boardroom authors and lucky to work with Marty's great Boardroom team, including the incomparable Brian Kurtz, our wonderful editors, Karen Daly and Amy Linkov, and the many people affiliated with Boardroom whose expertise and caring made this book possible. We'll list their names here, and give sincere thanks to each one for his or her contribution.

Marjory Abrams
Tom Dillon
Polly Stewart Fritch
Carolyn Gangi
Terri Kazin
Sandy Krolick
John Niccolls
Rich O'Brien, MD
Paula Parker
Kathi Ramsdell
Ken Sevey
Rebecca Shannonhouse
Jennifer Souder
Carmen Suarez
Melissa Virrill
Alexandra White
Michele Wolk
Phillis Womble

And the brilliant Arthur P. Johnson for working his magic. If there's anyone we inadvertently overlooked—well, we thank you, too! ■

A Word from the Authors

Human beings have been consulting healers for thousands of years. Whether it's a medicine man, shaman, naturopath, physician or some other type of health expert, what goes around seems to come around. *Consider this timeline...*

	"Doctor, I have a sore throat."
2000 BC	"Here, eat this root."
1000 BC	"That root is heathen. Say this prayer."
1850 AD	"That prayer is superstition. Drink this potion."
1940 AD	"That potion is snake oil. Swallow this pill."
1980 AD	"That pill is artificial and ineffective. Take this antibiotic."
2000 AD	"That antibiotic is artificial, causes side effects and you've built an immunity to it. Take this root!"

And so we've gone back to our roots. Being city dwellers, we get our roots at herb shops and health food stores. Actually, that's not all we get there. We also take advantage of modern-day technology, and buy vitamins and supplements that are commercially manufactured. You'll notice that, along with the classic folk remedies included in this book, we've added new remedies that may have you going to the health food store!

In this millennium, we've come to realize that we have lots of choices when it comes to health care. It shouldn't be a matter of *alternative medicine* vs. *allopathic medicine*. *Integrative medicine* combines traditional practices with alternative health treatments. Learn your options and, with the supervision of your health professional, take the best of both.

—Joan & Lydia ■

Introduction

Our experience with natural remedies goes back to our childhood. When we were growing up in Brooklyn, New York, each winter our mom would crochet little drawstring bags and our dad would make sure they were filled with camphor, which he then insisted we wear around our necks. It wasn't a fashion statement on our dad's part—he believed this would prevent us from catching colds. Of course, we reeked so from the camphor that none of our friends would come near us. And, as a result, we didn't catch their colds. So Daddy was right.

That camphor was our introduction to natural remedies…along with honey and lemon for a sore throat, sugar water for the hiccups, horseradish to clear the sinuses, garlic for a whole bunch of things—and chicken soup for everything else.

Our mom made the world's best chicken soup…when she wasn't crocheting little drawstring bags for the camphor. In fact, her soup recipe is in this book (*see* page 35). We have also included a very potent chicken soup recipe from a doctor (*see* page 36). How potent is it? It's so potent that the dosage is to take only two tablespoons at a time.

When we first started doing research for this book, we went to all our relatives and friends to ask for their home remedies. We heard wonderful "old country" stories about remarkable cures, but the times we live in are so different, and the world has changed dramatically. For example, who could have imagined that extra-virgin coconut oil could be used to treat diabetes? (For more details, *see* page 56.) And we knew we wanted the remedies in this book to be safe and effective, yet practical.

Yes, PRACTICAL! Every fruit, vegetable, herb, vitamin, mineral and liquid—in fact, all the ingredients mentioned in this book—can be found at your local health food store, supermarket, greengrocer or on the Internet—that is, if they aren't already in your home.

Most of the remedies in this book require only a few ingredients, and some require nothing more than your concentration or stimulating an acupressure point. Our directions are easy to follow and specific. However, if an exact amount or measurement is not indicated, then we could not verify it, but we felt that the remedy was effective enough to include.

OK, we've covered the practical aspects of this book…now for EFFECTIVE—do the remedies work? Yes! No one passes along or shares a remedy that doesn't work. Of course, we realize that not every remedy will work for every person. But these remedies are easy to use, inexpensive and have no side effects. In other words, while they may not always help —they certainly wouldn't hurt. *Which brings us to a very important point…*

Several esteemed medical doctors have reviewed each remedy in the book and deemed them SAFE. But you have to do your part for your own well-being—please consult a health professional whom you trust before trying any self-help treatment, including the remedies contained in this book.

Also, if you are pregnant or nursing, have any allergies and/or food sensitivities, or have been diagnosed with any serious illness or chronic condition—please!—talk to your physician, nurse/midwife, dentist, naturopath or other health specialist before trying any of these remedies. And keep in mind that most of these remedies are NOT meant for children. Please see "Healing Remedies for Children" (*see* page 207) for healing suggestions suitable for the wee ones in your life.

Please heed the "NOTE"s, "WARNING"s and "CAUTION"s found throughout the book. They stress the fact that our home-remedy suggestions are scientifically unproven and should not take the place of professional medical evaluation and treatment. Some remedies can be dangerous for people who are taking prescription medication or who suffer from a specific illness or condition.

Effective, proven, traditional health care is available for almost all of the conditions mentioned in this book. You may need to see a physician for certain ailments and/or persistent symptoms. These natural remedies should be used in addition to—but *never* as a substitute for—professional medical help.

One more thing…be sure to check out the "Six Sensational Superfoods" section beginning on page 257. These extraordinary foods have the power to help protect, improve, save and extend people's lives.

To find the most beneficial and tastiest ways to eat these foods, we did a lot of research and experimenting. We soaked, scrubbed, grated, minced, diced, spiced, blended, boiled, whipped, whisked, powdered, peeled, cooked, baked, roasted, toasted and tested…and came up with simple suggestions for incorporating these foods into your daily diet. (However, we have not personally kitchen-tested all of the recipes included in this book. We selected ones that we believed to be simple, healthful and delicious. We hope you enjoy them.)

Please know that we do not have formal medical training and we are not prescribing treatment. We're writers who are reporting what has worked for many generations of people who have shared their remedies with us. For your own safety, please consult your doctor before trying any self-help treatment or natural remedy.

Thank you for reading our book, and— every good wish for your good health!

The Wilen Sisters
Joan & Lydia ■

Remedies for What Ails You
A–Z
(*well*, W)

Remedies

ALLERGIES AND HAY FEVER

If you have a runny nose, sore throat and/or itchy eyes, you may be suffering from seasonal allergies. This type of allergy occurs when your body overreacts to pollen from trees or weeds, and sometimes household dust or mold. Hay fever is one variety of this type of allergy.

In addition, there is allergic asthma, conjunctivitis, hives, eczema, dermatitis and sinusitis as well as food allergies, latex allergies, insect-sting allergies and drug allergies. (We feel itchy just reading that list!)

There are almost as many different types of allergies as there are people who have them! Obviously, allergies need to be handled on an individual basis. We found a number of remedies that just may help people who suffer from seasonal allergies or hay fever. But—especially if you have allergies—be sure to check with your doctor first.

Allergy Relief

▶It is said that there are chemicals in bananas that repel allergies—that is, unless you're allergic to bananas. If not, eat a banana daily.

▶Vitamin-rich watercress is said to be an anti-allergen. Eat it in salads, sandwiches and sauces. It's potent stuff, so eat small portions at a time.

Allergy Prevention

▶We were told that licorice root (the herb, not the candy) helps build up an immunity to allergens. Add 3 ounces of cut licorice root (available at health food stores) to 1 quart of water. Boil it for 10 minutes in an enamel or glass pot, then strain into a bottle.

Dose: Take 1 tablespoon before each meal, every other day until you've taken the licorice-root water for six days. By then, we hope, it will make a difference in terms of your resistance to allergies.

CAUTION: Do not take licorice root if you have high blood pressure or kidney problems. It can cause renal failure.

3

Be Careful What You Crave

We met a woman who has a severe, life-threatening almond allergy. Her mother had eaten marzipan on a regular basis throughout her 9-month pregnancy, and marzipan is made of almonds. An allergy specialist later told the woman that it's not uncommon for a child to be allergic to a food that the mother craved and ate lots of for months at a time during her pregnancy.

Hay Fever Relief

▶ Several studies have shown that bioflavonoids—substances from plants that help maintain cellular health—help the body utilize vitamin C more effectively.

After the morning and evening meals, take one pantothenic acid tablet (50 milligrams [mg]) and one vitamin C tablet (500 mg) along with a bioflavonoid—a grapefruit, orange, a few strawberries, grapes or prunes. If you don't want the whole fruit, take a teaspoon of grated orange or lemon peel sweetened with a little honey. This remedy has been said to have brought relief to many hay fever sufferers.

Hay Fever Prevention

▶ The US Army tested honeycomb as a desensitizing and antiallergenic substance for hay fever. Their results were very encouraging, especially those from subjects who chewed the honeycomb.

Start this regime about two months before hay fever season. By the time the season rolls around, the honeycomb may have helped you build an immunity to the pollen in your area. (You can also chew a bite-sized chunk of honeycomb at the start of a hay fever attack.)

It's important to find a beekeeper in your vicinity and get local honeycomb. For prevention, chew a 1-inch square of it twice a day. The honey is delicious, and the comb part turns into a ball of wax. Chew the wax for about 10 to 15 minutes, then spit it out.

If you don't have access to a local beekeeper, look for honeycomb at your neighborhood health food store. Hopefully, it's from your neck of the woods.

CAUTION: People who are allergic to bee stings or honey should consult a doctor before chewing honeycomb.

▶ Starting three months before hay fever season, drink 1 cup of fenugreek-seed tea each day. The tea is available at health food stores. This remedy goes back to the ancient Egyptians and forward to Armenian mountaineers who drink 1 cup of fenugreek tea before each meal to clear and stimulate their senses of smell and taste.

ANEMIA

Blood is an extremely complex substance that consists of a variety of liquid and solid elements, including red blood cells, white cells and platelets.

The average adult has between 5 and 6 quarts of blood circulating through his/her body by way of the blood vessels.

Anemia is a condition in which the blood lacks iron, which reduces the blood's ability to carry oxygen. This may make a person feel weak and listless.

To combat anemia, it's important to increase your consumption of iron-rich foods (like beef or spinach) and supplement with B vitamins and minerals like copper.

To help circulation as well as purification of the blood and aid in elimination of iron-deficiency anemia, we offer suggestions *with* the suggestion that you *first* have appropriate professional blood tests performed. And always consult with a physician before embarking on any self-help program.

▶ Grape juice (no sugar or preservatives added) is a wonderful source of iron. Drink 8 ounces every day.

▶ Eat raw spinach salads often. Be sure to wash the spinach thoroughly to reduce the risk of food-borne illness. Combine any of the following in your spinach salad—watercress, radish, kohlrabi, garlic, chives, leek and onion. They're all high in iron.

▶ Every morning after breakfast and every evening after dinner, eat two dried apricots.

▶ Snack on raisins.

NOTE: In the case of a serious iron deficiency, you may require more iron than you can possibly get from any or all of these remedies. We suggest you seek help from a health professional.

Blood Fortifiers

▶ Raw (not canned) sauerkraut is said to do a super job of fortifying the blood. It also helps rejuvenate the body in other ways. Eat 2 to 4 tablespoons a day, right after a meal. (Raw sauerkraut can be found at health food stores, or *see* the "Preparation Guide" on page 252 and learn to make your own sauerkraut.)

▶ **Check with your medical adviser before going on this one-day fast!** Combine 2 tablespoons of lemon, 1 tablespoon of honey and a cup of warm water.

Dose: Every two hours, from morning until two hours before bedtime, take 2 tablespoons of the mixture. No food throughout the day, just the lemon/honey/water mixture.

▶ Raw (not cooked or canned) pumpkin pulp and squash are said to have purifying properties. Eat them in salads.

▶ When they're in season, a peach a day helps wash toxins away.

▶ Garlic is said to help thin and fortify the blood. Eat raw garlic and/or take garlic supplements daily.

CAUTION: Do not eat garlic or take garlic supplements if you have a bleeding disorder or ulcers, or are taking anticoagulants.

▶ Drink fresh carrot juice as often as once a day if you have access to a juicer, or eat raw carrots. They contain calcium, potassium, phosphorus and vitamins A, B$_1$, B$_2$ and C.

ANIMAL ENCOUNTERS

This section deals with remedies for a variety of animal bites (from spiders, jellyfish, Portuguese man-of-wars, hairy caterpillars, dogs and snakes) as well as insect stings (from bees, wasps, hornets, yellow jackets and mosquitoes).

CAUTION: If you have a history of allergies to stinging insects, have a physician-prescribed emergency sting kit on hand at all times!

Everyone knows that to avoid disease from biting insects and animals, you shouldn't bite any insects or animals! If they bite you, try these practical and effective suggestions.

▶ A paste made with water and baking soda can help draw out the heat of a sting, reduce the redness, inhibit the swelling and take the itch out of a bite. Every half-hour, alternate the baking soda paste with ice on the stung or bitten area.

▶ Wheat germ oil also helps soothe a sting. Every half-hour, alternate the wheat germ oil with ice on the stung area.

Animal Bites

An animal bite—even from your own pet dog, cat, hamster, guinea pig, ferret or parakeet—could be dangerous. If the bite breaks the skin, bacteria in the animal's saliva can cause infection.

First, wash the bitten area thoroughly with soap and water. Then apply pressure to stop the bleeding. Cover the wound loosely with a sterile bandage.

WARNING: If an animal bite breaks the skin, doesn't stop bleeding, or if it puffs up or is red and painful, get medical attention immediately. You will need antibiotics and possibly a tetanus shot.

Insect Stings

When an insect stings, its stinger usually remains in the skin while the insect flies away. However, if the insect stays attached to its stinger in your skin, flick it off with your thumb and forefinger. *Do not squeeze the insect*—not that anyone would want to do that.

Remove the stinger, but *do not* use your fingers or tweezers. Those methods can pump more poison into the skin. Instead, gently and carefully scrape the stinger out with the tip of a sharp knife. You can even use the edge of a credit card.

Kitchen Cupboard Soothers

▶ To relieve the pain and keep down the swelling of a sting, apply any one of the following for a half-hour, then alternate it with a half-hour of ice around the stung area...

- ◆ A slice of raw onion
- ◆ A slice of raw potato
- ◆ Grated or sliced horseradish root
- ◆ Wet salt
- ◆ Commercial toothpaste
- ◆ Wet, clean mud is one of the oldest and most practical remedies for stings.

If you haven't already removed the stinger, peeling off the dry mud will help draw it out.

- Vinegar and lemon juice—equal parts —dabbed on every five minutes until the pain disappears

- Diluted ammonia

- ⅓ teaspoon of (unseasoned) meat tenderizer dissolved in 1 teaspoon of water. One of the main ingredients in meat tenderizer is papain, an enzyme from papaya that relieves the pain and inflammation of a sting as well as lessens allergic reaction. *Use meat tenderizer only if you are MSG-allergy-free.*

- Oil squeezed from a vitamin E capsule

- A clump of wet tobacco (but don't tell the US Surgeon General or you'll have to print a warning on your arm)

- A drop of honey, preferably honey from the hive of the bee that did the stinging (of course, that's not too likely unless you're a beekeeper)

CAUTION: Do not put any foreign substance (mud, tobacco, ammonia, etc.) directly on broken skin. It could cause an infection that is *much* worse than the sting!

Other Stings

▶ If you are stung by a jellyfish, Portuguese man-of-war or hairy caterpillar, apply olive oil for fast relief...then seek medical attention immediately.

Mosquito Bites

WARNING: Mosquitoes can transmit the West Nile virus and other serious diseases, which can be serious and potentially fatal. Be sure to use mosquito repellent, wear long sleeves and pants when outdoors, eliminate mosquito breeding sites near your house, and repair any broken window and door screens.

▶ Mosquitoes prefer warm over cold, light over dark, dirty over clean, adult over child and male over female.

Once the mosquito bites the hand that feeds it, treat the bite with saliva. *Then apply any of the following...*

- Wet soap
- Wet tobacco
- Wet, clean mud
- Diluted ammonia
- Mixture of equal parts vinegar and lemon juice

As for the mosquito, after it bites you on one hand, be sure to give it the other hand— palm downward!

Mosquito and Gnat Bite Prevention

Remember how, when you were a child and got bitten up by mosquitoes, your mother would say, "That's because you're so sweet"? There may be something to it.

Experiments were conducted with people who completely eliminated white sugar and alcoholic beverages from their diets. They were surrounded by mosquitoes and gnats. Not only were those people not bitten, the insects didn't even bother to land on them.

If you're sugar-free, it's so long mosquitoes, and gnuts to gnats!

▶ Mosquitoes have been known to stay away from people whose systems have a high amount of vitamin B_1 (thiamine). Before you go to a mosquito-infested area, eat foods that are rich in B_1—sunflower seeds, brewer's yeast, Brazil nuts and fish.

Additionally, supplement with 100 mg of vitamin B_1 (thiamine) an hour before you reach your destination.

▶ Keep geraniums on porches and other places you like to sit. The potted geraniums keep mosquitoes away.

▶ If you dread mosquito bites more than you mind smelling of garlic, then we've got a remedy for you.

Rub garlic over all your exposed body parts before reaching a mosquito-infested area. Mosquitoes will not come near you. They hate garlic. Garlic is to mosquitoes what kryptonite is to Superman.

One university biologist tested garlic extract on five species of mosquitoes. The garlic got 'em. Not one mosquito survived.

▶ Eucalyptus oil will repel mosquitoes. Rub it over the uncovered areas of your body.

▶ Don't wear the color blue around mosquitoes. They're very attracted to it. They're also attracted to wet clothes. Keep dry!

▶ Rub fresh parsley on the exposed parts of your body to prevent insect bites.

▶ If you have an aloe vera plant, break off one of the stems. Squeeze out the juice and rub it on the uncovered areas of your body for protection against biting insects.

Snakebites

If you get a snakebite, chances are you're expecting you might get a snakebite. Think that over for a minute. As soon as it makes sense, please read on.

If you're going camping, or are placing yourself in a situation where there's a chance of being bitten by a snake, we recommend that you know the snakes in that area so that you can be prepared for how to handle a bite.

▶ If you get bit, make a poultice (*see* "Preparation Guide" on page 252) from two crushed onions mixed with a few drops of kerosene, and apply it to the bite. After a short time, it should draw out the poison, turning the poultice green.

Get to civilization as soon as possible and see a doctor!

▶ Mix a wad of tobacco with saliva or water. Apply this paste directly on the bite.

As soon as the paste dries, replace it with another wad of the paste and get to a doctor!

Rattlesnake Bites

▶ Don't get rattled. Wet some salt, put a hunk of it on the bite, then treat the area with a wet-salt poultice (*see* "Preparation Guide" on page 252). But don't stand around reading this. Get to a doctor!

⚡ **CAUTION:** Do not put any foreign substance (tobacco, salt, etc.) directly on broken skin. It could cause an infection that is *much* worse than the bite!

Spider Bites

There are four types of spiders that have bites that can be serious...

- ◆ *The black widow spider* has a black shiny body and a red or orange hour-glass marking on the underside of its abdomen.
- ◆ *The brown recluse spider* is also called the fiddle-back spider because of the violin-shaped marking on its back. It's found mainly in Southern and Midwestern states.
- ◆ *The hobo spider* is brown with a her-ringbone-like pattern on the top of its abdomen. It's found in the Pacific Northwest.
- ◆ *The yellow sac spider* is light yellow with a slightly darker stripe on the upper middle of its abdomen.

If you think the spider that bit you is any one of these four, try to remain as calm as possible. Call your doctor, a hospital and/or the Poison Help hotline (800-222-1222). If you can collect the spider, or any part of it, do so for identification purposes.

▶ Until you get professional help, apply ice to the bite to help prevent swelling.

▶ After you've been treated by a doctor, take nutrients that have anti-inflammatory action—vitamin C with bioflavonoids, 500 to 1,000 mg every six to eight hours for several days (cut back on the dosage if you get diarrhea)...bromelain, 500 mg three or four times a day on an empty stomach...and/or quercetin, 250 to 300 mg one to three times a day.

Tick Bites

▶ This is not a pleasant thought, but a remarkable remedy. If a tick has embedded itself in your skin—and it's been there less than 24 hours—take clear fingernail polish and put two drops on the insect. It will release its grasp and back out. Then just wipe it off your skin.

Unfortunately, you won't be able to do a Lyme culture on the tick because of the polish.

If it's still embedded, use tweezers to firmly pull the head of the tick straight out.

Keep a watchful eye on the site where the bug was pulled off—if a bull's-eye mark appears, you should go see your doctor and get tested for Lyme disease.

Skunk Spray

▶ When you've gotten in the path of a frightened skunk, add a cup of tomato juice to a gallon of water and wash your body with it. Do the same with your clothes. *Vinegar*

ARTHRITIS

One authority in the field feels that *arthritis* is a catchall term that includes *rheumatism* (inflammation or pain in muscles, joints or fibrous tissue), *bursitis* (inflammation of shoulder, elbow or knee joint) and *gout* (joint inflammation caused by an excess of uric acid in the blood). Another specialist believes that arthritis is a form of rheumatism. Still another claims there is no such ailment as rheumatism, that it's a term for several diseases, including arthritis.

No matter what it's called, everyone agrees on two things—the pain…and that all these conditions involve inflammation of connective tissue of one or more joints.

According to the US Centers for Disease Control and Prevention in Atlanta (*see* "Health Resources" on page 314), arthritis is the leading cause of disability in the United States. Approximately 66 million Americans are affected by arthritis—which has over 100 different forms.

Knowledge Is Power!

Check your local library and the Internet for books on arthritis (and there are lots of them). Also contact the Arthritis Foundation in Atlanta (*see* "Health Resources" on page 309) for more information. Learn about nonchemical treatments and low-acid diets.

These Veggies Are a Pain

There are foods that have been classified as nightshade foods—white potatoes, eggplants, green peppers and tomatoes are the most common ones—that may contribute to the pain of some arthritis sufferers.

Consider being professionally tested by a nutritionist or allergist for sensitivity to the nightshade foods. Work with a health professional to evaluate your condition and to help you find safe, sensible methods of treatment for relief.

Natural Remedies

Here are remedies that have been said to be successful for many arthritis sufferers—that is, *former* arthritis sufferers.

NOTE: These remedies are not substitutes for professional medical treatment. Talk to your doctor before trying any natural remedies.

It's the Cherries

▶ Cherries are said to be effective because they seem to help prevent crystallization of uric acid and to reduce levels of uric acid in the blood. It is also said that cherries help the arthritic bumps on knuckles disappear.

Eat any kind—sweet or sour, fresh, canned or frozen, black, Royal Anne or Bing. And drink cherry juice! It is available without preservatives or sugar added, and also in a concentrated form, at health food stores.

One source says to eat cherries and drink the juice throughout the day for four days, then stop for four days and then start all over again. Another source says to eat up to a dozen cherries a day in addition to drinking a glass of cherry juice. Find a happy medium by using your own good judgment. Listen to your body.

You'll know soon enough if the cherries seem to be making you feel better.

> **WARNING:** Eating an excess of cherries may cause diarrhea in some individuals.

Go Green

▶ Eat a portion of fresh string beans every day, or juice the string beans and drink a glassful daily. String beans contain vitamins A, B_1, B_2 and C and supposedly help relieve the excess-acid conditions that contribute to arthritis. (*See* recipe at right.)

▶ Steep 1 cup of fully packed, washed parsley in 1 quart of boiling water. After 15 minutes, strain the juice and refrigerate.

Dose: Drink ½ cup of parsley juice before breakfast, ½ cup before dinner and ½ cup anytime pain is particularly severe.

▶ Celery contains many nourishing salts and organic sulfur. Some modern herbalists believe that celery has the power to help neutralize uric acid and other excess acids in the body. Eat fresh celery daily (be sure to wash it thoroughly). The leaves on top of celery stalks are also good to eat.

If so much roughage is rough on your digestive system, place the tops and tough parts of the stalk in a nonaluminum pan. Cover with water and slowly bring to a boil. Then simmer for 10 to 15 minutes. Strain and pour into a jar.

■ Recipe ■

Papaya Salad with String Beans

1 cup green cabbage, cubed
2 cups green papaya, grated
½ lb string beans, julienned
3 garlic cloves, minced
3 dried red chilies, chopped
1 Tbsp granulated sugar
3 Tbsp soy sauce
3 Tbsp lime juice
3 small tomatoes, cut into wedges
5 Tbsp peanuts, roasted and crushed
4 Tbsp cilantro leaves, chopped

Place green cabbage pieces on a large serving platter and arrange the papaya and beans in layers. In a small bowl, mix together the garlic, chilies, sugar, soy sauce and lime juice.

Just before serving, pour the dressing over the salad and garnish with the tomatoes, peanuts and cilantro. Makes 4 servings.

Source: www.recipegoldmine.com

Dose: Take 8 ounces three times a day, a half-hour before each meal.

You can vary your celery intake by drinking celery seed tea and/or juiced celery stalks, or do as the Romanians do and cook celery in milk. Remember, celery is a diuretic, so plan your day accordingly.

Fishy Solution

▶ According to results published in the *Journal of the American Medical Association* (*www.jama.ama-assn.org*), based on experiments by a study team at the Brusch Medical Center in Cambridge, Massachusetts, cod-liver oil in milk helped to reduce cholesterol levels, improve blood chemistry and complexion, increase energy and correct stomach problems, blood sugar balance, blood pressure and tissue inflammation.

Mix 1 tablespoon of cod-liver oil (emulsified Norwegian cod-liver oil is nonfishy) in 6 ounces of milk.

Dose: Drink it on an empty stomach, a half-hour before breakfast and a half-hour before dinner.

> **NOTE:** Cod-liver oil is a source of vitamins A and D. If you are taking A and D supplements, check the dosages carefully. The daily recommended dosage of vitamin A is 10,000 international units (IU), for vitamin D, 400 IU. *Do not exceed these amounts.*

Applying cod-liver oil externally is said to help relieve the popping noises of the joints.

▶ Edgar Cayce, renowned psychic, said in one of his readings, "Those who would take a peanut oil rub each week need never fear arthritis."

Topical Treatments For Relief

▶ Garlic has been used to quiet arthritis pain quickly. Rub a freshly cut clove of garlic on painful areas. Also, take a garlic supplement—after breakfast and after dinner.

▶ Grate 3 tablespoons of horseradish and stir it into ½ cup of boiled milk. Pour the mixture onto a piece of cheesecloth, then apply it to the painful area. By the time the poultice cools, you may have some relief.

Temporary Relief—for Women Only

Arthritic pains often disappear when a woman is pregnant. This is probably due to hormonal changes, but as soon as researchers find the exact reason, they may also find a permanent cure for arthritis.

Dig a Potato

▶ Even if you have a sensitivity to nightshade foods, external potato remedies can be used, as they have been for centuries. Carry a raw potato in your pocket. Don't leave home without it! When it shrivels up after a day or two, replace it with a fresh potato. It supposedly relieves the inflammation that may be causing problems and pain.

▶ For dealing with the affected areas more directly, dice 2 cups of unpeeled potatoes and put them in a nonaluminum saucepan with 5 cups of water. Boil gently until about half the water is left. While the water is hot, but not scalding, dunk a clean cloth in the potato water, wring it out and apply it to the painful parts of the body. Repeat the procedure for as long as your patience holds out, or until the pain subsides—whichever happens first.

Rosy Relief

▶ When you're feeling twinges in the hinges all over your body, take a bath in rose petals. Take petals from three or four roses that are about to wither and throw them in your bathwater. It should give you a rosy outlook.

Bitter Makes It Better

Apple cider vinegar has been used in various ways to help arthritis sufferers. See which of the following remedies is most palatable and convenient for you. Have patience—and give it at least three weeks to work.

▶ Every morning and every evening, take 1 teaspoon of honey mixed with 1 teaspoon of apple cider vinegar.

Or, before each meal (three times a day), drink a glass of water containing 2 teaspoons of apple cider vinegar.

Or, between lunch and dinner, drink a mixture of 2 ounces of apple cider vinegar added to 6 ounces of water. Drink it down slowly.

Rub Salt on the Wound

▶ Prepare a poultice (*see* "Preparation Guide" on page 252) using coarse (kosher) salt that has been heated in a frying pan. Then apply it to the painful area. To keep the salt comfortably warm, put a hot water bottle on top of it. (Chances are, this old home remedy draws out the pain effectively with nonkosher salt, too.)

You can try more than one remedy at a time. While you're trying these remedies, pay attention to your body and you'll soon learn what makes you feel better.

Amazing Raisins

Joe Graedon, MS, pharmacologist, adjunct assistant professor at the University of North Carolina, Chapel Hill, is known as "The People's Pharmacist." He

is affiliated with the Research Triangle Institute (*www.rti.org*), and they tested "The Amazing Gin-Soaked Raisin Remedy" (*see* recipe below) for alcohol content.

The result: Less than one drop of alcohol was left in nine raisins. So when people who take the raisins are feeling no pain, it's not because they're drunk, it's because the remedy works.

■ Recipe ■

The Amazing Gin-Soaked Raisin Remedy

> 1 lb golden raisins
> Gin (approximately 1 pint)
> Glass bowl (Pyrex is good—crystal
>   is bad)
> Glass jar with lid

Spread the golden raisins evenly on the bottom of the glass bowl and pour enough gin over the raisins to completely cover them. Let them stay that way until all the gin is absorbed by the raisins. It takes about five to seven days, depending on the humidity in your area. (You may want to lightly cover the bowl with a paper towel so that dust or insects don't drop in.) To make sure that all of the raisins get their fair share of the gin, occasionally take a spoon and stir the mixture, bringing the bottom layer of raisins to the top of the bowl.

As soon as all the gin has been absorbed, transfer the raisins to the jar, put the lid on and keep it closed. *Do not refrigerate.* Each day, eat nine raisins—exactly and only nine raisins a day. Most people eat them in the morning with breakfast.

Even so, be sure to check with your health professional to make sure that gin-soaked raisins will not conflict with medication you may be taking, or present a problem for any health challenge you may have, particularly an iron-overload condition.

☛ **WARNING:** Do not give the gin-soaked raisins to children or women who are pregnant or nursing.

We've demonstrated this remedy on national television and the feedback has been incredible. One woman wrote to tell us that she had constant pain and no mobility in her neck.

Her doctor finally told her, "You'll just have to learn to live with the pain." Although that was unacceptable, she didn't know what else to do. And then she saw us on television, talking about a remarkable raisin remedy. We got her letter two weeks after she started "The Amazing Gin-Soaked Raisin Remedy." The woman had no pain and total mobility. She also had all of her friends waiting for their gin to be absorbed by their raisins.

This is one of dozens and dozens of success stories we've received. Some people have dramatic results after eating the raisins for less than a week, while it takes others a month or two to get results. There are some people for whom this remedy does nothing. But it's inexpensive, easy to do, delicious to eat and worth a try. Be consistent—eat the raisins every day. Expect a miracle…but have patience!

Grapes Are Good, Too

▶ White grape juice is said to absorb the system's acid. Drink one glass in the morning and one glass before dinner.

Camp Inside

▶ If you have morning stiffness caused by arthritis, try sleeping in a sleeping bag. You can sleep on your bed, but in the zipped-up bag. It's much more effective than an electric blanket because your body heat is evenly distributed and retained. Come morning, there's less pain, making it easier to get going.

▶ Corn-silk tea has been known to reduce acid in the system and lessen pain. Steep a handful of the silky strings that grow beneath the husk of corn in a cup of hot water for 10 minutes.

If it's not fresh-corn season, buy corn-silk extract in a health food store. Add 10 to 15 drops in 1 cup of water and drink. Dried corn silk can also be used. Prepare it as you would prepare an herbal tea. You can get dried corn silk at most places that sell dried herbs and spices (*see* "Sources" starting on page 297).

Herbal Relief

▶ Each of these herbs is known as a pain reducer—sage, rosemary, nettles and basil. Use any one, two, three or four of them in the form of herbal tea (*see* "Preparation Guide" on page 250). Have 2 cups each day, rotating them until you find the one that makes you feel best.

Coffee Cure

▶ Our friend's grandfather cleared up an arthritic condition (and lived to be 90) after he used a remedy given to him by a woman who brought it here from Puerto Rico. Squeeze the juice of a large lime into a cup of black coffee and drink it hot first thing each morning.

We're not in favor of drinking coffee, but who are we to argue with success?

▶ An old Native American arthritis remedy is a mixture of mashed yucca root and water. Yucca saponin, a steroid derivative of the yucca plant, is a forerunner of cortisone. The adverse effects of cortisone are too numerous and unpleasant to mention. The positive effects of yucca, according to a double-blind study done at a Southern California arthritis clinic, were relief from headaches as well as from gastrointestinal complaints.

In that study, 60% of the patients taking yucca tablets showed dramatic improvements in their arthritic condition. While it doesn't work for everyone, it works for enough people to make it worth a try.

Oceanside Resort

▶ For most people, this remedy is not practical—for many, it's not even possible. Then why take up all this space? The results reported to us were so spectacular that we feel if only one person reads this, follows through and is relieved of his/her painful, debilitating condition, it will have been well worth the space on the page.

Starting with the first set of directions, you will see why this is usually considered a "last resort" remedy.

Bring a couple of truckloads of ocean sand to your yard. (What did we tell you?) Select a sheltered spot away from the wind. Dig a hole about 12 feet by 12 feet and about 3 feet deep, then dump the sand in it.

You will, obviously, need help in setting up this arrangement. You will also need help in carrying out the treatment. Incidentally, treatment should take place on hot summer days.

Wear a brief bathing suit, lie on your stomach with your face to the side (so you can breathe, of course), and have your body completely covered with sand, except for your head. Have your assistant put sunscreen on your face. Stay in that position for 15 minutes. Next, turn over on your back and have your body completely covered with sand, except for your head and face. Stay that way for 15 minutes.

Then get out of the sandbath, quickly cover yourself with a warm flannel or woolen robe and head for the shower. Take a hot shower, dry off thoroughly and go to bed for several hours (three to four) and relax. During all of this, make sure there's no exposure to the wind or to any drafts.

According to an Asian saying—"Rheumatism goes out from the body only through sweating."

During the next couple of hours in bed, you may have to change underwear several times because of the profuse sweating. This is good. Be sure to keep rehydrating yourself by drinking lots of water.

One sandbath a day is sufficient. For some people, one week of treatments has been enough to help heal the condition completely.

> ✎ **NOTE:** The sandbath must have dry sand and be in your yard, in an area that's sheltered from the wind. The beach is too wet, too breezy and usually too far from home.

▶ If you do not have ulcers, drink ⅛ teaspoon of cayenne pepper in a glass of water or fruit juice (cherry juice without sugar or preservatives is best). If the pepper is just too strong for you, buy #1 capsules and fill them with cayenne, or you can buy already-prepared cayenne capsules at the health food store. Take two a day.

There's the Rub

▶ Combine ½ teaspoon of eucalyptus oil, available at health food stores, with 1 tablespoon of pure olive oil, and massage the mixture onto your painful areas.

▶ You may want to alternate the massage mixture (above) with this one—grate fresh ginger, then squeeze the juice through a piece of cheesecloth. Mix the ginger juice with an equal amount of sesame oil. Massage it on the painful areas. Ginger can be quite strong. If the burning sensation makes you uncomfortable, then tone down the ginger by adding more sesame oil to the mixture.

▶ Aloe vera gel is now being used for many ailments, including arthritis. You can apply the gel externally to the aching joint and you can take it internally—1 tablespoon in the morning before breakfast and 1 tablespoon before dinner.

▶ Vegetable juices are wonderful for everyone. They can be particularly helpful for arthritis sufferers. Use fresh carrot juice as a sweetener with either celery juice or kale juice. (Invest in a juicer or connect with a nearby juice bar.)

ASTHMA

During an asthma attack, bronchial tubes narrow and secrete an excess of mucus, making it very hard to breathe. It is a serious illness that can often be fatal.

Asthma in certain people may be attributed to exercise, allergies or emotional problems, or possibly a combination of all. (*See also* the "Allergies and Hay Fever" section on page 3.)

Renowned 19th-century British physician Peter Latham said, "You cannot be sure of the success of your remedy, while you are still uncertain of the nature of the disease." And so it is with asthma.

Worldly "Wisdom"

Folk medicine legends abound with curious asthma remedies from around the world. Although we are not advocating these unorthodox remedies, a few of them may have worked in the days before modern medicine. But be on the safe side and check with your doctor before trying any of them. Asthma is best treated by a health professional.

▶ European and Australian folklore advocates swallowing a handful of spiderwebs rolled into a ball.

▶ Deep in the heart of Texas, they are said to sleep on the uncleaned wool of recently sheared sheep. Legend has it that the asthma is absorbed by the wool.

▶ Another old Texas home remedy requires the asthmatic to get a chihuahua (Mexican hairless dog). The theory is that the asthma goes from the patient to the dog, but the dog does not suffer from it.

▶ According to Kentucky folklore, wearing a string of amber beads around the neck may cure asthma. With the cost of a full strand of amber these days, it would be cheaper to buy a chihuahua, have him get asthma, then buy that tiny dog a strand of amber.

These legendary folk remedies make for good conversation, but in the midst of an asthma attack, who can talk?

⚡ **CAUTION:** These remedies are not substitutes for professional medical treatment.

Natural Remedies

▶ We heard about a man who was able to ease off massive doses of cortisone by using garlic therapy. He started with one clove a day, minced, in a couple ounces of orange juice. He gulped it down without chewing any of the little pieces of garlic. That way, he didn't have garlic on his breath.

As he increased the number of garlic cloves he ate each day, his doctor decreased the amount of cortisone he was taking. After several months, he was eating six to 10 cloves of garlic a day, was completely off cortisone, and was not bothered by asthma.

▶ At the first sign of asthma-type wheezing, take a breath or two from your inhaler. Then saturate two strips of white cloth in white vinegar and wrap them around your wrists, not too tightly. For some people, it stops a full-blown attack from developing.

▶ Generally, dairy products are not good for asthmatics. They're too mucus-forming. We have heard, though, that cheddar cheese might be an exception. It contains *tyramine*, an ingredient that seems to help open up the breathing passages.

Sweet Solution

▶ Cut a 1-ounce stick of licorice root (the herb, not the candy) into slices and steep the slices in a quart of just-boiled water for 24 hours. Strain and bottle. At the first sign of heaviness on the chest, drink a cup of the licorice water.

⚡ **CAUTION:** Licorice root may cause renal failure in people with kidney conditions or high blood pressure.

✏️ **NOTE** (or should we say, **WARNING?**): In France, licorice water is used by women to give them more sexual vitality.

▶ We were on a radio show when a woman called in and shared her asthma remedy—cherry-bark tea. She buys tea bags in a health food store (if teas are alphabetically listed, it may be under "w" for "wild cherry-bark tea") and she drinks a cup before each meal and another cup at bedtime. The woman swore to us that it has changed her life. She hasn't had an asthma attack since she started drinking it five years ago.

▶ This remedy requires a juicer or a nearby juice bar. Drink equal amounts of endive (also called chicory), celery and carrot juice. One glass of the juice a day works wonders for some asthmatics.

▶ Remove the eggs from three eggshells. Then roast the eggshells for two hours at 400° F. The shells will turn light brown. (They'll also smell like rotten eggs.) Pulverize them and mix them into a cup of unsulfured molasses. Take 1 teaspoon before each meal. It just may prevent an asthma condition from acting up.

See It Disappear

▶ Visualization or mental imagery is a potent tool that can be used to help you heal yourself. Gerald N. Epstein, MD, assistant clinical professor of psychiatry, Mount Sinai Medical Center, and director of the American Institute for Mental Imagery (both in New York City), suggests that the following visualization be done to stem an asthma attack. Do it at the onset of an attack, for three to five minutes.

Sit in a comfortable chair and close your eyes. Breathe in and out three times and see yourself in a pine forest. Stand next to a pine tree and breathe in the aromatic fragrance of the pine. As you breathe out, sense this exhalation traveling down through your body and going out through the soles of your feet. See the breath exiting as gray smoke and being buried deep in the earth. Then open your eyes, breathing easily.

> ✎ **NOTE:** Learn this visualization and practice it when you're feeling fine so that you know exactly what to do and how to do it the second you feel a wheeze coming on.

▶ Ray C. Wunderlich, Jr., MD, PhD, director of the Wunderlich Center for Nutritional Medicine in St. Petersburg, Florida, recommends magnesium for helping take away bronchial spasms. Find a dose of a magnesium preparation that is tolerated (if you get diarrhea, you should cut back on the dosage) and use it to relieve asthma. Do not exceed a total dose of 400 mg of elemental magnesium per day, unless prescribed by a physician.

▶ Eat three to six apricots a day. They may help promote healing of lung and bronchial conditions.

▶ Jerusalem artichokes (*see* recipe below)—also called sunchokes because they're related to sunflowers—may be a real plus for nourishing the lungs of the asthmatic when eaten daily.

▶ Put 4 cups of shelled sunflower seeds in 2 quarts of water and boil it down to 1 quart of water. Strain out the little pieces of sunflower seeds, then add one pint of honey and boil it down to a syrupy consistency.

Dose: Take 1 teaspoon a half-hour after each meal.

■ Recipe ■

Sweet Pickled Jerusalem Artichokes

½ cup apple cider vinegar

½ cup water

3 Tbsp evaporated cane juice (available at health food stores)

¼ tsp salt

1½ cups sliced Jerusalem artichokes (½ lb)

1 large carrot, angle-sliced thinly

1 large stalk celery, sliced

Combine first four ingredients in a medium bowl and stir to combine flavors. Add vegetables, stir well and cover with plastic wrap. Store in the refrigerator to marinate for several hours or overnight. Makes about 4 cups.

Source: www.vegparadise.com

▶ Similar to, but more potent than, the sunflower-seed syrup is garlic syrup. Separate and peel the cloves of three entire garlic bulbs. Simmer them in a nonaluminum pan with 2 cups of water. When the garlic cloves are soft and there's about a cup of water left in the pan, remove the garlic and put it in a jar. Then, add 1 cup of cider vinegar and ¼ cup of honey to the water that's left in the pan, boiling the mixture until it's syrupy. Pour the syrup over the garlic in the jar. Cover the jar and let it stand overnight.

Dose: Swallow one or two cloves of garlic with a teaspoon of syrup every morning on an empty stomach.

(▶ **WARNING:** Infants, diabetics and people with honey allergies should not use honey.

Oldie, but a Goodie

▶ A relative told us that in the "old country," a remedy used at the onset of an asthma attack was to inhale the steam from boiling potatoes that were cut in pieces with the skin left on them. With or without the potatoes, inhaling steam can be beneficial.

Be careful: Steam is powerful and can burn the skin.

▶ Mix 1 teaspoon of grated horseradish with 1 teaspoon of honey and take it every night before bedtime.

▶ Slice two large raw onions into a jar. Pour 2 cups of honey over it. Close the jar and let it stand overnight. The next morning you're ready to start taking the "honion" syrup.

Dose: Take 1 teaspoon a half-hour after each meal and 1 teaspoon before bed.

▶ Buy either concentrated cranberry juice, sold at health food stores, or unconcentrated cranberry juice, sold at most supermarkets. Read the ingredients on the label and make sure there are no preservatives or sugar added. Or, you can make your own with 1 pound of cranberries in 1 pint of water. Boil until the cranberries are very mushy. Then, pour the mixture into a jar and keep it in the refrigerator.

Dose: Drink 2 tablespoons a half-hour before each meal and immediately at the onset of an asthma attack. Be sure to keep your inhaler handy, too.

ATHEROSCLEROSIS

Atherosclerosis is clogging of the arteries that is caused by deposits of fatty substances, cholesterol, calcium and other matter. This build-up is called *plaque*, and it develops over many years from poor diet, a sedentary lifestyle and smoking. It's important that you work with your doctor to treat this condition. Be sure to consult him/her before trying any natural remedies.

If you are developing atherosclerosis, do something to protect your arteries against the negative effects of improper diet, lack of exercise and bad habits (such as smoking). *These remedies may help...*

Natural Remedies

▶ Eating a few cloves of garlic each day has been known to help clear arteries. It seems to cleanse the system, and collect and cast out toxic waste.

Mince two cloves and put them in a half glass of orange juice or water and drink it down. There's no need to chew the pieces of garlic. By just swallowing them, the garlic smell doesn't stay on your breath.

In conjunction with a sensible diet, garlic can also help bring down cholesterol levels in the blood. No wonder this beautiful bulb has a fan club, appropriately called "Lovers of the Stinking Rose."

See the "Six Sensational Superfoods" on page 266 for more information on garlic.

▶ Rutin is one of the elements of the bioflavonoids. Bioflavonoids (substances from plants that help maintain cellular health) are necessary for the proper absorption of vitamin C. Taking 500 mg of rutin daily, with at least the same amount of vitamin C, is said to increase the strength of capillaries, strengthen the artery walls, help prevent hemorrhaging and help treat atherosclerosis.

▶ According to French folklore, eating rye bread made with baker's yeast supposedly prevents clogging of the arteries.

▶ It is reported that some Russians eat mature, raw potatoes at every meal to prevent atherosclerosis.

▶ Drinking a combination of apple cider boiled with garlic once a day is a Slavic folk remedy. This may not prevent atherosclerosis, but it certainly tastes like it should.

High Cholesterol Remedies

The US government recently changed the guidelines for what is considered a dangerous level of cholesterol. Previous levels were a maximum of 100 milligrams per deciliter (mg/dL) of low-density lipoprotein (LDL or "bad") cholesterol, and the new recommendation is to have LDLs no higher than 70 mg/dL.

These guidelines are meant for very high-risk people who have heart disease, plus diabetes, high blood pressure and smoke cigarettes. But even people with moderately high risk (for example, those who have already had a heart attack) should keep their LDL levels well below 100 mg/dL.

The only foods that have cholesterol are animal products—meat, poultry, fish, dairy. If you are diagnosed with high cholesterol, start a heart-smart diet immediately by cutting down or cutting out animal products. There are foods that can help lower your LDL and raise your HDL (good cholesterol).

✎ **NOTE:** Talk to your doctor about any dietary changes you make.

There have been a variety of cholesterol studies conducted over different periods of time with any number of test subjects. Some of the results are impressive, and all of the cholesterol-lowering foods are worth a try.

First—and most important—is to get that heart-smart diet in place, and incorporate the foods that have been shown to help. *According to the studies...*

◆ Eating half an avocado every day may lower cholesterol by 8% to 42%. Yes, avocados are high in fat, but it's monounsaturated fat that does good things for the system. An avocado also contains

13 essential minerals, including iron, copper and magnesium, and is rich in potassium. It tastes great, too.

◆ Eating two large apples a day may cause cholesterol levels to drop 16%. Apples are rich in flavonoids and pectin, which may form a gel in the stomach that keeps fats in food from being totally absorbed.

◆ Eating two raw carrots a day reduced cholesterol levels by 11%.

◆ People who consumed about ¾ cup of fenugreek daily for 20 days cut their LDL ("bad" cholesterol) levels by 33%. Their HDL ("good" cholesterol) stayed the same. Instead of eating table-spoons of ground fenugreek seeds, choose capsules (580 mg), which are available at health food stores. Take one or two with each meal.

◆ Eating four cloves of garlic a day can cut total cholesterol by about 7%. (While fresh garlic is best, garlic sup-plements are fine.)

◆ Men and women who started out with low blood levels of vitamin C and then took 1,000 mg of vitamin C every day for eight months had a 7% increase of their HDL (good choles-terol) readings.

◆ Kiwi has what it takes to help keep cholesterol down—magnesium, potas-sium and fiber. It makes a satisfying, energy-boosting afternoon snack.

◆ Omega-3 fatty acids have the uncanny ability to break down cholesterol in the lining of blood vessels, and also serve as a solvent for saturated fats in the diet. The end result is less choles-terol in the body and bloodstream, and a reduced likelihood of choles-terol/heart disease complications in the future.

Omega-3s are healthy polyunsat-urated fats found in many foods, including salmon, mackerel and other fatty fish. Flaxseed oil offers the most cost-effective and beneficial method for increasing the intake of omega-3 oils in the diet. (*See* "Six Sensational Superfoods" on page 262 for detailed flaxseed information.)

▶ Ray C. Wunderlich, Jr., MD, PhD, director of the Wunderlich Center for Nutritional Medicine in St. Petersburg, Florida, recom-mends grape seed oil (available at health food stores) as a reliable increaser of HDL (good cholesterol). Follow the dosage on the label.

▶ Impressive test results build a good case for the effectiveness of lecithin in lowering LDL levels and raising HDL levels.

Dose: Take 1 to 2 tablespoons of lecithin granules daily, available at health food stores.

▶ *The American Journal of Clinical Nutrition* (*www.ajcn.org*) mentions that raw carrots not only improve digestive elimination because of their high fiber content, but may also lower cholesterol. Test subjects who ate two carrots for breakfast for three weeks reduced their serum cholesterol level by 11%.

You may want to scrub the carrots you eat instead of peeling them. The peel is rich in B_1 (thiamine), B_2 (riboflavin) and B_3 (niacin). If you can get organically grown carrots, do so.

▶ It seems that very small amounts of chro-mium are vital for good health. A deficiency in chromium may be linked to coronary artery

■ Recipe ■

Banana Bread Oatmeal

3 cups fat-free milk

3 Tbsp firmly packed brown sugar

¾ tsp ground cinnamon

¼ tsp salt (optional)

¼ tsp ground nutmeg

2 cups quick or old-fashioned oats, uncooked

2 medium-size ripe bananas, mashed (about 1 cup)

2 to 3 Tbsp coarsely chopped toasted pecans*

Vanilla nonfat yogurt (optional)

Banana slices (optional)

Pecan halves (optional)

In medium saucepan, bring milk, brown sugar, spices and salt to a gentle boil (watch carefully); stir in oats. Return to a boil, and reduce heat to medium. Cook 1 minute for quick oats, 5 minutes for old-fashioned oats, or until most of liquid is absorbed, stirring occasionally.

Remove oatmeal from heat. Stir in mashed bananas and pecans. Spoon oatmeal into four cereal bowls. Top with yogurt, sliced bananas and pecan halves, if desired. Makes 4 servings.

*To toast pecans, spread evenly in shallow baking pan. Bake at 350° F for 5 to 7 minutes or until light golden brown. Or, spread nuts evenly on microwave-safe plate. Microwave on high for 1 minute, then stir. Continue to microwave, checking every 30 seconds, until nuts are fragrant and brown.

Source: www.recipegoldmine.com

disease. Take 1 to 2 tablespoons of brewer's yeast daily (be sure to read labels and select the brewer's yeast with the highest chromium content) or a handful of raw sunflower seeds.

The chromium, like the lecithin, is said to lower the LDL cholesterol level and raise the HDL cholesterol level. If you plan on doing this, get your doctor's approval.

▶ The results of one study conducted at Rutgers University in New Brunswick, New Jersey, showed that oats can bring down blood cholesterol levels. You can reap this benefit by eating oatmeal or any other form of oats two or three times a week. (*See* recipe at left.)

▶ According to James W. Anderson, MD, professor of internal medicine at the University of Kentucky College of Medicine in Lexington, "Including a cup of beans in your diet per day helps to stabilize blood sugars and lower cholesterol." This benefit can be attributed to dry beans, such as navy or pinto, rather than green beans.

▶ Scott Grundy, MD, director of the Center for Human Nutrition at the University of Texas Southwestern Medical Center in Dallas, says that research shows that *mono*unsaturated fatty acid, found in olive oil and peanut oil, is more effective in reducing artery-clogging cholesterol levels than *poly*unsaturated fats, such as corn oil and sunflower oil.

BACK PAIN

It is estimated that eight out of 10 people have, at some point in their lives, back pain that disables them. Also estimated is the money spent for diagnosis and treatment of back pain—more than $5 billion annually.

> **WARNING:** It's extremely important that any back pain be evaluated by a medical professional to rule out serious illness or injury. If your back pain is chronic, persistent or severe, see a doctor.

We have come across some remedies that are worth trying to relieve minor backaches. At best, they'll help—at least, they'll give you something to talk about the next time someone tells you his/her back went out.

Healing Position

▶ Thanks to the wise guidance of our cousin Linda, a physical therapist, many people who felt that their backs were on the verge of going out avoided the problem. If you've had back trouble, you know the feeling we're referring to.

When you get that feeling, carefully lie down on the floor, close enough to a sofa or easy chair so that you can bend your knees and rest your legs (knees to feet) on the seat of the sofa or chair. Your thighs should be leaning against the front of the sofa and your tush should be as close as possible, directly in front of it, with the rest of your body flat on the floor.

In position, you're like the start of a staircase. Your body is the lowest step, your thighs are the distance between the steps, and your knees-to-feet are the second step.

Stay in that position for 15 to 30 minutes. It's a restful and healing treatment for the back.

The best and safest way to get up is to lower your legs, roll over on your side, then slowly lift yourself up, letting your arms and shoulders do most of the work.

For Men Only

Do you have back or hip pain when you sit for any length of time? Is it something you and your doctor(s) can't quite figure out and so you label it "back trouble"?

According to doctors, you may need a "wallet-ectomy."

If you carry around a thick wallet in your hip pocket, it may be putting pressure on the sciatic nerve. Keep your wallet in your jacket pocket instead, and you'll find that sitting can be a pleasurable experience again.

Natural Remedies

▶ An Asian remedy for the prevention or relief of lower back problems is black beans (also called *frijoles negros*—although not in Asia!), which are available at supermarkets and health food stores.

Soak a cupful of black beans overnight. This softens the beans and is said to remove the gas-producing compounds. Then put them in a pot with 3½ cups of water. Bring to a boil, and let simmer for a half-hour over low heat. During that half-hour, keep removing the grayish foam that forms on top. After a half-hour, cover the pot and let it cook for another two hours. If, by the end of that time, there's still water in the pot, spill it out.

Eat 2 to 3 tablespoons of the black beans each day for one month, then every other day for one month.

Fresh beans should be prepared at least every three or four days.

Get a Friend

▶ You need to employ the buddy system for this remedy. Put 20 drops of eucalyptus oil in a cup and warm it in the microwave for a few seconds. Then have your buddy gently massage the warm oil on your painful area. The "hands on" are as healing as the oil.

Sciatica

Sciatica is a painful condition affecting the sciatic nerve, which is the longest nerve in the body. It extends from the lower spine through the pelvis, thighs, down into the legs and ends at the heels. When this nerve gets pinched or pulled (usually because of over-exertion), the resulting back pain can be excruciating.

The home remedies we describe may not cure the condition entirely, but they may help ease the pain.

Pain-Relieving Juices

▶ The juice from potatoes has been said to help sciatica sufferers. So has celery juice. If you don't have a juicer, a health food store with

a juice bar might be willing to accommodate you. Have them juice a 10-ounce combination of potato and celery juice. Add carrots and/or beets to improve the taste.

In addition to the juice, drink a couple of cups of celery tea throughout the day.

▶ Stimulate the sciatic nerve by applying a fresh minced horseradish poultice to the painful area. Keep it on for one hour at a time.

Add Some Garlic

▶ Vitamin B_1 and garlic may be very beneficial. Eat garlic raw in salads and use it in cooking. Also, take garlic supplements daily, plus 10 mg of vitamin B_1 along with a good B-complex vitamin.

⚡ **CAUTION:** Do not eat garlic or take garlic supplements if you have a bleeding disorder or ulcers, or are taking anticoagulants.

If you are taking any kind of medication, check with your health professional before taking garlic supplements.

▶ A hot water bag on the painful area may help you make it through the night with less pain and more sleep.

▶ Drink elderberry juice and elderberry tea throughout the day.

▶ Before bedtime, heat olive oil and use it to massage the painful areas.

▶ Eat lots of watercress and parsley every day. (*See* recipe on page 25.)

▶ According to many Germans, eating raw sauerkraut every day prevents sciatica.

■ Recipe ■

Emerald Sauce

2 Tbsp lemon juice

¼ cup chopped parsley

¾ cup lightly packed, rinsed and
  drained watercress sprigs

1 Tbsp chopped tarragon

1 cup sour cream (or half sour cream
  and half plain yogurt)

Salt to taste

In a blender or food processor, combine lemon juice, parsley, watercress, tarragon and sour cream. Whirl until mixture is smoothly puréed, scraping container sides as required. Add salt to taste. Serve over potatoes, fish or chicken.

Source: www.recipegoldmine.com

Be Well-Red

▶ Polish folk healers tell their patients who suffer from sciatica to wear woolen long underwear—red only—and carry a raw beet in their hip pocket.

▶ We heard about a man who went from doctor to doctor seeking help. Nothing worked. As a last resort, the man followed the advice of an alternative medicine practitioner who recommended garlic milk.

The man minced two cloves of garlic, put them in ½ cup of milk and drank it down (without chewing the pieces of garlic). He had the garlic milk each morning and each evening. Within a few days, he felt some relief. Within two weeks, all the pain had completely disappeared.

▶ Water has tremendous therapeutic value for a sciatic condition. It can reduce the pain and improve circulation. Take a long, hot bath or shower and follow it with a short cold shower. If you can't stand the thought of a cold shower, then follow up the hot bath with ice-cold compresses on the painful areas.

BODY ODOR

If you have a problem with bad-smelling armpits, raise your hand. Oops! Better not. Instead, try a few of the following remedies. They may help you combat stinky armpits—or whatever body parts are smelling bad.

▶ Take a shower, then prepare turnip juice. Grate a turnip, squeeze the juice through cheesecloth so that you have 2 teaspoons. Now raise your hand and vigorously massage a teaspoon of the turnip juice into each armpit.

Dietary Remedies

▶ A vegetarian friend's sense of smell is so keen, she can stand next to someone and tell whether that person is a meat eater.

If you are a heavy meat and fowl eater and are troubled by body odor, change your diet. Ease off meat and poultry and force yourself to fill up on green leafy vegetables. There will be a big difference in a short time. You probably won't perspire less, but the smell won't be as strong, and the change of diet will be healthier for you in general. It will also be appreciated by the people in the crowded elevators you ride. (*See* recipe on page 26.)

■ Recipe ■

Organic Garden Salad with Fresh Herbs

Mix of organic leafy greens (arugula, spinach, romaine, endive, etc.)

Organic tomatoes, diced

Sunflower sprouts

Mushrooms, sliced

Yellow peppers, sliced

Basil, minced

Oregano

Mint

Thyme

Parsley

Non-fat Italian dressing

1 Tbsp white balsamic vinegar

Fresh ground pepper, to taste

Mix equal parts of each type of greens in a large salad bowl or platter—adjust quantity based on the number of servings desired. Place the diced tomatoes, sunflower sprouts, sliced mushrooms, sliced yellow peppers and any other organic produce on top of the greens.

Next, sprinkle on the organic fresh herb leaves, minced or whole. Then cover the salad bowl or platter with plastic wrap or aluminum foil and refrigerate.

Just before serving, add 1 Tbsp of white balsamic vinegar to ¼ cup of non-fat Italian dressing. This will thin the dressing and give the characteristic flavor of balsamic vinegar. You could also use red balsamic vinegar or a fresh citrus juice. Add fresh ground pepper (especially red or green peppercorns) to taste.

Source: www.recipegoldmine.com

NOTE: Always thoroughly wash raw vegetables and produce to reduce the risk of food-borne illness.

The Grass Is Greener...

▶ In addition to eating green leafy vegetables, take a 500 mg capsule of wheat grass (powdered juice) daily. Or, if your local health food store sells fresh wheat grass juice, have an ounce first thing each morning. Be sure to take it on an empty stomach and drink it down with spring water. The chlorophyll can reduce body odor dramatically or eliminate it completely.

▶ If tension causes you to perspire excessively, which then causes unpleasant body odors, drink sage tea. Use 1½ teaspoons of dried sage, or two tea bags in 1 cup of water. Let the tea steep for 10 minutes. Drink it in small doses throughout the day. The tea should help you to relax, so don't sweat it.

▶ "Think Zinc—Don't Stink!" Credit for that slogan goes to a Pennsylvania man who rid himself of body odor by taking 30 mg of zinc every day. Within two weeks, he was smelling like a rose.

CAUTION: Some people get stomachaches from zinc. Also, high amounts of zinc may increase a man's risk of developing prostate cancer.

Consult your doctor for the proper dosage before supplementing with zinc.

BRUISES AND SKIN DISCOLORATION

Ouch! Bruises generally appear when the skin has undergone some form of trauma (minor or not) that caused little blood vessels to break. This can happen from bumping into the edge of a table or from something more serious like a car accident.

Most minor bruises will go away on their own with time (usually after going through a rainbow of colors), but these remedies may speed up the healing process.

Bruises

To prevent and heal common, everyday bruises…

▶ Apply a cold pack or ice wrapped in a washcloth as soon as possible after the injury. Hold for 20 minutes. Repeat several times. Cold constricts blood vessels, shortens clotting time and can reduce blood leakage from capillaries.

▶ Elevate the injured area higher than your heart. The longer you can do this, the better. It reduces blood flow to the injury.

▶ Take vitamin C. Vitamin C makes capillaries less fragile. Extra vitamin C is particularly important if you're taking aspirin or corticosteroids, drugs that can strip vitamin C from the body. The amount in a multisupplement, typically 60 to 100 mg, usually is adequate.

Bonus: Most multisupplements also contain zinc, a mineral that may reduce capillary leakage.

▶ If you close a door or drawer on your finger, prepare a poultice of grated onion and salt and apply it to the bruised area. The pain will disappear within seconds.

▶ Place ice on a bruise to help prevent the area from turning black and blue, and to reduce the swelling. If ice is not available, immediately press a metal knife (flat side only —we're talking bruises, not amputation) or spoon on the bruise for five to 10 minutes.

Easy Bruise Erasers

▶ Make a salve by mashing pieces of parsley into a teaspoon of butter. Gently rub the salve on the bruise.

▶ Grate a piece of turnip or a piece of daikon (Japanese radish). Apply the grated root to the bruise and leave it there for 15 to 30 minutes. These two roots have been known to help improve the look of the bruise.

▶ Spread a thin layer of blackstrap molasses on a piece of brown paper (grocery bag) and apply the molasses side to the bruise. Bind it in place and leave it there for a few hours.

▶ Peel a banana and apply the inside of the peel to the bruise. It will lessen the pain, reduce the discoloration and speed healing. Bind the peel in place with a bandage.

▶ Mix 2 tablespoons of cornstarch with 1 tablespoon of castor oil. Dampen a clean white cloth and make a cornstarch/castor oil poultice. (*See* "Preparation Guide" on page 252.) Apply the poultice to the bruise and leave it on until the damp cloth gets dry.

> **WARNING:** Most bruises are just evidence of an active life—but if you get a bruise and it doesn't go away or you keep getting bruises, it could be a sign of a dangerous medical condition. Schedule an appointment with your doctor.

Brown Spots

Large, flat brown spots on your face and hands may be called age spots or liver spots. Many fair-skinned people develop them in middle age from an accumulation of pigment (color) in the skin.

CAUTION: Any suspicious mark or skin discoloration should be evaluated by a dermatologist to rule out skin cancer.

The following remedies may not produce instant results. Keep in mind that these brown spots, thought to be caused by sun damage or a nutrition deficiency, took years to form. Give the remedy you use a few months to work. Then, if there's no change, try another remedy. It may take some trial and error to find what works best for you.

▶ Grate an onion and squeeze it through cheesecloth so that you have 1 teaspoon of onion juice. Mix it with 2 teaspoons of vinegar and massage the brown spots with this liquid. Do it daily—twice a day, if possible—until you no longer see spots in front of your eyes.

Banish Brown Spots with Beans

▶ This Israeli remedy calls for chickpeas. You may know them as garbanzo beans, ceci or arbus. If you don't want to prepare them from scratch, buy canned chickpeas. Mash about ⅓ cup and add a little water. Smear the paste on the brown spots and leave it there until it dries and starts crumbling off. Then wash it off completely. Do this every evening.

Gimme an E!

▶ Once a day, swallow a vitamin E capsule (check with your doctor for amount). In addi-

tion, at bedtime, puncture an E capsule, squish out the oil and rub it on the brown spots, leaving it on overnight. Wear white cotton gloves to avoid messing up your sheets.

▶ A variation of this remedy is to rub on castor oil and take the vitamin E orally.

Dark Undereye Circles

▶ If you have access to fresh figs, try cutting one in half and placing the halves under your eyes. You should, of course, lie down and relax for 15 to 30 minutes. Okay, fig face, time to get up and gently rinse the sticky stuff off with tepid water. Dab on some peanut oil.

▶ When figs are not in season, grate an unwaxed cucumber or a small scrubbed (preferably red) potato. Put the gratings on two gauze pads, lie down and put them under your eyes. Rinse thoroughly and dab on some peanut oil.

Black Eyes

We met a friend who had a shiner. We asked, "Did someone give you a black eye?" He answered, "No. I had to fight for it."

Black eyes are essentially bruises that are located around the eye socket. These remedies should help reduce the swelling and take away some of the color.

Hawaiian Treat

▶ Eat ripe pineapple and ripe papaya—lots of it—for two or three days, and let the enzymes in those fruits help eliminate the discoloration around the eye. If you can't get fresh pineapple or papaya, try papaya pills (available at health food stores). Take one after every meal. Both fruits are rich in vitamin C, which also promotes healing.

Steaks Are for Eating

▶ If you were a character in a movie and you got a black eye, in the following scene you would be nursing it with a piece of raw steak.

Cut! The steak may have bacteria that you don't want on your eye, and since the only reason it's being used is because it's cold, retake the scene with a package of frozen vegetables or a cold, wet cloth. Leave it on the bruised area for about 20 minutes, off for 10 minutes, on for 20, off for 10. Get the picture?

▶ Make a poultice (*see* "Preparation Guide" on page 252) by mixing 2 tablespoons of salt with 2 tablespoons of lard or vegetable shortening. Spread the mixture on a cloth and place it over the bruised eye. This poultice may help eliminate the bruised cells around the eye by stimulating the circulation. Be especially careful not to get the salty lard in your eye.

▶ Pour witch hazel on a cotton pad and apply it to the bruised, closed eye. Lie down with your feet slightly higher than your head for a half-hour while the witch hazel stays in place.

▶ Peel and grate a potato (a red potato is best). Make a poultice out of it (*see* "Preparation Guide" on page 252) and keep it on the black eye for 20 minutes. Potassium chloride is one of the most effective healing compounds, and potatoes are the best source of potassium chloride. (This remedy is also beneficial for blood-shot eyes.)

BURNS

The word "burn" applies to certain types of skin damage—caused by extreme heat or cold, chemicals, large doses of radiation or exposure to the sun.

Burns are classified by degree. In a first-degree burn, the skin is painful and red, but unbroken. In a second-degree burn, the skin is broken and there are painful blisters. A third-degree burn destroys the underlying tissue as well as surface skin. The burn may be painless because nerve endings have also been destroyed.

Second-degree burns that cover an extensive area of skin and all third-degree burns require *immediate medical attention*. Any kind of burn on the face should also receive immediate medical attention as a precaution against swollen breathing passages.

We'll deal mainly with superficial first-degree burns, which occur from things like grabbing a hot pot handle, grasping the iron side of an iron, having the oven door close on your forearm or getting splattered with boiling oil.

CAUTION: Do not use these topical remedies on broken skin due to the risk of infection.

Here are natural remedies using mostly handy household items.

First-Degree Burns

Apply cold water or cold compresses first! *Then you can...*

▶ Draw out the heat and pain by applying a slice of raw, unpeeled potato, a piece of fresh pumpkin pulp or a slice of raw onion. Leave the potato, pumpkin or onion on the burn for 15 minutes, off for five minutes and then put a fresh piece on for another 15 minutes.

▶ If you have either a vitamin E or garlic oil capsule, puncture one and squeeze the contents directly on the burn.

▶ Keep an aloe vera plant in your home. It's like growing a tube of healing ointment. Break off about a half-inch piece of stem. Squeeze it so that the juice oozes out onto the burned area.

The juice is most effective if the plant is at least two to three years old and the stems have little bumps on the edges.

▶ If you burn yourself while baking and happen to have salt-free unbaked pie crust around, roll it thin and place it on the entire surface of the burn. Let it stay on until it dries up and falls off by itself.

Good Enough to Eat

▶ Make a poultice (*see* "Preparation Guide" on page 252) of raw sauerkraut and apply it to the burned area. If you don't have sauerkraut, use crushed comfrey root with a little honey. In fact, according to research in India, just plain honey on the burn may ease the pain and help the healing process.

▶ Spread apple butter over the burned area. As it dries, add another coat to it. Keep adding coats for a day or two, until the burn is just about butter—uh, better.

CAUTION: Only put butter or other fatty substances on the most superficial, minor burns due to the risk of infection.

Second-Degree Burns

For at least 30 minutes, dip the burned area in cold water or apply a soft towel that has been drenched in ice-cold water. *Do not use lard, butter or a salve on the burn, especially if the skin is broken!* Those things are a breeding ground for bacteria. In addition, when you get medical attention, the doctor will have to wipe off the goo to examine the condition of the skin.

If the burn is on an arm or leg, keep the limb raised in the air to help prevent swelling.

Chemical and Acid Burns

Call for medical attention immediately. But until help arrives, put the affected area under the closest running water—a sink faucet, a garden hose or the shower. The running water will help wash the chemicals off the skin. Keep the water running on the burned skin for at least 20 minutes. You can stop when medical help arrives.

Minor Burns

Burnt Tongue

▶ Keep rinsing your mouth with cold water. A few drops of vanilla extract may relieve the pain, or try sprinkling some white sugar on it.

Rope Burns

▶ Soak your aching hands in salt water.

Burnt Throat

▶ If you've drunk something that was too hot, two teaspoons of olive oil will soothe and coat a burnt throat. A tablespoon of honey may also help.

Burning Feet

▶ For minor foot burns from walking on hot pavement or sand, wrap tomato slices on the soles of the feet (keep them in place with a bandage) and keep them elevated for a half-hour.

▶ Soak your feet in warm potato water (*see* "Preparation Guide" on page 252) for 15 minutes. Dry your feet thoroughly. If you're going right to bed, massage the feet with a small amount of sesame or almond oil. You might want to put on loose-fitting socks to avoid messing up the sheets.

▶ Bavarian mountain climbers, after soaking their feet in potato water, sprinkle hot, roasted salt on a cloth and wrap it around their feet. It not only soothes burning and tired feet, but relieves itchy ones as well.

Sunburn

See "Sunburn" on page 172.

CARPAL TUNNEL SYNDROME (CTS)

This condition results from swollen tendons that compress the median nerve within the carpal tunnel canal in the wrist. It's usually accompanied by odd sensations, numbness, swelling, soreness, stiffness, weakness, tingling, discomfort and pain...a lot of pain. It tends to be caused by continual, rapid use of your fingers, wrists and/or arms.

Many people feel the requirements of their job contribute to the onset of CTS. But people who spend each workday at a computer aren't the only ones doing repetitious work—musicians, supermarket checkers, factory workers, hair stylists, bus drivers, seamstresses, tailors and countless others are plagued by this repetitive motion injury.

Vitamin B$_6$ may help to ease symptoms of CTS. But too much B$_6$ can be toxic and harmful to the nervous system, so work with your health professional to determine a safe dosage of B$_6$ for you.

If your problem is computer-related, visit your local computer store and see what it has in the way of ergonomic products that will support your wrists when you use the computer.

Sleeping with CTS

The pain may be more severe while sleeping because of the way you fold your wrist. You may find it more comfortable to wear a splint or wrist brace to bed. Now that the problem is so common, you can find a selection of splints and

Carpal Tunnel Checklist

You may be predisposed to CTS if you are hypothyroid, have diabetes, are pregnant or if you're taking birth control pills. *The following things are situations you can begin to change immediately...*

- ◆ *Do you smoke?* Smoking worsens the condition because nicotine constricts the blood vessels and carbon monoxide replaces oxygen, reducing the blood flow to your tissues.

- ◆ *Are you overweight?* Being overweight can reduce the blood flow to your tissues. Also, the more weight, the more the muscles must support to move your hand and arm.

- ◆ *Do you exercise?* Aerobic exercise—30 minutes, four times a week—can increase the flow of oxygenated blood to your hands, and help remove waste products caused by inflammation.

wrist braces at most drugstores. You may want to wear the splint or brace during the day, too.

Exercise for CTS Prevention

A team of doctors from the American Academy of Orthopaedic Surgeons in Rosemont, Illinois, has developed special exercises that can help prevent carpal tunnel syndrome. The exercises, which decrease the median nerve pressure responsible for CTS, should be done at the start of each work shift, as a warmup exercise and again after each break.

▶ Stand up straight, feet a foot apart, arms outstretched in front of you, palms down. Then bring your hands and fingers up, pointing toward the sky. Hold for a count of five.

Straighten both wrists and relax the fingers. Make a tight fist with both hands. Then bend both wrists down while keeping the fists. Hold for a count of five. Straighten both wrists and relax the fingers for a count of five. The exercise should be repeated 10 times. Then let your arms hang loosely at your sides and shake them for a couple of seconds. *Don't rush through the exercise.* Let the 10 cycles take about five minutes.

One Expert's CTS Cure

▶ James A. Duke, PhD, a botanist formerly with the USDA's Agricultural Research Service in Beltsville, Maryland, and one of the world's leading authorities on herbal healing traditions, confesses that he uses a computer as much as 14 hours a day. But he hasn't developed any CTS symptoms. He gives some of the credit to the fact that he's a man.

"Women develop carpal tunnel problems more than men do," explains Dr. Duke, "because the cyclical hormone fluctuations of the menstrual cycle, pregnancy and menopause can contribute to swelling of the tissues that surround the carpal tunnel."

Another reason he thinks he's been spared the discomfort of CTS is hand exercises. "Adopting a Chinese technique that improves flexibility," says Dr. Duke, "I hold two steel balls in one hand and roll them around when I'm not typing. The Chinese balls provide a gentle form of exercise, and the rolling motion massages the tiny muscles and ligaments of the hands and wrists." When he's at the computer, he takes frequent breaks to twirl the Chinese balls in each hand.

Chinese balls are inexpensive and readily available at Chinese markets or on-line. Some health food stores may also carry them.

If You Use a Computer...

The National Institute for Occupational Safety and Health in Washington, DC, recommends that you...

◆ Position the screen at eye level, about 22 to 26 inches away.

◆ Sit about arm's length from the terminal. At that distance, the electrical field is almost zero.

◆ Face forward and keep your neck relaxed.

◆ Position the keyboard so that your elbows are bent at least 90 degrees and you can work without bending your wrists.

◆ Use a chair that supports your back, lets your feet rest on the floor or on a footrest, and keeps thighs parallel to the floor.

◆ If you can step away from the computer for 15 minutes every hour, it can help prevent eyestrain. Also, frequent blinking will help prevent eye irritation, burning and/or dry eyes.

For more information, go to *www.cdc.gov/niosh/homepage.html.*

Herbs for CTS

In his book *The Green Pharmacy* (St. Martin's), Dr. Duke reports on quite a few herbs that can help alleviate CTS.

▶ "Willow bark, the original source of aspirin, contains chemicals (salicylates) that both relieve pain and reduce inflammation. You might also try other herbs rich in salicylates, notably meadowsweet and wintergreen."

With any of these herbs, Dr. Duke steeps 1 to 2 teaspoons of dried, powdered bark, or 5 teaspoons of fresh bark, for 10 minutes or so,

■ Recipe ■

Sunrise Salsa

½ ripe papaya (about ½ pound), seeded, skinned and diced

½ ripe mango, seeded, skinned and diced

½ cup diced fresh pineapple (canned pineapple is fine)

1 medium cucumber, peeled, seeded and diced

1 or 2 jalapeño peppers, stemmed, seeded and minced

4 green onions, trimmed and thinly sliced

2 to 4 Tbsp finely chopped fresh basil or fresh mint

2 Tbsp fresh lime juice

Kosher salt and pepper, to taste

Combine papaya, mango, pineapple, cucumber, jalapeños, green onions, basil or mint and lime juice in a small glass bowl. Toss gently just to combine. Add salt and pepper to taste. Serve immediately or refrigerate, covered, for up to one hour. Makes about 2½ cups.

If making the salsa ahead of time, add the papaya and pineapple just before serving. Otherwise, the salsa will get watery.

Source: www.recipegoldmine.com

▶ Chamomile contains active compounds (bisabolol, chamazulene and cyclic esters) that also have potent anti-inflammatory action. Dr. Duke says, "If I had CTS, I'd drink several cups of chamomile tea a day."

▶ Ray C. Wunderlich, Jr., MD, PhD, director of the Wunderlich Center for Nutritional Medicine in St. Petersburg, Florida, adds devil's claw and burdock to the list of herbs that often help.

▶ Another option is to try bromelain, the *proteolytic* (protein-dissolving) enzyme found in pineapple. According to Dr. Duke, "Naturopaths suggest taking 250 to 1,500 mg of pure bromelain a day, between meals, to treat inflammatory conditions such as CTS." Bromelain is available at health food stores.

Since ginger and papaya also contain helpful enzymes, Dr. Duke, who favors food sources to store-bought supplements, suggests, "You might enjoy a proteolytic CTS fruit salad composed of pineapple and papaya and spiced with grated ginger." (*See* recipe on left.)

▶ One more suggestion from Dr. Duke— "Also known as cayenne, red pepper contains six pain-relieving compounds and seven that are anti-inflammatory. Especially noteworthy is capsaicin. You might add several teaspoons of powdered cayenne to ¼ cup of skin lotion and rub it on your wrists. Or you could make a capsaicin lotion by steeping 5 to 10 red (hot) peppers in 2 pints of rubbing alcohol for a few days. Just wash your hands thoroughly after using any topical capsaicin treatment, so you don't get it in your eyes. Also, since some people are quite sensitive to this compound, you should test it on a small area of skin before using it on a larger area. If it seems to irritate your skin, discontinue use."

then strains out the plant material. You can add lemonade to mask the bitter taste. Dr. Duke says to drink 3 cups of tea a day. He cautions that if you're allergic to aspirin, you probably shouldn't take aspirin-like herbs.

COLDS AND FLU

Having a cold or flu is nothing to sneeze at! The common cold can wipe you out, and the influenza virus—which is characterized by inflammation of the respiratory tract and fever, chills and muscular pains—can really knock you out.

If you're feeling down for the count with a red, runny nose, chest congestion and that achy-all-over feeling, instead of making much *achoo* about nothing, keep reading for some simple hints to fight back.

Hot Remedy for a Cold

▶ The first round of ammunition for fighting the cold war is chicken soup (also known as Jewish penicillin). Marvin A. Sackner, MD, retired medical director of the Mount Sinai Medical Center in Miami Beach, Florida, proved that chicken soup can help cure a cold.

Using a bronchofiberscope and cineroentgenograms and measurements of mucus velocity, Dr. Sackner tested the effectiveness of hot chicken soup versus both hot and cold water. *The results…*

Cold water lowered nasal clearance. Hot water improved it, but it was nothing compared with the improvement after hot chicken soup. Then, to negate the effects of the steam from the hot water and hot chicken soup, the fluids were sipped through straws from covered containers. Hot water had very little effect this way. But the hot chicken soup still had some benefit.

■ Recipe ■

Lillian Wilen's Essential Chicken Soup

4 to 5 lbs chicken parts

3 carrots, scrubbed or peeled, cut in thirds

2 parsnips, scrubbed, cut in thirds

2 celery stalks with leaves, cut in thirds

1 large onion, cut in half

1 green pepper, cut in half and cleaned out

10 cups water

1 to 2 tsp salt

2 sprigs dill (optional), or ½ teaspoon dill seeds

4 parsley sprigs

4 cloves garlic, crushed

Add the chicken, carrots, parsnips, celery, onion, green pepper, water and salt to a big pot. Wrap the dill or dill seeds, parsley and garlic in cheesecloth and add that to the pot. Bring it to a boil, clean off the scum from the top of the soup, cover and simmer for 2½ to 3 hours. Remove the chicken and the vegetables. Refrigerate the soup overnight.

The next day, before heating the soup, remove the top layer of fat, skimming the surface with a spoon. Add the chicken and vegetables, heat and eat! Before it gets cold!

The Proof Is in the Mayo

The respected Mayo Clinic in Rochester, Minnesota, printed the following in its *Health Letter…*

"There is now evidence that our ancestors may have known more about how to treat sniffles than we do. And that should not be surprising. Indeed, scientific study of folk medicines and cures often has proved to be remarkably rewarding.

"Moses Maimonides, a 12th-century Jewish physician and philosopher, reported that chicken soup is an effective medication as well as a tasty food.

"A report published in *Chest,* a medical journal for chest specialists, indicates that hot chicken soup is more effective than other hot liquids in clearing mucus particles from the nose. The cause of this beneficial effect is still not fully understood, but the soup does seem to contain a substance that prompts clearing of nasal mucus. And removal of nasal secretions containing viruses and bacteria is an important part of our body's defense against upper respiratory infections. The study gives scientific respectability to the long-standing contention that chicken soup might help relieve a head cold.

"Chicken soup—particularly the homemade variety—is a safe, effective treatment for many 'self-limiting' illnesses (those not requiring professional attention). It is inexpensive and widely available.

"What does it all add up to? Specifically, this recommendation: Next time you come down with a head cold, try hot homemade chicken soup before heading for the pharmacy. We believe chicken soup can be an excellent treatment for uncomplicated head colds and other viral respiratory infections for which antibiotics ordinarily are not helpful. Soup is less expensive and, most significantly, it carries little, if any, risk of allergic reactions or other undesirable side effects."

■ Recipe ■

Dr. Ziment's Chicken Soup

1 quart homemade chicken broth,
    or 2 cans low-fat, low-sodium
    chicken broth
1 garlic head—about 15 cloves, peeled
5 parsley sprigs, minced
6 cilantro sprigs, minced
1 tsp lemon pepper
1 tsp dried basil, crushed, or
    1 Tbsp chopped fresh basil
1 tsp curry powder
Optional: Hot red pepper flakes to taste,
    sliced carrots, a bay leaf or two

Place all ingredients in a pot without a lid. Bring to a boil, then simmer for about 30 minutes. (If the soup is for your own personal use, carefully inhale the fumes during preparation as an additional decongesting treatment.) Remove the solid garlic cloves and herbs and, along with a little broth, purée them in a blender or food processor. Return the purée to the broth and stir. Serve hot.

Chicken Soup (The Medicine)

Irwin Ziment, MD, professor emeritus of clinical medicine at the David Geffen School of Medicine, University of California at Los Angeles, is also an authority on pulmonary drugs. Considering the research, experience and expertise it took to earn his credentials, we believe that Dr. Ziment's chicken soup recipe for colds, coughs and chest congestion should be taken seriously and whenever you have a cold. (*See* recipe on page 36.)

⚡ **CAUTION:** This chicken soup is a medicine and is not to be eaten as one would eat a portion of soup. Please follow the dosage instructions.

Dose: Take 2 tablespoons of Dr. Ziment's Chicken Soup at the beginning of a meal, one to three times a day. (If you feel you want a little more than 2 tablespoons, fine, but do not exceed more than ½ cup at a time.)

Other Dietary Remedies

▶In Russia, garlic is known as Russian penicillin. It has been reported that colds have actually disappeared within hours—a day at most—after taking garlic.

Keep a peeled clove of garlic in your mouth, between the cheek and teeth. Do not chew it. Occasionally, release a little garlic juice by digging your teeth into the clove. Replace the clove every three to four hours.

The allicin in garlic is an excellent mucus-thinner and bacteria-killer. It's no wonder many cold remedies include garlic.

▶If taking garlic by mouth is not for you, then peel and crush six cloves of garlic. Mix them into ½ cup of white lard or vegetable shortening. Spread the mush on the soles of your feet and cover them with a (preferably warmed) towel or flannel cloth. Put plastic

wrap under your feet to protect bedding. Garlic is so powerful that even though it's applied to one's feet, it will be on one's breath, too.

Apply a fresh batch of the mixture every five hours until the cold is gone.

Liquid Measures

▶Prepare tea by steeping equal parts of cinnamon, sage and bay leaves in hot water. Strain, and before drinking the tea, add 1 tablespoon of lemon juice. If necessary, sweeten with honey.

▶Keep flushing out your system by drinking lots of nondairy liquids—unsweetened fruit juices, herbal tea and just plain water.

Contessa Knows Best

▶When our friend, a Contessa from the Italian hills, has a cold, she makes a mug of very strong, regular tea and adds 1 tablespoon of honey, 1 tablespoon of cognac, 1 teaspoon of butter and ¼ teaspoon of cinnamon. She drinks it as hot as she can and goes to bed between cotton sheets. If she wakes up during the night and is all sweaty, she changes her bedclothes and sheets and goes back to bed. By morning, she feels "*molto bene!*"

▶People have been known to fake a cold just to take this remedy—combine 4 teaspoons of rum with the juice of one lemon and 3 teaspoons of honey. Then add it to a glass of hot water and drink it before going to bed.

▶Mix ¼ cup of apple cider vinegar with an equal amount of honey. This elixir is particularly effective for a cold with a sore throat.

Dose: Take 1 tablespoon six to eight times a day.

▶ Boil down ½ cup of sunflower seeds (without the shells, of course) in 5 cups of water until there's about 2 cups of liquid left in the pot. Then stir in ¼ cup of honey and ¾ cup of gin. This potion is particularly good for chest colds.

Dose: Take 2 teaspoons three times a day at mealtime.

☞ **WARNING:** Infants, diabetics and people with honey allergies should not use honey.

Soothing Remedy

▶ Take 4 teaspoons of prepared mustard and rub it on the chest. Take a (preferably white) towel and dip it in hot water, then wring it out and place it on top of the mustard already on the chest. As soon as the towel is cool, redip it in hot water, wring it out and put it back on the chest. Reapply the towel four or five times. After the last application of the towel, wash off the chest, dry thoroughly, bundle up and go to bed.

▶ To stimulate appropriate acupuncture points that can help relieve a cold, place an ice cube on the bottom of both big toes. Keep them in place with an elastic bandage or piece of cloth. Place feet in a basin, in two plastic shoe boxes or on plastic to avoid a mess from the melting ice. Do this procedure for no more than 20 minutes at a time…morning, noon and night.

Mineral or Medicine?

▶ Zinc gluconate—available at health food stores and some pharmacies—works wonders for some people. It either nips the cold in the bud, considerably shortens the duration of the cold or lessens the severity of it.

For it to be effective, be sure to follow the dosage carefully: Adults, take two lozenges (23 mg each) at the outset and then one every two hours thereafter, but not more than 12 a day, and for no longer than two days.

Also, do not take them on an empty stomach. Even if you don't feel like eating, consume half a fruit before you take a lozenge. Suck on the lozenge so that it comes in prolonged contact with your mouth and throat. Honey-flavored are the best—lemon are the pits.

Zinc gluconate also comes in 46 mg tablets. If you get them instead of the 23 mg, take one at the outset of your cold and one every four hours, not exceeding six a day, and not for longer than two days.

⚡ **CAUTION:** Some people get stomachaches from zinc. Also, high amounts of zinc may increase a man's risk of developing prostate cancer.

Consult your doctor before supplementing with zinc.

For children's dosages, *see* "Healing Remedies for Children" on page 207.

Flowers to Help You Sniff

▶ Las Vegas–based herbalist Angela Harris (*www.angelaharris.com*) says that the combination of echinacea and goldenseal is effective in either stopping a cold from blossoming, or cutting short the duration and minimizing the severity of a cold.

The secret is to take two droppers of the extract (available at health food stores) in a few ounces of water every hour for the first four hours of the day you feel a cold coming on. After that, take two droppers every four hours. Do not take echinacea for more than two weeks at a time. (You shouldn't have to.)

Don't Blow It

▶ Another popular remedy for a head cold is to cut two thin-as-can-be strips of orange rind. Roll them up with the white spongy part (the pith) on the outside, and gently stick one in each nostril. Stay that way until your head cold is better, or you can't stand the rind in your nostrils anymore—whichever comes first. Be sure to leave a bit of orange rind sticking out of your nose so you can dislodge it easily.

▶ The first of our five senses to develop is our sense of smell. Eventually, the average human nose can recognize 10,000 different odors—but not when we have a head cold.

To clear your head and stop a runny nose, begin by cutting the crust off a piece of bread. Plug in your iron and put it on "hot"—wool or cotton setting. Carefully iron the bread crust. When it starts to burn, lift the iron off the crust and *carefully* inhale the smoke through your nostrils for two minutes. Repeat this procedure three times throughout the day. We've been told that the runny nose stops and the head cold clears up in a very short time—one or two days.

▶ The natural sulfur in broccoli and parsley is supposed to help us resist colds. Eat broccoli and/or parsley once a day.

▶ An apple a day…works! A university study showed that the students who ate apples regularly had fewer colds.

■ Recipe ■

Jade Green Broccoli

2 lbs broccoli (1 bunch)
1 Tbsp cornstarch
2 Tbsp soy sauce
½ cup water or vegetable stock
¼ cup oil
⅛ tsp salt
1 clove garlic, minced
2 Tbsp sherry

Clean broccoli. Cut stems on a ⅛" slant. Mix cornstarch, soy sauce and stock or water. Set aside.

Heat a wok or cast-iron pan until it is very hot. Add oil, then salt. Turn heat to medium and add garlic. When golden brown, turn up heat and add broccoli. Stir-fry for 3 minutes. Add sherry and cover the pan quickly. Cook, covered, for 2 minutes. Add cornstarch mixture and stir until thickened.

Source: www.recipegoldmine.com

▶ Before bedtime, take a ginger bath and sweat away your cold overnight. Put 3 tablespoons of grated ginger in a stocking and knot the stocking closed.

NOTE: It's easier to grate frozen ginger than fresh ginger.

Throw the grated-ginger stocking into a hot bath, along with the contents of a 2-ounce container of powdered ginger. Stir the bathwater with a wooden spoon. Then, get in and soak for 10 to 15 minutes.

Once you're out of the tub, dry yourself thoroughly, preferably with a rough towel. Put on warm sleep clothes and cover your head with a towel or woolen scarf, leaving just your face exposed. Get in bed under the covers and go to sleep. If you perspire enough to feel uncomfortably wet, change into dry sleepwear.

Gem of a Remedy

▶ Talking about "sweating it out," a gem therapist told us that wearing a topaz activates body heat and, therefore, helps cure ailments that may benefit from increased perspiration.

Healing Power of Onion

The onion is also a popular natural remedy to relieve colds. *Here are some ways in which the onion is used...*

▶ Cut an onion in half and place one half on each side of your bed so you can inhale the scent as you sleep.

▶ Eat a whole onion before bedtime in order to break up the cold overnight.

▶ Dip a slice of raw onion in a glass of hot water. After a few seconds, remove the onion and, when the water cools, start sipping it. Continue to do so throughout the day.

▶ If you like your onions fried, take the hot fried onions, put them in a flannel or woolen cloth and bind them on your chest overnight.

▶ Put slices of raw onion on the soles of your feet, and hold the slices in place with woolen socks. Leave them that way overnight to draw out infection and fever.

> **NOTE:** If you get colds often, your immune system may need a boost. Check out the immune system strengthener in "Remedies in a Class by Themselves" on page 244.

Fight the Flu

Before flu season starts (in early October), check with your doctor to see if you should get a flu shot. The flu can be deadly, and older people and those with compromised immune systems are especially at risk. *Then, if your doctor approves, try these remedies...*

▶ The second you feel fluish, take 1 tablespoon of liquid lecithin (available at health food stores). Continue to take 1 tablespoon every eight hours for the next two days. Some naturalists believe that these large doses of lecithin may prevent the flu from flourishing.

Old Family Recipe

▶ This formula was handed down from generation to generation by a family who tells of the many lives it saved in Stuttgart, Germany, during the 1918 flu pandemic. The family claims that this special elixir cleanses the harmful virus from the blood.

CAUTION: This remedy is only for people who do not have a problem with alcohol.

Peel and cut ½ pound of garlic into small pieces. Put the garlic and 1 quart of cognac (90 proof) in a dark brown bottle. Seal it airtight with paraffin wax or tape. During the day, keep the bottle in the sun or another light, warm place, like in the kitchen near the oven. At night, move the bottle to a dark, cool place.

After 14 days and nights, open the bottle and strain. Put the strained elixir back in the bottle. It is now ready to be used. The potency of this mixture is said to last one year, so label the bottle with the expiration date accordingly.

If you already have the flu, take 20 drops of the formula with a glass of water, one hour before each meal (three times a day), for five days.

To prevent the flu, take 10 to 15 drops with a glass of water, one hour before each meal, every day during the flu season. Also, be sure to wash your hands frequently and avoid crowds.

▶ The second you've been exposed to someone with the flu, try taking cinnamon oil.

Dose: Take 5 drops of cinnamon oil in a tablespoon of water, three times a day.

▶ By drinking raw sauerkraut juice once a day, you should avoid getting the flu. (It's also a good way to avoid constipation.)

▶ Move to the North Pole for the winter. None of the standard cold- and flu-causing microorganisms can survive there. The problem is, you might not be able to either.

Guggle-Muggle Drink

▶ Philosopher Friedrich Nietzsche once said, "Whatever does not destroy me makes me strong." That's the way we felt about the drink our grandmother (Bubbie) made the second someone in our family came down with a cold.

■ **Recipe** ■

The Koch Family (for adults only) Guggle-Muggle

1 grapefruit, juiced
1 lemon, juiced
1 orange (preferably Temple), juiced
1 Tbsp honey

Juice the grapefruit, lemon and orange. Combine the juices and put in a saucepan over medium heat. Add the honey. Bring the mixture to a boil while stirring. After it has boiled, take the mixture off the stove and let cool. Then pour it into a glass and add your favorite liquor* (brandy is Ed Koch's).

As with most guggle-muggles, drink it down, then get under the covers and go to sleep. Next morning, no cold!

*Women who are pregnant or nursing should not consume alcohol.

The dreaded drink was called a *guggle-muggle.* We thought it was a cute name that Bubbie made up. Imagine our surprise when Ed Koch, during his last term in office as mayor of New York City, talked about an ancient cure—his family's recipe for a guggle-muggle.

It seems that many Jewish families have their own guggle-muggle recipes—and some are more palatable than others. Our family's is among the worst, but Mr. Koch's is one of the best. As he told us, "It is not only medically superb, it is delicious!"

Fever Relievers

▶ Bind sliced onions or peeled garlic cloves to the bottoms of your feet. As we mentioned earlier, don't be surprised if it gives you onion or garlic breath. And don't be surprised if it brings down your temperature.

▶ Eat grapes (in season) throughout the day. Also, dilute pure grape juice and sip some of it throughout the day. Drink it at room temperature, never chilled.

▶ Boil 4 cups (1 quart) of water with ½ teaspoon of cayenne pepper. Just before you drink each of these cups (four consumed throughout the day), add to each cup 1 teaspoon of honey and ¼ cup of orange juice. Heat it up just a little and then drink it slowly.

☞ **WARNING:** Do not give honey to infants/ children, diabetics or someone who is allergic to honey.

Sore Throats

The trouble with sore throats is that each swallow tends to be a painful reminder that you have a sore throat.

Some sore throats are caused by allergies, smoking, postnasal drip, yeast overgrowth and varying severities of bacterial invasion into your throat tissues. Many sore throats are caused by a mild viral infection that attacks when your resistance is low. You may need a health professional to help you determine the cause.

If you have a sore throat right now, think about your schedule. Chances are, you've been

pushing yourself like crazy, running around and keeping later hours than usual.

If you take it easy, get a lot of rest, flush your system by drinking nondairy liquids and stay away from "heavy" foods, the remedies we suggest will be much more effective.

☞ **WARNING:** Chronic or persistent sore throat pain should be checked by a health professional. Severe sore throats need immediate treatment and possibly antibiotics.

Natural Remedies

▶ Add 2 teaspoons of apple cider vinegar to a cup of warm water.

Dose: Gargle a mouthful, spit it out, then swallow a mouthful. Gargle a mouthful, spit it out, then swallow a mouthful. Keep this up until the liquid is all gone. An hour later, start all over.

▶ Mix 1 teaspoon of cream of tartar with ½ cup of pineapple juice and drink it.

Dose: Repeat every half-hour until there's a marked improvement.

▶ A singer we know says this works for her every time—steep three nonherbal tea bags in a cup of just-boiled water. Leave them there until the water is as dark as it can get—almost black.

Dose: While the water is still quite hot but bearable, gargle with the tea. Do not swallow any of it. (No one needs all that caffeine.) Repeat every hour until you feel relief.

Salty Soother

▶ Warm ½ cup of kosher (coarse) salt in a frying pan. Then pour the warm salt in a large, clean, white handkerchief and fold it over and over so that none of the salt can ooze out. Wrap

the salted hanky around your neck and wear it that way for an hour.

This was one of our great-aunt's favorite remedies. The only problem was she would get laryngitis explaining to everyone why she was wearing that salty poultice around her neck!

Be a Sage

▶ Next time you wake up with that sore throat feeling, add 1 teaspoon of sage to 1 cup boiling water. Steep for three to five minutes and strain.

Dose: Gargle in the morning and at bedtime. It would be wise to swallow the sage tea.

▶ Relief from a sore throat can come from inhaling the steam of hot vinegar. Take special care while inhaling vinegar vapors or any other kind for that matter. You don't have to get too close to the source of the steam for it to be effective.

▶ What's a sore throat without honey and lemon? Every family has their own variation on the combination. Take the juice of a nice lemon (our family prefaces every noun with the word *nice*) and mix it with 1 nice teaspoon of some nice honey.

Dose: Take it every two hours.

▶ Add the juice from one lemon to a glass of hot water (our family drinks everything from a

glass) and sweeten to taste with honey—about 1½ tablespoons.

Dose: Drink one glass every four hours.

▶ Grate 1 teaspoon of horseradish and one piece of lemon peel. To that, add ⅛ teaspoon of cayenne pepper and 2 tablespoons of honey.

Dose: Take 1 tablespoon every hour.

> **WARNING:** Infants, diabetics and people with honey allergies should not use honey.

Act Like a Brat

▶ We came across a beneficial exercise to do when you have a sore throat. Stick out your tongue for 30 seconds, put it back in and relax for a couple of seconds.

Then stick out your tongue again for another 30 seconds. Do it five times in a row and it will increase blood circulation, help the healing process and make you the center of attention at the next executive board meeting.

Make a Tea Towel

▶ Prepare chamomile tea. As soon as it cools enough for you to handle, soak a towel (preferably white) in the tea, wring it out and apply it to the neck. As soon as it gets cold, reheat the tea, redip the towel and reapply it. The chamomile will help draw out the soreness, and the heat will relax some of the tension built up in that area.

▶ According to a gem therapist, yellow amber worn around the neck will protect against sore throats. If you already have a sore throat, it is said that the electric powers of this fossilized, golden resin will help cure it.

▶ Prepare a carrot poultice (*see* "Preparation Guide" on page 252) with a large, grated carrot. Put the poultice around your throat. On top of the poultice, apply a washcloth that has been dipped in hot water and wrung out. To keep the heat in, cover it all with a towel or wide elastic bandage. If it seems to soothe your throat, redip the washcloth in hot water as soon as it gets cold.

Hoarseness/Laryngitis

The trouble with laryngitis is that you have to wait until you don't have it before you can tell anyone you had it.

Rest your vocal cords as much as possible. If you must talk, speak in a normal voice, letting the sound come from your diaphragm instead of your throat. *Don't whisper!* Whispering tightens the muscles of your voice box, and puts more stress on your vocal cords than does talking in your normal voice.

▶ Drink a mixture of 2 teaspoons of onion juice and 1 teaspoon of honey.

Dose: Take 3 teaspoons every three hours.

▶ Drink a cup of hot peppermint tea with a teaspoon of honey. After a hard day at the office, it's very relaxing for the entire body as well as the throat.

▶ If your cold seemed to settle in your throat in the form of hoarseness and congestion, peel and mince an entire bulb of garlic. Cover all the little pieces with raw honey and let it stand for two hours. Take a teaspoon of the honey/garlic mixture every hour. Just swallow it down

without chewing the garlic. That way you won't have garlic on your breath.

☛ **WARNING:** Infants, diabetics and people with honey allergies should not use honey.

Buddhist's Secret

▶ In 1 cup of water, simmer ½ cup of raisins for 20 minutes. Let it cool, then eat it all. This is a Tibetan remedy. It must work because we've never met anyone from Tibet with laryngitis.

▶ Boil 1 pound of black beans in 1 gallon of water for one hour. Strain.

Dose: Take 6 ounces of bean water an hour before each meal. The beans can be eaten during mealtime. (If necessary, *see* "Gas/Flatulence" in the "Indigestion" section on page 125.)

▶ When you're hoarse and hungry, eat baked apples. To prepare them, core four apples and peel them about halfway down from the top. Place them in a greased dish with about ½ inch of water. Drop a teaspoon of raisins into each apple core, then drizzle a teaspoon of honey into each core and over the tops of the apples. Cover and bake in a 350° F oven for 40 minutes. Baste a few times with pan juices during the cooking time.

Dose: Eat the apples warm or at room temperature. As they say, an apple a day… you know the rest.

▶ *See* the apple cider vinegar remedy on page 42. After seven hours and seven doses of the vinegar and water, plus a good night's sleep, there should be a major improvement.

▶ Grate radishes and squeeze them through cheesecloth to get radish juice. Let a teaspoon of the juice slide down your throat every half-hour.

Singer's Solution

▶ This is a popular Russian remedy for what they call "singer's sore throat." It promises to restore the singer's voice to normal in a single day. Incidentally, you don't have to be a singer to try this formula.

Take ½ cup of anise seeds and 1 cup of water and boil them slowly for 50 minutes. Strain out the seeds, then stir ¼ cup of raw honey into the anise-seed water and add 1 tablespoon of cognac.

Dose: Take 1 tablespoon every half-hour.

WARNING: Infants, diabetics and people with honey allergies should not use honey.

Strep Throat

This illness is caused by Group A strepto-cocci bacteria. If you have an extremely sore throat, fever, chills and ache all over, then you might have strep.

CAUTION: Strep throat is a serious illness. If left untreated, it can lead to rheumatic fever. See a physician to diagnose and treat this condition.

▶ Do you have a dog or a cat? If you do and you're troubled by frequent bouts of strep throat, have a veterinarian examine the animal for streptococci. Once your pet is free of the bacteria, chances are you will be, too, after treatment by your health professional.

Tonsillitis

Tonsils are those two little bumps at the back of your throat. They are part of the lymph system and may help fend off respiratory infections. When they swell up for long periods of time—yet you don't feel any better—you probably have tonsillitis.

CAUTION: If you have tonsillitis, your immune system needs to be evaluated and treated by a physician. Be aware that untreated bacterial tonsillitis may have serious consequences, including rheumatic fever, scarlet fever or even kidney disease (nephritis).

Here are some simple remedies to help your tonsils feel less inflamed.

▶ Bake a medium-sized banana in its skin for 30 minutes at 350° F. Peel and mash the juicy banana, adding 1 tablespoon of extra-virgin, cold-pressed olive oil. Spread the mush on a clean white cloth and apply it to the neck. Leave it on for a half-hour in the morning and a half-hour in the evening.

▶ Juice garlic cloves (*see* "Preparation Guide" on page 250) so that you have 1 tablespoon of fresh juice. Add the juice and 2 ounces of dried sage to 1 quart of water in a glass or enamel pot. Cover the pot and bring the mixture to a boil. As soon as it starts to boil, turn off the heat and let it stand until it's lukewarm. Strain the solution.

Dose: Drink ½ cup of this sage-garlic tea every two hours. Gargle ½ cup every hour until the condition is better.

NOTE: The holistic health professionals we talked to believe that tonsils should not be removed unless it's absolutely necessary. They function as armed guards, destroying harmful bacteria that enter through the mouth. Asian medicine practitioners believe that when tonsils are unable to fulfill this function, the body's immune system needs to be strengthened—but the tonsils should not be removed.

CONSTIPATION

You are most likely reading this section because you're seeking a natural laxative. Therefore, you may already know that the commercial chemical laxatives can kill friendly bacteria, can lessen the absorption of nutrients, can stuff up the intestinal walls, can turn users into addicts, can get rid of necessary vitamins and can eventually cause constipation.

We offer easy-to-take, inexpensive, non-chemical constipation relievers that should not present any problem side effects if taken in moderation, using good common sense. In other words, don't try more than one remedy at a time.

✎ **NOTE:** Constipation is a common problem that may be a symptom of disease or lead to more major health problems. It is important to consult a medical professional before starting any self-help treatment.

Natural Remedies

▶ The most natural time to move your bowels is within the first few hours of the day. Drinking water on an empty stomach stimulates peristalsis by reflex. So, before breakfast, drink the juice of half a lemon in 1 cup of warm water. While it may help cleanse your system, it may also make you pucker a lot. If you find it hard to drink, sweeten it with honey.

If lemon and water is not for you, eat or drink any one of the following at room temperature (not chilled)...

- ◆ Prune juice or stewed prunes
- ◆ Papaya
- ◆ Two peeled apples
- ◆ Six to eight dried figs. Soak them overnight in a glass of water. In the morning, drink the water, then eat the figs.

▶ The combination of dried apricots and prunes is said to work wonders. Soak six of each overnight. The next morning, eat three of each. Then, in the late afternoon, an hour or two before dinner, eat the remaining three apricots and three prunes.

▶ Eat at least three raw fruits a day. One of them, preferably an apple, should be eaten two hours after dinner.

▶ Take two small beets, scrub them clean and eat them raw in the morning. You should have a bowel movement about 12 hours later.

▶ Flaxseed is a popular folk treatment for constipation. Take 1 to 2 tablespoons with lots of water right after lunch or dinner. (*See* "Six Sensational Superfoods" on page 262.)

▶ Sunflower seeds are filled with health-giving properties and have also been known to promote regularity. Eat a handful of shelled, raw, unsalted seeds every day.

Sensational Sauerkraut

▶ Raw sauerkraut and its juice have friendly bacteria and may aid digestion. It's also an excellent laxative. Heat destroys the important enzymes in sauerkraut, so make sure you eat it raw. (Raw sauerkraut is available at health food stores, or *see* "Preparation Guide" on page 252 and learn how to prepare your own sauerkraut.)

You can also drink an 8-ounce glass of warm sauerkraut juice and then an 8-ounce glass of grapefruit juice (unsweetened)—one right after the other. It should do the job.

WARNING: Grapefruit juice interacts with many medications. Talk to your doctor before trying the previous remedy.

▶ We were told about an acupressure technique that is supposed to encourage a complete evacuation of the bowels in 15 minutes. For three to five minutes, massage the area underneath your lower lip, in the middle of your chin.

Olive Oil—Olé!

▶ The findings of recent studies say that monounsaturated fatty acid—the kind found in olive oil—is best for lowering cholesterol levels. Olive oil is also a help when a laxative is needed. Take 1 tablespoon of extra-virgin, cold-pressed olive oil in the morning and 1 tablespoon an hour after eating dinner.

▶ For some people, a dose of brewer's yeast does the trick. Take 1 heaping teaspoon of brewer's yeast and 1 heaping teaspoon of wheat germ with each meal. (Both are available at health food stores.)

Start with small amounts of either or both brewer's yeast and wheat germ. Gradually increase your intake and stop when the amount you're taking works for you.

▶ Are persimmons in season? Try one. It's been known to relieve constipation.

▶ For a mild laxative, soak six dates in a glass of hot water. When the water is cool, drink it, then eat the dates. (*Also see* the fig remedy under "Fatigue" on page 83.)

▶ If you have a favorite brand of cereal, add raw, unprocessed bran to it. Start with 1 teaspoon and gradually work your way up to 1 or 2 tablespoons each morning, depending on your reaction to it.

Exotic, but Effective

▶ Two natural laxatives available at the greengrocer or produce aisle are escarole (eat it raw or boil it in water and drink the water) and Spanish onion (roast it and eat it at bedtime). The cellulose in onions gives intestinal momentum.

▶ Hippocrates (460–377 BC), the Greek physician and father of medicine, recommended eating garlic every day to relieve constipation. Cook with it and eat it raw (in salads) whenever possible.

Be Convincing

▶ Just as you're falling asleep, when the mind is most open to autohypnotic suggestion, say to yourself, "In the morning, I will have a good bowel movement." Keep repeating the sentence until you doze off. Pleasant dreams!

For a Gentle Approach

▶ Raw spinach makes a delicious salad, has lots of vitamins and minerals and is a mild laxative, too. Be sure to wash it thoroughly to reduce the risk of food-borne illness.

▶ Aerobic exercise is an excellent laxative. With your doctor's approval, try to move your body for 30 minutes every morning.

▶ One teaspoon of blackstrap molasses in ½ cup of warm water, drunk an hour before lunch, might do the trick.

▶ Soak your feet in cold water, 15 minutes at a time, once in the morning and once before bedtime. Be sure to dry your feet thoroughly.

▶ Okra acts as a mild laxative. Add chicken gumbo soup to your menu from time to time.

■ Recipe ■

Chicken Soup with Okra

1 small, cleaned chicken cut into
serving portions
2 Tbsp flour
1 onion, chopped
2 Tbsp vegetable oil
4 cups okra, chopped
2 cups tomato pulp
½ cup parsley, chopped
4 cups water
Salt and pepper to taste

Coat chicken pieces lightly with flour and sauté with onion in oil. Add okra, tomato, parsley and water as soon as chicken is browned. Season with salt and pepper to taste. Simmer for about 2½ hours, until chicken is tender and okra is well cooked. Be sure to add water as needed during the simmering. Serves 6.

Stool Softener

▶ Every night, before eating dinner, eat a tablespoon of raisins or three prunes that have been soaking in water for a couple of hours.

COUGHS

When the doctor examined her patient one morning, the doctor remarked, "I'm happy to say that your cough sounds much better."

The patient answered, "Well, it should. I had a whole night of practice."

This may be a joke, but it's not funny if you're the one who's coughing, especially at night when coughs seem to act up.

We all have a cough center in our brain. It's generally motivated by an irritation in the respiratory tract. In other words, a cough is nature's way of helping us loosen and get rid of mucus that's congesting our system.

Here are a few natural remedies that may quell the cough and help you sleep better.

NOTE: If cough is chronic or persistent, have it checked by a health professional. Coughs accompanied by a fever or shortness of breath can be serious.

Natural Remedies

▶ For five minutes, cook the juice of one lemon, 1 cup of honey and ½ cup of olive oil. Then stir vigorously for a couple of minutes.

Dose: Take 1 teaspoon every two hours.

▶ Combine ½ cup apple cider vinegar with ½ cup water. Add 1 teaspoon of cayenne pepper and sweeten to taste with honey.

Dose: Take 1 tablespoon when the cough starts acting up. Then swallow another tablespoon at bedtime.

WARNING: Infants, diabetics and people with honey allergies should not use honey.

Honion Syrup

▶ Peel and finely chop six medium onions. Put them and ½ cup of honey into the top of a double boiler, or in a pan over a pot of boiling water. Cover the mixture and let it simmer for two hours. Strain this concoction we call "honion syrup," and pour it into a jar with a cover.

Dose: Take 1 warm tablespoon every two to three hours.

▶ Grate 1 teaspoon of horseradish and mix it with 2 teaspoons of honey. (Or, one finely chopped clove of garlic can be used in place of horseradish.)

Dose: Take 1 teaspoon of the mix every two to three hours.

Lemony Fresh

▶ For a delicious, thirst-quenching and soothing drink, squeeze the juice of one lemon into a big mug or glass. Add hot water, 2 tablespoons of honey and either three whole cloves or a ½-inch piece of stick cinnamon.

Dose: Drink one glass every three hours.

▶ Cook a cup of barley according to the package directions. Then add the juice of one fresh lemon and some water to the barley. Liquefy the mixture in a blender. Drink it slowly.

Dose: Drink 1 cup every four hours.

Holy Rutabagas!

▶ Cut a hole through the middle of a rutabaga or a yellow onion and fill the hole with honey or brown sugar. Leave it overnight. In the morning, drink the juice and it will relieve the cough.

▶ Cut a deep hole in the middle of a large beet and fill the hole with honey or brown sugar. Bake the beet until it's soft. It's a treat to eat the beet…whenever you feel a cough coming on.

Mull This Over

▶ Adding spices and herbs to wine is called mulling. Into 3 cups of wine, add a 1-inch piece of stick cinnamon, 1 tablespoon of honey, three to six cloves (depending on how much you like the taste of cloves) and a few pieces of well-scrubbed lemon peel. Heat and stir.

Dose: Drink 3 cups a day.

Even if this mulled wine doesn't help, you somehow don't mind having the cough as much!

> **WARNING:** Do not give honey to infants/children, diabetics or someone who is allergic to honey. Women who are pregnant or nursing should not consume alcohol.

Ginger Gum

▶ Chew on a bite-sized piece of ginger root, just like you would chew gum. Swallowing the juice should help control a cough. Ginger is strong, and it might take some getting used to.

▶ Take a piece of brown grocery-bag paper, about the size of your chest, and soak it in vinegar. When it stops dripping, sprinkle black pepper on one side of the paper. Then place the peppered side on your bare chest.

To keep it in place overnight, wrap an elastic bandage or cloth around your chest. By morning, there may be a big improvement, particularly with a bronchial cough.

Oats to the Rescue

▶ Among other ingredients, the polyunsaturated fatty acids found in whole-grain oats have been said to soothe bronchial inflammation and relieve coughing spasms.

▶ Make a mash from the oats by following the directions on the whole-grain oats box, but reduce the amount of water by ¼ cup. Add honey to taste.

Dose: Eat 1 cup at a time, four times a day and whenever a coughing spell starts. Be sure the oat mash is eaten warm.

Turney Syrup?

▶ Peel and slice a large turnip. Spread honey between all the slices and let it stand for several hours while the turnip/honey syrup oozes out and collects at the bottom of the dish. Whenever the cough acts up, take a teaspoon of the syrup.

> **WARNING:** Infants, diabetics and people with honey allergies should not use honey.

▶ Add ½ cup of raw, shelled and unsalted sunflower seeds to 5 cups of water and boil in an enamel or glass pot until the water is reduced to about 2 cups. Strain, then stir in ¾ cup of gin and 1½ cups of honey. Mix well and bottle it. Whenever the cough acts up, take 1 to 2 teaspoons, but not more than four times a day.

> **WARNING:** People who have problems with alcohol should not try this remedy.

Love That Licorice!

▶ Licorice root contains saponins, natural substances known to break up and loosen mucus. When you have a hacking cough, drink a cup of licorice-root tea (*see* "Preparation Guide" on page 250).

> **NOTE:** Do not take licorice root if you have high blood pressure or kidney problems. It can cause renal failure.

Squeezin' Fights Wheezin'

▶ An acupressure point that has been known to stop a cough is the one near the end of the middle finger. With the fingers of your right hand, squeeze the top joint of the left hand's middle finger. Keep squeezing until you stop wheezing.

Beany Goodness

▶ This bean purée remedy is for one of those mean, deep-down coughs that nothing seems to reach. Put a cupful of kidney beans in a strainer and rinse them with water. Then put them in water and let them soak overnight (while you probably cough your head off, right?).

The next morning, drain the beans, tie them up in a clean cloth and bruise them—pound them with a blunt object like a rolling pin, frying pan or hammer. Place the bruised beans in an enamel or glass saucepan with three cloves of peeled and minced garlic and 2 cups of water. Bring the mixture to a boil, then simmer for one and a half to two hours, until tender. Add more water if necessary. Take 1 tablespoon of this bean purée whenever your cough acts up.

Types of Coughs

Bronchial Coughs

▶ Add 3 drops of oil of fennel and 3 drops of oil of anise to 6 tablespoons of honey. Shake vigorously and bottle it. Take 1 teaspoon when you start to cough.

WARNING: Infants, diabetics and people with honey allergies should not use honey.

▶ If you haven't prepared the syrup in advance of your cough and don't have the necessary ingredients, you may want to settle for second best. Do you have the liqueur called anisette? Take 1 teaspoon of anisette in 1 tablespoon of hot water, every three hours.

CAUTION: Women who are pregnant or nursing should not consume alcohol.

Just a Tickle...

▶ Many people are bothered by a tickling type of cough, usually at night in their sleep. Put 2 teaspoons of apple cider vinegar in a glass of water and keep it by your bedside. When the "tickling" wakes you up, swallow one or two mouthfuls of the vinegar water and go back to a restful sleep.

▶ Chew a couple of whole cloves to relieve a throat tickle.

▶ Eat a piece of well-done toast (preferably whole wheat).

Smoker's Cough

▶ This remedy is updated from the *Universal Cookery Book* (circa 1888). Pour 1 quart of boiling water over 4 tablespoons of whole flaxseed and steep for three hours. Strain, add the juice of two lemons and sweeten with honey (which replaces the crystals of rock candy used in the original remedy). Take a tablespoon whenever the cough acts up.

▶ An even better remedy for smoker's cough— stop smoking! (*See* "Smoking" on page 167.)

Dry Cough

▶ Take 1 to 2 tablespoons of potato water (*see* "Preparation Guide" on page 252) each time the cough acts up. You may also want to add honey to taste.

Nighttime Cough

▶ To help loosen phlegm, fry two finely chopped medium onions in lard or vegetable shortening. As soon as it's cool enough to touch, rub the mixture on the cougher's chest and wrap the chest with a clean (preferably white) cloth. Do this procedure in the evening. It may result in a good night's sleep.

▶ Right before bed, add 1 teaspoon of dry mustard powder to a half-filled bathtub of hot water. Prepare a hot drink of your choice— peppermint tea or hot water, honey and lemon. Wear bedclothes that leave the chest accessible.

Have two rough terrycloth towels and a comfortable chair or stool in the bathroom.

Dip your feet in water and keep them there for 15 minutes. (The rest of the body should be seated alongside the tub.) When the water cools, add more hot water. Sip the drink through this entire process.

After 15 minutes of sipping and dipping (no stripping), dunk one of the towels in the bathwater, wring it out and place it on the bare chest. Once the towel cools off, dunk it again, wring it out and place it back on the chest. Repeat this three times, then dry the body thoroughly, bundle up and go to bed.

According to Mark A. Stengler, ND, adjunct associate clinical professor at the National College of Natural Medicine in Portland, Oregon, and a naturopathic physician at La Jolla Whole Health Clinic in La Jolla, California, allergies and airborne irritants may cause postnasal drip. Mucous drainage irritates the throat, which can trigger a nighttime cough. Try propping up your pillows to provide more effective drainage. A high-efficiency particulate air (HEPA) filter in your bedroom can help reduce allergens, such as dust or pollen.

You might also try taking vitamin C (1,000 mg twice daily), along with *quercetin* (500 mg twice daily), a relative of vitamin C that acts as a natural antihistamine. Continue until your symptoms subside, typically in two to four days.

Nervous Cough

▶ We know a theatrical stage manager who wants to make this announcement before the curtain goes up....

"To stop nervous coughs, apply pressure to the area between your lip and your nose. If that doesn't work, press hard on the roof of the mouth. If neither works, please wait until intermission, then go outside and cough."

DEPRESSION AND STRESS

We all go through periods of depression and stress. Maybe it's because of the weather—you know, a change of season. Or for women, it could be "that time of month." Of course, pressures at the office don't help, nor do tense relationships or problems at home. Then there are additives in foods and side effects from medications that can cause chemical imbalances that may lead to depression and stress.

CAUTION: For cases of deep depression, extreme stress and/or chronic fatigue, we suggest you seek professional assistance to help pinpoint the cause and recommend treatment.

Whatever the reason, valid or not, when you're going through a bad time and you reach the point where you say to yourself, "I'm sick and tired of being sick and tired!"—then you're on the road to recovery.

Basic Solutions

If you are really ready to help yourself, you might start by cutting down on your sugar intake. Excessive sugar can help cause depression, nervous anxiety and spurts of energy followed by extreme fatigue.

Caffeine products (such as coffee, non-herbal tea, cola, chocolate and some medications), cigarettes and alcoholic beverages may also contribute to nervous anxiety, depression and highs and lows of energy. Take them out of your life. They're taking the life out of you.

Be sure to eat a sensible diet of whole grains, steamed green vegetables, lean meat and fish and raw garlic in big salads with onion and lots of celery. Have sunflower seeds, raisins, sauerkraut, whole wheat pasta and beans. What could be bad?

Meanwhile, here are some more anxiety-relieving recommendations that may help...

Dietary Remedies

▶ Have a pizza with lots of oregano. If you don't have the oregano, forget the pizza. In fact, forget the pizza and just have the oregano. Oregano may ease that depressed, heavyhearted feeling.

▶ If you have a juicer, whip up half a glass of watercress and half a glass of spinach. Throw in some carrots to make the juice sweeter. Then, bottoms up and spirits up.

▶ Eat two ripe bananas a day to chase the blues away. Bananas contain the chemicals serotonin and norepinephrine, which are believed to help prevent depression. (*See* recipe on page 54.)

Other Mood Lifters

▶ While running a warm bath, prepare a cup of chamomile tea. Add the used tea bag to the

■ Recipe ■

African Banana Fritters

6 well-ripened bananas

1 cup all-purpose flour

¼ cup granulated sugar

¼ cup water

1 tsp nutmeg

Mash bananas with a fork or use blender to make into a pulp. Add flour.

Mix water and sugar to make a syrup. Add syrup and nutmeg to bananas and flour (add more water, if needed, to make batter into pancake consistency.) Mix well. Fry like pancakes in oiled frying pan until golden brown.

Makes 24 small pancakes.

Source: www.recipegoldmine.com

bath, along with a new one. If you use loose chamomile, wrap the herb in cheesecloth before putting it in the tub to avoid messy cleanup. Once the bath is ready, take a pen and paper along with your cup of tea and relax in the tub. Make a list of a dozen wishes as you sip your tea. Be careful…the things you wish for may come true.

▶ To lighten a heavy heart, drink saffron tea and/or thyme tea that has been sweetened with honey. (Incidentally, "thyme" was originally called "wild time" because it was thought to be an aphrodisiac.)

▶ Sniffing citrus essential oils every hour you're awake may help you get out of a funk. You can buy lemon or orange oil at a health food store. *Do not* take the essential oils internally. If you have a citrus fruit in your kitchen, you can use a cardboard cutter to carefully make slits in the peel and squeeze it so that the volatile oil seeps out. Then take a whiff hourly.

▶ Cheer yourself up by wearing rose colors—pinks and scarlets. The orange family of colors are also picker-uppers.

▶ Making love can help people overcome feelings of depression—unless, of course, they have no one to make love to and that's why they're depressed.

▶ If you're mildly depressed, simply change your physiology and your emotions will follow suit. In other words, do the physical things you do when you're happy—and you'll feel happy. Smile! Laugh! Jump up and down! Sing! Dance! Get dressed up!

If you believe it will work, it will.

If you're not willing to go along with this suggestion, then you're not willing to let go of your depression. There's nothing wrong with staying in a funk for a brief period…as long as you understand that it is your choice.

Dietary Stress Relievers

▶ Juices seem to be calming to the nerves. Throughout the day, sip apple, pineapple, prune, grape or cherry juice. Make sure the juice has no added sugar or preservatives, and drink it at room temperature, not chilled.

▶ Chop a large onion into very small tidbits and add a tablespoon of honey. Eat half the

mixture with lunch and the other half with dinner. Onions contain prostaglandin, which is reported to have a stress-relieving effect.

> (☞ **WARNING:** Infants, diabetics and people with honey allergies should not use honey.

A Berry Good Idea

▶ If strawberries are in season, eat a few as a dessert after each meal (without the cream and sugar). You may *feel* a difference (you won't be as edgy), and you may *see* a difference (they'll make your teeth whiter).

▶ Acupressure away the pressure of the day by getting a firm grip on your ankle. Using your thumb and third finger, place one just below the inside of the anklebone, and the other finger on the indentation directly below your outer anklebone. Keep steady pressure on the spot as you count down from 100 to one, slowly (taking between one and two minutes in all).

▶ Peppermint tea has a wonderful way of relaxing the system and relieving moodiness. Drink it warm and strong.

Seeing Green...and Blue

▶ If you are on edge, high-strung and, generally speaking, a nervous wreck, try to surround yourself with calming colors. Green can have a harmonizing effect, since it's the color of nature. Earth colors should make you feel better. Wear quiet blues and gentle grays. Color helps more than we realize.

▶ Sage tea can help relieve the jitters. Steep a sage tea bag or 1 teaspoon of sage in 1 cup of

warm water for five minutes. Strain and drink three cups a day.

Bonus: Sage tea also helps sharpen one's memory and brain power.

▶ There's a reason why Epsom salt, an ancient natural healer, is still popular—it works! Pour 2 cups of Epsom salt into a warm-water bath. Set aside a half-hour for pure relaxation in the tub—no interruptions—just 30 minutes of stress-free fantasizing.

Phtheasy for You to Say

▶ According to European folklore, celery helps you forget your troubles from a broken heart and soothes your nerves at the same time. It's probably the *phthalide* in celery, which is known to have sedative properties.

Nervous Tics

▶ From time to time Joan gets a tic around her eye. She feels like she's winking at everyone. The tic-off switch that works like magic for her is vitamin B_6.

> ⚡ **CAUTION:** Be sure to consult with your naturopathic doctor about the correct dosage for you.

A nervous tic may also be your body's way of telling you that you need more calcium or magnesium—or both. A good supplement can help you get the 1,500 mg of calcium and 750 mg of magnesium you need daily.

DIABETES

In simplified terms, diabetes is a condition in which the pancreas does not produce an adequate amount of insulin to burn up the body's intake of sugars and starches from food.

You may have this condition if you urinate frequently and are thirsty all the time. The lack of insulin may also deplete your blood sugar, making you feel tired, weak and/or lightheaded. Be sure to consult your doctor if you have any of these symptoms.

Dietary Controls

Thanks to modern laboratory technology, diabetics can perform urinalysis and blood-sugar tests conveniently in their own homes. While it makes it easy to monitor oneself, remember—*diabetes is a serious condition. Do not embark on any plan of treatment without a doctor's supervision.*

Many cases of diabetes can be completely controlled—controlled, not cured—by sensible eating habits. By sticking to a healthy, well-balanced diet with plenty of fiber, and exercising (walking at a normal speed for a half-hour after every meal), many diabetics reduce or eliminate their need for medication and feel better than ever. Controlled weight loss, especially for the obese, is very important.

Joan's Amazing Blood Sugar Secret

▶ One of our most important remedies requires only one ingredient. As a diabetic, Joan needs to keep her blood sugar level down. When she's eaten something that caused her number to increase (even though she's taken her diabetic medication), she takes 1 to 2 table-

Get Choked Up

Sunchokes, also known as Jerusalem artichokes (although they're not from Jerusalem nor are they artichokes) have been said to help stimulate the production of insulin when eaten daily.

These tubers contain inulin and levulin, carbohydrates that do not convert to sugar in the body. Jerusalem artichokes are similar in texture to potatoes, but taste sweeter. They're great for helping you stick to a weight-loss diet because they satisfy your sweet tooth, and are low in calories and high in vitamins and minerals. Eat them raw as a snack or in salads, boiled in soups or baked in stews. (*See* the recipe on page 18.)

Some greengrocers now carry Jerusalem artichokes. They are easy to grow and worth the effort if you have the space. Ask your local nursery to help you get started.

spoons of that one special ingredient—organic extra-virgin coconut oil—and within an hour, Joan's blood sugar is dramatically lower.

Combination Plate

▶ Along with a well-balanced, sugar-free diet, the combination of garlic, watercress and parsley, eaten daily, might help regulate blood-sugar levels for some diabetics.

DIARRHEA

Diarrhea is a common condition that is often caused by overeating, a bacterial, viral or parasitic infection, mild food poisoning, emotional anxiety or extreme fatigue.

Even a quick and simple bout of diarrhea depletes the system of potassium, magnesium and even sodium, often leaving the sufferer tired, depressed and dehydrated. It's important to keep drinking clear fluids during and after a siege in order to avoid depletion and dehydration.

 CAUTION: If diarrhea persists, it may be a symptom of a more serious ailment. Get professional medical attention. Bloody diarrhea can be infectious and needs treatment immediately.

Dietary Remedies

Milk It

▶ A West Indian remedy for diarrhea is a pinch of allspice in a cup of warm water or milk. A Pennsylvania Dutch remedy is 2 pinches of cinnamon in a cup of warm milk. A Brazilian remedy calls for 2 pinches of cinnamon and 1 pinch of powdered cloves in a cup of warm milk.

A Different Kind of Charcoal

An adsorbent (that's right, *adsorbent*) substance attaches things to its surface instead of absorbing them into itself. Activated charcoal is the most powerful adsorbent known.

Charcoal capsules or tablets can help stop certain types of diarrhea quickly by adsorbing the toxins that may cause the problem. Follow the instructions on the box.

NOTE: Be sure to heed the warning and drug interaction precaution—charcoal can interfere with antibiotics. Activated charcoal is not for everyday use, as it adsorbs the vitamins and minerals you need to be healthy.

▶ We may as well "milk" this for all it's worth with a Welsh remedy that requires a cup of boiled milk and a redhot fireplace poker.

Carefully place the red-hot poker into the cup of milk. Keep it there for 30 seconds. The poker supposedly charges the milk with iron, which is a homeopathic treatment of diarrhea. Be careful and drink the iron-charged milk slowly—it may be hot!

▶ The combination of cinnamon and cayenne pepper is known to be very effective in tightening the bowels quickly. In fact, it probably takes longer to prepare the tea than for it to work.

Bring 2 cups of water to a boil, then add ¼ teaspoon of cinnamon and ⅛ teaspoon of cayenne pepper. Let the mixture simmer for 20 minutes. As soon as it's cool enough to drink, have ¼ cup every half hour.

▶ Add 1 teaspoon of powdered ginger to 1 cup of just-boiled water. To control diarrhea, drink 3 cups of the mixture throughout the day.

▶ Grate an onion and squeeze it through cheesecloth so you get 2 tablespoons (1 ounce) of onion juice. Take the onion juice every hour, along with 1 cup of peppermint tea.

Suited to a Tea

▶ Raspberry-leaf tea is a popular folk remedy for children and adults. Combine 1 ounce of dried raspberry leaves with 2 cups of water (a piece of cinnamon stick is optional), and simmer in an enamel or glass saucepan for 25 minutes. Strain, cool and drink throughout the day.

Hippocratic Oats

▶ According to Hippocrates, the Greek physician and father of medicine, everyone should drink barley water daily to maintain good health. One of the benefits is its effectiveness in treating diarrhea.

Boil 2 ounces of pearled barley in 6 cups of water until there's about half the water—3 cups—left in the pot. Strain. If necessary, add honey and lemon to taste. Not only should you drink the barley water throughout the day, you should also eat the barley.

Berry Good Berries

▶ Since biblical times, the common blackberry plant has been used to cure diarrhea and dysentery. And so the berry remedy, in one form or another, has been passed down through the generations. Don't be surprised if your neighborhood bartender recommends some blackberry brandy.

Dose: Drink 1 shot glass (2 tablespoons) every four hours.

⚡ **CAUTION:** Women who are pregnant or nursing should not consume alcohol.

▶ Blackberry juice or wine will also do fine.
Dose: Take 6 ounces blackberry juice every four hours—or 2 ounces (4 tablespoons) blackberry wine every four hours.

The Big Apple

▶ Scrape a peeled apple with a (preferably nonmetal) spoon and eat the scrapings. In fact, eat no other food but grated apple until the condition greatly subsides.

▶ Boil ½ cup of white rice in 6 cups of water for a half-hour. Strain and save the water, then sweeten with honey to taste.

Dose: Drink 1 cup of the rice water every other hour. Do not drink other liquids until the condition disappears.

Eating cooked rice with a dash of cinnamon is also helpful in controlling the problem.

An A-peeling Remedy

▶ Bananas may help promote the growth of beneficial bacteria in the intestine and replace some of the lost potassium.

Dose: Three times a day, eat one ripe banana that has been soaked in milk.

▶ Add 1 teaspoon of garlic (finely chopped) to 1 teaspoon of honey and swallow it down three times a day—two hours after each meal.

▶ Certain drinks are effective in treating diarrhea and help replenish the system's supply of friendly intestinal bacteria. Have 1 to 2 glasses of buttermilk or sauerkraut juice or kefir (found in health food stores).

Or eat a portion or two of yogurt with active cultures, along with pickled beets, pickled cucumbers or raw sauerkraut (*see* "Preparation Guide" on page 253 for sauerkraut recipe).

Press for Success

▶ The navel is an acupressure point for treating diarrhea. Using your thumb or the heel of your hand, press in and massage the area in a circular motion for about two minutes.

Chronic Diarrhea

This remedy goes to prove that you can't argue with success. A woman wrote to tell us that eating Archway coconut macaroons—two a day—put an end to her 12-year bout with diarrhea. She suffers from Crohn's disease, which is a chronic inflammation of the intestinal wall. Chronic diarrhea is one of the most common and debilitating symptoms of this condition. The woman asked that we include her remedy, hoping it will help others with this problem.

Upon further investigation, we found that Joe Graedon, MS, pharmacologist, adjunct assistant professor at the University of North Carolina, Chapel Hill, also reported on these cookies and the success many people had with them. One woman couldn't find the Archway cookies, so she made her own coconut macaroons and they, too, worked like magic. While they don't work for everyone, they may be worth a try.

NOTE: Take into consideration your dietary needs before trying the coconut macaroon remedy. The cookies are high in fat and contain sweeteners.

Dysentery

It is common for people traveling in foreign countries to get dysentery. All of the remedies for diarrhea may help treat bacterial dysentery. However, amoebic dysentery (which is caused by amoeba living in the raw green vegetables of some countries) and viral dysentery are more severe forms of dysentery. All types of dysentery should be treated by a health professional.

▶ To help prevent bacterial dysentery, two weeks before you travel to a foreign country, eat a finely chopped raw onion in a cup of yogurt every day.

Before you discard this preventive measure, try it. You may be surprised at how good it tastes. The yogurt somehow makes the onion taste sweet.

DRINKING PROBLEMS

Drinking alcohol in excess can make you look wrinkled and haggard, can destroy vital organs and, in general, ruin your life.

For the problem drinker, we strongly recommend the leading self-help organization for combating alcoholism—Alcoholics Anonymous. Headquartered in New York City, the organization is a support group for people with drinking problems. Go to *www.aa.org* for more information, or check the White Pages of the telephone book for your local chapter.

This section provides natural remedies for the social drinker who, occasionally, has one too many.

Dietary Remedies

▶ Before you have a drink, sprinkle nutmeg into a glass of milk and sip it slowly. It may help absorb and neutralize the effects of alcoholic beverages.

▶ The Greek philosopher and teacher Aristotle (384–322 BC) advised his followers to eat a big chunk of cabbage before imbibing. Cole slaw—which is made from cabbage and vinegar—is said to be an even more effective intoxication preventive.

▶ The best way to hold your liquor is in the bottle it comes in! One way to help you do that is, when sober, look at a man or woman who is drunk. It's not often a pretty sight.

Sober Up

The following suggestions are meant for people who have drunk too much alcohol—that is, these remedies may make them more alert and communicative.

However, DO NOT trust or depend on those people's reflexes, especially behind the wheel of a car. It generally takes one hour per 20 milligrams of alcohol consumed to sober up…in other words, wait an hour after each bottle of beer, glass of wine or shot of liquor.

▶ If a drunk person imagines that the room is spinning, have him/her lie down on a bed and put one foot on the floor to stop that feeling.

▶ Honey contains fructose, which promotes the chemical breakdown of alcohol. Start by giving the drunk person 1 or 2 teaspoons of honey. Follow that with 1 teaspoon of honey every half-hour for the next couple of hours.

WARNING: Do not give honey to someone who is diabetic or allergic to honey.

▶ To help sober up an intoxicated person, try feeding him cucumber—as much as he is willing to eat. The cuke's enzyme, erepsin, may lessen the effect of alcohol.

▶ Try sobering up someone who's tipsy by massaging the tip of his nose.

CAUTION: Stimulation of the tip of the nose can cause vomiting, so don't stand right in front of the person you're sobering up.

▶ This is a Siberian method of sobering up a drunk person. Have him lie flat on his back. Place the palms of your hands on his ears. Next, rub both ears briskly and strongly in a

circular motion. Within minutes, the person should start coming around.

While he may be a lot more sober than before you rubbed his ears, he should NOT be trusted behind the wheel of a car.

Hangover Help

In simplified terms, a hangover is the disagreeable physical effect—a headache or nausea, for example—caused by drinking too much alcohol. Hangovers can make a fun night turn into a bad morning.

▶ Hangovers can also be caused by an allergy or sensitivity to what you drank. Using homeopathic theory (like fights like), put 1 drop of the alcohol in a glass of water. Take three sips. If the hangover symptoms do not disappear within five minutes, then drink the rest of the glass of water. If you still don't feel better within a few minutes, then your hangover is not allergy-caused.

▶ For the morning after, take ⅛ teaspoon of cayenne pepper in a glass of water.

▶ Evening primrose oil (soft gels are available at health food stores) is said to help replenish the amino acids and gamma-linoleic acid that's lost when you drink alcoholic beverages. Take 1,000 milligrams (mg) with lots of water or orange juice before you go to sleep.

Too late for that? Okay then, take it when you wake up and are desperate for anything that will help you feel human again.

▶ According to the Chinese, a cup of ginger tea (*see* "Preparation Guide" on page 250) will help calm an unsettled stomach caused by a hangover. To relieve eye, ear, mouth, nose and brain pain from the hangover, knead the fleshy part of the hand between the thumb and the index finger on both hands. For a pounding hangover headache, massage each thumb, just below the knuckles.

Sweet Solution

▶ Take 1 tablespoon of honey every minute for five minutes. Repeat the procedure a half-hour later.

WARNING: Do not give honey to someone who is diabetic or allergic to honey.

▶ Rub ¼ lemon on each armpit. That may ease the discomfort of a hangover.

▶ If you insist on drinking, you may be interested to know that a research team from England advises drinkers to guzzle clear alcohols—gin, vodka or white rum—to lessen the chances of that "morning after" feeling. Red wine and whiskey seem to have more hangover-promoting elements.

Morning-After Breakfast

▶ Bananas and milk is the breakfast of choice of many hangover sufferers. It may be effective due to the fact that alcohol depletes the magnesium in one's body, and bananas and milk replenish the supply.

You may want to add tomato, carrot, celery and/or beet juice to replenish the B and C vitamins along with some trace minerals that alcohol may also deplete.

Listen to a Wise Old Owl

▶ The famed Roman naturalist Pliny the Elder (who lived from 23–79 AD and wrote a comprehensive encyclopedia called *Natural history*) recommended eating the eggs of an owl.

While owl eggs may be hard to come by, all eggs are a source of cysteine, which helps the body manufacture glutathione, an antioxidant that gets depleted when alcohol is present. So an omelet could be a helpful hangover breakfast.

Pliny may have eased the symptoms of many a hangover with those eggs. Look who was the wise old owl, after all.

▶ Have a hangover? Feel like pulling your hair out? Good idea, but don't go all the way. Just pull your hair, clump by clump, until it hurts a little (don't pull the hair out).

According to a noted reflexologist, hair-pulling is stimulating to the entire body and can help lessen the symptoms of a hangover.

▶ When you have a throbbing hangover headache, eat a raw persimmon for relief. From now on, if you insist on drinking, make sure it's persimmon season.

▶ Hangover sufferers are sometimes advised to just "sleep it off." That's smart advice, since a contributing factor to hangovers is the lack of REM (rapid eye movement) sleep which alcohol seems to suppress. So go ahead and sleep it off!

▶ A Chinese hangover remedy calls for eating 10 strawberries and drinking a glass of fresh tangerine juice. Hmmm—sounds good even if you don't have a hangover.

▶ Hungarian gypsies recommend a bowl of chicken soup with rice. What could be bad?

Another Chicken Soup Remedy

▶ Cysteine is an amino acid that helps the body manufacture glutathione, an antioxidant that gets depleted when it has the chore of contending with alcohol. According to a study performed at the University of California, San Diego (UCSD), cysteine is present in chicken. Therefore, chicken soup may help replenish the body's needed supply of cysteine, easing hangover symptoms at the same time.

▶ A glass of sauerkraut juice is said to be effective. If the pure juice is hard for you to take, add some tomato juice to it. Or, eat lots of raw cabbage. That's been known to work wonders.

Gimme a B!

▶ Some of the B-complex vitamins are B_1 (thiamine), B_2 (riboflavin), nicotinamide and pyridoxine. They are helpful in aiding carbohydrate metabolization, nerve function, the cellular oxidation process and the dilation of blood vessels, all of which are helpful for hangovers. Impressed?

If you have overindulged and are anticipating waking up with a hangover, take a vitamin B-complex supplement with two or three glasses of water before you go to bed. If you pass out before remembering to take the B-complex, take the vitamin as soon as possible after you awaken.

▶ There are some of you who will not be happy until you find a "hair of the dog" hangover remedy. Here's one we were told comes from a voodoo practitioner in New Orleans.

In a blender, add 1 ounce of Pernod, 1 ounce of white crème de cacao and 3 ounces of milk, plus three ice cubes. Blend, drink and good luck!

Easing the Urge to Drink

▶ A tangy beverage can ease and erase the urge to imbibe. Have a glass of tomato juice with the juice of one lemon added. You might also want to throw in a couple of ice cubes. Stir well. Sip slowly as you would an alcoholic drink.

▶ The supplement glutamine is helpful in easing the urge for alcohol. Take 500 mg three times a day.

Intoxication Prevention

We're reporting the remedies that supposedly prevent a person from getting drunk, but we ask that you please take full responsibility for your drinking. If you drink, DO NOT trust or test your reflexes—especially behind the wheel of a car—no matter how sober you seem to feel, or which preventive remedies you take. And women who are pregnant or nursing should not consume alcohol.

▶ Native Americans recommend eating raw (not roasted) almonds before drinking. Consume them on an empty stomach.

▶ Healers in West Africa suggest eating peanut butter before imbibing.

▶ Gem therapists tell of the power of amethysts. In Greek, *amethyst* is *ametusios* and means "remedy against drunkenness." Please don't take this to mean that if you carry an amethyst and you drink, you won't get drunk.

It's that carrying an amethyst should give one the strength to refuse a drink and, therefore, prevent intoxication.

Women, Take Heed

Women who drink right *before* menstruating—when their estrogen level is low—get drunk more easily, usually become more nauseated and experience rougher hangovers than at any other time during their cycle.

EAR PROBLEMS

riends, Romans, countrymen, lend me your ears…"—but not if you have an earache! Even Mark Antony (eulogizing Caesar in William Shakespeare's play *Julius Caesar*) would not want ears that are inflamed, painful and runny. Earaches and infections can be serious, but if your ears are burning…just tell people to stop talking about you!

Earaches

Earaches are generally caused by an infection of the middle ear as a result of a cold or the flu. The pain can be out of proportion to the seriousness of the problem.

> **WARNING:** An earache may be a sign of a serious infection. These remedies should not be considered a substitute for determining the cause of the earache or for getting proper medical treatment.
>
> If an earache persists, don't turn a deaf ear! See a health professional for diagnosis and treatment.

Whenever an ear is draining—discharging thick or thin liquid from the canal—it may be that the eardrum has ruptured, and there could be a potentially serious infection. If that's the case, get medical attention *immediately*. If your ear is draining, do not put anything in it unless medically instructed.

Natural Remedies

Occasionally, you may have an earache and can determine that medical care is not required at that moment. It is *only* at such times that you should consider the following remedies. And don't try them at all if there's broken skin in or around the ear.

▶ Fill the ear with 3 warm (not too hot) drops of olive oil and loosely plug the ear with a cotton ball. Do this three or four times a day until the earache is gone.

▶ Mix the juice from grated fresh ginger with an equal amount of sesame oil. Drop in 3 drops of the mixture and loosely plug the ear with a cotton ball. It might sting a bit, but try to keep it there for a few hours.

Please Bite Down

▶ This reflexology remedy requires an object that is sterile and hard to bite down on. The ideal item is one of those cotton cylinders the dentist uses. Or you can wad up a piece of cheesecloth, which works fine.

Place the hard, sterile item in back of the last tooth on the side of the aching ear, and bite down on it for five minutes. This stimulates the pressure point that goes directly to the ear.

Repeat this procedure every two hours until the earache is gone. This process relieves the pain of an earache and has been known to improve hearing as well.

▶ Another effective way of easing the pain of an earache is to place a soothing chamomile poultice (*see* "Preparation Guide" on page 252) over your ear. If you don't have the loose herb, use a couple of tea bags instead.

Onion Muffs

▶ Cut a large onion in half. Take out the inside of the onion so that the remaining part will fit over your ear. Warm the onion "earmuff" in the oven, then put it over your ear. Be sure it's not too hot. It should help draw out the pain.

▶ Mix ½ cup of unprocessed bran with ½ cup of kosher (coarse) salt and envelop it in a generous piece of folded-over cheesecloth. In other words, bundle it up so it doesn't spill all over the place. Then heat it in a low oven until it's warm but bearable to the touch. Place it over the painful ear and keep it on for an hour.

▶ Put castor oil on a piece of cotton. Sprinkle the oiled cotton with black pepper and apply it to the aching ear—not in the ear canal, but directly on the ear.

Rye to the Rescue

▶ If you're going to get an earache, try to get it when you're baking rye bread. All you have to do is take 1 ounce of caraway seeds and pummel them. Then add 1 cup of bread crumbs from a soft, hot, newly baked loaf of bread and wrap it all in a piece of cheesecloth. Apply it to the sore ear. If you use already-cooled bread, warm the bread in the oven before applying it.

Cold, Hot, Tea...Ahh!

▶ Most earache remedies say to put something *warm* on the ear. Las Vegas–based herbalist Angela Harris (*www.angelaharris.com*)

feels that the infection-causing bacteria thrive on warmth, and so her approach is to put *cold* on the ear.

While an ice pack is applied to the infected ear, put your feet in hot water—as hot as you can stand it without burning yourself—and slowly drink a mild laxative herb tea, available at health food stores. Do this cold/hot/tea remedy for about 15 minutes, long enough for the pain to be alleviated.

Ear Infections

WARNING: If your ear infection is painful and persistent, get medical attention. You may have a serious condition that needs professional treatment.

Inflamed Ear

▶ Mix 1 tablespoon of milk with 1 tablespoon of olive oil or castor oil, then heat the combination in a nonaluminum pan.

Dose: Once the mixture has cooled off, put 4 drops into the inflamed ear every hour and gently plug it up with cotton. Be sure the drops are not too hot.

Runny Ear Infection

▶ You'll need to go to a good, old-fashioned Italian fish store for this remedy. Get the soft, transparent beak from a squid. Bake it until it turns black and crush it into a powder. Taken orally—½ teaspoon before breakfast and another ½ teaspoon before dinner—it is said to help clear up a runny ear infection.

Swimmer's Ear

Soon after swimming, if you've noticed that it hurts when you touch or move your ear, you may have an infection of the ear canal known as "swimmer's ear." These remedies may bring some relief.

▶ Combine 1 drop of grapefruit extract, 1 drop of tea tree oil and 2 drops of olive oil, then put the mixture in your ear. Gently plug your ear with a cotton ball. This should help clear up the infection.

▶ To prevent infections, add 1 teaspoon of white vinegar to 4 tablespoons (2 ounces) of just-boiled water. Once the liquid is cool, store it in a bottle. Right after swimming, put 2 drops of the vinegar mixture in each ear. Plug each ear with a cotton ball and stay that way for about 10 minutes.

Ear Pressure

The key to relieving the pressure caused by airplane takeoffs and landings is chewing and swallowing.

▶ The American Academy of Otolaryngology in Alexandria, Virginia, advises that you should chew gum or suck on mints—whatever causes you to swallow more than usual. Stay awake as the plane ascends and descends so that you can consciously increase the amount of times you swallow.

▶ If you're sleepy, that's good. Hopefully, you'll start yawning, which is even better than swallowing because it activates the muscle that opens your eustachian tube. Then air can be forced in and out of your eustachian canal, and that's what relieves the pressure in your ears.

Other Ear Problems

Get the Bugs Out

▶ It happens! Not often, but once in a blue moon, an insect will get inside a person's ear. Since insects are attracted to light, if an insect gets in your ear, turn the ear toward the sun. Hopefully, the insect will fly out and away. If it occurs at night, shut off the lights in the room and shine a flashlight in your ear.

▶ If the insect in your ear doesn't respond to the light, pour 1 teaspoon of warm olive oil into your ear and hold it there a minute or two. Then tilt your head the other way so that the oil and the bug come floating out.

If that doesn't work, gently fill your ear with warm water. That should push out the insect and the oil.

If none of this debugs you, get professional medical help to remove the insect.

Waxy Buildup Begone!

▶ Sprinkle black pepper into 1 tablespoon of warm corn oil, then dip a cotton ball into it and gently put the cotton into your ear. Remove the cotton after five minutes.

▶ In the microwave, warm 1 tablespoon of 3% hydrogen peroxide. Put 10 drops in the ear and let it fizz there for three minutes. Then tilt your head so that the liquid runs out onto a tissue. The wax should be softened. Gently remove the wax with soft cotton. Repeat the procedure with the other ear.

You can also use a solution of half water and half hydrogen peroxide to irrigate and remove wax.

CAUTION: Only use cotton balls or swabs on the external part of the ear to prevent puncturing your eardrum.

▶ Warm 2 teaspoons of sesame oil and put 1 teaspoon of oil in each ear. *Be sure the oil is not too hot.* Gently plug the ear with a cotton ball, and allow the oil to float around for a while. Once the sesame oil softens the wax, you can wash out the ears completely. The results—no more oil, no more wax.

Tinnitus (Ringing in the Ears)

If the bells are ringing…and ringing…and ringing—you may have tinnitus.

NOTE: Although most tinnitus sufferers hear bells, others may hear clicking, hissing, roaring or whistling.

The exact cause of tinnitus is unknown, but may be brought on by noise-induced hearing loss, wax buildup, ear infection, jaw misalignment and even cardiovascular disease.

Ringing in the ears may also be the result of a mild overdose of salicylate, which is found in aspirin and other drugs. If this is what's causing the ringing, it should stop when the drug is discontinued.

▶ If you still hear ringing (and there are no bells nearby)…try onion juice.

Dose: Put 2 drops of onion juice in your ears, three times a week, to stop the ringing.

▶ Believe it or not, a heating pad on your feet and one on your hands may ease the ringing in your ears. It all has to do with blood being redistributed, improving circulation and lessening pressure in congested areas.

WARNING: If ringing persists, it might be a sign of a more serious illness, in which case you should seek medical attention.

▶ We heard about a woman who had constant ringing in her ears for years. None of the specialists could help her. As a last resort, she started using castor oil. After a month, the ringing subsided considerably. Within three months, it was completely gone.

Try 3 or 4 drops a day in each ear. To get the full benefit from the castor oil, plug the ear with cotton once you've put in the drops, and keep it there overnight.

Mix It Up

▶ In a blender, combine six large, peeled garlic cloves and 1 cup of almond oil or extra virgin, cold-pressed olive oil. Blend until the garlic is finely minced. Then clean a glass jar by pouring just-boiled water into it.

Once the jar is dry, pour the garlic and oil mixture into the jar, put the cover on and refrigerate it for seven days. Then strain the liquid from the jar into a clean eyedropper bottle.

At bedtime, take the chill out of a small amount of the liquid, then put 3 drops in each ear and plug the ears with cotton balls. Remove the cotton in the morning. Chances are, if the ringing is going to stop at all, it will do so within two weeks.

Always keep this preparation refrigerated, and do not keep it longer than a month.

Hearing Loss

> **NOTE:** Seek professional medical attention for a hearing impairment or any sudden hearing loss.

▶ A loud noise, a head cold or wax buildup can cause partial loss of hearing. In Sicily, where garlic is a cure-all, they stew a few cloves in olive oil, then press it and strain it. On a

daily basis, 3 or 4 drops of the garlic/olive oil juice are placed in the ear(s) and plugged up with cotton. It is said to restore one's hearing.

"Hey, I can hear now."

"Good. I've been wanting to tell you something…you smell of garlic!"

Improve Your Hearing

Aerobic exercise, including brisk walking or bicycling, can help prevent some age-related deterioration in the ears, as well as damage caused by exposure to loud noises. Exercise also increases the ability to hear faint sounds.

This good news comes from results of studies conducted at Miami University in Oxford, Ohio, which concluded that aerobic exercise improves hearing by circulating blood to inner ear cells and bringing them more oxygen and an increased supply of chemicals that prevent damage to them.

Be sure to check with your doctor before starting any new exercise program.

Just a Pinch

▶ Pinch the tip of your middle finger four times a day, five minutes each time. Before every meal, pinch the right finger. After every meal, pinch the left finger. When you get up in the morning, pinch the right finger. When you go to bed at night, pinch the left finger.

Your right finger is for your right ear and left finger for left ear, so if you want to improve only one ear, pinch accordingly. Make it easy on yourself and clip on a clothespin.

▶ This potent potion has been said to actually restore hearing—drink 1 ounce of garlic juice with 1 ounce of onion juice once a day. (*See* "Halitosis" [Bad Breath] on page 183 immediately!)

EMPHYSEMA

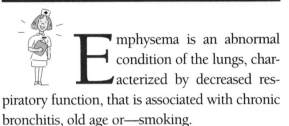

Emphysema is an abnormal condition of the lungs, characterized by decreased respiratory function, that is associated with chronic bronchitis, old age or—smoking.

If you've been diagnosed with emphysema and you're still smoking, don't bother reading this anymore. Turn to the "Smoking" section on page 167 and come back to read these remedies when you've stopped smoking.

▶ Now then…combine ½ teaspoon of raw honey with 5 drops of anise oil and take this dosage a half-hour before each meal. We've heard positive reports about this remedy.

▶ When you're having a hard time breathing, call 911 immediately. While you wait for help to arrive, sit down, lean forward and put your elbows on your knees. This position can make breathing easier because it elevates the diaphragm, the most important muscle used for breathing.

See "Exercise Your Lung Power" in the "Remedies in a Class by Themselves" section on page 243 and consider learning to play the harmonica.

WARNING: Emphysema is a very serious illness that should be treated by a qualified health professional.

EYE PROBLEMS

How very precious our eyes and vision are to each of us. Agreed? Agreed! Then what have you done for your eyes lately? Do you know there's eye food, eye-strengthening exercises, an acupressure eyestrain reliever, eyewashes to help brighten those baby blues, browns, grays or greens, and natural healing alternatives?

We once noticed a sign in an optometrist's office that said—"If you don't see what you want, you're in the right place."

Likewise. So read the following eye care suggestions, or get someone to read them to you.

Bloodshot Eyes

▶ If you don't drink in excess and you get enough sleep, but still have bloodshot eyes on a regular basis, you may be bothered by your contacts, allergic to the eye makeup you wear or you may be deficient in vitamin B_2 (riboflavin). Take 15 mg of B_2 daily. You might also want to have a tablespoon of brewer's yeast every day.

Use any of the eyewashes listed on pages 79–80, and you might want to try the grated potato remedy listed under "Black Eyes" on page 29.

Cataracts

When the lens of your eye becomes opaque (cloudy)—which occurs from old age, injury or a systemic disease like diabetes—then you have a cataract.

There are revolutionary new methods of removing cataracts, where the patient walks in and out of the doctor's office within a few hours. Cataracts should definitely be treated and removed by a qualified health professional.

Natural Remedies

While you're checking into today's modern techniques, you might want to try one or more of the following natural remedies to give you some relief until the cataract is professionally removed...

Mind Your Bs and Cs

▶ Research scientists have found that a deficiency of vitamin B_2 (riboflavin) can cause cataracts. So it serves to reason that B_2 supplements should help to prevent cataracts and may also clear up existing conditions.

Brewer's yeast is the richest source of riboflavin. Take 1 tablespoon a day and/or 15 mg of vitamin B_2. Along with a B_2 vitamin, take a B-complex vitamin to avoid high urinary losses of B vitamins. Also, eat foods high in vitamin B_2—broccoli, salmon, beans, wheat germ, turnip tops and beets.

▶ Vitamin C prevents damage in the watery portions of cells, particularly in the cornea and retina. A Tufts University study reported that women who supplemented their diets with 325 mg of vitamin C daily were 77% less likely to develop cataracts than women who did not supplement.

Take 1,000 mg of vitamin C every day or eat foods that contain it, such as broccoli, sweet potatoes, citrus fruits and bell peppers.

▶ For five minutes each day, massage the base of the index and middle (second and third)

■ Recipe ■

Beets in Orange Sauce

5 medium beets (1¼ lbs)

6 cups water

1 tsp salt

1 Tbsp packed brown sugar

2 tsp cornstarch

½ tsp salt

Dash of pepper

¾ cup orange juice

2 tsp vinegar

Cut off all but 2 inches of beet tops. Leave beets whole with root ends attached. Heat water and 1 tsp salt to boiling in 3-quart saucepan. Add beets. Heat to boiling, then reduce heat. Cover and cook until tender, 35 to 45 minutes. Drain. Run cold water over beets, then slip off skins and remove root ends. Cut beets into ¼-inch slices.

Mix brown sugar, cornstarch, ½ tsp salt and the pepper in 2-quart saucepan. Stir orange juice gradually into cornstarch mixture, then stir in vinegar. Cook, stirring constantly, until mixture thickens and boils. Boil and stir 1 minute. Stir in beets, and heat until hot. Makes 4 servings.

Source: www.recipegoldmine.com

fingers, as well as the webs between those fingers. The right hand helps the right eye and the left hand helps the left eye.

▶ The famed 17th-century English physician Nicholas Culpeper was a great believer in the healing effects of chamomile eyewashes to improve a cataract condition. (*See* "Eyewashes" on pages 79–80.)

Conjunctivitis (Pinkeye)

If your eyes are red, watery and itchy, you may have allergies or just some dust in your eye. But if your eyes are VERY irritated, you may have the serious (and extremely contagious) infection commonly known as pinkeye.

CAUTION: Conjunctivitis is a severe and contagious viral, fungal or allergic infection. If the condition doesn't show signs of improvement within a day or two, see a health professional.

▶ Once every day, make a poultice (*see* "Preparation Guide" on page 252) of grated apple or grated raw red potato and place it on your closed eye. Let it stay that way for a half-hour. Within two days—or three at the most—the condition should completely clear up.

▶ Prepare chamomile tea. When it cools, use it as an eyewash (*see* page 79) twice a day until the conjunctivitis is gone.

The Eyes Have It

▶ The plant eyebright is particularly effective in the treatment of conjunctivitis. Add 3 drops of tincture of eyebright (available at health food stores) to 1 tablespoon of just-boiled water. When cool enough to use, bathe the eye in the mixture.

Since this condition is a very contagious one, wash the eye cup thoroughly after you've washed one eye, then mix a new batch of eyebright with water before you wash the other eye. Do this three or four times a day until the condition clears up. Or, use the eyewashes listed on pages 79–80.

▶ Goat milk yogurt can also help clear up this uncomfortable condition. Apply a yogurt poultice (*see* "Preparation Guide" on page 252) over the infected eye(s) daily.

Also, eat a portion or two of the yogurt each day. The active culture in yogurt can provide you with healthy bacteria in your gastrointestinal tract. Goat's milk yogurt is available at some health food stores and specialty markets or can be ordered on-line.

Dry Eyes

Tear ducts that do not produce enough fluid to keep the eyes moist can result in an uncomfortable dry eye condition that is characterized by irritation, burning and a gravelly feeling.

Natural Tears

Check out homeopathic eyedrops for dry eye syndrome. Homeopathic medications are without side effects and are well-tolerated by even the most sensitive system. They work to restore health rather than to suppress symptoms.

NOTE: To get the most benefit from eyedrops, gently pull out your lower lid and let the liquid drop into the eye pocket. Then keep your eyes closed for about two minutes after putting in the drops. This will prevent the blinking process from pumping the drops out of your eyes.

Similasan Eye Drops, known throughout Europe, are available here in the US. For information about these homeopathic drops, go to *www.allaboutvision.com/similasan* or call Similasan at 800-426-1644.

▶ You may be able to eliminate artificial tears completely by adding omega-3 fatty acids to your diet, which may increase the viscosity of oils made by the body, mostly in the skin and eyes. Omega-3s are found abundantly in cold-water fish and flaxseed oil. This means eating several servings of fish a week—especially all varieties of salmon (except smoked) and canned white tuna—and/or taking flaxseed oil.

We suggest you read about the many benefits of flaxseed oil in the "Six Sensational Superfoods" section on page 262. And *see* the salmon recipe on page 73.

CAUTION: If you're on blood-thinning medication, have uncontrolled high blood pressure or bleeding disorders, or are going in for surgery, be sure to check with your doctor before taking flaxseed oil.

▶ Help your eyes do the work they're supposed to do by opening the clogged oil glands in the eyelids. Take a warm, white washcloth and place it on your closed eyelids. Leave it on until it turns cool—five to 10 minutes. Do this a few times a day—obviously, the more the better.

Dry Eye Don'ts

There are things you should avoid so that your dry eye condition doesn't become worse…

◆ Don't use a blow dryer on your hair unless you absolutely have to.

◆ Don't go outdoors without sunglasses. The wraparound kind are excellent for keeping the wind out.

◆ Don't dry out your eyes with heating or cooling systems in your home, office, car or even on an airplane. Keep the heat or air-conditioning to a minimum, and be sure the vents are not pointing in your direction. Turn it off completely if it isn't really necessary.

◆ Don't go for any length of time without blinking. People at computers have this problem. Every time you click the mouse, blink. Every time you save a document, blink. Every time you swallow, blink. Do whatever it takes to make yourself conscious of blinking often, especially when you're sitting in front of the computer.

◆ Don't wear contact lenses all the time.

◆ Don't smoke. Smoke exacerbates the burning and other symptoms of dry eyes.

◆ Don't cry about it. It makes the problem worse. Tears brought on by emotion wash away the oils that prevent dry eyes.

Eye Irritants

Chemicals

▶ When chemicals like hair dye get in the eye, immediately wash the eye thoroughly with lots of clean, tepid water. In most cases, you should have a doctor check your eye right after you've washed the damaging substance out.

Dust

▶ When something gets in your eye, try not to rub the eye. You'll irritate it, then it's hard to tell whether or not the foreign particle is out. Grasp your upper lid lashes firmly between your thumb and index finger. Gently pull the lashes toward the cheek, as far as you can without pulling them out. Hold them there, count to 10, spit three times and let go of the lashes.

Repeat the procedure one more time if necessary. If it still doesn't work, get an onion and try the next remedy.

▶ Mince an onion and let your natural tears wash away the dust in your eye.

Get a tissue ready. With one hand, pull your lashes so that the upper lid is away from your eye. With the other hand, appropriately position the tissue in the center of your face and blow your nose three times.

▶ Warm some pure olive oil in the microwave for a few seconds—long enough to *slightly* warm the oil. Then, using an eyedropper, put 2 drops in the irritated eye.

What? You don't have an eyedropper? Buy one at any health food store or pharmacy and keep it in your medicine chest for just such occasions.

▶ Until you get an eyedropper, you may want to try this—put 1 drop of fresh lemon juice in 1 ounce of warm water and wash your eye with it. It might sting at first, but it should remove the irritant.

▶ If your eyes are irritated from a foreign particle, cooking fumes, cigarette smoke, dust, etc., put 2 drops of castor oil or milk in each eye.

⚡ **CAUTION:** Be careful putting any foreign substance or liquid in the eye. It can be painful and may cause infection.

Eye Inflammation

▶ Peel and slice an overripe apple. Put the pieces of pulp over your closed eyes, holding

■ Recipe ■

Champagne-Poached Salmon

½ cup honey Dijon mustard
1½ tsp fresh tarragon, chopped
4 (6 to 8 oz) salmon steaks or fillets, skin and bones removed
Salt and pepper to taste
2 cups champagne
¼ cup fresh lime juice
4 slices red onion
1 Tbsp capers, optional
4 sprigs fresh tarragon

Mix together mustard and chopped tarragon. Set aside.

Season salmon steaks/fillets lightly with salt and pepper. Place in a pan just large enough to hold the salmon in one layer. Add the champagne, lime juice and just enough water to cover the fish. Remove the fish and bring the liquid to a boil.

Return the salmon steaks/fillets to the pan. Top each with an onion slice, capers and tarragon sprig. Reduce heat to a simmer, cover pan with foil and poach at no more than a simmer for 6 to 10 minutes (depending on the thickness of the salmon).

Remove salmon steaks/fillets from the liquid and place on four warm serving plates. Top each piece of fish with 1 ounce of the mustard mixture and serve.

Source: www.recipegoldmine.com

the pieces in place with a bandage or strip of cloth. Leave it on at least a half-hour to help alleviate irritation and inflammation.

▶ A poultice of either grated raw potato, fresh mashed papaya pulp or mashed cooked beets is soothing and promotes healing. Apply the poultice for 15 minutes, twice a day.

Fashion Statement

▶ Reuse steeped tea bags. Make sure they're moist and cool enough to apply to the closed eyelids for 15 minutes. (This remedy is a favorite for fashion models who wake up puffy-eyed.)

▶ Crush a tablespoon of fennel seeds and add it to a pint of just-boiled water. Let it steep for 15 minutes, then dunk cotton pads in the liquid and place them over your eyelids for about 15 minutes.

▶ There's an herb called horsetail that is helpful for inflamed eyes (see "Sources" on page 297 for vendors who might sell the herb).

Steep 1 teaspoon of dried horsetail in hot water for 10 minutes. Saturate cotton pads with it and apply the pads to your eyelids for 10 minutes. Redunk the pads in the liquid, then keep them on your eyes for another 10 minutes. Repeat again after a half-hour, and the inflammation should start calming down.

▶ Freshly sliced cucumber placed on eyelids for about 15 minutes is soothing and healing.

▶ Also, use any of the eyewashes on pages 79–80. Try the "palming" remedy, too. It's on page 79.

Eye Puffiness

We know a man who has so much puffiness under his eyes, it looks like his nose is wearing a saddle.

One reason for puffiness may be an excessive amount of salt in one's diet. Salt causes water retention and water retention causes puffiness. What can be done about it? Stay away from salt. *Here are some more suggestions...*

▶ When you want to look your best, set your clock an hour earlier than usual. Give yourself that extra time to depuff. Either that, or sleep sitting up so the puffs don't get a chance to form under your eyes.

▶ If you already have puffs, wet a couple of chamomile tea bags with tepid water and put them over your closed eyelids. Relax that way for 15 minutes.

Eyestrain/Tired Eyes

▶ Pinch the ends of your index and middle (second and third) fingers of each hand for 30 seconds on each finger. If your eyestrain isn't relieved after two minutes, do another round of pinching.

▶ Sunflower seeds contain vitamins, iron and calcium that may be extremely beneficial for eyes. Eat about ½ cup of unprocessed (unsalted) shelled seeds every day.

Put Up Your Feet

▶ If your eyes are strained and tired, chances are the rest of your body is also dragging. Lie down with your feet raised higher than your head. Relax that way for about 15 minutes. This

■ Recipe ■

Yogurt Fruit Salad with Sunflower Seeds

2 apples, chopped
2 oranges, chopped
2 bananas, chopped
2 pears, chopped
Handful of blueberries
2 peaches, chopped (can be frozen)
Seedless or seeded grapes, chopped
Canned pineapple chunks, drained
1 cup coconut, grated
½ cup unsalted sunflower seeds
¼ cup honey
1 to 2 cups unflavored yogurt

Combine all the ingredients (you may need to add a little more honey if you like it really sweet). Use your judgment as to how much yogurt to use to make it all stick together. Refrigerate until chilled and serve.

Source: www.recipegoldmine.com

gravity-reversing process should make you and your eyes feel refreshed and rarin' to go.

▶ Cut two thin slices of a raw red potato and keep them on your closed eyelids for at least 20 minutes. Red potatoes are said to have strong healing energy, but any other type of potato will work, too.

▶ Steep rosemary in hot water for 10 minutes. Use a rosemary tea bag or 1 teaspoon of the loose herb in a cup of just-boiled water. Saturate a cotton pad with the tea and keep it on your eyes for 15 minutes. Rosemary should help draw out that tired-eye feeling.

Also, *see* the "palming" remedy on page 79 (under "Vision Improvers").

Eyestrain Prevention

▶ Looking at red ink on white paper for long periods of time can cause eyestrain and headaches. Stay out of the red!

Eye Twitch

▶ Pressure and tension can cause eyelid twitching. Aside from taking a relaxing two-week vacation, you should try to eat more calcium-rich foods.

According to some nutritionists, adults can (and should) get all the calcium they require through nondairy foods—green vegetables, sesame seeds, whole grains, unrefined cereals, canned salmon and sardines, soy milk and other soy products, including tofu.

Glaucoma

Glaucoma is a loss of vision that usually occurs suddenly and without symptoms. Vision is impaired when there is damage to the optic nerve, but there may be other factors involved. If you are having trouble seeing, see a qualified eye specialist! Early detection and treatment can slow or halt the progression of glaucoma.

CAUTION: Glaucoma is a serious condition. Before using any home remedy, be sure to consult an eye specialist.

▶ Vitamin B₂ (riboflavin) deficiency is one of the most common vitamin deficiencies in the US. B₂ is also the vitamin that's most beneficial for eye problems like glaucoma. Take 100 mg every day, along with a B-complex supplement.

(The reason for the B-complex supplement is that large doses of any one of the B vitamins can result in urinary losses of other B vitamins.)

▶ Bathe the eyes morning and evening in an eyewash made with fennel seed, chamomile or eyebright. (*See* pages 79–80 for instructions on using these eyewashes.)

⚡ **CAUTION:** Be careful putting any foreign substance or liquid in the eye. It can be painful and may cause infection.

Night Vision

▶ Eat blueberries when they're in season. They can help restore night vision.

▶ You know the old joke about carrots being good for your eyes? Well, you've never seen a rabbit wearing glasses. Eat two or three carrots a day (raw or cooked) and/or drink a glass of fresh carrot juice. It's excellent for alleviating night blindness.

▶ Eat more watercress in salads and/or drink watercress tea.

Sties

If you have a painful red bump on your eyelid, then the sty's the limit! A sty occurs when the

---

■ Recipe ■

Chilled Czech Blueberry Soup

3 cups blueberries

4 cups water

Pinch of salt

¼ tsp cinnamon

1 Tbsp granulated sugar

1½ cups sour cream

6 Tbsp flour

Boil 2 cups of the blueberries in the water. Stir in salt, cinnamon and sugar. Remove from heat.

Whip flour into the sour cream, then whip both into the hot liquid. When well blended, return the pot to the heat and bring to a boil. Reduce heat and stir until thickened.

Remove from heat, stir in another ½ cup of blueberries and refrigerate.

When ready to serve, stir in the remaining ½ cup of blueberries and ladle into bowls.

Source: www.recipegoldmine.com

---

oil glands around the eyelid get infected and inflamed. Some natural remedies may help relieve the discomfort.

▶ Place a handful of fresh parsley in a soup bowl. Pour a cup of boiling water over the parsley and let it steep for 10 minutes. Soak a clean washcloth in the hot parsley water, lie down, put the cloth on your closed lids and relax for 15 minutes. Repeat the procedure before bedtime. Parsley water is also good for eliminating puffiness around the eyes.

▶ Moisten a regular (nonherbal) tea bag, put it on the closed eye with the sty, bandage it in place and leave it there for as long as possible. Hopefully, soon enough it will be "bye-bye sty."

Go for the Gold

▶ Rub the sty three times with a gold wedding ring. When we started compiling information for this book, we decided not to use any silly-sounding, superstition-based remedies. This remedy for sties, however, comes from so many reputable sources that it must have some credibility.

Fortunately for us, but unfortunately for research purposes, neither of us has had a sty since we began working on this book, so we haven't been able to test the wedding-ring remedy ourselves.

Banish Sties with Bancha

▶ Roasted-bancha leaves are used to make a popular Japanese tea—these tea bags are available at most US health food stores. Steep a tea bag in hot water for 10 minutes and add 1 teaspoon of sea salt (also available at health food stores as well as supermarkets). Saturate a cotton pad in the lukewarm liquid and apply it to your closed eye, keeping it there for 10 minutes at a time, three times a day.

▶ In addition to—or instead of—the roasted-blancha tea bag remedy, dab on some castor oil several times throughout the day until the sty disappears.

Sty Prevention

▶ Lydia went to school with a girl named Madeline whose nickname was "Sty." She always seemed to have a sty coming or going.

If you're like Madeline and are prone to sties, prepare a strong cup of burdock-seed tea every morning and take 1 tablespoon before each meal and 1 tablespoon at bedtime.

Sun Blindness

Sun blindness is caused by exposure to large expanses of snow or ice for a considerable length of time.

▶ **CAUTION:** Sun blindness is a serious condition that can lead to cataracts and retinal damage. It should be prevented by wearing protective sunglasses or goggles.

▶ Skiers find this remedy helpful in coping with large expanses of blinding, white snow. Eat a handful of sunflower seeds every day. (Buy them shelled, raw and unsalted.)

Within no time, the eyes may have a much easier time adjusting to the brightness of the snow, thanks to the sunflower seeds…and a good pair of sunglasses or goggles.

Eye Strengtheners

▶ Apply cold water on a washcloth to the eyelids, eyebrows and temples each morning, noon and night, five to 10 minutes at a time.

Get a Rosy Outlook

▶ Throw a handful of rose petals (the petals are more potent as the flower fades) into a pot and cover with water. Put it over a medium flame. When the water boils, take the pot off the flame and let it cool. Then strain the water into a bottle and close it tightly.

When your eyes feel tired and weak and appear red, treat them with the rose petal water. Pour the liquid on a washcloth or cotton pads and keep them on your closed eyes for 15 to 30 minutes. Your outlook might be a lot rosier.

▶ This is an interesting way to end the day. Prepare a candle, a straight-back chair and a five-minute timer. Light the candle and place it 1½ feet from the chair. Then sit in the chair, with your feet uncrossed and flat on the floor. The lit candle should be level with the top of your head.

Set the timer for five minutes. Then, using your index fingers, hold your eyelids open while you stare at the candle without blinking. There will be some tears. Do not wipe them away. Tough out the five minutes every other night for two weeks. Then discontinue the exercise for two weeks. Then start the exercise again, every other night for two weeks.

Once your vision is sufficiently strengthened, blow out the candle for good.

Vision Improvers

▶ You know all the talk about carrots being good for your eyes? They are! Drink 5 to 6 ounces of fresh carrot juice twice a day for at least two weeks. Obviously, you will need a juicer or access to a juice bar. After the two weeks, ease off to one glass of carrot juice a day...forever!

WARNING: If you have a Candida/yeast problem, skip the carrot juice. Its high sugar content can contribute to this condition.

▶ According to the late J.I. Rodale, organic-farming pioneer and founder of *Prevention* magazine, sunflower seeds are a miracle food. We agree. Eat a handful (shelled, raw and unsalted) every day.

Eye, Eye Matey

▶ We've heard that wearing a gold earring in your left ear improves and preserves one's eyesight, but we thought it was a useless superstition.

Then we read in David Louis's book, *2201 Fascinating Facts* (Greenwich House) that

■ Recipe ■

Lemon–Parsley Carrots

1 lb carrots sliced ¼-inch thick
    (about 3 cups)
2 Tbsp water
2 Tbsp butter or margarine
1 Tbsp granulated sugar
1 Tbsp parsley, freshly chopped
½ tsp lemon peel, grated
2 tsp lemon juice
¼ tsp salt

Place carrots and water in a 2-quart covered glass casserole. Microwave, covered, at 100% power (700 watts) for 8 to 9 minutes until crisp-tender, stirring once after 5 minutes. Drain. Stir in butter, sugar, parsley, lemon peel and juice, and salt. Microwave, covered, at 100% power for 1 to 1½ minutes until heated through.

Makes 4 servings.

Source: www.recipegoldmine.com

pirates believed that piercing their ears and wearing earrings improved their eyesight—and the swashbucklers may have been right.

The idea, which had been scoffed at for centuries, has been reevaluated in light of recent acupuncture theory, which holds that the point of the lobe where the ear is pierced is the same acupuncture point that controls the eyes.

Hmmmm. Get out the gold earrings.

Palm Power

▶ We've thoroughly researched "palming" and no two of our resources agree on the procedure. We'll give you a couple of variations. Test them and see what works for you.

Sit. (They all agree on that.) Rub your hands together until you feel heat. Place your elbows on the table in front of you, then put the heels of your hands over your eyes, blocking out all light. Some feel it's better to keep one's eyes open in the dark while others advocate closed eyes. The length of time to sit this way also ranges—from two minutes to 10 minutes.

"Palming" is beneficial for improving vision, for nearsightedness, tired eyes, astigmatism and inflammation…and it may even help squinters stop squinting.

Eyeglass Cleaners

▶ To avoid streaks on your eyeglass lenses, clean them with a lint-free cloth and a touch of vinegar or vodka.

Eyewashes

Commercial eyedrops eliminate the redness because of a decongestant that constricts the blood vessels. Using these drops on a regular basis can worsen the problem. The blood vessels will enlarge again in less and less time. Make your own eyedrops from the following herbs, or just bathe your eyes with these eyewashes.

✎ **NOTE:** It's important to make sure that all the ingredients are hygienic—boiled and/or sterilized.

Eyebright

▶ To make an eyebright eyewash, add 1 ounce of the whole dried herb eyebright to 1 pint of boiling-hot water and let it steep for 10 minutes. Strain the mixture thoroughly through a superfine strainer or through unbleached muslin. Wait until it's cool enough to use.

▶ Add 3 drops of tincture of eyebright to a tablespoon of boiled water and wait until it's cool enough to use.

Chamomile

▶ Add 1 teaspoon of dried chamomile flowers to 1 cup of just-boiled water. Steep for five minutes and strain the mixture thoroughly through a superfine strainer or through unbleached muslin. Wait until it's cool enough to use.

▶ Add 12 drops of tincture of chamomile to 1 cup of boiling-hot water. Wait until it's cool enough to use.

Fennel Seeds

▶ Add 1 teaspoon of crushed fennel seeds to 1 cup of boiling-hot water. Steep for five minutes and strain the mixture thoroughly through a superfine strainer or through unbleached muslin. Wait until it's cool enough to use.

Red (Eye) Alert

If you use artificial tears, *do not* use any product that also "gets the red out." When your eyes are red or bloodshot, it's because there's a problem. Your body's way of handling the problem is by enlarging the delicate veins or blood vessels in your eyes. The eye drops that "get the red out" are vasoconstrictors that shrink those veins so that they're not visible. This is not a good thing and is only a temporary masking of the problem.

Also, your eyes can become dependent on those drops and, when you stop using them, the problem will worsen and the blood vessels in your eyes will be more dilated than before.

When you use artificial tears, make sure the box says *preservative-free* or *non-preserved*. Preservatives in artificial tears can be harmful to your eyes.

Carrots

▶ Carefully wash a bunch of carrots and cut off the tops. Place a handful of the clean carrot tops in a jar of distilled hot water. Let it stand. When it's cool, use the carrot water as an eyewash.

You can also drink the remaining liquid. This drink should help your eyes and also help strengthen your kidneys and bladder. (*See* recipe on page 78.)

▶ Mix 1 drop of lemon juice in 1 ounce of warm distilled water and use it as an eyewash. It's particularly effective when your eyes have been exposed to dust, cigarette smoke, harsh lights and chemical compounds in the air.

Eyewash Directions

✎ **NOTE:** Always remove contact lenses before doing an eyewash.

You'll need an eye cup (available at drugstores). Carefully pour boiling water over the cup to sterilize it. Without contaminating the rim or inside surfaces of the cup, fill it half full with whichever eyewash you've selected.

Lean forward, apply the cup tightly to the eye to prevent spillage, then tilt your head backward. Open your eye wide and rotate your eyeball to thoroughly wash the eye.

Lean over again and remove the cup. Clean the cup again, and use the same procedure with the other eye.

FAINTING

When you feel dizzy and light-headed as though you're going to faint, lie down. If possible, lie with your feet and torso elevated so that your head is lower than your heart. That's the secret of preventing a faint—getting your head lower than your heart so that blood can rush to your brain.

Natural Remedies

▶In India, instead of smelling salts, people take a couple of strong whiffs of half an onion to bring them around.

▶If you're in a very warm room that's making you feel faint, just run cold tap water over the insides of your wrists. If there are ice cubes around, rub them on your wrists. Relief is almost immediate.

▶A friend of ours is a paramedic. When one of her patients is about to faint, she pinches the patient's philtrum—the fleshy part between the upper lip and nose. That may help to prevent the faint from happening.

▶If you're prone to fainting spells—a case of the vapors, perhaps—keep pepper handy. Sniff a grain or two and sneeze. The sneeze stimulates the brain's blood vessels and may help prevent fainting. It's good to remember, since not many households have smelling salts, but just about all have black pepper.

▶Check your eating habits. Are you eating regularly at mealtimes? Are you eating good, wholesome meals with a sufficient amount of protein, and without an excess of sweets and refined foods? Sometimes low blood sugar or a poor diet can cause a person to faint.

⚡ **CAUTION:** If you faint and don't know why, consult a doctor. Fainting can be a symptom of an ailment that needs medical attention.

FATIGUE

If you're sick and tired of being tired, then you need to figure out the reason for your fatigue. Too many late nights at the office? A crying baby? Poor diet? Check in with your doctor to make sure there's not a medical condition causing your fatigue. Once you get a clean bill of health, try these remedies to help you perk up.

Natural Remedies

▶We've read case histories in which, within a few weeks, the intake of bee pollen not only increased a person's physical energy, but restored mental alertness and eliminated lapses of memory and confusion.

Suggested dosage: Take 1 teaspoon of granular bee pollen after breakfast, or two 500 mg bee pollen pills after breakfast. (Read more about bee pollen in the "Six Sensational Superfoods" section on page 258.)

Start by taking just a few granules of bee pollen each day to make sure you have no allergic reaction to it. If all is well after three days, increase the amount to ¼ teaspoon every day. Gradually, over the next month or two, work your way up to 3 teaspoons of bee pollen taken throughout the day.

▶If you're tired the second you wake up in the morning, try this Vermont tonic—in a blender, put 1 cup of warm water, 2 tablespoons of apple cider vinegar and 1 teaspoon of honey. Blend thoroughly, then sip it slowly until it's all gone. Have this tonic every morning before breakfast and, within days, you may feel a difference in your energy level.

☞ **WARNING:** People who are allergic to bee stings should consult a doctor before taking bee pollen.

In addition, infants, diabetics and people who are allergic to honey should not use any remedies that contain honey.

▶A quick picker-upper is ⅛ teaspoon of cayenne pepper in a cup of water. Drink it down and get a second wind.

▶If you're suffering from mental fatigue, try this Austrian recipe—thoroughly wash an apple, cut it into small pieces, leaving the peel on and place the pieces in a bowl. Pour 2 cups of boiling water over the apple and let it steep for an hour. Then add 1 tablespoon of honey. Drink the apple/honey water and eat the pieces of apple.

Take Off Your Shoes

▶If possible, walk barefoot in dewy grass—just watch out for critters! The next best thing is to carefully walk up and back in six inches of cold bathwater. Do it for five to 10 minutes twice a day—in the morning and late afternoon.

▶If you have a bad case of the drowsies, puncture a garlic pearle (soft gel) or cut a garlic clove in half, and take a few deep whiffs. That ought to wake you up.

Energy Boosters

▶A Chinese theory is that "tiredness" collects on the insides of one's elbows and the backs of one's knees. Wake up your body by slap-slap-slapping both those areas.

▶You don't have to depend on caffeine to stay awake. Mix 1 teaspoon of cayenne pepper to 1 quart of juice—any kind of juice with no sugar or preservatives added. Throughout a long drive, or a night of cramming, as soon as you feel sleep overcoming you, take a cup of the cayenne-laced juice to keep awake and alert.

▶Tough day at the office? Need to get that second wind? Ready for a drink? Tired of all these questions? Add 1 tablespoon of blackstrap molasses to a glass of milk (regular, skim, soy or rice milk) and bottoms up.

Reach for the Sky

▶Call on your imagination for this visualization exercise. Sit up with your arms over your head and your palms facing the ceiling. With your right hand, pluck a fistful of vitality out of the air. Next, let your left hand grab its share. Open both hands, allowing all that energy to flow down your arms to your neck, shoulders and chest.

Start over again. This time, when you open your hands, let the energy flow straight down to your waist, hips, thighs, legs, feet and toes. There! You've revitalized your body. Now stand up feeling refreshed.

Get Figgy with It

▶A bunch of grapes can give you a bunch of energy. But grapes may be too perishable for you to carry around. If so, try dried figs. They sure can pack an energy punch! They're delicious, satisfying, have more potassium than bananas, more calcium than milk, have a very high dietary fiber content and no cholesterol, fat or sodium.

Most important, figs have easily digestible, natural, slow-burning sugars that will get you going and keep you going, unlike the quick-fix, fast-crash processed sugar in junk food.

Herbalist Lalitha Thomas, who lists figs as one of the *10 Essential Foods* (in her book of the same name, published by Hohm Press), recommends making a serious effort to get unsulfured figs. Eat a few at a time—but don't overdo it. Figs are also known to help prevent or relieve constipation.

▶When you just can't keep your eyes open or your head up and you don't know how you'll make it to the end of the workday, run away from it all. Go to the bathroom or a secluded spot and run in place. Run for two minutes—this should help you keep going the rest of the day.

Three Cheers for Chia

▶According to a study of American Indians, a pinch of chia seeds helped the braves brave their arduous round-the-clock days of hunting.

Ground chia seeds, available at health food stores, can be sprinkled on salads or in soup for those on-the-go, around-the-clock days when stamina counts.

Start Your Day the Energy Way

▶Wake up your metabolism in the morning by squeezing the juice of half a grapefruit into a glass. Fill the rest of the glass with warm water. Drink it slowly, then eat the fruit of the squeezed-out half grapefruit. Now that your thyroid is activated, have a productive day!

⚡ **CAUTION:** Grapefruit can interfere with some prescription medications. Be sure to check with your doctor before trying this remedy.

▶If, after a full night's sleep, you get up feeling sluggish, it may be due to a tired liver. Stand up. Place your right hand above your waist, on the bottom of your ribs on your right side, with your fingers apart, pointing toward your left side. Place your left hand the same way on your left side. Ready?

You press your right hand in, then bring it back in place. You press your left hand in, then bring it back in place. You do the Hokey-Pokey and you turn your—no! Sorry...we got carried away.

Press your right hand in, then bring it back in place. Press your left hand in, then bring it back in place. Do it a dozen times on each side when you get up each morning. In a couple of weeks, this liver massage may make a big difference in your daily energy level.

▶Cutting out heavy starches and sweets from your diet can also go a long way in adding to your get-up-and-go.

FOOT AND LEG PROBLEMS

Our feet carry a lot of weight and are probably the most abused and neglected part of our anatomy. They get cold, they get frost-bitten, they get wet, they burn, they blister, they itch and they sweat…as we walk, jog, run, dance, climb, skate, ski, hop, skip and jump. Also, at some time or other, we're all guilty of the Cinderella Stepsister Syndrome—pushing our feet into ill-fitting shoes.

We put our poor, tired tootsies under all kinds of stress and strain. And then we wonder why our feet are "just killing us!" Well, we killed them first.

CAUTION: If you have circulation problems or diabetes, do not use any of these remedies without the approval and supervision of your health professional.

Let's get to the bottom of our troubles with some remedies for the feet…

Aching Feet

▶During a busy day when your "dogs are barking" and you feel like you're going to have to call it quits, cayenne pepper comes to the rescue! Sprinkle some cayenne into your socks or rub it directly on the soles of your aching feet. Now get going or you'll be late for your next appointment!

▶After a long day, when your nerves are on edge, your feet hurt and you're tired—too tired to go to sleep—soak your feet in hot water for 10 to 15 minutes. Then (and this is the important part) massage your feet with lemon juice.

After you've done a thorough job of massaging, rinse your feet with cool water. As always, dry your feet completely, then take five deep breaths. You and your pain-free feet should be ready and able to settle down for a good night's sleep.

Super Soaker

▶This remedy requires two basins or dishpans or four plastic shoe boxes. Fill one basin (or two shoe boxes) with ½ cup Epsom salts and about 1 gallon of hot (not scalding) water. Fill the other basin (or the other two shoe boxes) with ice cubes. Sit down with a watch or timer. Put your feet in the hot water for one minute and then in the ice cubes for 30 seconds.

Alternate back and forth for about 10 minutes. Your feet will feel better. This procedure also helps regulate high blood pressure and may prevent varicose veins, improve circulation and, if done on a regular basis, relieve chronic "cold feet."

Modified version: Stand in the bathtub and first let hot water run on your feet for one minute, then let ice-cold water run on your feet for 30 seconds, alternating the hot/cold water for a total of 10 minutes.

Do not exceed one minute of hot or cold water on your feet!

▶Add 1 cup of apple cider vinegar to a basin (or two plastic shoe boxes) filled halfway with lukewarm water. Then soak your feet for at least 15 minutes. The heat and hurt should be gone by then.

Boil or roast a large turnip until it's soft. Then mash it and spread half of it on a white cotton handkerchief. Spread the other half on another handkerchief. Apply the turnip mush to the bottoms of your bare feet, bandage them in place and sit with your feet elevated for about half an hour. This "sole food" should draw out the pain and tiredness.

Corns and Calluses

Believe us, this is a type of corn you really don't want to eat!

Corns are hard, thick layers of skin that form on the top or side of a toe—calluses form on the soles of your feet. Neither is a serious condition, but you'll probably be more comfortable if you get rid of the shoes (or whatever else) that are causing the friction that leads to corns and calluses.

These remedies should help, too.

You can soften your calluses by applying any of the following oils—wheat germ oil, castor oil, sesame seed oil or olive oil. Apply the oil as often as possible throughout the day, day after day.

Walking barefoot in the sand, particularly wet sand, is wonderful for your feet. It acts as an abrasive and sloughs off the dead skin that leads to corns and calluses.

If you're not near the beach, add 1 tablespoon of baking soda to a basin or to two plastic shoe boxes filled halfway with lukewarm water…and soak your feet for 15 minutes. Then take a pumice stone (available at health food stores and pharmacies) and carefully file away the tough skin.

Foot Salad

Cut an onion in half—the size of the onion should be determined by the size of the callused area the onion's surface has to cover. Let the onion halves soak in wine vinegar for four hours, then take the onion halves and apply them to the calluses. Bind them in place with plastic wrap, put on socks and leave them on overnight.

The next morning, you should be able to scrape away the calluses. Be sure to wash and rinse your feet thoroughly to get rid of the onion/vinegar smell.

Corn Remedies

The difference between an oak tree and a tight shoe is that one makes acorns, the other makes corns ache. *What to do for those aching corns…*

Rub castor oil on the corn twice a day and it will gradually peel off, leaving you with soft, smooth skin.

Every night, put one piece of fresh lemon peel on the corn (the inside of the peel on the outside of the corn). Put a bandage around it to keep it in place. In a matter of days, the corn should be gone.

Make a poultice (*see* "Preparation Guide" on page 252) of one crumbled piece of bread soaked in ¼ cup of vinegar. Let it stand for a half-hour, then apply it to the corn and tape it in place overnight. By morning, the corn should peel off. If it's a particularly stubborn corn, you may have to reapply the bread/vinegar poultice a few nights in a row.

Fresh Fruit for the Feet

►Every day, wrap a strip of fresh pineapple peel around the corn (the inside of the peel taped directly on the corn). Within a week, the corn should disappear, thanks to the enzymes and acid content of the fresh pineapple.

►Don't throw away used tea bags. Tape a moist one on the corn for a half-hour each day and the corn should be gone in a week or two.

►To ease the pain of a corn, soak the feet in oatmeal water. Bring 5 quarts (20 cups) of water to a boil and add 5 ounces of oatmeal. Keep boiling until the water boils down to about 4 quarts. Then pour off the clear water through a strainer, into a large enough basin for your feet, or into two plastic shoe boxes. Soak your feet for at least 20 minutes.

►Make a paste out of 1 teaspoon of brewer's yeast and a few drops of lemon juice. Spread the mixture on a cotton pad and apply it to the corn, binding it in place and leaving it overnight. Change the dressing daily until the corn is gone.

►A paste of powdered chalk and water should also take care of the corn.

Corn Cures from Afar

►A Hawaiian medicine man recommends pure papaya juice on a cotton pad, or a piece of papaya pulp directly on the corn. Bind in place and leave it on overnight. Change daily until the corn is gone.

►Australian shepherds squeeze the juice from the stems of dandelions and apply it to the corn every day until it disappears, usually within a week or so.

Cold Feet

►If you can't get inside to warm up, then stand on your toes for a couple of minutes, then quickly come back down on your heels. Repeat the toes/heels maneuver several times until your blood tingles through your feet and warms them up.

►Before going to bed, walk in cold water in the bathtub for two minutes. Then briskly rub the feet dry with a coarse towel. To give the feet a warm glow, hold each end of the towel and run it back and forth along your feet's arches.

Spice Up Your Feet

►If the thought of putting cold feet into cold water is not appealing to you...add 1 cup of table salt to a bathtub that is filled ankle-high with hot water, and soak your feet for 15 minutes. Dry the feet and then massage them with damp salt.

This will remove dead skin and stimulate circulation. After you've massaged each foot for three to five minutes, rinse them in lukewarm water and dry thoroughly.

►Warm your feet by sprinkling black pepper or cayenne pepper into your socks before putting them on. It's an old skier's trick, but you don't have to be an old skier to do it. If you use cayenne, your socks and feet will turn red.

Your feet will be fine, but your socks may never be the same again.

Also, if you're at a restaurant and the meal is too bland, you can always take off a sock and season the food to taste.

Athlete's Foot

▶ The fungus that causes athlete's foot dies in natural sunlight. So, spend two weeks barefoot in the Bahamas. If that's a bit impractical, then for one hour a day, expose your feet to sunlight. It might eliminate a mild case of athlete's foot.

▶ In between sunbaths, keep the feet well aired by wearing loose-fitting socks.

▶ At night, apply rubbing alcohol (it stings for a couple of seconds), then wait until your feet are completely dry and sprinkle them with talcum powder (the unscented kind is preferable).

▶ Apply one clove of crushed garlic to the affected area. Leave it on for a half-hour, then wash with water. If you do this once a day, within a week, you'll be smelling like a salami, but you may not have athlete's foot.

> **WARNING:** When you first apply the garlic, there will be a sensation of warmth. If, after a few minutes, that warm feeling intensifies and the garlic starts to burn, wash the area with cool water. The next day, dilute the garlic juice with plain water and try again.

Sweet Feet

▶ Every evening, apply cotton or cheesecloth that has been saturated with honey to the infected area. Tape it in place. To avoid a gooey mess (a possibility even with the tape in place), wear socks to bed.

In the morning, wash with water, dry thoroughly and sprinkle them with talcum powder (preferably unscented).

▶ Grate an onion and squeeze it through cheesecloth to get onion juice. Massage the juice into the fungus-infected areas of your foot.

Leave it on for 10 minutes, then rinse your foot in lukewarm water and *dry it thoroughly* (fungi thrive in moist conditions). Repeat this procedure three times a day until the condition clears up.

▶ To avoid reinfecting yourself with athlete's foot, soak your socks and pantyhose in white vinegar. Also wipe out your shoes with vinegar.

The smell of vinegar will vanish after being exposed to the air for about 15 minutes.

Ingrown Toenails

We were surprised to learn that a tendency toward ingrown toenails is inherited. If the toe is red, swollen and/or painful, see a doctor.

▶ If you have an ingrown toenail, relieve the pain with a footbath. In a plastic shoe box, add ½ ounce of comfrey root to ½ gallon (2 quarts) of warm water. Soak your foot in it for 20 minutes.

Once the nail is softened from soaking, take a piece of absorbent cotton and twist it so that it's like a thick strand of thread. Or twist together a few strands of unwaxed dental floss. Gently wedge the "thread" under the corner of the nail. That should prevent the nail from cutting into the skin. Replace the strands a couple of times a day, every day, until the nail grows out.

Once it grows out, the nail should be cut straight across, not down into the corners, and not shorter than the toe. You might want to have a podiatrist trim the toenail properly. Pay careful attention so you'll be able to take care of your toes yourself and avoid another ingrown nail (and another podiatrist bill).

Pigeon Toes

▶ If you are slightly pigeon-toed and an orthopedist hasn't helped you...as a last resort, buy a pair of shoes one size larger than you usually take. Wear them to bed every night with the right shoe on the left foot and the left shoe on the right foot. Give it a month to get results.

Cracked Heels

▶ Before bedtime, wash your feet with warm water and dry them. Liberally apply petroleum jelly on your feet, massaging it into the rough and cracked areas. Wrap each foot with plastic wrap. Put socks on and sleep that way. Repeat the process nightly until your feet are fine. It shouldn't take more than a week...probably less.

Sweaty Feet

The average pair of feet gives off about ½ pint of perspiration daily. It's amazing we don't all slosh around. *Well, for those of you who feel like you do...*

▶ Put some bran or uncooked oat flakes into your socks. It should absorb the sweat and make you feel more comfortable. Start conservatively, with about 1 tablespoon in each sock. Add more if needed.

Numb Toes

▶ Daily doses of vitamin B_6 and B-complex have been known to eliminate tingling and numbness in toes.

⚡ **CAUTION:** Check the amount of B_6 in the B-complex—high doses can be toxic. Check with your naturopathic doctor.

Varicose Veins

The word *varicose* comes from the Latin word varix, which means "twisted." When the little veins in your legs start looking like squiggly worms, you might wish those old Romans had picked another word.

We hope these remedies bring some relief to whatever discomfort or swelling your veins are causing.

▶ Folk medicine practitioners throughout Europe have been known to help shrink varicose veins by recommending the application of apple cider vinegar.

Once every morning and once every evening, soak a cheesecloth bandage in the vinegar and wrap it around the affected area. Lie down, raise your legs and relax that way for at least a half-hour. (This will benefit more than just your varicose vein condition!)

After each vinegar-wrap session, drink 2 teaspoons of the vinegar in a cup of warm water. The practitioners tell us that by the end of one month, the veins shrink enough for there to be a noticeable difference.

Easy Ways to Ease the Veins

Heed these simple suggestions to keep varicose veins from getting worse...

◆ Keep your feet elevated as much as possible. It's ideal to elevate your legs at or above the level of your heart for 20 minutes a few times every day.

◆ Never sit with your legs crossed.

◆ Don't wear knee-high stockings or tight socks.

◆ Wear flats or very low heels, not high heels.

◆ If you're overweight, do your legs a favor and lose those extra pounds.

◆ Exercise. Just walking a half-hour every day will help with circulation.

▶ In between the vinegar wraps, don't forget to sit properly. You may be surprised to know that you can stop varicose veins from getting worse simply by fixing the way you sit.

Never sit with your legs crossed. In a relaxed way, keep your knees and ankles together and slightly slant your legs. It's graceful-looking and doesn't add to the congestion that promotes varicose veins.

Natural Remedies

Here are some suggestions that may help improve the condition of your varicose veins.

▶ Take vitamin C with bioflavonoids daily. Herbs may also be very helpful, particularly butcher's broom, horse chestnut and hawthorn. You can find them in health food stores. Follow the recommended dosage on the label.

▶ Take 1 bilberry capsule (80 mg) and 1 bromelain capsule (500 to 1,000 mg) with each meal. Once a day, take 1 capsule (150 mg) of butcher's broom. All are available at health food stores.

These herbs have many wonderful benefits, including improving your blood circulation and helping the walls of your veins maintain their shape.

▶ Reduce the swelling and constriction of varicose veins by wrapping a cheesecloth bandage soaked in witch hazel around the affected area. Lie down, raise your legs and relax.

▶ At the end of every day, stand in a tub filled with cold water. (The water should be up to your knees.) After two or three minutes, dry your legs thoroughly with a coarse towel, then walk around at a brisk pace for two or three minutes.

▶ Take horse chestnut capsules (which are available at health food stores), 300 mg, once or twice a day.

Phlebitis

▶ If you know you have superficial varicose vein inflammation (superficial thrombophlebitis), usually in the leg—chances are that you are under a doctor's care and should be.

You probably developed this type of inflammation because you were recovering from childbirth, surgery or were somehow incapacitated and inactive for a long period of time. This inactivity decreased the blood flow in your veins and allowed clots to form. Blood clots are potentially very dangerous.

After the acute care has been medically completed, pay strict attention to optimal diet, optimal bowel function, optimal weight and exercise and meticulous body hygiene—nose, ears, mouth, tongue and gums, fingernails,

■ Recipe ■

Broccoli Slaw

4 broccoli stems, washed and peeled

6" piece of daikon radish, peeled

2 large carrots, peeled

½ bunch green onions, chopped

2 kiwis, peeled and diced

2 Tbsp pine nuts, toasted

2 cloves garlic, minced

1 tsp salt

¼ tsp ground black pepper

2 Tbsp organic canola oil

Black sesame seeds

Coarsely grate the broccoli stems, daikon radish and carrots, and put them into a bowl.

Add green onions, kiwis, pine nuts, garlic, salt, pepper and canola oil to bowl and toss together. Adjust seasoning to taste, and transfer to a serving bowl.

Garnish with a generous sprinkling of black sesame seeds. This slaw tastes best when made 3–4 hours ahead. Use as a side dish.

Makes 6–8 servings.

Source: www.vegparadise.com

legs, feet, toes, toenails, scrotum or vulva—to prevent complications and recurrence.

Natural Remedies

Herbs that assist in vein health include butcher's broom, hawthorn and horse chestnut. All are available at health food stores. Follow the recommended dosage on the label.

And be sure to check with your doctor about the following suggestions.

▶Apply a comfrey poultice on the outside of the affected area. (*See* "Preparation Guide" on page 252.)

▶You should be eating a raw vegetable diet. It's important to have leafy greens, plus lots more roughage.

▶Drink lots of fresh juices.

▶Take 1 tablespoon of lecithin every day.

▶Follow your physician's instructions and elevate the affected area for as many hours a day as possible. This will keep the blood circulating properly.

Weak Ankles

This exercise will promote toe flexibility and strengthen the arches as well as the ankles.

▶Get a dozen marbles and a plastic cup. Put them all on the floor. Sit down and then pick up each marble with the toes of your right foot—one by one, drop them in the cup. Then do the same with the toes of your left foot.

You may want to add to the fun by timing yourself and seeing if you can keep breaking your previous record. Whatever happens, try not to lose your marbles.

FROSTBITE/FROSTNIP

Frostbite occurs when the skin of a person's extremities (usually hands, feet and nose) has been exposed to cold temperatures for too long. If the skin is cold, pale or numb, there may be frostbite.

The extent of frostbite varies greatly, depending on the length of time a person has been exposed to the cold...the intensity of the cold, humidity and winds...the kinds and amount of clothing worn...a person's natural resistance to cold...as well as his/her general state of health. The minor chilling of skin is usually considered "frostnip."

CAUTION: People with circulation problems, vascular disease, diabetes and other conditions where blood flow is compromised should do everything possible to prevent frostbite. Bundle up and stay dry!

One big problem with frostbite is that it's hard to know you have it until it's already on its way to being serious.

At some ski resorts, the ski patrol does occasional nose-and-cheek checks of skiers. Thanks to those checks, lots of mild frostbite victims are sent indoors to defrost.

CAUTION: Seriously frostbitten victims should be placed under a doctor's care and/or hospitalized immediately.

Be sure the frostbite sufferer is in a warm room while waiting for medical help. If the person is conscious, give him or her a warm drink. Do not give alcoholic beverages! They can worsen the condition.

The frozen body parts must be warmed immediately. Be careful, when touching the skin, not to break the frostbite blisters. Cover the frostbitten areas with a blanket. Call 911 and get medical treatment as soon as possible.

For mild cases of frostnip, the following remedies are worth a try...

▶ Get inside to warm up, then steep a teaspoon of sage in a cup of hot water for five minutes and drink it. Sage tea will help improve circulation.

▶ Warm some olive oil and gently dab it on the chilled skin or apply it with a kitchen pastry brush.

▶ If you have an aloe vera plant or bottled aloe vera gel, gently apply it to the chilled area.

▶ Boil and mash potatoes. Add salt and apply the mixture to the chilled areas.

GALLBLADDER PROBLEMS

The gallbladder is the liver's companion and assistant. Its job is to store bile produced by the liver, then release it to dissolve fats. Your job is to keep the gallbladder healthy and functioning. *These remedies may help...*

CAUTION: Pain and/or vomiting can be signs of a serious illness. See a doctor before trying any of these natural remedies.

Natural Remedies

▶An inflamed, irritated or clogged gallbladder can be very painful and make you feel sluggish and tired, even when you first wake up in the morning. Take 3 tablespoons of fresh lemon juice in half a glass of warm water, a half-hour before breakfast. Try this for one week and see if there's a difference in your morning energy level. Lemon juice is known to stimulate and cleanse the gallbladder.

▶The most popular folk remedy for the gallbladder is black radish. Juice the radish either with a juice extractor or by grating the radish and squeezing it through cheesecloth. Take 1 to 2 tablespoons of black radish juice before each meal. Do it for two weeks or more. Your digestion should improve and so should the condition of your gallbladder.

▶If you have had gallbladder surgery, you may help the healing process by drinking peppermint tea—1 cup one hour after eating each of the two biggest meals of the day. Menthol, the active ingredient in peppermint, gives the liver and gallbladder a workout by stimulating bile secretion.

GOUT

Isn't it amazing how much pain you can have from one toe? Gout comes on suddenly, but you know it when you have it. Caused by a build-up of uric acid in the joints, it usually settles in a person's big toe. Gout is extremely painful, but also extremely treatable. Be sure to see a doctor for an evaluation and diagnosis. Severe gout conditions can be very serious.

If you have gout, you probably know it's time to change your diet. Once known as "the disease of kings," it's often brought on by a steady diet of rich foods like red meat, wine, cream sauces and sweets. The closer you stick to vegetarian cuisine, the faster the gout will go. You can eat some fish and lean chicken now and then, but stay away from red meat for a while. Also, avoid alcohol and eliminate sugar and white flour from your diet. You may start feeling so good that you'll never want to go back to consuming those things.

Best Remedy

It's the Cherries

The one remedy that everyone seems to agree is very effective—cherries! Eat them fresh or frozen. Also, drink cherry juice daily. You can get pure juice (concentrate) at health food stores. (*See* the recipe on page 93.)

Other Remedies

▶Soak your gouty foot in comfrey tea (*see* "Preparation Guide" on page 250).

▶A Russian remedy is raw garlic—two cloves a day. The best way to take raw garlic is to mince the cloves, put them in water (better yet, in cherry juice) and drink them down. Chewing is not necessary. The garlic will not linger on your breath. It may repeat on you— but then, so does a salami sandwich, and this is a lot healthier.

> ✎ **NOTE:** Eat garlic with a few sprigs of parsley to decrease repeating and smelly breath.

▶Eating strawberries and very little else for a few days is said to be a possible cure for gout. Strawberries are a powerful alkalizer and contain calcium, iron and an ingredient known as salacin, which soothes inflammatory conditions.

■ Recipe ■

Three-Cherry Jam

2 cups light sweet cherries
2 cups dark sweet cherries
2 cups tart red cherries
6 cups sugar
Juice of 1 lemon

Pit and measure cherries. Grind coarsely. Simmer about 5 minutes to soften skins. Add sugar and juice. Cook until thickened, about 15 to 20 minutes, but no longer than 20 minutes. Skim and pour into hot sterilized jars. Adjust lids at once and process in boiling water bath, 212° F, for 5 minutes. Remove from canner and complete seals, unless closures are self-sealing type.

Makes about 6 pints.

Source: www.homecooking.about.com

It worked so well for 18th-century botanist Carl Linnaeus (who developed the modern system for classifying plants) that he referred to strawberries as "a blessing of the gods."

HAIR PROBLEMS

According to a French proverb, "A fool's hair never turns white." The Russians say, "There was never a saint with red hair." According to the German Pennsylvanians, "Pull out a gray hair, and seven will come to its funeral."

The biggest hair worries are having too much or too little. Too much hair, especially in the wrong places, can be permanently removed by electrolysis. It's expensive and painful, but worth every penny and ounce of pain in exchange for a better self-image.

Too little hair, especially in men, is usually hereditary baldness (*alopecia*). If none of the available hair-restoring treatments, including cosmetic surgery (implants and transplants) and the drugs currently on the market are for you, then you may want to try a natural remedy.

People claim that these remedies have stopped the loss of hair as well as restored hair that's already been lost. So they may be worth a try. After all, what do you have to lose—that you aren't already losing?

Stopping Hair Loss/ Promoting Hair Growth

In an average lifetime, the hair on a person's head grows about 25 feet.

Each of us loses about a hundred hairs a day from our scalp. Mostly, the hairs grow back. When they don't, the hairstyle changes from "parted" or "unparted" to "departed."

Ninety percent of baldness cases can be attributed to hereditary factors. Can something be done to prevent it or overcome it? The people who gave us these remedies say, "Yes!"

▶ An hour before bedtime, slice open a clove of garlic and rub it on the hairless area. An hour later, massage the scalp with olive oil, put on a cap and go to bed. The next morning, shampoo.

Repeat the procedure for a few weeks and, hopefully, hair will have stopped falling out and there will be regrowth showing.

Fingernail Buffer

▶ Three times a day, five minutes each time, buff your fingernails with your fingernails. Huh? In other words, rub the fingernails of your right hand across the fingernails of your left hand. Not only is it supposed to stop hair loss, it's also supposed to help encourage hair growth and prevent hair from graying.

Great Hair

Human hair is almost impossible to destroy. Other than its vulnerability to fire, it cannot be destroyed by changes of climate, water or other natural forces. When you think of all the ways some of us abuse our hair—with bleaches, dyes, rubber bands, permanents, mousses, sprays and that greasy kid stuff—you can see how resistant it is to all kinds of corrosive chemicals. No wonder it's always clogging up sinks and drainpipes.

While hair may not be destroyed by this abuse, it may look lifeless and become unmanageable and unhealthy.

One way to tell whether or not hair is healthy is by its stretchability. A strand of adult hair should be able to stretch to 25% of its length without breaking. If it's less elastic than that, it's less than healthy.

▶ Prepare your own hair-growing elixir by combining ¼ cup of onion juice with 1 tablespoon of honey. Massage the scalp with the mixture every day. We heard about a man who had a bottle of this hair tonic. One day, he took the cork out of the bottle with his teeth. The next day, he had a mustache that needed to be trimmed. *But seriously…*

Russian Hair Restorer

▶ We heard a similar remedy from a man who emigrated to the United States from Russia. He told us that many barbers in the former Soviet Union recommend this to their customers.

Combine 1 tablespoon of honey with 1 jigger of vodka and the juice from a medium-size onion. Rub the mixture into the scalp every night, cover, sleep, awaken, shampoo and rinse.

Open Sesame

▶ An Asian remedy to stop excessive amounts of hair from falling out is sesame oil. Rub it on your scalp every night. Cover your head with a cap or wrap a dish towel around it. In the morning, wash with an herbal shampoo (available at most stores where shampoo is sold). Your final rinse should be with 1 tablespoon of apple cider vinegar in 1 quart of warm water.

▶ Another version of this nightly/daily treatment calls for equal amounts of olive oil and oil of rosemary. Combine the two in a bottle and shake vigorously. Then massage it into the scalp, cover the head, sleep, awaken, shampoo and rinse.

▶ Yet another version—garlic oil. Puncture a couple of garlic pearles, squish out all the oil and massage it into your scalp. Then follow the routine of covering the head overnight and, in the morning, be sure to shampoo and rinse.

▶ Mix 1 jigger of vodka with ½ teaspoon of cayenne pepper and rub it on the scalp. The blood supply feeds the hair. The vodka and pepper stimulates the blood supply.

▶ And still another version of these massage scalp remedies…take half of a raw onion and massage the scalp with it. It's known to be an effective stimulant. Cover the head overnight, then shampoo and rinse in the morning.

If these remedies don't work, there is a plus side to baldness—it prevents dandruff.

Natural Remedies
Dandruff

▶ If you are brunette, wash your hair with a combination of 1 cup of beet juice and 2 cups of water, plus 1 teaspoon of salt. This is an Arabian remedy, and most Arabs have dark hair. Since beets contain a dye, this is not recommended for light-haired people who want to stay that way. To be safe, do a test on a patch of hair.

▶ Squeeze the juice of one large lemon and apply half of it to your hair. Mix the other half with 2 cups of water. Wash your hair with a mild shampoo, then rinse with water. Rinse again with the lemon and water mixture. Repeat these steps every other day until the dandruff disappears.

▶Massage 4 tablespoons of warm corn oil into your scalp. Wrap a warm, wet towel around your head and leave it there for a half-hour. Shampoo and rinse. Repeat this treatment once a week.

Good Enough to Eat

▶Grate a piece of ginger and squeeze it through cheesecloth, collecting the juice. Then mix the ginger juice with an equal amount of sesame oil. Rub the ginger/sesame mixture on the entire scalp, cover the head with a cap or wrap with a dish towel, and sleep with it on.

In the morning, wash with an herbal shampoo (available at most stores where shampoo is sold). The final rinse should be with 1 tablespoon of apple cider vinegar in 1 quart of warm water. Repeat this treatment three or four times a week until the dandruff or other scalp problems vanish.

▶Prepare chive tea by adding 1 tablespoon of fresh chives to 1 cup of just-boiled water. Cover and let it steep for 20 minutes. Strain and—making sure it's cool—rinse your hair with it right after you shampoo.

Dry Hair

▶Shampoo and towel-dry your hair. Then evenly distribute 1 tablespoon of mayonnaise through your hair. (Use more if your hair is long.) Leave the mayonnaise on for an hour, wash hair with a mild shampoo and rinse. The theory is that the flow of oil from the sebaceous glands is encouraged as the natural fatty acids of the mayonnaise help nourish the hair.

Dull, Permed Hair

▶After shampooing, rinse with a combination of 1 cup of apple cider vinegar and 2 cups

Hairy Standing Pose

Do not do this exercise if you have high or low blood pressure! Do not do this exercise without your doctor's approval if you are significantly beyond young adulthood!

If you know how to do it properly, stand on your head. If not, then get down on all fours, with your hands about two feet away from your knees. Then carefully lift your rear end in the air so that your legs are straight and your head is between your outstretched arms.

Stay in that position for a minute each day and, after a week, gradually work your way up to five minutes each day. The theory behind this is that you will bring oxygen to the hair follicles, which will rejuvenate the scalp and encourage hair to grow.

of water. Your hair will come alive and shine. This treatment is especially effective on permed hair, but can be used on any lifeless-looking hair.

Frizzy, Dry Hair

▶After shampooing, rinse with 1 tablespoon of wheat germ oil, followed by a mixture of ½ cup of apple cider vinegar and 2 cups of water. It will tame the frizzies.

Remedies for Bad-Hair Days

If your self-esteem is in the cellar and you're feeling less than confident, capable or sociable, it may be because you're having a bad hair day.

The findings of a study conducted at Yale University in New Haven, Connecticut, confirmed the negative effect of a crummy coif on the psyche.

The fascinating aspect of the study was that men were more likely to feel less smart and less capable than women when their hair stuck out, was badly cut or was otherwise a mess.

Here are natural remedies to help you have healthy hair, be the best-tressed person around and boost your self-esteem…

A Rinse for Shinier Dark Hair

▶Prepare a rinse in a glass or ceramic bowl. Add 3 tablespoons of either parsley, rosemary or sage (available at health food stores) to 8 cups of just-boiled water. Let it steep until it gets cool. Strain through muslin or a superfine strainer. After shampooing, massage the herb water into your scalp as you rinse with it.

A Rinse for Shinier Fair Hair

▶Prepare a rinse in a glass or ceramic bowl. Add 3 tablespoons of either chamomile, calendula or yarrow (available at health food stores) to 8 cups of just-boiled water. Let it steep until it gets cool. Strain through muslin or a superfine strainer. After shampooing, massage the herb water into your scalp as you rinse with it.

Dry Shampoo

▶If your home is having plumbing problems, your city is having a water shortage or you just don't feel like washing your hair, you can dry-shampoo it using cornmeal or cornstarch. Sprinkle some on your hair. Then put a piece of cheesecloth or pantyhose on the bristles of a hairbrush and brush your hair with it. The cornmeal/cornstarch will pull out the dust from your hair, and the cloth will absorb the grease.

Shine your hair with a silk scarf, using it as you would a buffing cloth on shoes. After a few minutes of this, if your hair doesn't look clean and shiny, tie the scarf around your head and no one will know the difference.

Get the Grease Out

▶Coarse or kosher salt is known to be an effective dry shampoo. Put 1 tablespoon of the salt in aluminum foil and in the oven to warm for five minutes. Using your fingers, work the warm salt into the scalp and throughout the hair.

As soon as you feel that the salt has had a chance to absorb the grease and dislodge the dust, patiently brush it out of your hair. Wash the brush thoroughly, or use a clean brush and brush again to make sure all the salt has been removed.

✎ **NOTE:** Do not use table salt for a dry shampoo. Not only will you still have dirty hair, but it will look as though you have dandruff, too.

Hair Revitalizers

▶This was our mom's favorite hair treatment. (Actually, it was the only hair treatment she ever used.) Slightly warm ½ cup of olive oil. You may want to add a few drops of an extract like vanilla to make it more fragrant. Mom put it in an eyedropper bottle and let it stand in very hot water for a few minutes. Then, using the eyedropper, she'd put the warm oil on the hair and massage it into the scalp. Once the whole head is oiled, shampoo the oil out.

According to reflexology expert Mildred Carter, "To energize the hair roots, grab a handful of hair and yank gently. Do this over the whole head. This is also said to help a hangover, indigestion and other complaints.

"To further stimulate these reflexes in the head, lightly close your hands into loose fists. With a loose wrist action, lightly pound the whole head. This will not only stimulate the hair, but also the brain, bladder and other organs."

An experienced reflexologist, Ms. Carter believes that tapping the reflexes in the head with a wire brush can add even greater electrical stimulation to the hair, as well as other parts of the body.

Green Hair

Don't you just hate it when you get out of the pool and your blonde hair has a greenish tinge? Next time, take a clean sponge, dip it in red wine and dab it on your hair. The chemicals in a chlorinated pool will be neutralized by the tannic acid in the wine.

Keep a bottle of lemon juice and a box of baking soda near the pool. After your swim, and before you hit the shower, mix ½ cup of the baking soda into a cup of lemon juice. Wet your hair, then rinse it with this bubbly mixture to get the green out. (Maybe blondes *don't* have more fun.)

Dissolve six aspirin tablets in a pint of warm water, massage this into your wet hair and the green will never be seen. Rinse thoroughly with clear water.

"Natural" Hair Coloring

Herbal or vegetable dyes take time because the color must accumulate. Look at it this way—if you get the gray out gradually, no one will realize you ever had any gray to begin with.

Brunette Beauty

We have two hair-darkening formulas that use dried sage, which helps to add life to hair and prevents dandruff.

Prepare dark sage tea by adding 4 tablespoons of dried sage to 2 cups of just-boiled water and letting it steep for two hours. Strain. This dark tea alone will darken gray hair—but for an even stronger hair color, add 2 cups of bay rum and 2 tablespoons of glycerine (available at pharmacies). Bottle this mixture and don't forget to label it.

Every night, apply the potion to your hair, starting at the roots and working your way to the ends. Stop the applications when your hair is as dark as you want it to be.

If you're a teetotaler and don't want to use the rum remedy, combine 2 tablespoons of dried sage with 2 tablespoons of black tea and simmer in 1 quart of water for 20 minutes. Let it steep for four hours, then strain and bottle. Massage it into your hair daily until your hair is the color you desire. When you need a touch-up, mix a fresh batch of the teas.

Taking sesame-seed tea internally has been known to darken hair. Crush 2 teaspoons of sesame seeds and bring them to a boil in 1 cup of water. Simmer for 20 minutes. As soon as it's cool enough to drink, drink the potion, seeds and all. Have 2 to 3 cups daily, and keep checking the mirror for darkening hair.

▶ Add a little life to your hair color right after you shampoo by pouring a cool cup of espresso through your hair. Let it stay there for five minutes and rinse.

Blonde Bombshell

▶ Dried chamomile can help add golden highlights to wishy-washy, bland blonde hair. Add 4 tablespoons of dried chamomile to 2 cups of just-boiled water and let it steep for two hours. Strain and use it as a rinse. Have a basin set up so you can save the chamomile and use it again for the next two or three shampoos.

> ✎ **NOTE:** As with most herbal rinses, you mustn't expect dramatic results overnight—if ever. Chamomile tea, no matter how strong you make it, will not cover dark roots.
>
> That reminds us of something we've wondered about for a while. In Sweden, are there brunettes with blonde roots?

▶ Squeeze the juice out of two lemons, strain and dilute with 1 cup of warm water. Comb the juice through your hair. Be very careful not to get any of it on your skin. Why? Because you should sit in the sun for 15 minutes in order to give your hair the glow of a summer day. If your skin has lemon juice on it, it can cause a burn and give your skin mottled stains.

After the sunbath, rinse your hair thoroughly with warm water or, better yet, with chamomile tea.

> ✎ **NOTE:** Be sure your skin is properly protected in the sun with sunscreen with a sun protection factor (SPF) of at least 15 (higher is better).

Ravishing Red

▶ Add radiance to your red hair right after you shampoo by pouring a cup of strong Red Zinger tea (available at health food stores and many supermarkets) through your hair. Let it remain there for five minutes and rinse.

▶ Juice a raw beet (in a juice extractor) and add three times the amount of water as there is juice. Use this as a rinse after shampooing.

> ✎ **NOTE:** Since there are many shades of red, we suggest you do a test patch with the beet juice to see how it reacts on your specific color.

Gray, Gray—Go Away!

▶ Many vitamin therapists have seen proof positive that taking a good B-complex vitamin daily can help change hair back to its original color over a period of two months or more.

▶ In a glass of water, mix 2 tablespoons each of apple cider vinegar, raw unheated honey and blackstrap molasses. Drink this mixture first thing in the morning. Not only should it help you get rid of gray hair, but it should also give you a lot more energy than people who haven't gone gray yet.

> ☞ **WARNING:** Do not give honey to someone who is diabetic or allergic to honey.

▶ According to the Chinese, a combination of fresh gingerroot juice and ground cloves should be massaged into the scalp to prevent gray hair.

Setting Lotions

If you want your hair to hold its curls, sometimes it's best to use a setting lotion before making waves...

▶ Don't throw away beer that's gone flat. Instead, dip your comb in it, comb it through your hair and you have a wonderful setting lotion. Incidentally, the smell of beer seems to disappear quickly.

▶ A friend of ours is a professional fashion model and she knows many tricks of the trade. Her favorite hair-setting lotion is fresh lemon juice. The hair takes longer to dry with the juice on it, but the setting stays in a lot longer. When she runs out of lemons, she uses bottled lemon juice from her fridge and that works well, too.

▶ If beer or lemon isn't your cup of tea, try milk. Dissolve 4 tablespoons of skim-milk powder in 1 cup of tepid water. Use it as you would any commercial hairsetting lotion. But, unlike most commercial products, the milk helps nourish the scalp and hair.

Helpful Hair Hints

Prevent Gray from Yellowing

▶ By adding a couple of teaspoons of laundry bluing to a quart of warm water and using it as your final rinse after shampooing, you can prevent gray hair from turning that yucky yellow.

No-No #1—Rubber Bands

▶ We've always been told not to wear rubber bands in our hair. We just found an explanation for this—the rubber insulates the hair and stops the normal flow of static electricity, so hair elasticity is reduced and the hair breaks more easily.

No-No #2—Combing Wet Hair

▶ Combing wet hair stretches it out, causing it to be less elastic and break more easily.

Gum Remover

▶ To remove gum from hair, take a glob of peanut butter, put it on the gummed area, then rub the gum and peanut butter between your fingers until the gum is on its way out. Use a comb to finish the job, then get that careless kid (is it you?) under the faucet for a good shampooing.

A Permanent's Pungent Odor Remover

▶ The distinctive smell of a permanent has a habit of lingering. Tomato juice to the rescue! Saturate your dry hair with tomato juice. Cover your hair and scalp with a plastic bag and stay that way for 10 minutes. Rinse hair thoroughly, then shampoo and rinse again.

Hair Spray Remover

▶ When you are in the middle of shampooing, massage 1 tablespoon of baking soda into your soaped-up hair. Then rinse thoroughly. The baking soda should remove all the nasty hair spray buildup.

Improvised Setting Rollers

▶ If you have long hair and want to experiment setting it with big rollers, try used frozen-juice cans, opened at both ends. Be careful not to cut yourself with the open edges.

Grounding Your Hair

▶When static electricity makes your hair temporarily unmanageable, you might want to zap it with static spray used on records (that is, if you still have any records!).

Or, rub a sheet of fabric softener on your hair as well as on your brush or comb.

HAND AND NAIL PROBLEMS

Like our feet, hands and fingernails suffer a lot of daily abuse. From washing dishes in hot water to typing on a computer keyboard, our hands and nails seem to touch everything. If your hands and nails are feeling a little rough, dry or brittle, some of these remedies may bring soothing relief.

▶Chapped hands will be greatly soothed when you massage wheat germ oil into them.

▶Red, rough and sore hands (feet, too) should be relieved with lemon juice. After you rinse off the lemon juice, massage the hands with olive, coconut or wheat germ oil.

✎ **NOTE:** Give a moisturizer time to work by keeping it on your hands overnight. To maximize the moisturizer's effectiveness, and to protect your bedsheets, put on white cotton gloves after you've applied the moisturizer. If you don't have white cotton gloves, then go to a photographic-supply store and pick up the inexpensive gloves that photographers and film editors wear when handling film.

Rough Hands

▶For those chapped hands, try some honey. Wet your hands and shake off the water without actually drying them. Then rub some honey all over your hands. When they're completely honey-coated, let them stay that way for five minutes. (We would recommend you read the paper to pass the time, but turning the pages would definitely present problems.)

Next, rub your hands as you rinse them under tepid water. Then pat your hands dry. Do this every day until you want to clap hands for your unchapped hands.

▶Tired of being called "lobster claw"? Take 1 teaspoon of granulated sugar in the palm of your hand and add a few drops of castor oil and enough fresh lemon juice to totally moisten the sugar. Vigorously massage your hands together for a few minutes. Rinse with tepid water and pat dry. This hand scrub should leave hands smooth and, in the process, remove stains.

Hand Cleansers

▶One simple cleanser consists of scrubbing your hands with a palmful of dry baking soda, then rinsing with tepid water.

▶For another cleanser, take a palmful of oatmeal, moistened with milk. Rub and rinse.

Farmer's Friend

▶This remedy for rough, chapped and soiled hands is a favorite among farmers. In a bowl, combine about ¼ cup of cornmeal, 1 tablespoon of water and enough apple cider vinegar to make the mixture the consistency of a loose paste. Rub this mildly abrasive mixture all over your hands for 10 minutes. Rinse with tepid water and pat dry.

This treatment not only can remove dirt, it can also soften, soothe and heal the hands.

▶ In a jar, combine equal parts of tomato juice, lemon juice and glycerin (available at drugstores). Let one hand massage the other with the mixture. Rinse with tepid water.

▶ The ideal remedy for people with dry hands is having their own sheep as a pet. This is because sheep's wool contains lanolin. By rubbing your hands across the animal's back every so often, you'll keep them in great shape.

Clammy Hands

▶ In a basin, combine ½ gallon of water with ½ cup of alcohol and put your palms in the mixture. After a few minutes, rinse your hands with cool water and pat dry. This is especially useful for clammy-palmed politicians on the campaign trail.

Fingernail Remedies

If you're having problems with breaking, splitting and thin nails, you may need to supplement your diet with a B-complex vitamin and zinc sulfate (follow the directions on the bottle for the dosage), along with garlic—raw and/or supplements. Be sure to consult your doctor first!

The following remedies for strengthening fingernails can help if they're used in addition to a well-balanced diet.

▶ Daily, soak your fingers for 10 minutes in any one of these oils…
  ◆ Warm olive oil
  ◆ Warm sesame-seed oil
  ◆ Warm wheat germ oil

As you wipe off the oil, give your nails a mini-massage from top to bottom.

▶ If your nails are very brittle, use a juice extractor to juice parsnip—enough for ½ cup at a time. Drink parsnip juice at least once a day. Be patient for results—give it a couple of weeks or more.

▶ While tapping your nails on a table can be very annoying to people around you, it is very good for your nails. The more you tap, the faster they will grow. Which is good because you may need long nails to defend yourself from those annoyed people around you.

Stained Nails

Want natural, healthy-looking, pinkish nails? *Some helpful advice from a New York City nail salon…*

▶ Stop using colored nail polish directly on the nail. Instead, wear a protein-based coat under nail polish to protect your nails from the polish's color pigments, which cause staining and oxidation.

▶ To get rid of polish stains, toss two denture-cleansing tablets into ¼ cup of water. Soak your fingertips in the solution for about 15 minutes.

If your nails are not as stain-free as you had hoped, gently brush them with a nail-brush. Rinse and dry.

▶ Put tooth-whitening paste on a toothbrush and gently distribute the paste on your nails. Leave it on for about 15 minutes…then brush as you rinse off the paste. Gently dry.

> ✎ **NOTE:** It may take several tries, day after day, before the stains are completely gone. But keep working at it—your appearance is worth it!

Nicotine Nails

▶ If your nails are cigarette stained, we'll tell you how to bleach them back to normal—as long as you promise to stop smoking, okay? (*See* "Smoking" starting on page 167.)

Now then…to remove the stains, rub half a lemon over your nails. Then remove the lemon's pulp and, with the remaining rind, concentrate on one nail at a time, rubbing each one until it looks nice and pink.

> ✎ **NOTE:** If you have citrus juice on your skin and you go in the sun, your skin may become permanently bleached or discolored.
> Be sure to completely wash off the lemon juice before you go outdoors.

Finger Sores (Whitlows)

▶ When you have a painful inflammation around your fingernail, soak it in hot water. Then heat a lemon in the oven, cut a narrow opening in the middle and sprinkle salt in it. Take the infected finger and stick it in the lemon. After an initial sting, the pain should disappear within minutes.

Be sure to discard the lemon and cover your finger—whitlows can be contagious.

HEADACHES

Take a holistic approach to your headache. Step back and look at the past 24 hours of your life. Have you eaten sensibly? Did you get a decent night's sleep? Have you moved your bowels since waking up this morning? Are there deadlines you need to meet? Do you have added pressures at home or at work? Is there something you're dreading?

Now that you probably realize the reason for your headache, what should you take for it? Don't refuse any offer.

Studies show that more than 90% of headaches are brought on by nervous tension, so most of our remedies are for the common tension headache. Only a few are for the more serious migraines.

> ☛ **WARNING:** In the case of regularly recurring headaches, they can be caused by eyestrain, an allergy or something more serious. Seek professional medical attention, especially if the headache comes on suddenly or is accompanied by nausea, vomiting and/or a fever.

Natural Remedies

Headaches are such a headache! Use your instincts, common sense and patience to find which one of these remedies works best for you and your headache.

▶ Research scientists tell us that almonds contain salicylates, the pain-relieving ingredient in aspirin. Eat 15 raw almonds to do the work of one aspirin. While it may take a little longer for the headache to vanish, you won't

Exotic Edibles

The fact that you are reading this book leads us to believe that you're a person who's interested in and open to all kinds of alternatives, variety and new adventures. Usually, when a person is adventurous, it extends to his/her eating habits. And so we would like to introduce you to *daikon*, a Japanese radish (if you aren't already familiar with it). It's delicious eaten raw in salads and wonderful for digestion, especially when eating oily foods.

▶ Grate a piece of daikon and squeeze out the juice through cheesecloth onto a washcloth. Apply the washcloth to your forehead and bandage in place. It should help draw out the headache pain.

While we're talking "exotic edibles" as remedies, you should know about *gomasio*—that's Japanese for sesame salt. You can find it at health food stores. The interesting thing about this seasoning is that the oil from the crushed sesame seeds coats the sea salt so that it doesn't cause an excessive attraction for water. In other words, you can season food with it and it won't make you thirsty like regular table salt.

▶ To get relief from a headache, eat 1 teaspoon of gomasio. Chew it thoroughly before swallowing.

run the risk of side effects. (What the scientists need to find now are fast-acting almonds.)

▶ Get a little bottle of essence of rosemary and rub a small amount of the oil on your forehead and temples, and also behind your ears. Then inhale the fumes from the open bottle four times. If your headache doesn't disappear within a half-hour, repeat the rubbing and inhaling once more.

Relief from the East

▶ This remedy seems to be a favorite of some Indian gurus. In a small pot, combine 1 teaspoon of dried basil with 1 cup of hot water, and bring it to a boil. Take it off the stove, then add 2 tablespoons of witch hazel. Let it cool, then saturate a washcloth with the mixture, wring it out and apply it to the forehead. Bandage it in place and keep it there until the washcloth dries or your headache disappears, whichever comes first.

▶ This will either work for you—or it won't. Either way you'll find out quickly and easily. Dunk your hands into water that's as hot as you can stand—be careful not to scald yourself! Keep them there for one minute. If you don't start feeling relief within 15 minutes, try another remedy.

▶ If your tension headache seems to stem from the tightness in your neck, use an electric heating pad or a very warm, wet cloth around your neck. The heat should relax you and improve circulation.

Pass the Mint

▶ A Mexican folk remedy says to paste a fresh mint leaf on the part of the head where the pain is most severe.

▶ In England, the mint leaf is juiced and the juice is used as eardrops to relieve a headache.

Mr. Potato Head

▶Grate a potato (a red one if possible) or an apple, and make a poultice out of it (*see* "Preparation Guide" on page 252). Apply the poultice to your forehead and bandage it in place, keeping it there for at least an hour.

Bite Your Tongue—Really!

▶You might want to try some acupressure to get rid of that headache. Stick out your tongue about ½ inch and bite down on it as hard as you can without hurting yourself. Stay that way for *exactly 10 minutes*—not a minute more!

▶Some people rid themselves of headache pain by taking a low dose of vitamin C every hour—just be aware that too much vitamin C can cause diarrhea.

If, after a few hours, you still have a headache, then stop taking vitamin C and try another remedy.

▶Add ½ teaspoon of angelica (available at health food stores) to ¾ cup of hot water and drink. It not only helps ease the pain of a headache, but it is said to give a person a lighter, happier feeling.

▶In Jamaica, a popular headache remedy uses the leaf of an aloe vera plant. Carefully cut it in half the long way, and place the gel side on your forehead and temples. Keep it in place with a handkerchief or bandage and let it stay there until your headache is gone.

Ask Your Headache to Go Away

We were once told that whatever you fully experience, disappears. The following exercise can help you experience away your headache. *Ask yourself the following questions and answer them honestly…*

◆ *Do I really want to get rid of the headache?* (Don't laugh. A lot of people want to hang on to their headaches. It's a great excuse and cop-out from all kinds of things.)

◆ *What kind of headache do I have?* Be specific. Is it pounding over one eye? Does it throb each time you bend down? Do you have a dull ache at the base of your neck?

Now, either memorize the next questions or have someone read them to you. ("Why?" you wonder.) Close your eyes. ("Aha!" That's why.)

◆ *What size is my headache?* Figure out the exact dimensions of it. Start with the length from the front of your face to the back of your head, the width from ear to ear and the thickness of it from the top of your head down toward your neck.

◆ *What color is my headache?*

◆ *How much water will it hold?* (This is done in your mind through visualization.) Fill a cup with the amount of water needed to fill the area of the headache. Then, pour the water from the cup into the space of your headache. When you've completed that, open your eyes. You should have experienced away your headache.

The first time we used this exercise, our results were quite dramatic. If we hadn't experienced it ourselves, we'd probably think it's as crazy as you're probably thinking we are right now.

V Is for Vinegar

▶ When our grandmother had a headache, she would dip a large white handkerchief in vinegar, wring it out and tie it tightly around her forehead until the headache disappeared.

A variation of soaking a handkerchief in vinegar is to soak a piece of brown grocery-bag paper in vinegar. Shake off the excess liquid and place it on your forehead. Tie it in place and keep it there for at least 30 minutes.

▶ We used this remedy with great success on the host of a famous TV morning show…he had a monster headache that he'd been suffering with for two days. He tried our "tie a yellow lemon" remedy and felt better by the end of the interview!

Peel the rind off a lemon. Make the pieces as wide as possible. Rub the rind (the inside of the skin should touch your skin) on your forehead and temples. Then place the pieces of rind on the forehead and temples, securing them with a scarf or bandage. Keep it there until the headache goes away, usually within a half-hour.

Take a Walk

▶ Let ice-cold water accumulate in the bathtub until it's ankle-high. Dress warmly except for your bare feet. Take a leisurely stroll in the tub—from one to three minutes—as long as it takes for your feet to start feeling warm in the ice-cold water. When that happens, get out of the tub, dry your feet and go directly to bed. Cover up, relax and within no time, your headache should be a pain of the past.

▶ Press your thumb against the roof of your mouth for four to five minutes. Every so often, move your thumb to another section of the roof of your mouth. The nerve pressure in your head should be greatly relieved. While this remedy is highly impractical during a speaking engagement, it's worth a try in the privacy of your home.

Getting Steamy

▶ Mix a cup of water with a cup of apple cider vinegar and bring it to a slow boil in a medium-sized pot. When the fumes begin to rise, turn off the stove and remove the pot. Put a towel over your head and bend over the pot.

Inhale and exhale deeply through your nose about 80 times or for about 10 minutes. Be very careful—steam can burn if you get too close. And make sure you hold the towel so that it catches the vapor for you to inhale, but that it doesn't touch the hot pot or stove.

▶ If strawberries are in season, eat a few. They contain organic salicylates, which are related to the active ingredients in aspirin. (Do not try this remedy if you are allergic to aspirin.)

▶ Vigorously rub the second joint of each thumb—two minutes on the right hand, two minutes on the left hand—until you've done it five times each, or for 10 minutes. Use hand lotion on the thumbs to eliminate friction.

▶ A very old American remedy is to swallow a teaspoon of honey mixed with ½ teaspoon of garlic juice.

☛ **WARNING:** Infants, diabetics and people with honey allergies should not use honey.

▶ Enlist the help of someone who will slowly move his/her thumb down the right side of your back, alongside your shoulder blade and toward your waist. Let that person know when he hits a sore or tender spot. Have your helper exert steady pressure on that spot for a minute. This should bring relief from the headache.

CAUTION: See your doctor immediately if your headache is worse or "different" than usual...comes on rapidly and severely...first occurs after age 50...and/or is accompanied by neurological symptoms, such as paralysis, slurred speech or loss of consciousness. These symptoms may indicate an aneurysm, brain tumor, stroke or some other serious problem.

Migraine Headaches

If you suffer from migraines, sometimes the only thing you can do to relieve the throbbing pain, double vision and nausea is to lie down in a dark, quiet room.

To prevent the onset of an attack, it helps to eat a healthy diet, avoid caffeine and get enough sleep. These remedies may provide some additional relief.

CAUTION: Chronic migraine sufferers should seek medical attention. You may need medication to treat your headaches.

▶Dip a few cabbage leaves in boiling hot water to make them soft. As soon as they're cool enough, place one or two thicknesses on your forehead and on the back of your neck. Secure them in place with a scarf or bandage. Then relax as the cabbage draws out the pain.

▶Boil two Spanish onions. Eat one and mash the other for a poultice (*see* "Preparation Guide" on page 252). Then place the poultice on your forehead.

Anti-Migraine Massage

▶Apply pressure to the palm of one hand with the thumb of the other hand. Then reverse the order. If you feel a tenderness in either palm, concentrate the massage on that area. Keep up the firm pressure and massage for 10 minutes—five minutes on each hand.

▶We heard about a woman who would eat a tablespoon of honey the second she felt a migraine coming on. If the headache wasn't gone within a half hour, she'd take another tablespoon of honey with three glasses of water and that would do it.

WARNING: Infants, diabetics and people with honey allergies should not use honey.

▶Bathe your feet in a basin or two plastic shoe boxes filled with very strong, warm, black coffee. Some medical professionals recommend drinking a cup or two of coffee as well. Or, for the same effectiveness, but with less caffeine, drink yerba maté, also called Jungle Punch (*see* page 131). It is available at health food stores.

NOTE: Be aware that yerba maté contains caffeine, although less than coffee or regular tea.

Head to the Salon

▶Ready for this one? Sit under a hair dryer. The heat and high-pitched hum of the dryer may relax the tension that brought on the headache.

■ Recipe ■

Apple Salsa with Cinnamon Tortilla Chips

Apple Salsa

2 medium tart apples, chopped
    (preferably Granny Smith)
2 tsp lemon juice
1 cup fresh strawberries, chopped
2 medium kiwi fruit, peeled and chopped
1 small orange
2 Tbsp brown sugar, firmly packed
2 Tbsp apple jelly, melted

Cinnamon Tortilla Chips

8 eight-inch flour tortillas
Water
¼ cup granulated sugar
2 to 4 tsp ground cinnamon

In a large bowl, toss the chopped apples with the lemon juice to keep them from browning. Add the chopped strawberries and kiwi.

Grate about 1 Tbsp of orange peel (the zest) into the bowl. Then slice the orange in half and squeeze out about 3 Tbsp of the orange juice. Make sure to remove the seeds from the orange so they do not get into your salsa. Stir in the brown sugar and jelly. Set aside.

To prepare the cinnamon tortilla chips, brush both sides of the tortillas with a tiny bit of water (just enough to allow the sugar and cinnamon to stick.)

Blend together the sugar and cinnamon and sprinkle it lightly over the tortillas, turning to cover both sides. If you have an empty spice shaker, it works well to double the mixture and sprinkle it over the tortillas from the shaker. Any leftover sugar and cinnamon is perfect for preparing cinnamon toast, quick and easy.

Cut each tortilla into 8 equal pie-shaped wedges and place the pieces in a single layer on a baking sheet that has been lightly coated with a non-stick cooking spray or a thin brush of butter.

Bake the cinnamon-coated tortillas in a preheated 400° F oven for 6 to 8 minutes or until lightly browned. Cool until crisp, then serve with the apple salsa on the side.

Makes 4 servings.

Source: www.recipegoldmine.com

According to one physician, the dryer brings relief to two-thirds of the migraine sufferers who try it. Your local beauty salon will probably be happy to accommodate you as long as you don't have a headache during their busy time.

WARNING: If you have chemical sensitivities, stay out of a hair salon. It could make your headache worse.

▶ Open a jar of strong mustard and slowly inhale the fumes several times.

▶ Some people have migraines without having severe headaches. Instead, they are troubled by impaired vision—spots in front of their eyes or seeing double. We heard about a simple remedy for this—chew a handful of raisins. Chew them thoroughly before swallowing.

Headache Prevention... Sort of

A three-year study conducted at the University of Michigan in Ann Arbor showed that students who ate two apples a day had far fewer headaches than those who didn't eat any apples. The apple eaters also had fewer skin problems, arthritic conditions and colds.

You might want to have an apple for breakfast and one as a late afternoon snack, or one a couple of hours after dinner.

Did we mention that apples contain natural salicylates, substances that are related to the active ingredient in aspirin?

Chances are, eating two apples a day will also prevent constipation, which can be a leading cause of headaches. (*See* recipe on page 108.)

HEART PROBLEMS

The heart is a four-chambered, hollow muscle and double-acting pump that is located in the chest between the lungs. This hardworking, fist-sized muscle pumps blood through the blood vessels to all parts of the body at the rate of about 4,000 gallons a day. (No wonder so many of us have "tired blood.")

The heart is so complex—and heart trouble is so serious—that the best suggestions we can offer are...

♦ If you feel as though you're having a heart attack, call for professional medical help IMMEDIATELY!

♦ If you have a history of heart problems, follow an eating plan that will promote a healthy heart.

♦ To learn how to help others, take a cardiac pulmonary resuscitation (CPR) course through the local chapter of the American Heart Association or the Red Cross.

♦ Don't smoke!

Heart Attack

If you or someone you're with feels as though he/she is having a heart attack, call 911 for professional medical help *immediately*. Symptoms may not seem serious at first, but don't delay.

▶Unlock your door and, while you're waiting for help to arrive, squeeze the end of the pinky finger on the left hand. Squeeze it HARD! Keep squeezing it. This acupressure procedure has been said to save lives.

▶If he/she is not allergic or taking blood thinners, have the person having a heart attack chew one full-strength (325 mg) aspirin tablet or four baby aspirin tablets.

NOTE: When you receive medical attention, be sure to tell the person treating you about any medication or natural supplements you have taken.

▶A cup of peppermint tea a day is said to help prevent a heart attack.

CAUTION: Beware that peppermint is a powerful herb that can undermine or negate the effectiveness of homeopathic medicine.

Heart Palpitations

Many healthy people get heart palpitations (*arrhythmia*). You may feel as though your heart has skipped a beat or is beating very fast or strong. The heart is powered by electrical pulses that aren't always perfect. Be sure to see your doctor for an evaluation and diagnosis.

> **WARNING:** Seek medical attention if the palpitations persist or are accompanied by dizziness, chest pain or fainting/passing out.

▶ If you are given a clean bill of health, but you experience a minor bout of palpitations (and who hasn't at one time or another?), take a holistic approach to find the cause. Was it the MSG in the Chinese food you had for lunch? The caffeine in the chocolate you pigged out on? Pressure at the office? Cigarette smoke? Sugar? Work on figuring it out so that you learn what not to have next time.

▶ Here's a natural sedative to subdue the thumping. Steep two chamomile tea bags in 2 cups of just-boiled water. Steam a few shredded leaves of cabbage. Then, in a soup bowl, combine the steamed leaves with the chamomile tea. This tea-soup may not taste good, but it can help overcome those skipped heartbeats.

▶ If you have heart palpitations occasionally, drink peppermint tea. Have a mug every day. It seems to have a calming effect on people, especially since it is an herbal tea that does not contain caffeine.

Heart Helpers

▶ According to the results of a study, orchestra conductors live an average of 7½ years longer than the average person.

To strengthen your heart, tone up your circulatory system and have some fun, go through the motions of conducting an orchestra. Do it for at least 10 minutes a day, or 20 minutes three days a week. Conduct to music that inspires you. If you don't have a baton, use a ruler or a chopstick. Pretend each day of exercise is a command performance. Throw your whole self into it physically and emotionally.

> **NOTE:** If you have a history of heart problems, be sure to check with your doctor before you begin conducting.

Healing Honey

▶ Two teaspoons of raw honey a day, either in a glass of water or straight off the spoon, is thought by many nutritionists to be the best tonic for strengthening the heart, as well as for general physical repair.

> **WARNING:** Infants, diabetics and people with honey allergies should not use honey.

▶ Okay, so you don't want to join a gym. You don't have to. For the best exercise and the perfect body stimulator, just take an old-fashioned walk—make it a *brisk* walk—daily. (Just be sure to check with your doctor before starting a new exercise program.)

Brisk means walking a mile every 20 minutes (three miles an hour). It's slower than running or race-walking, but generally faster than a stroll.

▶ *The New England Journal of Medicine* (*www.nejm.org*) reported the findings of a long-term study of 72,000 women ages 40 to 65. Heart attack risk was reduced 30% to 40% in the women who did at least three hours of brisk walking a week. The women who walked briskly for five hours or more a week cut their heart attack risk by more than 40%.

In addition to the walking, those who did vigorous exercise for 90 minutes a week cut their risk almost in half. Gardening and housework are considered vigorous exercise. So you can have a clean house, a beautiful garden and a healthy heart.

CAUTION: Broccoli and turnip greens are rich in vitamin K, the clot-promoting vitamin. If you take anticlotting medication prescribed by your physician, be aware that eating big portions of these vegetables can counteract the effects of the medicine.

▶This remedy is recommended for people who have a history of heart problems—right before going to bed, take a 10-minute footbath. Step into calf-high water, as hot as you can take it without scalding yourself. As the minutes pass and the water cools, add more hot water. After 10 minutes, step out of the tub and dry your feet thoroughly, preferably with a rough towel.

Once your feet are dry, give them a one-minute massage, manipulating the toes as well as the entire foot. This footbath/massage may help circulation, remove congestion around the heart and lead you to a peaceful night's sleep.

▶We recently read a list of supposed benefits of hawthorn berries. We followed up by researching the herb and, as a result, we now take hawthorn supplements daily.

Benefits: Normalizes blood pressure by regulating heart action...improves heart valve defects...helps people with a lot of stress...

strengthens weakened heart muscle...and prevents atherosclerosis. (*See* page 19.)

NOTE: Check with your health professional for dosage, depending on your size and the state of your heart health.

▶Omega-3 fatty acids impact many factors linked to cardiovascular disease. They help lower LDL ("bad") cholesterol levels and triglycerides, inhibit excessive platelet aggregation, lower fibrinogen levels and lower both systolic and diastolic blood pressure in individuals with high blood pressure.

Omega-3s are found in many foods, including salmon, mackerel and other fatty fish. Flaxseed oil offers the most cost-effective and beneficial method for increasing the intake of omega-3 oils in the diet. (*See* "Six Sensational Superfoods" on page 262 for detailed flaxseed information.)

▶For a healthier heart, eat wheat germ every day. You might also want to supplement with vitamin E. It's said to help reduce hardening of the arteries. Be sure to check with your doctor for the amount that is right for you.

▶Take a garlic supplement every day to protect and strengthen the heart and help thin the blood. Also, use garlic in cooking and eat it raw in salads.

That's Nothing to Wine About

▶Moderate consumption of red wine, as reported in the respected British medical journal *The Lancet* (*www.thelancet.com*), is directly associated with lower rates of heart disease.

▶According to wine therapists, a little champagne sipped daily helps strengthen the heart.

The champagne's tartrate of potassium content supposedly has a positive effect on one's cardiac rhythm.

> ✎ **NOTE:** Please remember—*everything in moderation, especially alcohol!*

▶ We've been told that massaging the pads at the base of the last two fingers of the left hand, or massaging the left foot under the third, fourth and fifth toes, can relieve heart pain within seconds.

Red Roses for Love

▶ If someone wants to give you an edible treat, instead of candy, suggest red roses. They're said to help strengthen the heart as well as other organs of the body, not to mention what they do for a relationship.

Remove the bitter white part on the bottom of the rose petals and eat the rest of the petals raw, or make rose-petal tea to drink. Be sure the roses are organically grown and haven't been sprayed.

▶ Eat onions once a day. According to Russian scientists, onions are beneficial for all kinds of heart problems.

▶ Every morning, before breakfast, drink the juice of half a lemon in a cup of warm water. It's reputed to be helpful for all kinds of body functions, from proper fluid action in the blood to regularity in the bathroom.

Rev Up Your Circulation

▶ Once a day, mix ⅛ teaspoon of cayenne pepper in a cup of water and drink it down. It's not easy to take, but it may be beneficial to the circulatory system, since cayenne pepper is reputed to be the purest herbal stimulant.

▶ Japanese medicine recommends ginger footbaths to improve circulation. Add a cup of fresh, minced ginger to a basin with 2 quarts of warm water, or divide the water and ginger into two plastic shoe boxes. Soak your feet in the water until they're rosy red. Then dry thoroughly and notice a more energized feeling.

HEMORRHOIDS

According to the American College of Surgeons, hemorrhoids (also known as piles) are fibromuscular cushions that line the anal canal. When irritated, infected or strained, they are literally a pain in the anus.

Two out of every three adults have had, currently have or will have a case of hemorrhoids. Chances are, if you're reading this, you are one of the two out of the three.

Along with treating your condition with natural, nonchemical remedies, there are ways to speed up the healing process...

♦ Keep the bowels as clear as possible. Drink lots of fruit juices and vegetable juices. Stay away from hard-to-digest, overly processed foods—especially those that contain white flour and sugar—as well as alcoholic beverages.

♦ Eat six or seven servings of fruits and vegetables a day.

- ◆ Do not strain or hold your breath while having a bowel movement. Make an effort to breathe evenly.
- ◆ Take a brisk walk as often as you can, especially after meals.

Natural Remedies

Heed these suggestions and, hopefully, in a few days, you'll have this problem behind you.

▶ Apply liquid lecithin directly on the hemorrhoids, once a day, until they disappear.

▶ Eat a large boiled leek every day as an afternoon snack or with dinner.

▶ Eat three raw unprocessed almonds every day. Chew each one about 50 times.

▶ In a blender, finely chop ¼ cup cranberries. Place 1 tablespoon of the blended cranberries in a piece of cheesecloth and place it over the anus. An hour later, remove the cheesecloth and replace it with another tablespoon of cranberries in cheesecloth for another hour. This is a great pain reliever. By the end of two hours, you should feel much better.

Faster Than a Speeding Bullet

▶ How are you at ice carving? Carefully carve or melt an ice cube down to the size and shape of a bullet. Use it as a suppository. The cold may give you a start, but it may also reduce the swelling and heal the hemorrhoids.

Witchy Water

▶ Add ¼ cup of witch hazel to a basin of warm water. If it's not irritating, sit in it for at least 15 minutes at a time, at least two times a day.

Complete cures have been reported within three days.

▶ Psychic healer Edgar Cayce recommended this exercise to a hemorrhoid sufferer…

- ◆ Stand with feet about six inches apart, hands at sides.
- ◆ Raise your hands up to the ceiling.
- ◆ Bend forward and bring your hands as close to the floor as you can.
- ◆ Go back to the first position.

Repeat the entire procedure 36 times. It should take just a few minutes to do. Perform this exercise every day, an hour after breakfast and an hour after dinner, until the hemorrhoids are history.

Tobacco That's Good for You

▶ Put the tobacco from two cigarettes in a warm pan, add 4 teaspoons of butter and let the mixture simmer for a couple of minutes. (This is a much better use for cigarettes than smoking them!) Next, pour the hot liquid through a strainer onto a sanitary napkin. When it's cool enough, apply it to the hemorrhoid area. Whip up a fresh batch and reapply three times a day.

▶ A consulting physician for the Denver Broncos and Denver Nuggets athletic teams has had success in speeding up the healing process of hemorrhoids with vitamin C baths.

Put 1 cup of ascorbic acid powder to every 5 quarts of cool bath water. Sit in the tub for 15 minutes at a time, two or three times a day.

✎ **NOTE:** Ascorbic acid powder is expensive. If you can fit your tushy into a basin with ½ cup of the powder and 2½ quarts of cool water, you'll save a fortune.

▶Take advantage of the healing properties of the enzymes in papaya by drenching a wad of sterilized cotton in pure papaya juice. Position it on the hemorrhoid area and secure it in place with a bandage. The juice should help stop the bleeding and bring the irritation under control.

Hemorrhoid Prevention

To *prevent* hemorrhoids, it's best to increase the fiber and fluids in your diet.

▶According to psychic healer Edgar Cayce, eating three raw almonds a day will help prevent hemorrhoids.

▶Since hemorrhoids are a sitter's ailment, it may help to take a long walk every day at a fairly fast pace. A yoga class two or three times a week is also a good preventive measure.

HERPES

The herpes virus is a common infection that affects the body's nerve cells, making them "break out" in painful sores. *Herpes simplex 1* generally affects the mouth (cold sores and fever blisters) and *simplex* 2 affects the genitals. Each type tends to be recurrent (you have an outbreak whenever you are sick or under stress), and each can be contagious during intimate contact—kissing, oral sex or intercourse.

Forty-five million Americans (one out of every five sexually active adults) have genital herpes. Each year, up to one million more get this virus. The best way to prevent transmission of the virus is to abstain from intimate contact during an outbreak.

We spoke with a man who did extensive research and came up with a remedy for overcoming the symptoms of herpes simplex 1. He tested it and had friends test it. The results were impressive.

But first the remedy, next the explanation and then more about the results.

Dietary Remedy

▶Do not eat nuts, chocolate or (sorry, Mom!) chicken soup. At the first sign of a herpes flare-up, eat 1 pound of steamed flounder. That's it. That's the remedy.

The explanation—in simple terms, as best as we understand it—is that there's a certain balance in the body between two amino acids …arginine and lysine. To contract herpes and to have the symptoms recur, one's body has to have a high level of arginine compared with the level of lysine.

The secret, then, is to reduce the amount of arginine (eliminate nuts, chocolate and chicken soup) and increase the amount of lysine (eat flounder). One pound of flounder has 11,000 mg of lysine. You can take lysine tablets, but you would have to take lots of them, and they contain binders and other things you just don't need. Also, the tablets are not as digestible or as absorbable as the lysine found naturally in flounder.

By steaming the fish, you help to retain the nutrients. An added bonus is that you can add the sauce of your choice to the flounder after it's been steamed. That way, you won't even think of it as medicine!

As for results, the man and his friends have had symptoms disappear overnight after eating flounder and never eating nuts, chocolate and chicken soup.

Cold Sores and Fever Blisters

▶Speed up the healing process of a cold sore by cutting a clove of garlic in half and rubbing it on the sore. Not pleasant, but effective.

▶Combine 1 tablespoon of apple cider vinegar with 3 tablespoons of honey (preferably raw honey) and dab the sore with the mixture in the morning, late afternoon and at night.

⚡ **CAUTION:** Open sores are infectious to hands, eyes and genitalia. They are best left alone to dry and heal. Foreign substances may cause further irritation and infection.

▶Grind up a few walnuts and mix them with 1 teaspoon of cocoa butter. Apply this "nutty-butter" salve to the sore twice a day. The sore should be gone in three or four days.

▶Lysine may inhibit the growth of herpes viruses that cause cold sores and fever blisters. Take one L-lysine 500 mg tablet daily with dinner. Or eat flounder for dinner!

▶This remedy came to us from several people across the country. (If they weren't embarrassed to tell it to us, we won't be embarrassed to tell it to you.) Use earwax (your own, of course) on your cold sore or fever blister.

▶When a cold sore is on its way, there's often a peculiar tingling sensation. At the first sign of that tingle, take _colorless_ nail polish and paint it lightly on the area where the cold sore is about to emerge. The nail polish prevents the sore from blossoming.

Cyndi Antoniak, a producer for MSNBC, got this unique remedy from her dermatologist. Since Cyndi first used this remedy successfully some time ago, she hasn't needed to use it again. Incidentally, the polish peels off naturally within a short time.

Shingles

Did you have the chicken pox when you were a kid? _Herpes zoster virus_ is the chicken pox virus, which is also the shingles virus, revisited. The chicken pox virus stays dormant until your immune system falls down on the job. The resulting painful, blistery flare-up is shingles.

▶St. John's wort is an antiviral, anti-inflammatory herb that can also strengthen the nervous system. Drink St. John's-wort tea to help you de-stress, and gently massage the tincture directly on the affected area. Both tea and tincture are available at health food stores.

⚡ **CAUTION:** Check with your health professional before taking St. John's wort. It may interfere with some medications.

▶Aloe vera gel is a soothing, cooling antiseptic. You can buy a bottle at a health food store or you can buy an aloe vera plant. They're inexpensive, easy to grow and they look a lot prettier than a refrigerated bottle.

Look for aloes that have little spikes on the edge of the leaves.

When using the plant, cut off the lowest leaf, then cut that leaf into 2-inch pieces. Slice one of the pieces in half and apply the gel directly to the affected area. Individually wrap the remaining pieces of the leaf in plastic wrap and keep them in the freezer. Every few hours, take a piece of leaf from the freezer and apply the soothing gel.

▶ In order to get a healthy dose of a beneficial amino acid, lysine, eat flounder. (*See* "Dietary Remedy" on page 114.)

⚡ **CAUTION:** Shingles that affect the face or forehead—anywhere near the eyes—can lead to cornea damage and/or temporary facial paralysis. Be sure to see your health professional immediately for treatment.

▶ Make a paste of baking soda and water, and apply to the affected area for some relief.

▶ Prepare a paste of Epsom salts and water. Place the paste directly on the affected area. Repeat the procedure as often as possible.

▶ Apply any of the following to relieve the itching and speed the healing—witch hazel (an astringent), apple cider vinegar (an infection fighter), red raspberry tea (particularly good for viral eruptive problems) or aloe vera gel.

▶ According to Frank L. Greenway, MD, professor and chair of the outpatient clinic at Pennington Biomedical Research Center in Baton Rouge, Louisiana, shingles pain can be eased by geranium oil.

Applied directly on the affected area, 100% geranium oil relieved pain dramatically in 25% of patients whose pain after a case of shingles had lasted for three months or more and was not relieved by standard pain medications. Fifty percent of the patients showed some relief, and 25% did not benefit. Geranium oil is available in health food stores.

HICCUPS

A hiccup is a spastic contraction of the diaphragm—the large circular muscle that separates the chest from the abdomen.

Hiccups are a great conversation starter. If you're in a room with 30 people, ask each one of them how they get rid of the hiccups and you will probably get 30 different remedies.

According to the *Guinness Book of World Records* (Guinness), the longest recorded attack of hiccups is that which afflicted Charles Osborne of Anthon, Iowa. He was born in 1894 and got the hiccups in 1922, when he was slaughtering a hog.

The hiccups continued but didn't stop him from marrying twice and fathering eight children. (Who knows, maybe they helped.)

In 1983, *Guinness* reported that Charles Osborne had hiccupped—and was still hiccuping—about 420 million times. By the time he died in 1990, the hiccupping had slowed down from 40 times a minute to 20 times a minute. You do the math.

Natural Remedies

To prevent a case of the hiccups, do not slaughter a hog. To cure a case of the hiccups, try one or more of the following remedies.

▶ Drink a glass of pineapple or orange juice.

▶ Make believe your index finger is a mustache. Place it under your nose and press in hard for 30 seconds.

▶ Drink a glass of water that has a tablespoon in it—the bowl of the spoon being the part that's in the water. As you drink, be sure the metal handle of the spoon is pressed against your left temple.

▶ Swallow a teaspoon of fresh onion juice.

▶ Mix a teaspoon of apple cider vinegar in a cup of warm water and drink it down.

▶ Drink a glass of water from the far side of the glass. You have to bend far forward to do this without dribbling all over yourself.

Pep It Up

▶ When children between the ages of seven and 14 have the hiccups, promise to double their allowance if they can hiccup once more after you say "Go!" Chances are there will not be one more hiccup after you say "Go!" We don't know why, but it works…most of the time.

▶ Men should place an ice cube right below their Adam's apple and count to 150.

▶ Take a mouthful of water and keep it in your mouth while you stick the middle fingers of each hand into your ears and press fairly firmly. Count to 100, then swallow the water and unplug your ears.

Do You Know La Bohème?

▶ Pretend you're singing at New York City's Metropolitan Opera House without a microphone, and the foremost opera critic is in the last row of the uppermost tier. One aria and the hiccups should disappear. (Of course, so might your roommate.)

▶ Take seven drinks of water without taking a breath in between swallows. While you're drinking the water, keep turning the glass to the left.

▶ Put a handkerchief over a glass of water and suck the water through it as you would with a straw.

▶ Stick out your tongue as far as possible and keep it out for three minutes. Be careful, one big hiccup and—ouch!

Sole Solution

▶ The sole of the foot is an acupressure point for curing the hiccups. Massage the center of the sole for as long as it takes for the hiccups to stop.

▶ Mix ½ teaspoon of sugar in ½ glass of water and drink it slowly.

▶ Place a pencil between your teeth so that it sticks out on both sides of your mouth. Chomp down on it while drinking a glass of water. (You might want to wear a bib.)

▶ Locate the area about two to three inches above your navel and between the two sides of your rib cage. Press in with the fingers of both of your hands and stay that way long enough to say to yourself—"One, two, three, four, I don't have the hiccups anymore."

If you still have them, try reciting "The Rime of the Ancient Mariner"—it's a very, very long poem written by Samuel Taylor Coleridge in 1798.

Bald and Beautiful

▶ Close your eyes, hold your breath and think of 10 bald men. Let us start you off—Sean Connery, Montel Williams, Howie Mandel, Paul Shaffer, Michael Jordan, etc.

▶Pardon our name-dropping, but...television news journalist Jane Pauley told us that her husband, Garry Trudeau (creator of the "Doonesbury" comic strip), gets painful hiccups. His remedy is to put a teaspoon of salt on half a lemon and then suck the juice out of the lemon.

▶Our great-aunt Molly used to soak a cube of sugar in fresh lemon juice and then let it dissolve in her mouth. She did it to get rid of the hiccups. She also did it as a shortcut whenever she drank tea.

Think of Peter Rabbit

▶Just visualizing a rabbit—its cute little face, quivering nose and white whiskers—has been known to make the hiccups disappear.

▶One of the most common remedies for hiccups is a teaspoon of granulated sugar. It supposedly irritates the throat, causing an interruption of the vagus nerve impulse pattern that is responsible for triggering the spasms of the diaphragm. (Just reading the previous sentence aloud may help you get rid of the hiccups.)

In Arabia, people have been known to use sand in place of sugar.

▶Another way you might interrupt the diaphragmatic spasms is by holding your arms above your head and panting like a dog. Well, you might not get rid of the hiccups, but you may end up with some table scraps.

▶Lay a broom on the floor and jump over it six times. If you want to update this remedy, try jumping over a vacuum cleaner. For all of you rich people, jump over your maid.

▶Turn yourself into a "T" by spreading out your arms. Then give a big yawn.

▶Pretend you're chewing gum while sticking your fingers in your ears, gently pressing inward. "What did you say? I can't hear you. My fingers are in my ears."

▶If nothing else works, take a hot bath. This has helped cure severe cases of hiccups.

When Someone Else Has Hiccups...

▶Take something cold that's made of metal—a spoon is good—tie a string around it and lower it down the hiccupper's back.

▶Suddenly accuse the hiccupper of doing something he/she did not do—"You left the water running in the tub!"..."You borrowed money from me and forgot to pay it back!"... "You skipped the best part!"

HYPERTENSION

More than 65 million Americans have been diagnosed with hypertension (high blood pressure). If you're one of those people, obviously you're not alone.

We urge you to take a look at your lifestyle and, once and for all, do something to change whatever is causing the blood pressure problem.

The most important dietary recommendation for lowering blood pressure is to increase the consumption of plant foods in the diet, according to Jade Beutler, RRT, RCP, San Diego–based CEO of Lignan Research LLC and a licensed health care practitioner. A primarily vegetarian diet typically contains less saturated fat and refined carbohydrates, and more potassium, complex carbohydrates, fiber, calcium, magnesium, vitamin C and essential fatty acids.

Basic Solutions

To help combat the effects of hypertension, start with these suggestions—after consulting your doctor.

- ◆ If you're overweight, diet sensibly (without diet pills).
- ◆ Eliminate salt (use sea salt in moderation), and cut down on or cut out red meat.
- ◆ To reduce the stress of your everyday life, try meditation or a self-help program. Ask a health professional for guidance and reputable contacts.
- ◆ If you smoke, stop! (*See* "Smoking" on page 167.)
- ◆ If you drink alcohol, stop! Or at least cut down drastically.

Double-blind studies have demonstrated that either fish oil supplements or flaxseed oil, both rich in omega-3 fatty acids, are very effective in lowering blood pressure. (*See* "Six Sensational Superfoods" on page 262 for detailed information on flaxseed.)

When blood pressure is measured, there are two numbers reported. The first and higher number is the systolic. It measures the pressure inside the arteries when the heart beats (constricts). The diastolic is the lower number and measures the pressure in the arteries when the heart is at rest in between beats.

Hypertension is ranked in stages...

	Systolic	Diastolic
Prehypertension	120 to 139	80 to 89
Stage 1	140 to 159	90 to 99
Stage 2	greater than 160	greater than 100

We saw a woman wearing a T-shirt that said—"Anybody with normal blood pressure these days just isn't paying attention."

Read on for more strategies that will help to improve your blood pressure...

If Your Blood Pressure Is High...

▶ Eat two apples a day. The pectin in apples may help lower high blood pressure.

▶ Eat raw garlic in salads and use it in cooking. Also take garlic supplements daily—one after breakfast and one after dinner.

Go Fish

▶ According to a university study, blood pressure can be reduced by staring at fish in a fish tank. The relaxation benefits of fish-watching are equal to biofeedback and meditation.

If caring for a tank of fish isn't for you, check the Internet or your local video store for tapes of aquariums and fish swimming in their natural habitats.

▶ Cucumbers are rich in potassium, phosphorus and calcium. They're also a good diuretic and calming agent. To help bring down blood pressure, try eating a cucumber every day. If you have a juicer, drink ½ cup of fresh cucumber juice. You can also include some carrots and parsley, which is another good diuretic.

▶ Drink 2 cups of potato water daily. (*See* "Preparation Guide" on page 252.)

▶ Cayenne pepper is a wonderful blood pressure stabilizer.

■ Recipe ■

Cucumbers in Sour Cream

2 large cucumbers, sliced

1 tsp salt

1 cup sour cream

2 Tbsp vinegar

1 Tbsp chopped chives

1 tsp dill weed

¼ tsp granulated sugar

Dash of pepper

Peel cucumbers and slice thin. Sprinkle with 1 tsp salt and let stand 30 minutes.

Drain well. Combine sour cream, vinegar, chives, dill weed, sugar and pepper. Pour over cucumbers. Taste and add additional salt, if needed. Chill in refrigerator for at least 30 minutes.

Source: www.recipegoldmine.com

▶Add ⅛ teaspoon to a cup of goldenseal tea (*see* "Preparation Guide" on page 250) and drink a cup daily.

Don't Spit Out the Seeds

▶In a blender, or by using a mortar and pestle, crush 2 teaspoons of dried watermelon seeds. Put them in a cup of just-boiled water and let them steep for one hour. Stir, strain and drink the watermelon-seed tea a half-hour before a meal.

Repeat the procedure before each meal, three times a day. After taking the tea for a few days, have your pressure checked and see if it has improved. Watermelon-seed tea can be bought at health food stores.

More Accurate Blood Pressure Readings

When measuring blood pressure, it's important to make sure your reading is as accurate as possible. One way to ensure you get a proper reading is to keep your arm bent.

According to investigators from the University of California, San Diego (UCSD) School of Medicine and the Medical College of Wisconsin in Milwaukee, blood pressure readings can be 10% higher if a person's arm is held parallel to the body.

So bend that arm! Make sure your elbow is at a right angle to your body with the elbow flexed at a heart level. This should give the most precise reading. And for the record, it doesn't matter if you're sitting, standing or laying down for the test—as long as you're in the same position every time you're tested, results should be accurate.

✎ **NOTE:** Watermelon seeds are known to strengthen kidney function—and increase urine production. Be prepared to use bathroom facilities often.

▶How would you like a hot or cold cup of raspberry-leaf tea? It may help bring down your blood pressure. Combine 1 ounce of raspberry leaves to 2 cups of boiling water and simmer for 20 minutes in an enamel or glass saucepan. Drink 1 cup a day, hot or cold (no ice cubes). After a week, check the results by having your blood pressure taken.

▶The faster you talk, the less oxygen you have coming in. The less oxygen, the harder your heart has to work to maintain the supply of oxygen in your body. The harder the heart has to work, the higher your blood pressure seems to go.

The bottom line here is that if you talk slowly, you should need to take bigger and better breaths, giving you more oxygen and preventing your blood pressure from climbing.

If Your Blood Pressure Is Low...

Just as there are people with high blood pressure, there are people (not as many) with low blood pressure. These remedies are said to be effective blood pressure regulators and stabilizers.

▶Scientific studies have shown that five to 10 minutes of laughter first thing in the morning improves blood pressure levels. What's there to laugh at first thing in the morning? Listen to a funny local radio DJ, or go on-line and type in "jokes" at any Internet search engine (Yahoo!, Google, AltaVista, Dogpile, Excite).

▶We heard from a Russian folk healer who recommends drinking ½ cup of raw beet juice when a person feels that his/her blood pressure may be a little too low. This healer also told us that a person with low blood pressure knows that feeling.

7–14–7 Exercise

▶Deep breathing may help to bring your blood pressure levels up to normal. First thing in the morning and last thing at night, perform this breathing exercise.

Let all the air out of your lungs—exhale, squeezing all the air out—then let the air in through your nostrils slowly, to the count of seven. When no more air will fit in your lungs, hold tight for the count of 14. Next, gently let the air out through your mouth to the count of seven—all the way out. Inhale and exhale this way 10 times.

Even when your blood pressure is normal, continue this breathing exercise for all kinds of physical benefits.

INDIGESTION

The famous actress and comedienne Mae West once said, "Too much of a good thing…is wonderful!" We say, "Too much of a good thing… can cause indigestion!"

There are several different types of indigestion—mild, severe and persistent. Persistent indigestion may be caused by a food allergy. The best course of action is to get professional medical help and have it checked out.

That said, severe indigestion or stomach pain may be something a lot more serious than you think, so it's also important to seek professional help immediately.

CAUTION: Never take a laxative when you have severe stomach pain.

Mild indigestion usually produces one or a combination of the following symptoms—stomachache, heartburn, nausea and vomiting, or gas (flatulence). If you are feeling minor tummy troubles, here are some remedies to try.

Natural Remedies

The first thing a person suffering from a mild case of indigestion usually does is promise never to overindulge again. That takes care of next time. As for now, relief may be just a few paragraphs away.

▶ When you have stomach cramps caused by indigestion, sip some peppermint or ginger tea as your after-dinner drink.

Roll Some Relief

▶ In the case of acid indigestion, thoroughly chew a teaspoon of dry rolled oats, then swallow them. The oats not only soothe the acid condition, they also neutralize it.

▶ We keep *daikon* in the refrigerator at all times. It's a Japanese radish—white, crisp, delicious and available at your greengrocer or Asian market. It's an effective digestive aid, especially when eating heavy, deep-fried foods.

Either grate 1 to 2 tablespoons or have a couple of slices of the daikon with your meal. It also helps detoxify animal protein and fats.

▶ When you have a white-coated tongue, bad breath and a headache, it's probably due to an upset stomach. A wise choice of herbs would be sage. Sip a cup of herbal sage tea slowly. (*See* "Preparation Guide" on page 250.)

Red-String Relief

▶ We have come across some strange-sounding remedies for which there seems to be no logical explanation. We've included a few of them, simply because they sometimes work.

This is certainly one of them—when your stomach aches, tie a red string around your waist. (If the pain disappears, fine. If not, try another remedy.)

▶ When you have a sour stomach, chew a few anise seeds, cardamom seeds or caraway seeds. All will sweeten your stomach and your breath as well.

▶ Like rolled oats, raw potato juice also neutralizes acidity. Grate a potato and squeeze it through cheesecloth to get the juice. Dilute 1 tablespoon of potato juice with ½ cup of warm water. Drink it slowly.

Brush It Off

▶ Take a wire hairbrush or a metal comb and brush or comb the backs of your hands for three to four minutes. It's supposed to relieve that sluggish feeling you get from eating one of those old-fashioned, home-cooked, the-cholesterol-can-kill-ya meals.

▶ This remedy was recommended to us for a nervous stomach. Add ¼ teaspoon of oregano and ½ teaspoon of marjoram to 1 cup of hot water. Let it steep for 10 minutes. Strain and sip slowly. Two hours later, if you still have stomach uneasiness, drink another fresh cup of the mixture.

International Relations

▶ This remedy from India is recommended for quick relief after a junk-food binge. Crush 1 teaspoon of fenugreek seeds and steep them in 1 cup of just-boiled water for five minutes. Strain and drink slowly. You should feel better in about 10 minutes.

▶ According to a Chinese massage therapist, if you are having stomach discomfort, there will be tender areas at the sides of your knees, just below the kneecaps. As you massage those spots and the tenderness decreases, so should the corresponding stomachache.

▶ Mix 1 tablespoon of honey and 2 teaspoons of apple cider vinegar into a glass of hot water and drink the mixture.

WARNING: Diabetics and people with honey allergies should not use honey.

▶ By eating one large radish, all the symptoms and discomfort of indigestion may disappear,

■ Recipe ■

Papaya Shake

>   1 ripe papaya, peeled, seeded and cut
>   into chunks
>   1 tsp vanilla extract
>   3 Tbsp granulated sugar
>   ⅛ to ¼ tsp ground cinnamon
>   1 cup milk
>   12 ice cubes
>   Fresh mint leaves

Combine the first five ingredients in a blender and process until smooth. Add ice cubes and process until frothy. Garnish with mint leaves, if desired.
Makes 3 cups.

Source: www.recipegoldmine.com

unless radishes do not agree with you. In that case, move on to the next remedy.

Mellow Yellow

▶ Put on a yellow slicker, not because it's raining, but because color therapists claim that the color yellow has rays that can help heal all digestive problems. Eat yellow foods like bananas, lemons, pineapple, squash and grapefruit. Lie down on a yellow sheet and get a massage with some yellow oil. What could be bad?

▶ Chamomile and peppermint teas are very soothing. At the first sign of indigestion, drink a cup of either one.

▶ Eat, drink or take some form of papaya after eating. Fresh papaya (the *yellow* ones are ripe), papaya juice or papaya pills help combat

indigestion, thanks to papain, the potent digestive enzyme they contain. (*See* recipe on page 123.)

▶ In moderation, drink some white wine *after*—not during—a meal to help overcome indigestion. (Women who are pregnant or nursing should not drink alcohol.)

Hits the Bullseye

▶ Arrowroot is a wonderful stomach settler. Combine 1 tablespoon of arrowroot with enough water to make a smooth paste. Boil the mixture. Let it cool, then add 1 tablespoon of lime juice and take it when you have "agita."

▶ Garlic helps stimulate the secretion of digestive enzymes. If you're plagued by indigestion, take garlic supplements after lunch and after dinner. Use garlic in salads and, whenever possible, in cooking—unless garlic gives you indigestion.

✎ **NOTE:** Eating garlic with parsley can help prevent the indigestion from garlic.

▶ Scrub an orange and eat some of the peel five minutes after finishing a meal.

▶ Boiled or steamed zucchini sprinkled with raw grated almonds is a side dish that will ensure better digestion.

▶ Cayenne pepper sprinkled sparingly (no more than ¼ teaspoon) on food or in soup will aid digestion.

Herbal Helper

▶ Add fresh basil to food while cooking. It will make the food more digestible and also help prevent constipation.

If you really have a taste for basil, add ⅛ to ¼ teaspoon to a glass of white wine and drink it *after*, not during, the meal. (Women who are pregnant or nursing should not drink alcohol.)

Indigestion Prevention

▶ If you have trouble digesting raw vegetables, at least three hours before eating, sprinkle the veggies with fresh lemon juice. Somehow the lemon, as wild as this sounds, partly digests the hard-to-digest parts of the greens.

▶ A doctor we know practices preventive medicine on himself before eating Szechuan or Mexican food or any other "hot" food that would ordinarily give him an upset stomach. He takes 1 tablespoon of extra-virgin, cold-pressed olive oil about 15 minutes before the meal.

The Quick Kick Test

Are you sure it's gas and not your appendix? To test for appendix problems, in a standing position, lift your right leg and then quickly jut it forward as though kicking something. If you have an excruciating, sharp pain anywhere in the abdominal area, it may be your appendix.

If this is the case, seek medical attention immediately. If there is no sharp pain when you kick, it's probably just gas, but you should check with your doctor to be sure.

▶ We've heard that 1 teaspoon of whole white mustard seeds taken before a meal may help prevent stomach distress.

▶ Add 1 cup of bran and 1 cup of oatmeal to a gallon of water. Let it stand for 24 hours, then strain, keeping the liquid. Drink a cup 15 minutes before each meal to prevent indigestion.

▶ To prevent indigestion by aiding digestion, see if this helps—try not to drink any beverages during or after meals. Wait at *least* one hour—preferably two or three hours—after eating to drink any liquids.

Gas/Flatulence

By now, you probably know which foods give you gas, and which meals may prove lethal. But do you know about food combining? The library has lots of books with information on the subject, and there are simple, inexpensive charts available at health food stores. If you follow proper food combining—for example, wait two hours after eating regular food before eating fruit—you shouldn't ever have a problem with gas. But it's not always convenient to stick to good combinations.

Here are some remedies for when your food combining is less than perfect and, as a result, you're cooking with gas.

Charcoal, Not Gas

▶ When you know you're eating food that's going to make you and everyone around you

sorry you ate it, take two charcoal tablets or capsules as soon as you finish your meal.

Just be aware that activated charcoal will adsorb medication you may be taking, such as birth-control pills, aspirin and many prescription drugs. (*See* page 57 for more information.)

It's important to take the charcoal quickly because gas forms in the lower intestine and if you wait too long, the charcoal can't get down there fast enough to help.

> **WARNING:** Do not take charcoal capsules or tablets more often than directed. Charcoal is a powerful adsorbent and will rob you of important nutrients you get from food.

▶ A strong cup of peppermint tea will give you relief quickly, especially if you walk around as you drink it.

▶ A hot water compress placed directly on the abdomen can relieve gas pains.

▶ Add 1 teaspoon of anisette liqueur to a cup of warm water. Stir and sip.

Try the Dagwood Special

▶ An old home remedy for gas and heartburn is a raw onion sandwich. Some people would rather have gas and heartburn than eat a raw onion sandwich, and some people get gas and heartburn from a raw onion sandwich. That said, if onions agree with you, it's worth a try.

▶ Add ½ teaspoon of bay leaves to a cup of boiling water. Let it steep, then strain it and drink it down slowly.

▶ Get rid of a gas condition with mustard seeds and lots of water. The first day, take two seeds, the second day take four and so on until you take 12 seeds on the sixth day. Then work it down until you're taking two seeds on the eleventh day. By then, you should be fine. Continue to take two seeds a day. Always take the mustard seeds on an empty stomach.

▶ Add 1 cup of bran and 1 cup of oatmeal to a gallon of water. Let it stand for 24 hours, then strain, keeping the liquid. Drink a cup 15 minutes before each meal to prevent indigestion.

Soothing Seeds

▶ Each one of the following seeds is known to give fast relief from the pain of gas—anise seeds, caraway seeds, dill seeds and fennel seeds (all are available at health food stores).

To release the essential oils, gently crush the seeds and add 1 teaspoon to a cup of just-boiled water. Let it steep for 10 minutes. Strain and drink. If the gas pains don't disappear right away, drink another cup of the seed tea before eating your next meal.

▶ The unripe berries of a pimento evergreen tree are called allspice. It was given its name because it tastes like a combination of spices— cloves, juniper berries, cinnamon and pepper. Allspice is said to be effective in treating flatulent indigestion. Add 1 teaspoon of powdered allspice to a cup of just-boiled water and drink. If you have the dried fruit, chew ½ teaspoon, then swallow.

Pretzel Logic

▶ This gas-expelling yoga technique should be done in the privacy of your bedroom. Lie on the bed face down with one leg tucked under you. Got the picture? Your knee is under your chest.

Stay that way for three or four minutes, then stretch out that leg and bring the other leg up, with the knee under your chest. Every

three or four minutes, reverse the legs. When you've expelled the gas, you can stop.

▶ If you feel you have a gas pocket, or trapped gas, lie down on the floor or on a bed and slowly bring your knees up to your chest to the count of 10, then back down, and relax. While you're relaxing, massage your stomach in a circular motion with the top half of your fingers, pressing hard to move that gas around and out.

If that doesn't do it, repeat the entire process, by bringing your knees up to your chest and—you know the rest.

▶ Drink ginger tea after a heavy, gassy meal. Steep ¼ teaspoon of powdered ginger in a cup of hot water for five minutes, or let a few small pieces of fresh gingerroot steep, then drink the tea slowly.

▶ To prevent beans from giving you gas, soak dried beans overnight. In the morning, pour off the water. Add fresh water and an onion, then boil them.

When the liquid comes to a boil, pour off the water and throw away the onion. Then, cook the beans the way you ordinarily cook them—only this time, they may not create gas.

Belching Relief

▶ This is a Taoist remedy that dates back to the 6th century BC. Scrub a tangerine, then peel it and boil the pieces of peel for five minutes. Strain, let cool and drink the tangerine tea. The tea should stop you from belching. You can also eat the tangerine peel as a digestive aid.

Heartburn

Certain foods may not agree with you, causing the stomach acid to back up (reflux). That's when you have heartburn (you literally feel like your heart is burning). Our mother used to get heartburn a lot. We remember asking her, "How do you know when you have it?" And our mother would always answer, "You'll know!" She was right.

Natural Remedies

When you have heartburn, it's best not to lie down. The backflow of stomach acid into the esophagus increases when you lie on your right side, so if you have to lie down, stay on your left side. If that doesn't work, stay on your feet and try one of the following remedies.

▶ Eat six blanched almonds. Chew each one at least 30 times.

▶ Eat a slice of raw potato.

▶ Mix 1 tablespoon of apple cider vinegar and 1 tablespoon of honey into a cup of warm water. Stir and drink.

> **WARNING:** Diabetics and people with honey allergies should not use honey.

▶ Grate a raw potato and put it in cheese-cloth. Squeeze out the juice in a glass. Add twice the amount of warm water as potato juice and drink it down.

▶ Peel and eat a raw carrot. Chew each bite 30 times.

Lemon Aid

▶ If you have heartburn from eating something sweet, squeeze the juice from half a lemon into a cup of warm water. Add ½ teaspoon of salt and drink it slowly.

▶ Keep chewable papaya tablets with you and, at the first sign of heartburn or any kind of indigestion, pop papaya pills in your mouth, chew and swallow.

▶ A cup of peppermint tea has been known to relieve the discomfort of heartburn. It helps relieve gas, too.

▶ Eat 1 teaspoon of *gomasio* (sesame seeds and sea salt, available at health food stores). Chew thoroughly before swallowing.

Be a Flake!

▶ This may not be too appetizing, but it works —swallow a teaspoon or two of uncooked oat flakes, after chewing thoroughly.

▶ The flow of saliva can neutralize the stomach acids that slosh up and cause heartburn.

According to the late Wylie J. Dodds, MD, who was a professor of radiology and medicine at the Medical College of Wisconsin in Milwaukee, chewing gum (we suggest sugarless) can increase the production of saliva eight or nine times, and reduce the damage caused by stomach acids.

Heartburn Prevention

▶ Turmeric, a basic ingredient in Indian curry dishes, is also a digestive aid. It stimulates the flow of saliva (saliva neutralizes acid and helps push digestive juices back down to where they belong). If you're about to eat something that typically gives you heartburn, spice up the food with turmeric.

If it's not an appropriate ingredient for the meal, take two or three turmeric capsules, (available at health food stores) before eating.

Stomach Cramps

▶ Steep 1 teaspoon of fresh or dried parsley in 1 cup of hot water. After five minutes, strain and slowly drink the parsley tea. Remember that parsley tea also acts as a diuretic, so make sure you plan accordingly, because you may have to "eat and run."

▶ Slice one medium-sized onion and boil it in 1 cup of milk. Drink this concoction warm. It sounds awful and probably is, but it's an old home remedy that may work.

▶ American Indians used this one for stomachaches—pour 1 cup of boiling water over 1 teaspoon of cornmeal. Let it sit for five minutes. Add salt to taste and drink slowly.

▶ Water has amazing healing power. Get in a hot shower and let the water beat down on your stomach for 10 to 15 minutes. By the time you dry off, you should be feeling a lot better.

JET LAG

When you travel by air, it generally takes one day to recover for every time zone that you pass through. New York to California—that's three time zones, so three days of jet lag. Actually, going east to west and gaining a few hours is better jet-lag-wise than west to east when you lose a few hours.

In terms of getting that first good night's sleep at your destination, it seems best to plan on arriving in the evening.

England's Royal Air Force School of Aviation Medicine (King's College, London) suggests that when flying east, fly early…when heading west, fly late.

Surely you've heard that alcohol is one of the most powerful dehydrators there is. And you must know that just being in an airplane is dehydrating. But do you know that dehydration makes jet lag worse?

Conclusion: Do not drink any alcoholic beverages while airborne. Instead, try to drink lots of water and juice—as much as possible. If you have to keep going to the lavatory, good. Walking up and down the aisles will help refresh and prepare you for your new time zone.

Natural Remedies

▶ A couple of days before flying, take ginkgo-hawthorn tincture (available at health food stores) and follow the dosage on the label.

▶ It's been reported that taking ½ to 1 mg of melatonin right before boarding the plane has prevented jet lag. If you know that you really suffer from jet lag, ask your doctor about taking melatonin before your upcoming flight. But be careful—some studies in animals suggest that people with high blood pressure or cardiovascular disease should not take melatonin. Again,

---

Anti–Jet Lag Diet

This diet was developed by the US Department of Energy's Argonne National Laboratory in Argonne, Illinois, to help air travelers quickly adjust their bodies' internal clocks to new time zones. Start the program three days before departure day.

Day 1: Have a high-protein breakfast and lunch, and a high-carbohydrate (no meat) dinner. No coffee except between 3 pm and 5 pm.

Day 2: Have very light meals—salads, light soups, fruit and juices. Coffee only between 3 pm and 5 pm.

Day 3: Same as Day 1.

Day 4: Departure. If you must have a caffeinated beverage (such as coffee or cola) you can have a cup in the morning when traveling west, or between 6 pm and 11 pm when traveling east. Have fruit or juice until your first meal. To know when to have your first meal, figure out when breakfast time will be at your destination.

If your flight is long enough, sleep until your destination's normal breakfast time, *but no later* (that's important). Wake up and eat a big, high-protein breakfast. Stay awake and active. Continue the day's meals according to mealtimes at your destination, and you'll be in sync when you arrive.

For more information on the diet, go to *www.antijetlagdiet.com.*

always consult with your health professional before taking melatonin.

Play Make-Believe

▶ As soon as you board the plane, pretend it's whatever time it actually is at your destination. In other words, if you board the plane at 7 pm in New York, and you're headed for London where it's 1 am, pull down your window shade or wear dark glasses and, if possible, go to sleep.

If you board a plane late that night and it's already daylight at your destination, force yourself to stay awake during the flight. Making believe that you're in the new time zone at the very start of your trip should help you acclimate more quickly.

▶ William F. Buckley, the late "conservative intellectual" and founder of the *National Review* magazine, got this remedy from a world traveler friend of a British doctor specializing in jet lag. The theory is that jet lag comes from internal perspiring, which causes a deficiency of salt in the body.

According to Buckley, the doctor said to put a heaping teaspoon of salt in a cup of coffee as soon as you get onto the plane and drink it. Five hours later, drink another cup with salt and you will experience a miracle. The salted coffee will taste like ambrosia. That is your body talking, telling you how grateful it is that you have given it the salt it so badly needs.

✎ **NOTE:** This salty coffee remedy is *not* for anyone who is watching his/her sodium and/or caffeine intake.

MEMORY PROBLEMS

I keep misplacing my house keys, I can't remember anyone's name—I finally told my doctor that my memory has been getting terrible lately."

"What did the doctor do about it?"

"He made me pay in advance."

Sure, it's easy to make jokes, but we know how frustrating it is to feel like your memory is slipping. One remedy for remembering a familiar name, place or fact is to simply relax and forget that you can't remember. When you're not thinking about it, it will pop into your mind.

Neither of us believes a good or not-so-good memory is a matter of age. We think we're all victims of data overload.

The genius scientist and physicist Albert Einstein didn't believe in remembering anything he could look up. While that's not always practical, it is a tension-relieving thought.

Meanwhile, we have some remedies that may help you re-create a wonderful memory.

Natural Remedies

▶ Choline is used by our brains to make the important chemical acetylcholine, which is required for memory.

At a health food or vitamin store, buy choline chloride or choline hydrochloride—*not* choline bitartrate. (The latter sometimes causes diarrhea.) Taking choline may improve your memory and your ability to learn. You should also notice a keener sense of mental organization.

Dose: Take 500 mg of choline twice a day. (Set your alarm clock so you won't forget to take it.)

▶ Here's a memory-improving drink—combine half a glass of carrot juice with half a glass of milk, and drink daily.

▶ Three prunes a day supposedly improves memory. It can also help prevent constipation, and since constipation paralyzes the thinking process, take three prunes a day.

▶ Daily doses of fresh ginger used in cooking and for tea may heighten memory.

▶ Add four cloves to a cup of sage tea. Sage and cloves have been said to strengthen memory. Drink a cup every day.

Try This Jungle Punch

▶ Yerba maté (pronounced *mah-tay*) is considered the beverage of choice in many South American countries, including Paraguay, Uruguay, Argentina and parts of Chile and Brazil. The herb is cultivated from leaves of a tree that is related to holly and is grown today mainly in Paraguay and Argentina.

One of the many positive effects of the herb, according to South American medical authorities, is that it strengthens one's memory. It's also been proven in European studies to boost the body's immunity, make people feel better both physically and mentally, and it can

actually help them lose weight. It's no wonder that this amazing drink is guzzled with as much gusto in South America as coffee is in the US. Drink one cup of yerba maté early in the day. It is available at health food stores.

To read more about this near-magical drink, *see* page 195.

NOTE: Be aware that yerba maté contains caffeine, although less than coffee.

▶ Take 1 teaspoon of apple cider vinegar in a glass of room-temperature water before each meal. Not only is it said to be an excellent tonic for the memory, but it also curbs the appetite.

▶ Ah, the healing powers of almonds. Eat six raw almonds every day to help improve your memory.

Eye-Opening Discovery

▶ Our research led us to a Japanese doctor whose records show that he successfully treated more than 500 patients who were having memory problems. How? By recommending they take eyebright, an herb best known for treating eye disorders...until now.

Add ½ ounce of eyebright and 1 tablespoon of clover honey to 1½ cups of just-boiled water. When it's cool, strain the mixture and put it in a bottle. Drink ¾ cup before lunch and ¾ cup before dinner.

▶ Two mustard seeds, taken as you would take pills, first thing every morning, are said to revive one's memory.

▶ Eat a handful of sunflower seeds daily. These seeds are beneficial in many ways, one being memory improvement.

■ Recipe ■

Cinnamon-Roasted Almonds

1 egg white
1 tsp cold water
4 cups almonds
½ cup granulated sugar
¼ tsp salt
½ tsp ground cinnamon

Preheat oven to 250° F . Lightly grease one 15" x 10" x 1" jellyroll pan.

Lightly beat the egg white, then add water and beat until frothy but not stiff. Add the nuts and stir until well coated.

Sift together the sugar, salt and cinnamon. Sprinkle over the nuts and toss to mix.

Spread on pan and bake for one hour, stirring occasionally.

Source: www.recipegoldmine.com

▶ According to a gem therapist, wearing an amethyst helps strengthen one's memory. You just have to remember to wear the amethyst.

Walk This Way

▶ Walking increases oxygen flow to the brain ...and it's never too late! Researchers experimented on adults between the ages of 60 and 75. The group that walked briskly three days a week, starting with 15 minutes each day and working their way up to 45 minutes a day, had a 15% boost in mental functioning. That 15% could mean an end to the frustration of not remembering things...at any age.

What's the most prevalent color in legal pads? In Post-Its? Notice a pattern forming here? According to color therapy research, the color yellow most stimulates the brain. Writing on yellow paper may help you better remember whatever it is you've written.

The Case for Color

If you don't think that color has an impact on us, think again after you read the following—Alexander Schauss, PhD, president of the Life Sciences Division of the American Institute for Biosocial and Medical Research in Tacoma, Washington, recommended that Blackfriars Bridge in London be painted a particular shade of blue. Called Ertel Blue, the color was supposed to reduce the incidence of suicides off the bridge, the highest of any bridge on the Thames River.

The bridge was painted Ertel Blue and the effect was dramatic. No suicides were reported from that point on.

MUSCLE ACHES

Muscle strain, a tight, sore neck...leg cramps...an achy body can be such a pain! But most minor muscle aches seem to loosen up quite well when treated to a massage or a nice, hot bath. In addition, these remedies may help ease your aches and pains.

▶ Prepare strong ginger tea with 2 teaspoons of ginger powder or fresh, grated ginger root in 2 cups of water. Let it simmer until the water turns yellowish in color. Add the ginger tea to a bathful of warm water. Relax in the tub for 20 to 30 minutes. This ginger tea bath may relieve muscle stiffness and soreness and is wonderful for one's circulation.

Charley Horse

▶ When you have sudden muscle stiffness or pain (charley horse), soak in a tub of "old faithful"—Epsom salts. Pour 3 cups into warm water. Stay in the water 20 to 30 minutes and your charley-horse pain may start to ease.

▶ This remedy is said to be particularly effective for a charley horse. Vigorously scrub three small lemons, two small oranges and one small grapefruit. (If you can get organic produce, do so.) Cut up the six fruits and put them into a blender—peel and all. Add 1 teaspoon of cream of tartar and blend. Store the mixture in a covered jar in the refrigerator.

Dose: To relieve the stiffness, take 2 tablespoons of the concoction with 2 tablespoons of water twice a day—first thing in the morning and right before bedtime.

Neck Tension

It's quite common for those of us who are under pressure to have a pain in the neck. People tend to tense up in that area, which is the worst thing to do to yourself. Your neck connects your brain and nervous system to the rest of your body. When you create tension in your neck, you impair the flow of energy throughout your system.

▶ To prevent tension buildup, do neck rolls. Start with your chin on your chest and slowly rotate your head so that your right ear reaches for your right shoulder, then head back, left ear to left shoulder, and back with your chin on your chest. Do these rolls, slowly, six times in one direction and six times in the opposite direction, morning and evening. You may hear lots of crackling, crunching and gravelly noises coming from your neck. As tension is released, the noises will quiet.

▶ If, when you roll your neck around or just turn from side to side, you hear and feel like there's gravel in your neck, eat three or four cloves of raw garlic every day. You may have to work your way up to that amount. (*See* "Six Sensational Superfoods" on page 266 for the easiest way to take raw garlic cloves.)

Stiff Neck

▶ The medicine men and healers from several Native American tribes prescribe daily neck rubs with fresh lemon juice, as well as drinking the juice of half a lemon first thing in the morning and last thing at night.

▶ According to the ancient principles of reflexology, the base of the big toe affects the neck. Rub your hands together vigorously until you feel heat. Now you're ready to massage your big toes with circular motions. Spend a few minutes massaging the bottom of your feet at the base of the toes and the area surrounding them. As a change of pace, you might want to massage the base of your thumbs, also for a few minutes at a time. Keep at it, at least two times a day, every day.

Whiplash

Whiplash is the result of neck muscles that were too tense to absorb a sudden thrust (like from a car accident). We've been told by medical professionals that wearing a neck collar is the worst thing you can use for whiplash. It doesn't help realign the neck and it doesn't let the body help realign itself.

Instead, a naturopath, chiropractor or osteopath can realign the neck vertebrae properly. During this uncomfortable time, wear a silk scarf. It has been known to help blood circulation and relieve muscle pain and tension in the neck.

☞ **WARNING:** If you've been in an accident and experience neck pain, get medical attention immediately. You could have a fracture that can result in paralysis if not treated.

Leg Cramps

We've learned that leg cramps can be caused by certain nutritional deficiencies. For instance, a lack of magnesium, potassium, vitamin E, calcium or protein. Are you eating lots of greens? (And we don't mean having two or three olives in your martini.)

Cut down on fatty meats, sugar and white flour. After a week, see if there's a difference in the incidence of leg-cramping.

Go Bananas!

▶ If you take a diuretic, you may be losing too much potassium from your system, which may be causing leg cramps. If that's the case, eat a banana or two every day. You might also want to ask your doctor to take you off the chemical diuretic and find a natural one, like cucumber, celery or lettuce.

▶ Drink a glass of tonic water. It may have enough quinine to help you and not enough to harm you.

▶ If you get leg cramps while you sleep, keep a piece of silverware—a spoon seems the safest—on your night table. When the cramp wakes you up, place the spoon on the painful area and the muscle should uncramp. Incidentally, the spoon doesn't have to be silver—stainless steel will work as well.

▶ Cramp bark is an herb that—you guessed it—is good for any sort of cramping. The tincture is available at health food stores. Take 1 to 2 teaspoons, three to five times a day.

▶ Muscular cramps that tend to occur at night may often be relieved within 20 minutes by taking this combination—1 tablespoon of calcium lactate, 1 teaspoon of apple cider vinegar and 1 teaspoon of honey in half a glass of warm water.

▶ The late D.C. Jarvis, MD, suggested taking 2 teaspoons of honey at each meal, or honey combined with 2 teaspoons of apple cider vinegar in a glass of water before each meal, as a way to prevent muscle cramps.

> **WARNING:** Diabetics and people with honey allergies should not use honey.

Walk on the Wall Side

▶ Before you get out of bed in the morning, turn yourself around so that you can put your feet against the wall, higher than your body. Stay that way for 10 minutes. Do the same thing at night, right before you go to sleep. It will improve blood circulation and may help to prevent muscle cramps. It's also an excellent stretch that in itself may prevent cramps.

▶ *The Lancet*, the prestigious British medical journal (*www.thelancet.com*), reports that vitamin E is helpful in relieving cramps in the legs. Take vitamin E before each meal, daily (check with your doctor for amount). Within a week or two, there should be a positive difference.

▶ Take advantage of the therapeutic value of a rocking chair. Rock whenever you watch television and for at least one hour before bedtime. For those of you who sit most of the time, a rocking chair may prevent varicose veins (*see* pages 88–89) and blood clots. It may also improve circulation as well as relieve you of leg cramps.

▶ Drink 1 cup of red raspberry-leaf tea in the morning and 1 cup at night. Do this every day and you may no longer have leg cramp attacks.

▶ According to one doctor, three weeks after prescribing vitamin B_6 to his patients suffering from leg cramps, they were no longer bothered by them. The B_6 also took care of numb and tingling toes.

Pinch It

▶ We were told about a simple acupressure technique called "acupinch." It may help relieve the pain of muscle cramps almost instantly.

The second you get a cramp, use your thumb and your index finger and pinch your philtrum—the skin between your upper lip and your nose. Keep pinching for about 20 seconds. The pain and cramp should disappear.

▶ Try drinking an 8-ounce glass of water before bedtime.

Jogger's Leg Cramps

▶ After your run, find a cool stream of moving water in which to soak for 15 to 20 minutes.

For those of you who can only dream of that…every night, right before going to bed, walk in about 6 inches of cold water in your bathtub for three minutes.

The feedback from runners who do this has been very convincing—cold water walks prevent leg cramps. Be sure to have those non-slip stick-ons on the floor of the tub.

NAUSEA AND VOMITING

The conditions nausea and vomiting can both be symptoms of a variety of illnesses. Nausea is an uneasiness in the stomach that may lead to vomiting (throwing up)—but not always. In any case, few things are more uncomfortable than a prolonged bout of nausea and/or vomiting. These remedies may help to settle your stomach and bring relief.

Natural Remedies

▶When you have an upset stomach and you're feeling nauseated, take a carbonated drink—seltzer, club soda, Perrier or some ginger ale. If you don't have any of those, and you're not on a sodium-restricted diet, mix 1 teaspoon of baking soda with 8 ounces of cold water and drink slowly. Within a few minutes, you should burp and feel better.

▶Drink 1 cup of yarrow tea (available at health food stores). This herb is known to stop nausea in next to no time. It's also wonderful for helping tone up the digestive system.

Gourmet Cure

▶When the food you ate seems to be lying on your chest—or you have a bad case of stomach overload and you know you'd feel much better if you threw up—reach for the English mustard. It's available at food specialty shops.

Dose: Drink 1 teaspoon in a glass of warm water. If you don't vomit in 10 minutes, drink another glass of this mustard water. After another 10 minutes, if it still hasn't worked, the third time should be the charm.

▶To help ease a severe bout of vomiting, warm ½ cup of vinegar, saturate a washcloth in it and place the moist cloth on your bare abdomen. Put a hot water bottle on top of the cloth for extra relief.

WARNING: Severe or prolonged vomiting may be a symptom of a serious illness (and can lead to dangerous dehydration). Consult a doctor for prompt medical treatment.

▶Drink a cup of chamomile tea to calm your stomach and stop vomiting.

Spices That Are Nice

▶A few cloves steeped in boiling water for five minutes may do the trick. If the taste of cloves reminds you too much of the dentist, then steep a piece of cinnamon stick or 1 teaspoon of powdered ginger in boiling water. All of these are fine for stopping nausea and vomiting.

▶Crack an ice cube and suck on the little pieces. It's worth a try when you have nothing else in the house.

▶This remedy is the pits—the armpits. Peel a large onion and cut it in half. Place one half under each armpit. As nauseating as it sounds, we've been told it stops vomiting and relieves nausea in no time.

► A cup of warm water drunk a half-hour before each meal may prevent nausea.

► If you're on the road, feeling nauseated, stop at the nearest luncheonette and ask for a teaspoon of pure cola syrup with a water chaser.

► If you're home and have some cola or even root beer, let the soda go flat by stirring it. Once the fizz is gone, drink 2 or 3 ounces to ease the nausea.

WARNING: Seek medical attention if your stomach pain is severe or is accompanied by repeated vomiting.

Motion Sickness

The story is told about the captain of the ship who announced, "There is no hope. We are all doomed. The ship is sinking and we'll all be dead within an hour." One voice was heard after that dire announcement. It was the seasick passenger who cried, "Thank heavens!"

If you have ever been seasick, you probably anticipated that punchline.

Natural Remedies

Most people think air, land and sea sickness start in the stomach. Wrong! Guess again. Constant jarring of the semicircular canals in the ears cause inner balance problems that produce those awful motion sickness symptoms.

What to do? Go suck a lemon! Really! That's one of the time-tested remedies.

Here are a few more that might help you get through that miserable feeling.

► Pull out and pinch the skin in the middle of your inner wrist, about an inch from your palm. Keep pulling and pinching alternate wrists until you feel better.

► A cup of peppermint or chamomile tea may calm the stomach and alleviate nausea.

Make Things Spicy

► Mix ⅛ teaspoon of cayenne pepper in a cup of warm water or a cup of soup and force yourself to finish it, even if you think it'll finish you. It won't. But it may stop the nausea.

► At the first sign of motion sickness, take a metal comb or wire brush and run the teeth over the backs of your hands, particularly the area from the thumb to the first finger, including the web of skin in between both fingers. You may have relief in five to 10 minutes.

► Briskly massage the fourth and fifth fingers of each hand, with particular emphasis on the vicinity of the pinkie's knuckle. You may feel relief within 15 minutes.

► During a bout of motion sickness, suck a lemon or drink some fresh-squeezed lemon juice to relieve the queasiness.

► To avoid the misery of motion sickness, a doctor at Brigham Young University in Provo, Utah, recommends taking two or three capsules of powdered ginger a half-hour before the expected motion.

Or stir ½ teaspoon of ginger powder into 8 ounces of warm water and drink it about 20 minutes before you travel.

▶ Here's a we-don't-know-why-it-works-but-it-does remedy—tape an *umeboshi* (that's a Japanese pickled plum) directly on your navel, right before you board a bus, train, car, plane or ship, and it should prevent motion sickness. Umeboshi plums are available at health food stores and at Asian markets.

Incidentally, the plums are very rich in calcium and iron. Of course, to reap those benefits, one must eat them, rather than tape them to one's tummy.

Far-out Idea

▶ On any form of transportation, sit near a window so you can look out. Focus on things that are far away, not on nearby objects that move past you quickly.

▶ On a plane, to assure yourself of the smoothest flight possible, select a seat that's over the wheels, not in the tail. There's a lot more movement in the tail end of a plane.

▶ A Mexican method of preventing motion sickness is to keep a copper penny in the navel. It is supposed to work especially well on crowded bus rides over bumpy roads.

▶ For at least half a day before leaving on a trip, have only liquid foods that are practically sugar-free and salt-free.

▶ This remedy came to us from Hawaii, Afghanistan and Switzerland. Take a big brown paper bag and cut off and discard the bag's bottom. Then slit the bag from top to bottom so that it's no longer round, but instead a long piece of paper. Wrap the paper around your bare chest and secure it in place. Put your regular clothes on top of it and travel that way. It's supposed to prevent motion sickness.

Seasickness

▶ Marjoram tea is believed to help prevent seasickness. Drink a cup of warm tea before hitting the deck.

▶ Take a teaspoon of *gomasio* (sesame seeds and sea salt, available at health food stores and Asian markets) and keep chewing it as long as you can before swallowing. It should help get rid of that queasy feeling.

NEURALGIA

The average human body contains 45 miles of nerves. Neuralgia is an inflammation of a nerve—it can result from shingles, fractures or pinched nerves. A neuralgia attack is an excruciating sharp pain in the torso, but can also occur in the face area, usually near the nose, lips, eyes or ears.

Neuralgia is a serious medical condition that should be diagnosed and treated by a physician. But with your doctor's approval, these remedies might help.

Natural Remedies

▶ To ease the pain of an attack, hard-boil an egg. Take off the shell, cut the egg in half and when it cools enough not to burn you, apply both halves to the trouble spot. By the time the egg cools completely, the pain should be gone.

▶ If you have neuralgic pains in your face, take a shower and let the hot streams of water beat against the problem area. Or, just try a hot water compress if the shower is too much for you to take.

NOSEBLEEDS

Most people have had a nosebleed. They tend to be minor and can be brought on by allergies, cold weather, sinus infection and other illnesses. When the nasal passages are irritated by rubbing, picking or blowing, the tiny blood vessels break and the nose, it starts a-flowin'!

⚡ **CAUTION:** Nasal hemorrhaging—blood flowing from both nostrils—requires immediate medical attention. Rush to the nearest doctor or hospital emergency room.

Also, recurrent nosebleeds may be a symptom of an underlying ailment. Seek appropriate medical attention.

Natural Remedies

For the *occasional* nosebleed, the first thing to do is to gently blow your nose. It will help rid your nostrils of blood clots that may prevent a blood vessel from sealing. Then try any of the following remedies.

▶ When you have a nosebleed, sit or stand. Do not lie down. Do not put your head back. It will cause you to swallow blood.

▶ The best way to stop a nosebleed is to apply direct pressure. Grasp your nose at the bridge, then move your fingers just above the fleshy part of your nose and squeeze—gently but firmly. Stay this way for 10 to 20 minutes.

If your nose is still bleeding after 20 minutes of direct pressure—get to the hospital.

Tie Things Up

▶ This is a remedy that came to us from the Caribbean islands—take the pinkie finger of the hand opposite the bleeding nostril and tightly tie a string under the pinkie's fingernail.

▶ We know that cayenne pepper stops the bleeding of a cut or gash. We've been told that drinking ⅛ teaspoon of cayenne in a glass of warm water will help to stop a nosebleed.

▶ Gem therapists say that a nosebleed can be stopped by placing a piece of pure amber on top of the nose.

■ Recipe ■

Garlicky Greens

    1 bunch kale (about 10 cups)
    1 bunch collard greens (about 10 cups)
    2 Tbsp olive oil
    1 large onion cut into thin half-moons
        (2 cups)
    ½ cup garlic, minced
    ½ Tbsp sea salt
    1 Tbsp tamari (dark Japanese soy sauce)

De-vein the kale and collard greens. Cut into ½" pieces. In a steamer basket, steam greens for about 2 minutes.

In a large skillet, heat the oil. Add onions, garlic and sea salt.

Sauté for 5 minutes or until the onions are well cooked. Add tamari.

Add the cooked greens. Then toss with the onions and garlic. Sauté for 3 minutes.

Serve immediately.

Source: www.vegparadise.com

▶ Vinegar is said to be very helpful in getting a bloody nose under control. Pour some distilled white vinegar on a cloth and wash the neck, nose and temples with it. Also, mix 2 teaspoons in half a glass of warm water and drink it.

Nosebleed Prevention

▶ If you're prone to minor nosebleeds and you're otherwise in good health, take bioflavonoids. Eat at least one citrus fruit a day, and be sure to include the white rubbery skin under the peel. It's called the "pith" and it's extremely rich in bioflavonoids.

In addition, take a vitamin C supplement with bioflavonoids. And add green leafy vegetables—lots of them—to your diet. They're rich in vitamin K, needed for the production of prothrombin, which is necessary for blood clotting.

CAUTION: Broccoli and turnip greens are rich in vitamin K, the clot-promoting vitamin. If you take anticlotting medication prescribed by your doctor, be aware that these vegetables may counteract the effects of the medicine.

RASHES AND ITCHY SKIN

Dry skin is the most common cause of minor itches…and if you keep scratching it, it might turn into a rash. Other itches are caused by more serious conditions, like eczema or poison ivy.

It's a good idea to keep your nails short and—most important—try not to scratch! (Scratching can lead to infection.) If the itch or rash is persistent, see a doctor.

Eczema

Eczema is a chronic skin disease that is very uncomfortable, but not contagious. It tends to show up on elbows, knees and wrists, and may be triggered by allergies.

▶ We've been told that eating raw potatoes—at least two a day—has worked miracles in clearing up eczema. Wear gloves, and be sure the potatoes are thoroughly cleaned and scrubbed. If you don't see an improvement after a couple of weeks (or if you start to get sick of eating raw potatoes!), try something else.

NOTE: People with eczema should avoid touching raw potatoes with their bare hands. Persistent or chronic eczema is best treated by a health professional.

Brew Up a Batch

▶ Every morning and night, mix a few tablespoons of brewer's yeast with water, enough to form a paste that will cover the affected area. Gently apply it and leave it on until it dries out and crumbles off.

Psoriasis

Psoriasis may be caused by a problem with the immune system. Skin cells grow too quickly and build up into hard, itchy, crusty patches.

▶ A cabin at the shore and frequent dips in the surf or a trip to Israel's Dead Sea seems to work wonders for psoriasis sufferers.

The next best thing is to dissolve ½ cup of sea salt in 1 gallon of water. Soak the psoriasis patches in the salty water several times a day—whenever possible.

▶ A leading authority on herbs, James A. Duke, PhD, a botanist formerly with the USDA's Agricultural Research Service in Beltsville, Maryland, explains in his book, *The Green Pharmacy* (St. Martin's), "Several plant oils are chemically similar to fish oils, which have a reputation for helping to relieve psoriasis. Flaxseed oil contains the beneficial compounds eicosapentaenoic acid and alpha-linolenic acid."

Dr. Duke reviewed studies showing that 10 to 12 grams (5 to 6 teaspoons) of flaxseed oil can help treat psoriasis. (*See* "Six Sensational Superfoods" on page 262 for more details on flaxseed oil and how to take it.)

▶ Every evening, pat garlic oil on the affected area. You can do this by puncturing a garlic pearle (soft gel) and squishing out the oil. It may help clear up the condition.

▶ Add 1 teaspoon of sarsaparilla root (available at health food stores) to 1 cup of just-boiled water and let it steep for 15 minutes. If it's cool enough by then, strain and saturate a white washcloth in the liquid and apply it to the trouble spot.

You may need to use more than one washcloth, depending on the extent of the condition.

If it seems to agree with you, do it morning and night for an entire week and watch for an improvement.

Pruritis and Hives

Pruritis is the fancy term for itching. This form is usually associated with some type of illness, as opposed to the itch from hives (known as *urticaria*), which is from an allergic reaction or skin sensitivity.

WARNING: Any persistent or chronic itch should be examined by a doctor.

'Tis better than riches to scratch when it itches! For relief, apply any one of the following to your itchy areas.

- Fresh sliced carrots
- 1 vitamin C tablet dissolved in 1 cup of warm water
- Lemon juice (for genital areas, dilute the juice with water)
- Raw onion slices
- A paste of uncooked oatmeal with a little water
- Apple cider vinegar (for genital areas or areas near the eyes, use diluted apple cider vinegar)

▶ If you're itching to bathe, add 2 cups of apple cider vinegar to the bathwater. Or add 3 tablespoons of baking soda to your bathwater.

Or add a pint of thyme tea to your bathwater. Thyme contains thymol, which is an antiseptic, antibacterial substance that can make your itch disappear.

▶ If you prefer a shower to a bath, take a quick shower under hot water—as hot as you can tolerate without burning yourself. The hot water has been known to stop the itching for hours at a time.

Lydia recently had an itchy patch on her back. The way she found relief was by taking a

■ Recipe ■

Sweet and Spicy Pumpkin Seeds

1 cup pumpkin seeds (from one
  5- to 7-lb pumpkin)
5 Tbsp granulated sugar, divided
¼ tsp coarse salt
¼ tsp ground cumin
¼ tsp ground cinnamon
¼ tsp ground ginger
Pinch cayenne pepper, or to taste
1½ Tbsp peanut oil

Preheat oven to 250° F. Line a baking sheet with parchment paper.

Cut pumpkin open from the bottom, removing seeds with a long-handled spoon. Separate flesh from seeds and discard. Spread seeds on parchment in an even layer. Bake until dry, stirring occasionally, about one hour. Let cool.

In a medium bowl combine 3 Tbsp of the sugar, salt, cumin, cinnamon, ginger and cayenne. Heat peanut oil in a large nonstick skillet over high heat. Add pumpkin seeds and the remaining 2 Tbsp sugar. Cook until the sugar melts and the pumpkin seeds begin to caramelize, about 45 to 60 seconds. Transfer to bowl with spices and stir well to coat. Let cool.

These may be stored in an airtight container for up to one week.

Makes about 1 cup.

Source: www.recipegoldmine.com

fast, hot shower and—for a few seconds before ending the shower—letting the c-c-c-c-cold water run on her back. It stopped the itching, and she was able to sleep through the night. See what works best for you.

▶ To stop an itch, wash the itchy part with strong rum. This remedy is from—where else?—Jamaica, mon!

▶ Do you have a drawstring bag made of cotton? You can sew one easily, using a white handkerchief. Fill the bag with 1 pound of uncooked oatmeal and close it tightly. Throw it in your tub as you run the warm bathwater. Then take a bath and, with the oatmeal-filled bag, gently massage the dry, itchy skin. Enjoy staying in the bath for at least 15 minutes.

Hives

You don't have to be a bee to have hives! These pale red bumps usually appear in response to an allergy—from food, medicines, insect stings or sun exposure.

▶ Hives usually disappear almost as fast and as mysteriously as they appear. If yours are hanging on, rub them with buckwheat flour. That ought to teach 'em to hang around!

▶ Combine 3 tablespoons of cornstarch and 1 tablespoon of vinegar. Mix well and apply the paste to the hives.

▶ Form a paste by mixing cream of tartar and water. Apply the paste to the red marks. As soon as the paste gets crumbly dry, apply more paste.

▶ Add 1 cup of baking soda to a bath and soak in it for 20 minutes. Also, drink ¼ to ½ teaspoon of baking soda in a glass of water.

NOTE: None of these remedies offer relief from the Seven-Year Itch.

Genital Itching

▶ Sprinkle cornstarch all over the area to stop the itching.

▶ Buttermilk is known to stop the itching and help heal the area. Dip a cotton pad in some buttermilk and apply it to the problem spot.

NOTE: Genital and rectal itching may be due to an allergy, yeast overgrowth, poor hygiene or parasites. Go to the doctor and find the cause, then it will be easier to eliminate the problem.

Rectal Itching

▶ Soak a cotton pad in apple cider vinegar and place it on the itching area. If the area is raw, be prepared for a temporary burning sensation. Leave the soaked cotton pad on overnight. (You can keep it in place with a sanitary napkin.) You should have instant relief. If itching starts again during the day, repeat the procedure—instead of scratching.

▶ Before bedtime, take a shower, then pat dry the itchy area and apply wheat germ oil. To avoid messy bedclothes and sheets, put a sanitary napkin over the oily area.

▶ For years, pumpkin seeds have been used as a folk treatment to control and prevent intestinal parasites (which may result in an itchy bottom). Buy the shelled and unsalted seeds, and eat a handful daily. (*See* also the recipe on page 143.)

Heat Rash (Prickly Heat)

Heat rash can develop anytime your body over-heats—typically in very hot, humid conditions. Stay cool and don't let the heat get to you!

▶ Make a soothing powder by browning ½ cup of regular flour in the oven. Then apply to the rash.

▶ Take a vitamin C supplement regularly. It helps relieve the itch.

▶ Rub the prickly-heated area with the inside of watermelon rind.

Shaving Rash

Men, ever get a shaving rash, particularly on your neck? And women, all we need to say are two words—bikini area. These remedies may provide some relief.

▶ Puncture a vitamin E capsule, squish out the contents and mix with a little petroleum jelly. Then gently spread the mixture on the irritated skin.

▶ Cornstarch makes a soothing powder for underarms and other rash-ridden areas.

Ringworm

Ringworm is a fairly minor fungal infection of the skin's outer layer that is related to athlete's foot, jock itch, nail infections and some forms of diaper rash.

The ringworm rash produces red, scaly patches of blisters, and it can spread quickly.

▶ A woman called us to share her ringworm remedy—mix blue fountain-pen ink with cigar ashes and put the mixture on the fungus-infected area. The woman said she has never seen it fail. Within a few days, the ringworm completely disappears.

But if this remedy is going to get you into the habit of smoking cigars, you may be better off with the ringworm!

▶ Mince or grate garlic, apply it to the trouble spots and cover with gauze. Leave it overnight.

Throughout the day, puncture garlic pearles and rub the oil on the afflicted areas. The garlic should stop the itching and help heal the rash.

> ☞ **WARNING:** Be careful when putting anything wet on a fungal infection. Fungi thrive in moist conditions.

Seborrhea

This chronic skin rash occurs most often in babies and teenagers (life stages when the oil glands are active). The rash usually causes red patches of skin and greasy, crusty scales. The itching tends to be mild, but these remedies may provide some relief.

▶ Apply cod-liver oil to blotchy, scaly and itchy skin. Leave it on as long as possible. When you finally wash it off, use cool water. Health food stores should carry Norwegian emulsified cod-liver oil that doesn't smell.

▶ Rub on some liquid lecithin and leave it on the problem areas as long as possible. Use cool water to wash it off. Repeat the procedure as often as possible…several times a day.

Poison Ivy

At least one of the three poison weeds—ivy, oak and sumac—grows in just about every part of the United States. And these weeds all produce the same sort of uncomfortable reactions. Chances are, if you're allergic to one, you're allergic to all. It's estimated that as many as 10 million Americans are affected by these plants.

CAUTION: Poison ivy on the face or any large area of skin is extremely serious and should be treated by a doctor as soon as possible.

Poison Ivy Prevention

The best way to avoid getting poison ivy is to know what the plant looks like and to avoid touching it. It also helps to be able to recognize jewelweed, the natural antidote. Chances are, if you know what jewelweed looks like, then you'll also know what poison ivy looks like and, therefore, you'll have no need for jewelweed.

If you do have occasion to use jewelweed, crush the leaves and stems to get the flower's juice. Apply the juice on the poison ivy rash every hour throughout the day.

▶ If possible, as soon as you think that you may have poison ivy, let cold, running water wash the plant's urushiol oil off the affected

What to Do with the Poison Ivy Plant

Never burn poison ivy. The plant's oil gets in the air and can be inhaled. That can be very dangerous and harmful to lungs. Instead, while wearing gloves, uproot the plants and leave them on the ground to dry out in the sun.

Or kill them with a solution of 3 pounds of salt in a gallon of soapy water. Spray, spray, spray the plants and then spray them some more. Wash your garden tools thoroughly with the same solution.

Once you've gotten rid of the poison ivy and cleaned your tools, carefully take off your gloves, turn them inside out and dispose of them. You may want to dispose of your clothes, too. Poison ivy oil may not wash out completely and can stay active for years.

skin. You have a very short window of opportunity to do this—about three minutes—so just hope the poison ivy patch you stepped in is near a waterfall or a garden hose.

▶ This may be a little *iffy*, but…*if* you know you're going into poison ivy territory, and *if* it's green-tomato season, take some green tomatoes with you.

The second you know that poison ivy sap is on your skin, cut up the green tomato and squeeze the juice on the affected area. It may save you the anguish of the poison ivy itch.

▶ If you have a poison ivy rash, use a mixture made from equal parts of white vinegar and rubbing alcohol. Dab on the solution each time the itching starts. It should relieve the itching and, at the same time, dry up the rash.

▶ Mash a piece of white chalk so that it's powdery. Then mix the powder in a pint of water. With a clean cloth, apply the mixture onto the poisoned parts. Repeat the procedure several times a day. This is an especially convenient cure for schoolteachers.

Waste Not, Want Not

▶ Rub the inside part of a banana skin directly on the affected skin, using a fresh banana skin every hour for a full day.

> **NOTE:** Take the leftover bananas, cut them into 2-inch pieces, put them in a plastic bag and freeze them. They're great as an ingredient in a smoothie, along with a couple of strawberries, a dollop of yogurt and 10 ounces of pineapple juice.
>
> Or blend frozen banana pieces in a high-powered blender until the mixture is the consistency of soft ice cream and have it as a delicious, low-calorie dessert.
>
> On a hot day, it's refreshing to munch on plain frozen banana pieces.

▶ Apply fresh mud to the infected areas. At the end of each day, shower off the mud (not that we have to tell you to do that).

Keep up this daily procedure until the redness caused by the poison ivy disappears.

▶ Slice one or two lemons and rub them all over your affected areas. It should stop the itching and help clear up the skin.

▶ Chop four cloves of garlic and boil them in 1 cup of water. After the mixture cools, apply it with a clean cloth to the poison ivy areas.

Repeat often—but that's the way it is with garlic...repeating often.

▶ Place ice-cold, whole-milk compresses on the affected areas. Once the rash calms down, wash off the milk with cool water. If you don't have whole milk, put ice cubes on your skin.

▶ Take an oatmeal bath to ease the itching and help dry out the eruptions.

▶ Put mashed pieces of tofu directly on the itchy areas, and bind them in place with a cloth or bandage. They should help stop the itching and cool off the poison ivy flare-up.

▶ Don't be a crab, just get one. Cook the whole crab in boiling water, let it cool and then use the water to wash the poison ivy area. Or look inside the crab shell for the green stuff. Apply that green gunk directly on the rash.

▶ If none of these poison ivy remedies work and you're stuck with the itch—its usual duration is about 10 days—then rub on four-leaf clovers, and have a "rash of good luck!"

Poison Ivy Test

The white paper test will tell you if that patch of plants you just brushed up against is poison ivy. Take hold of the plant in question with a piece of white paper (DO NOT touch it with your bare hands!). Schmush the leaves, causing liquid from the plant to wet the paper. If it's poison ivy, the juice on the paper will turn black within five minutes.

SEXUAL PROBLEMS

During our appearances on dozens of radio and television shows, we have been asked many sex-related questions. As a result, we decided to give people what they want—more sex! That is, remedies for sexual dysfunctions and some fuel to help rev up the sex drive.

Researchers tell us that about 90% of the cases of decreased sexual ability are psychologically caused. Since a psychological placebo has been known to evoke a prize-winning performance, we're including rituals, recipes, potions, lotions, charms and all kinds of passion-promoting spells.

Natural Remedies

For history buffs and for history in the buff, we culled the ancient Greek, Egyptian, Indian and Asian sex secrets that are still being used today.

So, if you did but don't...should but won't...can't but want to...or do but don't enjoy it—please read on. Help and newfound fun may be waiting.

Heighten a Man's Orgasm

Touching a man's testicles before his orgasm is a wonderful way for a woman to greatly excite her lover. It also may hasten—as well as heighten—the orgasm.

NOTE: Touching the testicles just after orgasm is a no-no. It may give an unpleasant, almost painful sensation.

■ Recipe ■

Love Elixir

Ancient Teuton brides drank honey-beer for 30 days after their wedding ceremony. It was said to make the bride more sexually responsive. The custom of drinking honey-beer for a month, poetically referred to as a "moon," is the way we got the term "honeymoon."

Rather than go through the bother of preparing honey-beer the way they did way back when, herbalists simplified it to a tea made from hops and honey.

1 oz hops
1 pint water, boiled
1 tsp raw honey

Place the hops (available at health food stores) in a porcelain or Pyrex container. Pour the boiling water over the hops, cover and allow to stand for 15 minutes, then strain. Add the honey to a wineglass of the tea and drink it an hour before each meal. If you prefer warm hops and honey, heat the tea before drinking.

Honey contains aspartic acid and vitamin E. Honey and hops contain traces of hormones. All these ingredients are said to stimulate female sexuality. We'll drink to that!

WARNING: Diabetics and people with honey allergies should not use honey.

Fertili-tea

▶ Add 1 teaspoon of sarsaparilla to 1 cup of just-boiled water and let it steep for five minutes. Strain and drink 2 cups a day.

While sarsaparilla tea may be helpful to a woman who wants to conceive, it should not be given to a man who wants to be potent. Sarsaparilla (available at health food stores) seems to inhibit the formation of sperm.

Fertility Charm

▶ Hundreds of years ago, witches wore necklaces of acorns to symbolize the fertile powers of nature. In some circles, it is still believed that by carrying an acorn you will promote sexual relations and conception.

Muscle Strengthener

▶ The ancient Japanese, masters of sensuality, invented Ben Wa Balls. Later, 18th-century French women referred to them as *pommes d'amour* ("love apples"). Doctors throughout the world have recommended them for their therapeutic value.

When these small brass (or sometimes gold-plated steel) balls are placed in the vagina, they create a stimulating sensation upon the vaginal-wall muscles. To keep the balls from falling out, the muscles have to be contracted. This exercise strengthens the vaginal muscles, supposedly giving a woman greater control over her orgasms.

✎ **NOTE:** Make sure Ben Wa Balls have been thoroughly cleaned before inserting them in the vagina.

A strong vaginal muscle is also beneficial to pregnant women. They have more control over their bladders, and it's said to make the birth process a little easier. A strong vaginal muscle also helps prevent incontinence.

You can also do Kegel exercises to strengthen these muscles. Read about Kegels under "Bladder Control" in "Healing Remedies for Women" on page 225.

It Makes Scents

▶ Have your favorite fragrance linger in the air and help set the mood for romance. Lightly spray your perfume on a lightbulb—one you plan to leave on. In cold weather, spray your radiator, too.

Time for Love

▶ Testosterone, the hormone that stimulates sexual desire, is at its lowest level in the human body at 11 pm. It's at its highest level at sunrise. (No wonder you may not want to make love during *The Tonight Show*.)

Instead, try getting up with the roosters, and maybe you and your mate will have something to crow about.

Tea for Two

▶ Turkish women believe fenugreek tea makes them more attractive to men. Besides the sexual energy it may give them, the tea has a way of cleansing the system, sweetening the breath and helping eliminate perspiration odors. (If body odor is affecting your sex life, *see* the remedies on pages 25–26.)

▶ Men suffering from lack of desire and/or inability to perform have also turned to fenugreek tea with success.

Many men with sexual problems lack vitamin A. Fenugreek contains an oil that's rich in vitamin A. Trimethylamine, another substance found in fenugreek, and currently being tested on men, acts as a sex hormone in frogs. Fenugreek is available at health food stores.

If you want to do your own testing, add 2 teaspoons of fenugreek seeds to a cup of just-boiled water. Let it steep for five minutes, stir and strain, then add honey and lemon to taste. Drink a cup a day and don't be surprised if you get the urge to make love on a lily pad.

Sexy Clam Bake

▶ Bake the meat of a dozen clams for about two hours at 400° F. When the clam meat is dark and hard, take it out of the oven, let it cool and pulverize it to a powder, either in a blender or with a mortar and pestle. Take ½ teaspoon of the clam powder with water, two hours before bedtime, for one week. This Japanese remedy is supposed to restore sexual vitality.

Aphrodisiacs

We heard about a married couple whose idea of "sexual compatibility" is for both of them to get a headache at the same time.

They're the ones who asked us to include aphrodisiacs. The word itself means "any form of sexual stimulation." It was derived from the name of Aphrodite, the Greek Goddess of Love, who earned her title by having one husband and five lovers, including that handsome Greek guy Adonis. But enough about her!

After much research, we've come up with a list of foods said to have aphrodisiacal effects. At the top of the list is, believe it or not, celery. Eat it every day.

Of course, we've all heard about eating oysters. Do eat them! But beware of contaminated sources! And always make sure they are thoroughly cooked to reduce the risk of food-borne illness. Oysters contain zinc and, like pumpkin seeds, are said to be wonderful for male genitalia.

The list continues with peaches, honey, parsley, cayenne pepper, bran cereals and truffles. In fact, the 19th-century French general and emperor Napoleon Bonaparte credited truffles for his ability to sire a son.

Here are remedies that you and your mate can try to add new vigor and uninhibited sensuality to your love life.

▶ Many Native Americans use ginseng as an aphrodisiac. The Chinese also use ginseng. This herb should be taken sparingly, about ¼ teaspoon twice a month. It is said to stimulate the endocrine system and be a source of male hormones. Ginseng has also been said to help men who have had a sterility problem.

▶ Contrary to what we've been led to believe about cold showers, they might help stimulate sexual desire. Every day for about two months, take a cold shower or cold sitz bath and notice a rejuvenated you.

Sexual Power Pose

▶ To improve sexual potency, do this yoga exercise before breakfast and before bedtime—sit on the floor with your back straight, head up and feet crossed in front of you. Tighten all the muscles in the genital area, including the anus. Count to 20, then relax and count to 20 again. Repeat this procedure five times in a row, twice each day.

▶ The English have a commercial preparation called "Tonic for Happy Lovers." The recipe used to make it consists of 1 ounce of licorice root mixed with 2 teaspoons of crushed fennel seeds (both of which you should be able to get at a health food store) and 2 cups of water. Bring the mixture to a boil, lower the heat, cover and simmer slowly for 20 minutes. After it has cooled, strain it and bottle it.

Dose: Take 1 to 3 tablespoons twice a day.

CAUTION: Do not take licorice root if you have high blood pressure or kidney problems. It can cause renal failure.

The Curse That Renews Sexual Bliss

Ancient mystics used "curses" as a positive way to reverse the negative flow of physical manifestations. In other words, if you're not hot to trot, Curses!

The secret of success lies in the emotional charge behind the incantation as you repeat it morning, noon and right before bedtime. *Here's one to try...*

Eros and Psyche, Cupid and Venus, restore to me passion and vitality.

Mars and Jupiter, Ares and Zeus, instill in me strength and force.

Lusty waters and penetrating winds, renew my vigor, my capacity, my joy.

Cursed be weakness, cursed be shyness,

Cursed be impotence, cursed be frigidity,

Cursed be all that parts me and thee!

Sensation Stirrer

▶ To get in the mood, prepare a warm bath to which you've added 2 drops of jasmine oil, 2 drops of ylang-ylang oil and 8 drops of sandalwood oil. These essential oils are natural, organic substances that work in harmony with the natural forces of the body. Health food stores carry these "oils of olé"! You might want to save water by bathing together.

Passion Fruit

▶ Fruits beginning with the letter "p" are said to be especially good for increasing potency in men and enhancing sexual energy in women. The fruits we recommend are peaches, plums, pears, pineapple, papayas, persimmons and bananas—uh, pananas.

Potion and Chant for Enduring Love

▶ Stir a pinch of ground coriander seeds into a glass of fine red wine while repeating this chant with your partner...

Warm and caring heart

Let us never be apart.

Each of you should sip the wine from the same glass, taking turns. When the wine is all gone, your love should be here to stay.

Native American Passion Promoter

▶ Add 2 tablespoons of unrefined oatmeal and ½ cup of raisins to 1 quart of water and bring it to a boil. Reduce heat, cover tightly and simmer slowly for 45 minutes. Remove from heat and strain. Add the juice of two lemons and stir in honey to taste. Refrigerate the mixture. Drink 2 cups a day—one before breakfast and another an hour before bedtime.

Oatmeal is rich in vitamin E. Is that where "sow wild oats" comes from?

A Gem of a Gem

▶ According to a gem therapist we know, wearing turquoise is supposed to increase the wearer's sexual drive.

The Honeymoon Picker-Upper

▶ This is an updated recipe of an ancient Druid formula. Sex therapists who prescribe it believe that taking it on a regular basis can generate a hearty sexual appetite.

Mix the following ingredients in a blender for several seconds—2 level tablespoons of skim milk powder and water (according to the skim milk instructions), ¼ teaspoon of powdered ginger, ⅛ teaspoon of powdered cinnamon, 2 tablespoons of raw honey and a dash of lemon juice, plus any fresh fruit or pure fruit juice you care to add.

Blend and pour into a glass. It's a great drink to have "before the games begin."

WARNING: Diabetics and people with honey allergies should not use honey.

SINUS PROBLEMS

Ip dor node id stupped up... you probably have sinus problems. Your nose may be runny, stuffy and red from a cold or allergies, and it can really make you feel run down. It may also give you a headache from all the congestion. Keep the tissues handy and try these remedies.

Natural Remedies

▶ Slowly, cautiously and gently inhale the vapors of freshly grated horseradish. While you're at it, mix grated horseradish with lemon juice (equal amounts of each).

Dose: Eat 1 teaspoon one whole hour before breakfast and at least one hour after dinner. It gives long-lasting relief to some sinus sufferers who are good about taking it every day without fail.

▶ Crush one clove of garlic into ¼ cup of water. Sip up the garlicky water into an eyedropper. (Make sure no garlic pieces get into the dropper.)

Dose: Use 10 drops of clear garlic water per nostril, three times a day for three days. At the end of the three days, there should be a noticeable clearing up of the sinus infection.

▶ Buy garlic pills and parsley pills.

Dose: Take two garlic pills and two parsley pills four times a day, separating the doses by four hours. After six days, you should be breathing a lot easier.

▶ To stop sniffling, swallow 1 teaspoon of honey with freshly ground pepper sprinkled on it. Don't inhale the pepper or you'll get rid of the sniffles and start sneezing.

> **WARNING:** Diabetics and people with honey allergies should not use honey.

▶ If you feel a sneeze coming on and you're in a situation where a sneeze would be quite disruptive, put your finger on the tip of your nose and press in.

Sinus Headaches

▶ Sniff some horseradish juice—the stronger the horseradish, the better. Try to do it slowly.

▶ Prepare poultices of either raw grated onion or horseradish (*see* the "Preparation Guide" on page 252). Apply the poultices to the nape of the neck and the soles of the feet. Leave them on for an hour.

SKIN PROBLEMS

Skin is the largest organ of the human body. An average-sized adult has about 17 square feet of skin. Thick or thin, it weighs about five pounds.

Five pounds of skin covering 17 square feet of body surface...that's a lot of room for eruptions, cuts, sores, grazes, scrapes, scratches and itches.

Someone named Anonymous once said, "Dermatology is the best specialty. The patient rarely dies—and never gets well."

We hope these treatments will prove Mr. Anonymous wrong about that last point.

Acne

When dirt and oil plug up your skin's pores, you can get acne (whiteheads and blackheads). If bacteria gets trapped, then the skin gets red and inflamed—and you get pimples.

Washing your skin regularly with a gentle soap and warm water is the best way to prevent acne break-outs. But for a quick zit-zapper, try one of the following solutions.

Acne Antidotes

These remedies may not produce dramatic results overnight. Select one and stay with it for at least two weeks. If there's no improvement by then, try another remedy.

▶ Combine 4 ounces of grated horseradish with a pint of 90-proof alcohol. Add a pinch of grated nutmeg and a chopped up bitter orange peel (available at health food stores). With sterilized cotton, dab some of this solution on each pimple every morning and every evening.

▶ This South American remedy was given to us by Las Vegas–based herbalist Angela Harris (*www.angelaharris.com*), who has used it to clear up the faces of many.

Wash with mild soap and hot water. Then apply a thin layer of extra-virgin, cold-pressed olive oil. Do not wash it off. Let the skin completely absorb the olive oil. (Angela emphasized the importance of using "extra-virgin olive oil.")

Do this three times a day. Angela's experience has been that the skin clears up within a week. For maintenance, wash and oil once a day.

▶ Once a day, take ⅓ cup uncooked oats and, in a blender, pulverize them into a powder. Then add water—a little less than ⅓ cup—so that it becomes the consistency of paste. Apply the paste to the pimples. Leave this soothing and healing mush on until it dries up and starts crumbling off. Wash it all off with tepid water.

> **NOTE:** Always wash your face with tepid water. Hot water can cause the breaking of capillaries (small veins), as can cold water.

▶ Using a juice extractor, juice one cucumber. With a pastry brush, apply the cucumber juice to the trouble spots. Leave it on for at least 15 minutes, then wash off with tepid water. Do this daily.

▶ Once a day, boil ⅓ cup of buttermilk. While it's hot, add enough honey to give it a thick, creamy consistency. With a pastry brush, brush the cooled mixture on the acne. Leave it on for at least 15 minutes. Wash off with tepid water.

▶ This is an industrial-strength acne remedy taken internally. Before breakfast—or as you eat breakfast—on the first day, start with 2 teaspoons of brewer's yeast, 1 tablespoon of lecithin granules and 1 tablespoon of cold-pressed safflower oil, all mixed in one glass of pure apple juice.

On the second day, add another teaspoon of brewer's yeast and another teaspoon of lecithin granules. Each day, add another teaspoon of brewer's yeast and lecithin granules until you're taking 2 tablespoons (6 teaspoons) of brewer's yeast and almost the same amount of lecithin, along with the 1 tablespoon of safflower oil, all mixed in one glass of apple juice.

As this detoxifies your system and rids you of acne, it should give you added energy and shiny hair.

> **NOTE:** It is advisable to do this process only with medical supervision—and if you can stay near a bathroom.

▶ Mix the juice of two garlic cloves with an equal amount of vinegar and dab it on the pimples every evening. The condition may clear up in a couple of weeks.

▶ Simmer one sliced medium onion in ½ cup of honey until the onion is soft. Then mash the mixture into a smooth paste. Make sure it's cool before applying it to blemishes. Leave it on at least one hour, then rinse off with warm water. Repeat the procedure every evening until you can say, "Look Ma, no pimples!"

▶ Eat brown rice regularly. It contains amino acids that are good for skin blemishes.

▶ About four hours before bedtime, steep 1 cup of mashed strawberries in 2 cups (1 pint) of distilled white vinegar. Let it steep until you're ready for bed. Then strain the pulp and seeds. Massage the remaining liquid on your face and have a good night's sleep.

It's not as messy as it sounds. The liquid dries on your face before you touch the pillow. In the morning, wash off the mix with cool water. This is an excellent cleanser and astringent for blemished skin.

Acne Scars

▶ To help remove acne scars, combine 1 teaspoon of powdered nutmeg with 1 teaspoon of honey and apply it to the scarred area. After 20 minutes, wash it off with cool water.

Do this twice a week, and hopefully within a couple of months you will see an improvement.

Blackheads

▶ Before going to bed, rub lemon juice over the blackheads. Wait until morning to wash off the juice with cool water. Repeat this procedure several evenings in a row, and you'll see a big improvement in the skin.

Dead Skin and Enlarged Pores

▶ A friend of ours uses Miracle Whip salad dressing to remove dead skin cells and to tighten her pores. She puts it on her face and leaves it there for about 20 minutes. Then she washes it off with warm water, followed by cold water.

Our friend claims that no other mayonnaise works as well as Miracle Whip. Maybe that's where the "Miracle" comes in.

▶ Papaya contains the enzyme papain, which is said to do wonderful things for the complex-

ion. Wash your face and neck. Remove the meat of the papaya (it makes a delicious lunch) and rub the inside of the papaya skin on your skin. It will dry, forming a see-through mask. After 15 minutes, wash it off with warm water.

Along with removing dead skin and tightening the pores, it may make some light freckles disappear.

▶ To help refine pores, put ⅓ cup of almonds into a blender and pulverize them into a powder. Add enough water to the powder to give it the consistency of paste. Rub the mixture gently across the enlarged pores from your nose outward and upward. Leave it on your face for a half-hour, then rinse it off with tepid water.

As a final rinse, mix ¼ cup of cool water with ¼ cup of apple cider vinegar and splash it on to tighten the pores.

For best results, treat your skin to this almond rub on a regular basis.

Extra-Large Pores

▶ We're talking *really big* pores here. Every night for one week, or as long as one container of buttermilk lasts, wash your face, then soak a wad of absorbent cotton in buttermilk and dab it all over your face. After 20 minutes, smile. It's a very weird sensation. Wash the dried buttermilk off with cool water.

✎ **NOTE:** The smile is optional.

Wounds and Sores

Sores that are open and/or infected are best treated by a medical professional. Keep the wound clean and consult a doctor as soon as possible.

> ⚡ **CAUTION:** If a wound is bleeding profusely, apply direct pressure, preferably with a sterile dressing, and seek medical attention immediately. If a sore doesn't start to heal within a few days, see a doctor.

If a bleeding wound or sore is NOT severe, the following remedies may help. But be aware that there is a risk of infection when applying raw and/or natural substances to an open sore or wound. If an infection persists or a sore does not heal, consult a health professional.

That's Gotta Sting!

▶ Lemon is an effective disinfectant and also stops a cut from bleeding. Squeeze some juice on the cut and get ready for the sting.

▶ Sprinkle on some cayenne pepper or black pepper to stop the flow of blood from a cut within seconds. Put it directly on the cut. Yes, it will sting.

Don't Smoke It

▶ A clump of wet tobacco will stop the bleeding. So will wet cigarette paper.

▶ Cobwebs on an open wound can stop the bleeding instantly. In fact, they are so good at clotting a wound that they've been used for years on cows right after they've been dehorned.

However, all kinds of bacteria carried by the cobwebs might infect the open wound. Use cobwebs *only* when there is absolutely nothing else to use—like the next time you get a gash in a haunted house.

▶ The crushed leaves of a geranium plant applied to the cut act as a styptic pencil and help stop the bleeding.

Weeping Sores

▶ Place a piece of papaya pulp on a weeping sore. Keep it in place with a sterile bandage. Change the dressing every two to three hours until the sore clears up.

▶ Dab on lavender oil with a cotton swab or cotton ball throughout the day. It should help heal the sore and also help you feel more relaxed.

▶ Apply a poultice of either raw, grated carrots or cooked, mashed carrots to stop the throbbing and draw out the infection.

▶ A honey poultice is disinfecting and healing. Use raw, unprocessed honey.

> ✎ **NOTE:** *See* "Preparation Guide" on page 252 for instructions on preparing poultices.

Sores and Lesions

▶ Some nonmalignant sores need help healing. Put pure, undiluted Concord grape juice on a sterile cotton ball or gauze pad and apply it to the sore, binding it in place with a sterile bandage.

Do not wash the sore. Just keep the grape juice on it, changing the dressing at least once in the morning and once at night. Be patient.

> ☞ **WARNING:** Diabetics should see a health professional to receive antibiotic treatment for any infected sores that do not heal.

Boils

Skin boils usually begin as a red, tender area from an infection deep in the skin. Boils can get large, firm and hard as they fill with pus—which may need to be drained surgically.

![CAUTION icon] **CAUTION:** If pain gets progressively worse, or if you see a red streak in the boil, get professional medical attention. Don't wait!

If your boil hasn't started to simmer, try these remedies for relief.

▶ Slowly heat 1 cup of milk. Just as slowly, add 3 teaspoons of salt as the milk gets close to boiling. Once the salt has been added, remove the milk from the heat and add flour to thicken the mixture and make a poultice (*see* "Preparation Guide" on page 252). Apply it to the boil. The heat of the poultice will help bring it to a head, but be careful that it's not too hot.

▶ Gently peel off the skin of a hard-boiled egg. Wet that delicate membrane and place it on the boil. It should draw out pus and relieve the inflammation.

▶ Apply several fresh slices of pumpkin to the boil. Replace the slices frequently until the boil comes to a head.

▶ A poultice of cooked, minced garlic or raw, chopped garlic applied to the boil will draw out the infection.

▶ Heat a lemon in the oven, then slice it in half and place the inside part of one half on the boil. Secure it in place for about an hour.

Fig-get About Boils

▶ "And Isaiah said, 'Take a lump of figs.' And they took and laid it on the boil, and he recovered."—*2 Kings 20:7.*

Roast a fresh fig. Cut it in half and lay the mushy inner part on the boil. Secure it in place for a couple of hours. Then warm the other half of the roasted fig and replace the first half with it. And thou shalt recover when the boil runneth over.

▶ Mix 1 tablespoon of honey with 1 tablespoon of cod-liver oil (Norwegian emulsified cod-liver oil is nonsmelly) and apply it to the boil. Bind it with a sterile bandage. Change the dressing every eight hours.

▶ To draw out the waste material painlessly and quickly, add a little water to about 1 teaspoon of fenugreek powder, making it the consistency of paste. Put it on the boil and cover it with a sterile bandage. Change the dressing twice a day.

Glop It On

▶ This Irish remedy requires four slices of bread and a cup of milk. Boil the bread and milk together until it's one big, gloppy mush.

As soon as the mush is cool enough to handle, slop a glop on the boil and cover with a sterile bandage. When the glop gets cold, replace it with another warm glop. Keep redressing the boil until you've used up all four slices of bread. By then, the boil should have opened.

When the Boil Breaks...

▶ The boil is at the brink of breaking when it turns red and the pain increases. When it finally does break, pus will be expelled, leaving a big hole in the skin. But almost magically, the pain will disappear.

Boil 1 cup of water and add 2 tablespoons of lemon juice. Let it cool. Clean and disinfect the area thoroughly with the lemon water. Cover with a sterile bandage.

For the next few days, two or three times a day, remove the bandage and apply a warm, wet compress, leaving it on for 15 minutes at a time. Re-dress the area with a fresh sterile bandage.

Dry Elbows and Knees

▶ Take the skin from half an avocado and rub the inside of it against the rough areas of your elbows and/or knees. Keep rubbing for a few minutes. Don't clean off the area until bedtime.

▶ Rest your elbows in grapefruit halves to get rid of alligator skin. Make yourself as comfortable as possible and keep your elbows in the citrus fruit for at least a half-hour.

▶ Make a paste by combining salt and lemon juice. Rub this abrasive mixture on rough and tough areas such as elbows, feet and knees. Wash the paste off with cool water.

Freckles

Freckles tend to run in families, but you can also get them if you've spent a lot of time in the sun. Of course, if you get a whole lot of freckles very close together, you'll have a nice suntan and won't have to bother with all this stuff.

▶ If you're determined to do away with your freckles, bottle your own freckle remover. Get four medium-sized dandelion leaves (either pick them yourself, or buy them at the greengrocer), rinse them thoroughly and tear them into small

pieces. Combine the leaves with 5 tablespoons of castor oil in an enamel or glass pan.

Over low heat, let the mixture simmer for 10 minutes. Turn off the heat, cover the pan and let it steep for three hours. Strain the mixture into a bottle. (Don't forget to label the bottle.)

Massage several drops of the oil on the freckled area and leave it on overnight. In the morning, wash your skin with tepid water. Do this daily for at least a week and watch the spots disappear.

▶ Potato water (*see* "Preparation Guide" on page 252) can help fade summer freckles. Dip a washcloth in it, wring it out and apply it to the freckles. Leave it on for 10 minutes daily.

▶ Apply lemon juice, juice of parsley or juice of watercress.

▶ Combine 6 tablespoons of buttermilk with 1 teaspoon of grated horseradish. Since this is a mild skin bleach, coat the skin with a light oil before applying the mixture.

Leave it on for 20 minutes, then wash it off with warm water. Follow up with a skin moisturizer on the bleached area.

▶ If you ever wake up in the morning, look in the mirror and see freckles you never had before, try washing the mirror.

Cuts and Scrapes

▶ The first thing to do when you get a scratch, small cut or graze is to rinse it with water.

Put honey on the opening and let its healing enzymes go to work.

▶ Put the inside of a banana peel directly on the wound and secure it in place with a bandage. Change the peel every three to four hours. We've seen remarkable and rapid results with banana peels. It might be a good idea to carry bananas when you go camping.

Paper Cuts

▶ Clean the cut with the juice of a lemon. Then, to ease the pain, wet the cut finger and dip it into powdered cloves. Since cloves act as a mild anesthetic, the pain should be gone in a matter of seconds.

Scars

▶ According to Las Vegas–based herbalist Angela Harris (*www.angelaharris.com*), you can fade scars by applying a light film of extra-virgin, cold-pressed olive oil every day. Be consistent and be patient. It won't happen overnight.

Splinters

If you get a tiny piece of wood, metal or glass under your skin, it can really hurt. Remove it carefully to prevent infection. Keep in mind that wood swells when it's wet, so most of these suggestions work best on other types of splinters.

▶ Boil water, then carefully fill a wide-mouthed bottle to within half an inch of the top. Next, place the splintered part of the finger over the top of the bottle and lightly press down. The pressing should allow the heat to draw out the splinter.

▶ If the splintered finger is very sore, tape a slice of raw onion around the area and leave it on overnight. The swelling and the splinter should be gone by morning.

▶ Make a paste of oatmeal, banana and a little water, and apply it to the splintered area. Alternate this with salad oil compresses and, by the end of the day, you should be able to squeeze out the splinter.

▶ Make a poultice from the grated heart of a cabbage. Apply it to the splinter and in an hour or two, it should draw the sliver out.

▶ For real tough splinters, sprinkle salt on the splintered area, then put half a cherry tomato on it. Bind the tomato on the salted skin with a bandage and a plastic covering to keep from messing up the bedsheets.

Oh, we forgot to mention, you're supposed to sleep with the tomato overnight. The next morning, the splinter should come right out.

Stretch Marks

The skin is very elastic, but it doesn't always recover properly from stretching—such as from pregnancy or weight gain/loss.

▶ After a shower or bath, gently massage sesame oil—about a tablespoon—all over your stretch-marked areas. Eventually, the marks may disappear.

Wrinkles

It took years to get the folds in your face, and it will take time and persistence to unfold. We know a man who has so many wrinkles in his forehead, he has to screw his hat on. That's a lot of wrinkles!

He can start to smooth them by relaxing more, by staying out of the sun, by not smoking (smokers have far more wrinkles than nonsmokers) and by trying one of the following remedies.

▶ Before bedtime, take extra-virgin, cold-pressed olive oil and massage the lined areas of your neck and face. Start in the center of your neck and, using an upward and outward motion, get the oil into those dry areas. Work your way up to and include your forehead. Let the oil stay on overnight.

In the morning, wash with tepid, then cool, water. You may want to add a few drops of your favorite herbal essence to the olive oil, then pretend it costs $60 a bottle.

▶ This is an internal approach to wrinkles. No, it doesn't mean you'll have unlined insides, it means that the nutritional value of brewer's yeast may make a difference in overcoming the external signs of time.

Start with 1 teaspoon a day of brewer's yeast in a pure fruit juice, and gradually work your way up to 2 tablespoons—1 teaspoon at a time.

Some people get a gassy feeling from brewer's yeast. We were told that that means the body really needs it, and the feeling will eventually go away when the body requirements for the nutrients are met. Huh? We're not sure what it all means, but we do know that brewer's yeast contains lots of health-giving properties, and it may help dewrinkle the face. Seems to us it's worth trying.

▶ The most popular wrinkle eraser we found requires 1 teaspoon of honey and 2 tablespoons of heavy whipping cream. Mix them together vigorously. Dip your fingertips in the mixture and, with a gentle massaging action, apply it to the wrinkles, folds, lines, creases, crinkles—whatever.

Leave it on for at least a half-hour—the longer the better. You'll feel it tighten on your face as it becomes a mask. When you're ready, splash it off with tepid water. By making this a daily ritual, you may become wrinkle-free.

Eye Wrinkles

▶ For those of you who haven't had an eye tuck, applying castor oil on the delicate area around the eyes every night may prevent the need for cosmetic surgery.

Wrinkle Prevention

▶ To reduce the tendency to wrinkle, mash a ripe banana and add a few drops of peanut oil. Apply it to your face and neck (remember, upward and outward), and leave it on for at least a half-hour. Wash it off with tepid water. If you do this daily—or even every other day—it should make your skin softer and less likely to get lined.

▶ If you eat oatmeal for breakfast, have we got a remedy for you! Separate some of the cooked oatmeal. Add a bit of vegetable oil—enough to make it spreadable—and massage it into your face and neck. Leave this on for a half-hour, then wash it off with tepid water. If you want to be wrinkle-proof, you must repeat the procedure on a regular, daily basis.

▶ Buttermilk is a good wrinkle-preventing facial. Keep it on for about 20 minutes, then splash it off with warm water and pat dry.

Au Revoir, Wrinkles!

▶ This is supposedly the secret formula of a renowned French beauty—combine together and boil 1 cup of milk, 2 teaspoons of lemon juice and 1 tablespoon of brandy. While the mixture is warm, paint it on the face and neck with a pastry brush. When it is thoroughly dry, wash it off with warm water and pat dry.

▶ The best way to prevent wrinkled skin is to avoid excessive sun exposure and always apply sunscreen before going outside.

Lip Line Prevention

▶ The way to prevent those little crinkly lines around the mouth is by exercising the jaw muscle. Luckily, the jaw muscle can work the longest of all the body's muscles without getting tired. So whistle, sing and talk.

Tongue twisters are like aerobics for the mouth, especially ones with "m," "b" and "p" sounds. *Here are a couple to start with…*

- ◆ Pitter-patter, pitter-patter, rather than patter-pitter, patter-pitter.
- ◆ Mother made neither brother mutter to father.

SLEEP PROBLEMS

Yaaaawn! Not getting enough sleep can really make you tired! Most people have trouble sleeping every once in a while—but for others, the problem is chronic. If you have trouble dozing off (or staying dozed off), try these remedies.

Insomnia

▶ A popular folk remedy for insomnia is counting sheep. We once heard about a garment manufacturer who had trouble sleeping. Not only did he count the sheep, he sheared them, combed the wool, had it spun into yarn, woven into cloth, made into suits, which he distributed in town, watched as they didn't sell, had them returned and lost thousands on the deal. Of course, that's why he had trouble sleeping in the first place.

Treating Insomnia

We have some other remedies to help the garment manufacturer—and you—get a good night's sleep.

▶ In England, it is believed that a good night's sleep will be ensured if you lie in bed with your head to the north and your feet to the south.

▶ Nutmeg can act as a sedative. Steep half of a crushed nutmeg (not more than that) in hot water for 10 minutes, and drink it a half-hour before bedtime. If you don't like the taste of it, you can use nutmeg oil externally. Rub it on your forehead.

▶ Try drinking a glass of pure, warmed grapefruit juice. If you need to have it sweetened, use a bit of raw honey.

⚡ **CAUTION:** Grapefruit can interfere with certain medications—check with your doctor before trying this remedy. In addition, diabetics and people with honey allergies should not use honey.

▶ This Silva Method exercise seems to…zzzzzzz. Where were we? Oh yes, once you're in bed, completely relax. Lightly close your eyes. Now picture a blackboard. Take a piece of imaginary chalk and draw a circle. Within the circle, draw a square and put the number 99 in the square. Erase the number 99. Be careful you don't erase the sides of the square. Replace 99 with 98. Then erase 98 and replace it with 97, then 96, 95, 94, etc. You should fall asleep long before you get to zero.

For more information about the Silva Method, go to *www.silvamethod.com.*

▶ Michio Kushi, pioneer of the macrobiotic diet and founder of the Kushi Institute in Becket, Massachusetts, says that when you can't sleep, put a cut, raw onion under your pillow. No, you don't cry yourself to sleep. There's something in the onion that scurries you off to dreamland.

▶ Cut a yellow onion in chunks and place it in a glass jar. Cover the jar, and keep it on your night table. When you can't fall asleep—or when you wake up and can't fall back asleep—open the jar and take a deep whiff of the onion. Close the jar, lie back, think lovely thoughts and within 15 minutes…zzzzzzzz.

▶ A relaxing bath may help you fall asleep. Before you take your bath, prepare a cup of sleep-inducing herb tea to drink as soon as you get out of the tub. Use chamomile, sage or fresh ginger tea. (*See* "Preparation Guide" on page 250.) Then take a bath using any one or a combination of the following herbs—lavender, marigold, passionflower or rosemary. All of these calming herbs should be available at health food stores.

By the time you finish your bath and the tea, you should feel wound down and ready to doze off.

▶ A gem therapist told us about the power of a diamond. Set in a silver ring, it supposedly prevents insomnia. The therapist also said that wearing a diamond—in any setting—protects the wearer from nightmares. Well, there's one of the best arguments for getting engaged!

Elderberriezzzz...

▶ A glass of elderberry juice, at room temperature, is thought of as a sleep inducer. You can get pure elderberry concentrate at health food stores. Just dilute it, drink it and hit the hay.

▶ According to the record (please don't ask us which one), King George III of England (1738–1820) was plagued with insomnia until a physician prescribed a hop pillow. Hops have been known to have a tranquilizing effect. Lupulin, an active ingredient in hops, has been used to treat a variety of nervous disorders.

Here's how you can use hops to help you sleep better—buy or sew together a little muslin or fine white cotton bag. Fill it with hops and tack it to your pillow. Change the hops once a month.

▶ You may want to try placing a pillow, filled with flaxseed, on your eyes to help you fall asleep. Many health food stores carry them,

▣ Recipe ▣

Elderberry Pie

2½ cups elderberries

3 Tbsp lemon juice

¾ cup granulated sugar

2 Tbsp all-purpose flour

⅛ tsp salt

1 9" double crust pie pastry

Preheat oven to 425° F. Line a 9" pie pan with pastry.

Combine berries and lemon juice. Pour into pie shell.

Mix sugar, flour and salt. Sprinkle over berries. Cover with top crust, then seal and flute edges. Cut a few small steam vents in the top. Bake for 10 minutes, then reduce oven temperature to 350° F and bake 30 minutes longer.

Source: www.recipegoldmine.com

and you can find them on-line. The eye pillow applies just enough pressure to the eyes and orbits to help you relax.

From Baaa to Zzzz

▶ A naturopath we met has had great success in treating patients who suffer from severe insomnia—with goat's milk! He recommends they drink 6 ounces before each meal and 6 ounces before bedtime.

Within a week, he has seen patients go from getting two hours of sleep a night to sleeping eight restful hours night after night. Some supermarkets and most health food stores sell goat's milk.

The Rabbit Sleeps Tonight

▶ Galen, a Greek physician, writer and philosopher (129–216 AD), was able to cure his own insomnia by eating lots of lettuce in the evening. Lettuce has lactucarium, a calming agent. The problem with eating lots of lettuce is that it's a diuretic. So, while it may help you fall asleep, you may have to get up in the middle of the night to go to the bathroom.

Avoid Sleep

▶ Worried about not being able to fall asleep? Okay then, don't let yourself go to sleep. That's right—try to stay awake. Sleep specialists call this technique "paradoxical intent." (When we were children and our father used it on us, we precociously called it "reverse psychology.") So, take the worry out of trying to go to sleep, and try hard to stay awake. We bet you'll be asleep in no time.

▶ Keep the temperature of the room cool and your feet warm. Wear socks to bed, or rest your feet on a hot water bottle.

According to a study done at the Chronobiology and Sleep Laboratory in Basel, Switzerland, sleepiness is caused by a drop in core body temperature. That happens as your body heat slowly dissipates through dilated blood vessels in the feet. Aside from falling asleep faster, warm feet are more comfortable for you and your bedmate.

Sleep Lives of the Rich and Famous

Renowned British author Charles Dickens (1812–1870) believed it was impossible to sleep if you crossed the magnetic forces between the North and South Poles. As a result, whenever Mr. Dickens traveled, he took a compass with him so he could sleep with his head facing north.

American statesman, inventor and writer Benjamin Franklin (1706–1790) believed in fresh-air baths in the nude as a sleep inducer. During the night, he would move from one bed to another because he also thought that cold sheets had a therapeutic effect on him. (At least, that's what he told his wife!)

Abraham Lincoln (1809–1865), the 16th president of the United States, took a midnight walk to help him sleep.

Celebrated American writer and notorious wit Mark Twain (1835–1910) had a cure for insomnia—"Lie near the edge of the bed and you'll drop off."

According to American journalist and radio personality Franklin P. Adams (1881–1960), "Insomniacs don't sleep because they worry about it and they worry about it because they don't sleep."

▶ Exercise *during the day.* Get a real workout —take a class or follow an exercise plan from a book or a videotape at home. Do not exercise right before bedtime. And be sure to check with your doctor before starting a new exercise program.

▶ Try using an extra pillow or two. This works for some people.

▶ Stay in one position. (Lying on the stomach is more relaxing than on the back.) Tossing and turning acts as a signal to the body that you're ready to get up.

▶ In a pitch-black room, sit in a comfortable position with your feet and hands uncrossed. Light a candle. Stare at the lit candle while relaxing each part of your body, starting with the toes and working your way up. Include ankles, calves, knees, thighs, pelvis, stomach, waist, midriff, rib cage, chest, fingers, wrists, elbows, arms, shoulders, neck, jaw, lips, cheeks, eyes, eyebrows, forehead and top of the head. Once your entire body is relaxed, take care to extinguish the candle properly and go to sleep.

▶ Take your mind off having to fall asleep. Give yourself an interesting but unimportant fantasy-type problem to solve. For instance—if you were to write your autobiography, what would be the title?

▶ Steep 1 teaspoon of chamomile in a cup of boiling water for 10 minutes and sip it right before bedtime.

▶ Do not go to bed until you're really sleepy, even if it means going to bed very late when you have to get up early the next morning. Nothing will happen to you if you get less than eight, seven, six or even five hours of sleep just one night.

▶ Get into bed. Before you lie down, breathe deeply six times. Count to 100, then breathe deeply another six times. Good night!

▶ An hour before bedtime, peel and cut up a large onion. Place the onion in a heat-resistant receptacle and pour 2 cups of boiling water over it. Let it steep for 15 minutes. Strain the water, then drink as much of it as you can. Do your evening ablutions (which might include freshening your breath) and go to sleep.

Tryptophan Toddy

▶ Folk-remedy recipes always include warm milk with ½ teaspoon of nutmeg and 1 or 2 teaspoons of honey before bedtime to promote restful sleep.

The National Institute of Mental Health (*www.nimh.nih.gov*) believes this concoction works because warm milk contains tryptophan. Tryptophan is an essential amino acid (link of protein) that increases the amount of serotonin in the brain. Serotonin is a neurotransmitter that helps to send messages from brain to nerves and vice versa.

The advantage of a tryptophan-induced sleep over sleeping pills is that you awaken at the normal time every day and do not feel sleepy or drugged.

▶ The feet seem to have a lot to do with a good night's sleep. One research book says that before going to bed, put your feet in the refrigerator for 10 minutes. If you're brave (or silly) enough to try this, please proceed with care. Talk about getting cold feet!

▶ Try a little Chinese acupressure. Press the center of the bottoms of your heels with your thumbs. Keep pressing as long as you can—for at least three minutes. (Well, it beats sticking your feet in the fridge.)

▶ If you've reached the point where you're willing to try just about anything, then rub the soles of your feet and the nape of your neck with a peeled clove of garlic. It may help you fall asleep—and it will definitely keep the vampires away.

▶ Prevent sleepless nights by eating salt-free dinners and eliminating all after-dinner snacks. Try it a few nights in a row and see if it makes a difference in your sleep.

▶ It is most advisable, for purposes of good digestion, not to have eaten for two or three hours before bedtime. However, a remedy recommended by many cultures throughout the world as an effective cure for insomnia requires you to eat a finely chopped raw onion before going to bed.

▶ Having an orgasm is a wonderful relaxant and sleep inducer.

That said, totally satisfying sex can help you sleep. But unsatisfying sex can cause frustration that leads to insomnia. So (with apologies to the wonderful English poet, Alfred Lord Tennyson), is it better to have loved and lost sleep than never to have loved at all?

Nightmares

If you've ever woken up with a start—heart racing and sweating—you may have had a nightmare. These scary dreams can be frightening, but are generally harmless.

▶ Right before going to sleep, soak your feet in warm water for 10 minutes. Then rub them thoroughly with half a lemon. Don't rinse them off, just pat them dry. Take a few deep breaths and have pleasant dreams.

As you're dozing off to sleep, tell yourself that you want to have happy dreams. It works lots of times.

▶ This nightmare-prevention advice comes from Switzerland—eat a small evening meal about two hours before bedtime. When you go to bed, lie on your right side with your right hand under your head. *Then dream of the Alps…*

▶ Before you go to sleep, drink thyme tea and be nightmare-free.

▶ Simmer the outside leaves of a head of lettuce in 2 cups of boiling water for 15 minutes. Strain and drink the lettuce tea right before bedtime. It's supposed to ensure sweet dreams and is also good for cleansing the system.

▶ Lightly sprinkle essence of anise (available at health food stores) on your pillow so that you inhale the scent as soon as you lie down. It is said to give one "happy" dreams, restful sleep—and an oil-stained pillowcase.

Sleepwalking

▶ A Russian professor who studied sleepwalkers recommended a piece of wet carpeting, placed right by the sleepwalker's bed. In most cases, the sleepwalker awoke the second his or her feet stepped on the wet carpet.

Snoring/Sleep Apnea

A friend told us he starts to snore as soon as he falls asleep. We asked if it bothers his wife. He said, "It not only bothers my wife, it bothers the whole congregation."

Actually, snoring is not a joking matter. Chronic snoring—that is, snoring every night and loudly—may be the start of a serious condition known as sleep apnea.

Apnea is Greek for "without breath." During the night, the windpipe keeps blocking the air as the throat relaxes and closes, making it difficult to breathe. After holding one's breath for an unnatural amount of time (anywhere from 10 seconds to a couple of minutes), the snore occurs as the person gasps for air. The person wakes up slightly each time it happens, and it can happen dozens and dozens of times during the night, without the person realizing it. The interrupted sleep causes that person to be tired all day.

If you have this condition, it is dangerous to drive a car, operate heavy machinery or just cross a street. Aside from the daytime accident aspect, sleep apnea may lead to high blood pressure, heart problems and stroke.

If you think that you may have sleep apnea, ask your doctor to recommend a sleep specialist right away. There are sleep clinics throughout the country.

For bouts of routine snoring, here are some helpful remedies to try…

▶ You may want to sew a tennis ball on the back of the snorer's pajama top or nightgown. This stops the snorer from sleeping on his or her back, which prevents snoring.

▶ Snoring can be caused by very dry air—a lack of humidity—in the bedroom. If you use

Three Strikes Against Snoring

All snorers can minimize or completely eliminate their nighttime noise three ways...

◆ *If you smoke, stop!* Let your smoker's inflamed, swollen throat tissues heal.

◆ *If you drink, don't!* Alcoholic beverages relax the respiratory muscles, making it harder to breathe and, in turn, promoting snoring.

◆ *If you're overweight, trim down!* Fat deposits at the base of the tongue may contribute to the blocking of an already-clogged airway. You should also wait a couple of hours after you've eaten before going to sleep, and avoid eating anything that will create additional congestion.

a radiator in cold weather, place a pan of water on it, or simply use a humidifier.

Snore Stopper

▶ Lightly tickle the snorer's throat and the snoring should stop. Of course, the laughing may keep you up.

SMOKING

A smoking habit can cause, contribute to or worsen backaches, bronchitis, cataracts, emphysema, gum problems, hangovers, infertility, osteoporosis, phlebitis, sleep disorders (including sleep apnea), sore throats, tinnitus, ulcers, varicose veins, endometriosis, heartburn, diverticulosis...and—believe us—that's just for starters.

Smoking has been linked to every serious disease. We'll spare you the statistics from the American Heart Association (*www.americanheart.org*), the American Lung Association (*www.lungusa.org*) and the American Cancer Society (*www.cancer.org*) on the approximate number of Americans who die because of smoking—before they reach retirement age.

All the talk about sickness and premature death doesn't seem to motivate smokers—especially teenagers or young adults—to stop. James A. Duke, PhD, a botanist formerly with the USDA's Agricultural Research Service in Beltsville, Maryland, has a wake-up call. He likes to remind young smokers that the habit hits men in the penis and women in the face.

"Smoking damages the blood vessels that supply the penis, so men who smoke have an increased risk of impotence. Smoking also damages the capillaries in women's faces, which is why women [and men] smokers develop wrinkles years before nonsmokers."

Ready to stop smoking? Hopefully the following suggestions will help make it easier.

Stop Smoking...Seriously

We are antismoking advocates, so much so that Lydia belongs to an organization that lobbies for nonsmokers' rights. We were happy to find one more reason not to smoke—a condition called "smoker's back."

According to a study conducted at the University of Vermont in Burlington, back pain is more common and more frequent among smokers. Researchers theorize that the effect of nicotine on carbon monoxide levels in the blood causes the smoker to cough. This puts a tremendous strain on the back.

Yup! That's one more good reason to STOP SMOKING!

Natural Ways to Help You Quit

▶ Make a list of all the reasons you want to quit smoking. You may want to divide the list into "short-term reasons," such as wanting to be more kissable, and "long-term reasons," such as wanting to walk your daughter down the aisle at her wedding. Keep the list handy and refer to it each time you're about to give in and have a smoke.

▶ A professor of behavioral medicine suggests that when a craving comes over you, pick up a pen instead of a cigarette, and write a letter to loved ones, telling them why smoking is more important than they are.

Tell them how you choose to die young and how you'll miss sharing in their happiness. Apologize for having to have someone take care of you when you're no longer well enough to take care of yourself.

Got the picture? These, hopefully, *unfinished* letters may give you the strength to pass up a cigarette one more time, each time, until you no longer feel the horrible craving and want to smoke.

▶ The late Nobel laureate and chemist Linus Pauling, PhD, suggested eating an orange whenever you have the urge to smoke. A research group in Britain conducted experiments with smokers and oranges. The results were impressive.

■ Recipe ■

Apricot Snowballs

　1 8-oz package dried apricots
　1½ cups flaked coconut
　2 Tbsp confectioners' sugar
　2 tsp orange juice
　Sugar (optional)

Grind apricots using the medium blade of a food processor.

In a separate small bowl, combine the apricots, coconut, confectioners' sugar and orange juice with your hands. Shape into ½-inch balls. Roll in sugar. Store in a tightly covered container.

Makes 30 snowballs.

Source: www.recipegoldmine.com

By the end of three weeks, the orange-eating cigarette smokers smoked 79% fewer cigarettes than they ordinarily would have, and 20% kicked the habit completely. It seems that eating citrus fruit has a kick that's similar to smoking a cigarette.

Incidentally, when you take a piece of orange instead of smoking a cigarette, first suck the juice out and then eat the pulp.

▶ For many smokers, the thought of smoking a cigarette after they've had a citrus drink is unpleasant. If you feel that way—good! Carry a small bottle of citrus juice with you and, whenever you feel like lighting up, take a swig of the juice. And since each cigarette robs your body of between 25 and 100 mg of vitamin C, the juice will help replenish it as well as keep you from smoking.

Red Clover, Red Clover

▶ To help cleanse your system of nicotine, and to help prevent tumors from forming, take ½ teaspoon of red clover tincture (available at health food stores) three times a day. Drinking a cup of red clover tea once or twice a day may also help.

▶ To help detoxify your liver, drink 2 cups of milk thistle seed tea before every meal. In case you're worried about gaining weight now that you're not going to be smoking, these 6 cups of tea before meals may help you cut down on the amount of food you eat.

▶ Marjoram tea (available at health food stores) makes your throat very dry, so smoking will not be nearly as pleasurable. Marjoram is naturally sweet—nothing needs to be added to it. Have 1 cup of tea when you would ordinarily have your first cigarette of the day. Try ½ cup after that…whenever you have an uncontrollable urge to smoke.

▶ According to some Chinese herbalists, magnolia-bark tea is effective in curbing the desire to light up. You might want to alternate between magnolia-bark and marjoram teas.

▶ If you want to stop or at least cut down on your tobacco habit, after your next cigarette or cigar, replace the nicotine taste in your mouth by sucking on a small clove. After an hour or two, replace the clove with another one. Without that lingering nicotine taste in your mouth, your desire for another smoke should be greatly reduced.

Bugs Bunny's Secret

▶ James A. Duke, PhD, a botanist formerly with the USDA's Agricultural Research Service in Beltsville, Maryland, smoked three packs of unfiltered, king-sized cigarettes a day—until the day he quit cold turkey. That was close to three decades ago.

According to Dr. Duke, carrots helped him quit. He would munch on raw carrots instead of puffing on a cigarette. "If cigarettes are cancer sticks," says Dr. Duke, "carrots are anticancer sticks."

He explains that carotenoids, the chemical relatives of vitamin A, are abundant in carrots. The carotenoids help prevent cancer, especially if they come from carrots or other whole foods rather than from capsules. Carrots also help lower cholesterol levels.

Buy a bunch of baby carrots and munch on them throughout the day.

▶ Apricots are rich in minerals like beta-carotene, potassium, boron, iron and silica. Not only do they help prevent cancer, they are also good for the heart, for promoting estrogen production in postmenopausal women, for preventing fatigue and infection and for healthy skin, hair and nails. Apricots are especially helpful in minimizing the long-term potential harm caused by nicotine.

Start eating a few dried apricots every day and continue eating them even as a non-smoker. (*See* recipe on page 168.) Purchase unsulfured, dried apricots. Sulfur (sulfite) preservatives can produce allergic reactions,

especially in asthmatics. Also, the long-term accumulation of sulfites can cause unhealthy conditions.

▶ In addition to eating carrots and apricots, unsalted, raw sunflower seeds are another wonderful munchie.

Tobacco releases stored sugar (glycogen) from the liver and it perks up one's brain. Sunflower seeds provide that same mental lift.

Tobacco also has a sedative effect that tends to calm a person down. Sunflower seeds stabilize the nerves because they contain oils that are calming and B-complex vitamins that help nourish the nervous system. (Maybe that's why baseball players often eat them during a game.)

Tobacco increases the output of adrenal gland hormones, which reduces the allergic reaction of smokers. Sunflower seeds have the same effect.

Keep in mind that the seeds are fairly high in fat, so don't overdo it. Consider buying sunflower seeds with shells. The shelling process will slow down your consumption of the seeds.

The Dreadful Withdrawal Time

▶ During the worst time, the dreaded first week or two of withdrawal, push yourself to exercise—walk, swim, bowl, play table tennis, clean your house, do gardening, play with a yo-yo. *Just keep moving.* It will make you feel better. It will help prevent weight gain.

Incidentally, gaining five to 10 pounds because you stopped smoking is worth it when you consider the health risks of smoking. But if you follow these suggestions, and also start eating the foods in the "Six Sensational Superfoods" section (*see* page 257), you may stop smoking and not gain any weight.

◆ *Be kind to yourself and don't place temptation in your face.* Do not frequent bars or other places where people smoke, smoke, smoke. Hang out at places where smoking is not permitted—movie theaters, museums, the library, houses of worship, adult education courses at schools, etc.

◆ *Figure out how much money you'll end up saving each year by not smoking.* Decide on exactly what you want to do with that money—special treat(s) for yourself or your loved ones—and actually put that money away every time you *don't* buy a pack of cigarettes when you ordinarily would have.

Once You Quit...

A nicotine-dependency researcher reported that nicotine causes smokers to process caffeine two and a half times faster than non-smokers.

So, once you quit smoking and the nicotine is washed out of your system, you'll need only about a third as much coffee to get the same buzz you got from drinking coffee while still smoking.

The same goes for alcoholic beverages. Take into consideration that you'll get drunk faster without nicotine in your body.

Think of the additional money you'll be saving on coffee and booze!

Clearing the Air

▶ If cigarette smokers are at your home and you don't want to ask them not to smoke, place little saucers of vinegar around the room in inconspicuous spots. The vinegar absorbs the smell of tobacco smoke.

▶ Lit candles add atmosphere to a room and absorb cigarette smoke at the same time. Scented candles emit a lovely aroma that can mask the tobacco stench.

SPRAINS AND STRAINS

You may have sprained an ankle playing sports or running to catch a bus. Any sudden twist to a ligament causes a sprain. Strains are more minor injuries that affect tendons and muscles.

According to Ray C. Wunderlich, Jr., MD, PhD, director of the Wunderlich Center for Nutritional Medicine in St. Petersburg, Florida, as soon as you get a sprain, take large amounts of enzymes hourly, in the form of fresh vegetable juices and/or bromelain, papaya and pancreatic supplements (available at health food stores). The sooner you start taking enzymes, the better! Then read on to decide what to do next.

Treating Sprains

We questioned a number of medical professionals about what works best for a sprain, and here is the consensus…

▶ Don't use the injured joint, and treat it with the RICE method (Rest, Ice, Compression, Elevation). During the first 12 hours after the injury, starting as soon as possible, apply an ice-cold water compress to the hurt area. This will reduce the swelling.

Leave the compress on for 20 minutes, then take it off for 20 minutes. Extend the 12 hours of cold compresses to 24 hours if it seems necessary.

☛ **WARNING:** Seek medical attention as soon as possible to make sure the sprain is just a sprain and not a fractured, chipped or dislocated bone.

Natural Remedies

We've also heard about other remedies that have worked wonderfully well. *For example…*

▶ Put the sprained area in a basin of ice-cold water, and keep it there for five minutes. Then bind the area with a wet bandage and cover the wet one with a dry bandage.

▶ Warm a cupful of apple cider vinegar, saturate a washcloth with it and apply the cloth to the sprain for five minutes every hour.

▶ Take the peel of an orange and apply it to the sprained area—put the white spongy side on the skin—and bind it in place with a bandage. It should reduce the swelling of a sprain.

▶ Add 1 tablespoon of cayenne pepper to 2 cups of apple cider vinegar and bring it to a slow boil in an enamel or glass saucepan. Bottle the liquid and use it on sprains, pains and sore muscles.

▶ Grate ginger (frozen ginger is easier to grate) and squeeze the grated ginger through cheesecloth, getting as much juice as you can. Measure the amount of ginger juice and add an equal amount of sesame oil. Mix it thoroughly, and massage it on your painful parts.

▶ Add 1 teaspoon of catnip to 1 cup of just-boiled water and steep it for five minutes. Saturate a washcloth with the catnip tea and apply it to the sprained area to reduce swelling. When the washcloth gets to be room temperature, resaturate the cloth in the heated liquid and reapply it.

Catnip is available at most health food stores—and pet stores.

Comfrey Comfort

▶ Comfrey is popular among professional athletes and their smart coaches. This herb helps speed up the healing process and relieve the pain of pulled tendons and ligaments, strains, sprains, broken bones and tennis elbow.

Use a comfrey poultice (*see* "Preparation Guide" on page 252) on the sprained area, changing it every two to three hours. Comfrey is safe to use topically, if there is no open wound. It's always best to consult with your naturopathic doctor, of course.

Leek-y Relief

▶ To help relieve the pain from a severe sprain, rub on leek liniment. To prepare the liniment, simmer 4 leeks in boiling water until they're mushy. Pour off the water and mash 4 tablespoons of coconut butter into the leek. As soon as it's cool, massage it into the sprained area. Keep the remaining liniment in a covered container. It can also be used for most muscle aches and pains.

Recurrent-Sprain Prevention

▶ This applies mostly to athletes and dancers who keep spraining the same weakened parts of their bodies.

Before a warm-up session, saturate a washcloth with hot water and apply it to your vulnerable area for about 10 to 15 minutes. In other words, preheat the trouble spot before you work out.

Tennis Elbow

▶ *See* the comfrey remedy on this page.

SUNBURN

It's important to protect your skin from the ultraviolet (UV) rays of the sun. Use sunscreen with a sun protection factor (SPF) of at least 15—more is better. Use it all year long, not just in the summer. In fact, during the day, don't leave home without it!

For optimal effectiveness, apply sunscreen a half-hour before going outside, to give it time to soak in. While you're enjoying the sunny outdoors, reapply sunscreen often, especially if you perspire and/or go swimming. Don't hesitate to slather it on. One ounce of sunscreen should cover the exposed skin of an average-sized adult wearing a swimsuit. It's worth it, especially when you consider the cost of skin problems down the road.

WARNING: If you're on any kind of medication, ask your doctor or pharmacist about interactions with sunscreen.

▶ Do *not* use sunscreen on infants six months or younger. The chemicals in it may be too harsh for their delicate skin. Babies that young should never be exposed to the sun for any length of time. The melanin in their skin will not offer them proper protection. When you take a baby out, dress him/her in a tightly woven long-sleeved shirt, long pants and a wide-brimmed hat.

Soothing the Burn

▶ When you've gotten more than you've basked for, fill a quart jar with equal parts of milk and ice and 2 tablespoons of salt. Soak a washcloth in the mixture and place it on the sunburned area. Leave it on for about 15 minutes. Repeat the procedure three to four times throughout the day. This cooling compress can be very soothing.

▶ Empty a package of powdered nonfat milk or a quart of regular low-fat milk into a tub of warm water, and spend the next half-hour soaking in it.

CAUTION: Severe sunburns can be second-degree burns (*see* "Burns" starting on page 29). If the skin is broken or blistering, treatment should include cold water followed by a dry and sterile dressing. See a doctor as soon as possible.

The Shadow Knows

If you have any question about whether or not you are at risk for being sunburned, look at your shadow. If your shadow is shorter than your height, you can get sunburned.

Don't be surprised to see that your shadow can be shorter than your height as late in the day as 4 pm. The sun is strongest at about 1 pm (daylight savings time). If you're going outdoors, be sure to use sunscreen starting at least three hours before and until three hours after 1 pm.

▶ Steep six regular (nonherbal) tea bags in 1 quart of hot water. When the tea is strong and cool, drench a washcloth in the liquid and apply it to the sunburned area. Repeat the procedure until you get relief.

▶ Spread sour cream over the sunburned area, particularly the face. Leave it on for 20 minutes, then rinse off with lukewarm water. The sour cream is said to take the heat out of the sunburn and tighten pores, too.

CAUTION: Do not put sour cream on broken skin. It can cause an infection.

▶ Apply cool raw slices of cucumber, apple or potato skin.

▶ Use aloe vera, either in commercial gel form or squeezed fresh from a plant.

Preventing the Pain

One way to prevent a sunburn from hurting is by taking a hot—yes, hot—shower right after sunbathing. According to homeopathic principle, the hot water desensitizes the skin.

Sunburned Eyes and Eyelids

▶ Make a poultice (*see* "Preparation Guide" on page 252) of grated apples and rest it over your closed eyelids for a relaxing hour.

▶ Take vitamin C—500 mg—twice a day to help take out the burn.

▶ Soothe burned eyelids with tea bags soaked in cool water.

▶ To make a compress for inflamed skin, soak a clean washcloth in apple cider vinegar, witch hazel or a mixture of one part skim milk to four parts water and wring halfway. Apply the cloth for five to 10 minutes.

CAUTION: If blisters develop, do not treat the sunburn yourself—see a doctor.

Sun-Abused Skin

▶ Soften that leathery look with this centuries-old beauty mask formula. Mix 2 tablespoons of raw honey with 2 tablespoons of flour. Add enough milk (2 to 3 tablespoons) to make it the consistency of toothpaste.

Be sure your face and neck are clean and your hair is out of the way. Smooth the paste on the face and neck. Stay clear of the delicate skin around the eyes. Leave the paste on for a half-hour, rinse it off with tepid water and pat dry.

▶ Now you need a toner. May we make a suggestion? In a juice extractor, juice two cucumbers, then heat the juice until it's boiling, skim off the froth (if any), bottle the juice and refrigerate it.

Dose: Twice daily, use 1 teaspoon of juice combined with 2 teaspoons of water. Gently dab it on your face and neck and let it dry.

▶ Now you need a moisturizer. Consider using a light film of extra-virgin, cold-pressed olive oil or castor oil.

TENSION AND ANXIETY

Sweaty palms, indigestion, a stiff neck, hyperventilating, an ulcer, a dry mouth, a tic—yes, even a canker sore —all of these conditions can be caused by nervous tension, anxiety and stress.

There are as many symptoms and outward manifestations of anxiety as there are reasons for it. Throughout this book, we generally address ourselves to the problem at hand, like sweaty palms. In this section, we address the problem that may have caused the symptom—nervous tension and anxiety.

Psychologist Joyce Brothers, PhD, unwinds by doing heavy gardening on her farm. Sailing is a great release for former CBS News anchor Walter Cronkite. Actor John Travolta pilots his own plane for relaxation.

Natural Remedies

While not all of us have a plane, a sailboat or a farm, most of us have a kitchen, a neighborhood health food store—and the following tension-relieving remedies.

▶ A good first step would be to cut out caffeine. Substitute herbal teas for regular tea and coffee. If you're a chocoholic, check out carob bars when you get a craving for chocolate. Health food stores have a big selection of carob treats that contain no caffeine. The taste and texture of some carob brands are similar to chocolate.

▶ Harried homeowners, do not paint your kitchens yellow to cheer you up. According to the Wagner Institute for Color Research, a yellow room contributes to stress and adds to feelings of anxiety.

Pressure Relieves Pressure

▶ Here's a little acupressure to relieve life's pressure. For at least five minutes a day, massage the webbed area between your thumb and index finger of your left hand. Really get in there and knead it. It may hurt. That's all the more reason to keep at it.

Gradually, the pain will decrease, and so should the tightness in your chest and shoulders. Eventually, you should have no pain at all, and you may notice a difference in your general relaxed state of well-being.

▶ For a burst of energy without the tension that's usually attached to it, add ⅛ teaspoon of cayenne pepper to a cup of warm water and drink it down.

It's strong stuff and may take a while to get used to, but cayenne is so beneficial, it's worth it. Once you get used to using it, you can increase the amount to ¼ teaspoon and then to ½ teaspoon.

▶ Make two poultices out of a large, raw, grated onion. (*See* "Preparation Guide" on page 252.) Place a poultice on each of your calves and leave them there for a half-hour. We know, it's hard to believe that onions on your legs can eliminate nervous anxiety, but don't knock it until you try it.

▶ If all of your tension is preventing you from falling asleep, try the tranquilizing effect of a hop pillow. (*See* "Sleep Problems" on page 161 for details.)

▶ Let's talk about something some of you may already know about—Valium (brand name *diazapam*). Often prescribed to relieve tension, it can have side effects. But there is an alternative that is said to have no side effects. It's called valerian root, and it's the natural forerunner to Valium. Capsules and tablets are available at health food stores. Follow the dosage on the label.

Cut and powdered valerian root is available, but the smell is so vile, we can't imagine anyone wanting to make their own tea with it.

▶ Did you know there's a Center for the Interaction of Animals and Society? Well, there is, and it's at the University of Pennsylvania School of Veterinary Medicine in Philadelphia. Results of a study conducted at the Center showed that looking at fish in a home aquarium is as beneficial as biofeedback and meditation, in terms of relaxation techniques. Yup, just sitting in front of a medium-sized fish tank—watching ordinary, nonexotic little fish—relaxed people to the point of considerably improving their blood pressure.

Get a few guppies and pull up a chair! Or, if you have a VCR or DVD player, there are videos of fish in aquariums and in the ocean. Go to *http://research.vet.upenn.edu/cias* for more information on the Center.

▶ Chia seeds are a calmative. Drink a cup of chia-seed tea before each meal. You can also sprinkle the seeds on salads.

Switch Nostrils to Relax

▶ Alternate-nostril breathing is a well-known yoga technique that is used to put people in a relaxed state with a feeling of inner peace.

Pay attention—it sounds more complex than it is.

- Place your right thumb against your right nostril.

- Place your right ring finger and right pinkie against your left nostril. (This is not an exercise for anyone with a stuffed nose.)

- Inhale and slowly exhale through both nostrils.

- Now press your right nostril closed and slowly inhale deeply through your left nostril to the count of five.

- While your right nostril is still closed, press your left nostril closed.

- Holding the air in your lungs, count to five.

- Open your right nostril and exhale to the count of five. Inhale through your right nostril to the count of five.

- Close both nostrils and count to five. Exhale through the left nostril to the count of five.

Keep repeating this pattern for—you guessed it—five minutes. Do it in the morning when you start your day and again at day's end.

▶ *Kombu* is a type of seaweed. Kombu tea can be a potent nerve tonic. Add a 3-inch strip of kombu to a quart of water and boil it for 10 minutes. Drink ½ cup at a time throughout the day. Kombu is available at health food stores and Asian markets.

Pin Up Your Hands

▶ Do you have some clothespins hanging around? Take a handful of them and clip them to the tips of your fingers, at the start of your nails of your left hand. Keep them there for seven minutes. Then put those clothespins on the fingers of your right hand for another seven minutes. Pressure exerted on nerve endings is known to relax the entire nervous system.

Do this clothespin bit first thing in the morning, and before, during or right after a particularly tense situation.

Relax—From Head to Toe

▶ Here's a visualization exercise used by hypnotherapists and at many self-help seminars. Make sure you're not going to be disturbed by telephones, pagers, cell phones, doorbells, dogs, whistling teapots, etc.

Sit in a comfortable chair. Close your eyes and...wait! Read these directions first, then close your eyes. Once your eyes are closed, put all your awareness in your toes. Concentrate on feeling as though nothing else exists but your toes. Completely relax the muscles in your toes. Slowly move up from your toes to your feet, ankles, calves, knees, thighs, pelvis, hips, back, stomach, chest, shoulders, arms, hands, neck, jaw, mouth, cheeks, ears, eyes and brow. Yes, even relax the muscles of your scalp. Now that you're relaxed, take three slow, deep breaths, then slowly open your eyes.

Stage Fright

Most of us get nervous when we have to do any kind of public speaking. In fact, lots of professional performers get a bad case of butterflies before the curtain goes up.

Here are a couple of exercises that can make nervousness a thing of the past...

▶ Before "showtime," stand squarely in front of an immovable wall. Put both your palms on the wall, elbows bent slightly. With your right foot a step in front of the left one, bend both legs at the knees and push, push, push! Be sure to tighten your abdominal muscles. This flexing of your diaphragm somehow dispels the butterflies.

One time, Lydia thought a TV studio wall was immovable and it turned out to be part of a set that was quite movable. (That's one show to which we probably won't be invited back.)

▶ A minute before "You're on!" slowly take a deep breath. When no more air will fit into your lungs, hold it for two seconds, then let the air out very fast, in one big "whoosh." Do this two times in a row, and you should be ready to go out there in complete control.

Dry Mouth

▶ When it's time to make that all-important speech—or pop that critical question—you want to seem calm and sound confident. That's hard to do when your mouth is dry.

When this happens, do not drink cold beverages. Doing so may help your dry mouth, but it will tighten up your already-tense throat.

Also, stay away from drinks with milk or cream. They can create phlegm and more problems talking. Warm tea is your best bet.

If there's none available, gently chew on your tongue. In less than 20 seconds, you'll manufacture all the saliva you'll need to end your dry mouth condition.

▶ Mix 1 tablespoon of honey with ½ cup of warm water, and swish and gargle with the mixture for about three to five minutes. Then rinse away the sweetness with water. The levulose in honey increases the secretion of saliva, relieving dryness of the mouth and making it easier to swallow.

WARNING: Diabetics and people with honey allergies should not use honey.

TOOTH AND MOUTH PROBLEMS

Be true to your teeth or they will become false to you! Irish dramatist and Nobel prize–winner George Bernard Shaw (1856–1950) once said, "The man with toothache thinks everyone happy whose teeth are sound."

Natural remedies can help ease the pain of a toothache and, in some cases, alleviate problems caused by nervous tension and low-grade infections.

Since it is difficult to know what is causing a toothache, make an appointment to see

your dentist as soon as possible. More important, have the dentist see your teeth.

Tooth Problems

▶ If your teeth are loose, strengthen them with parsley. Pour 1 quart of boiling water over 1 cup of parsley. Let it stand for 15 minutes, then strain and refrigerate the parsley water.

Dose: Drink 3 cups a day.

Toothache

Until you get to the dentist for the drilling, filling and billing, try one of these remedies to ease the toothache pain.

▶ Prepare a cup of chamomile tea and saturate a white washcloth in it. Wring it out, then apply it to your cheek or jaw—the outside area of your toothache. As soon as the cloth gets cold, redip it and reapply it. This chamomile compress should draw out the pain before it's time to reheat the tea.

▶ Soak your feet in hot water. Dry them thoroughly, then rub them vigorously with bran.

No, this didn't get mixed into the wrong category. We were told this is a Cherokee Indian remedy for a toothache.

Papa Wilen's Pig Fat Story

▶ Whenever the subject of toothaches came up in our home, we would prompt our dad to tell the "pig fat" story.

He would begin by telling us that one time, when he was a teenager, he had dental work done on a Thursday. Late that night, there was swelling and pain from the work the dentist did. In those days, dentists were not in their offices on Friday, and the thought of waiting until Monday was out of the question because the pain was so severe.

Friday morning, our grandmother went to the nonkosher butcher in the neighborhood and bought a piece of pig fat. She brought it into the house (something she had never done before, since she kept a strictly kosher home), heated it up and put the melted fat on a white handkerchief, which she then placed on top of Daddy's cheek. Within a few minutes, the swelling went down and his pain vanished.

At this point in the telling of the story, our father would get up and demonstrate how he danced around the room, celebrating his freedom from pain.

Recently, we've come across another version of that same remedy (we promise, no more stories). Take a tiny slice of pork fat and place it between the gum and cheek, directly on the sore area.

Keep it there for 15 minutes, or however long it takes for the pain to subside. (The dance afterward is optional.)

▶ Make a cup of stronger-than-usual sage tea. If your teeth are not sensitive to "hot," hold the hot tea in your mouth for half a minute, then swallow and take another mouthful. Keep doing this until you finish the cup of tea and, hopefully, have no more pain.

▶ Grate horseradish root and place a poultice of it behind the ear closest to the aching tooth. To ensure relief, also apply some of the grated horseradish to the gum area closest to the aching tooth.

▶ Pack powdered milk in a painful cavity for temporary relief. But see a dentist pronto!

Let Your Fingers Do the Healing

▶ Acupressure works like magic for some people—hopefully, you're one of them. If your toothache is on the right side, squeeze the index finger on your right hand (the one next to your thumb), on each side of your fingernail. As you're squeezing your finger, rotate it clockwise a few times, giving that index finger a rapid little massage.

▶ Apply just a few grains of cayenne pepper to the affected tooth and gum. At first it will add to the pain, but as soon as the smarting stops (within seconds), so should the toothache.

▶ Soak a cheek-sized piece of brown paper (grocery bag) in vinegar, then sprinkle one side with black pepper. Place the peppered side on the outside of the face next to the toothache. Secure it in place with a bandage and keep it there at least an hour.

▶ Split open one fresh, ripe fig. Squeeze out the juice of the fruit onto your aching tooth. Put more fig juice on the tooth in 15-minute intervals, until the pain stops or until you run out of fig juice.

This is an ancient Hindu remedy. And it must really work well…because when was the last time you saw an ancient Hindu with a toothache?

▶ Roast half an onion. When it is comfortably hot, place it on the pulse of your wrist, on the side opposite your troublesome tooth. By the time the onion cools down completely, the pain should be gone.

Sweet Relief from Cloves

▶ An old standard painkiller is cloves. You can buy oil of cloves or whole cloves. The oil should be soaked in a wad of cotton and placed directly on the aching tooth. The whole clove should be dipped in warm honey.

Then chew the clove slowly, rolling it around the aching tooth. That will release the essential oil and ease the pain.

> **WARNING:** Diabetics and people with honey allergies should not use honey.

▶ Saturate a slice of toast with alcohol, then sprinkle on some pepper. The peppered side should be applied externally to the toothache side of the face.

▶ If you love garlic, this one's for you. Place one just-peeled clove of garlic directly on the aching tooth. Keep it there for a minimum of one hour. (Follow up with "Bad Breath" remedies on pages 183–185.)

▶ If you are scheduled to go to the dentist, take 10 mg of vitamin B_1 (thiamine) every day, starting a week before your dental appointment. You may find that the pain during and after dental procedures will be greatly reduced.

It is thought that the body's lack of thiamine might be what lets the pain become severe in the first place.

Preparing for Dental Work

▶ As soon as you know you're going to the dentist to have work done, start eating pineapple. Have fresh pineapple or a cup of canned pineapple in its own juice, and drink a cup of 100% pineapple juice every day.

Continue the pineapple regimen for a few days after the dental work is completed. The enzymes in pineapple should help reduce pain and discomfort. They can also help speed the healing process.

Tooth Extractions

To Stop Bleeding

▶ Dip a tea bag in boiling water, squeeze out the water, and allow it to cool. Then pack the tea bag down on the tooth socket and keep it there for 15 to 30 minutes.

To Stop Pain

▶ Mix 1 teaspoon of Epsom salts with 1 cup of hot water. Swish the mixture around in your mouth and spit it out. (Do not swallow it—unless you need a laxative.) One cup should do the trick. But if the pain recurs, get the Epsom salts and start swishing again.

▶ Wrap an ice cube in gauze or cheesecloth. (Hopefully you'll figure out this remedy before the ice melts.)

When your thumb is up against the index finger, a meaty little tuft is formed where the fingers are joined. Acupuncturists call it the "hoku point."

Spread your fingers and, with the ice cube, massage that tuft for seven minutes.

If your hand starts to feel numb, stop massaging with the ice and continue with just a finger massage. It should give you from 15 to 30 minutes of "no pain."

This is also effective when you have pain after root canal work.

Gum Problems

▶ It's helpful to brush your teeth and massage the gums with goldenseal tea (available at health food stores).

▶ Myrrh (yes, one of the gifts brought by the wise men) is a shrub, and the gum from that shrub is an antiseptic and astringent used on bleeding or swollen gums to heal the infection that's causing the problem.

Myrrh oil can be massaged directly on gums, or use myrrh powder on a soft-bristled toothbrush and gently brush your teeth at the gum line. Do this several times throughout the day for relief.

Pyorrhea

Pyorrhea is a degeneration of the gums and tissues that surround the teeth. This disease is marked by severe inflammation, bleeding gums and a discharge of pus. As pyorrhea advances, the gums may recede altogether.

Pyorrhea is a serious condition that should be treated by a dentist. But the following remedies may provide some temporary relief for those aching gums.

▶ In parts of Mexico, pyorrhea is treated by rubbing gums with the rattle from a rattlesnake. (We'd hate to think of how they do root canals.)

▶ Make your own toothpaste by combining baking soda with a drop or two of hydrogen peroxide. Brush your teeth and massage your gums with it, using a soft, thin-bristled brush.

▶ Take Coenzyme Q-10—15 mg twice a day. Also, open a CoQ-10 capsule and use the powder to brush your teeth and massage your gums.

Each time you take a CoQ-10, also take 500 mg of vitamin C with bioflavonoids.

▶ Brian R. Clement, director of the Hippocrates Health Institute in West Palm Beach, Florida, reports that garlic is the first and foremost remedy for clearing up gum problems.

He also warns that raw garlic can burn sensitive gums. It is for that reason the Institute's professional staff mixes pectin with garlic before impacting the gums with it. The garlic heals the infection while the pectin keeps it from burning the gums. Suggest this line of defense to a (new age or holistic) periodontist.

Bleeding Gums

▶ Bleeding gums may be your body's way of saying you do not have a well-balanced diet. After checking with your dentist, consider seeking professional help from a vitamin therapist or nutritionist, who can help you supplement your food intake with the vitamins and minerals you're lacking. Meanwhile, take 500 mg of vitamin C twice a day.

✎ **NOTE:** Persistent bleeding gums should be checked by a health professional.

Cleaning Teeth and Gums

▶ Cut one fresh strawberry in half and rub your teeth and gums with it. It may help remove stains, discoloration and tartar without harming the teeth's enamel. It may also strengthen and heal sore gums.

Leave the crushed strawberry and juice on the teeth and gums as long as possible—at least 15 minutes. Then rinse with warm water. Use only fresh strawberries which are kept at room temperature.

▶ If you can't brush after every meal, kiss someone. Really—kiss someone! It starts the saliva flowing and helps prevent tooth decay.

▶ Actually, the best way to clean your teeth is the way you do it right before leaving for your dental appointment.

Cavity Prevention

▶ To avoid being "bored" to tears by the dentist, eat a little cube of cheddar, Monterey Jack or Swiss cheese right after eating sugary, cavity-causing foods. It seems that cheese reduces bacterial acid production, which causes decay.

■ Recipe ■

Peanut Slaw

3½ cups cabbage, shredded
¾ cup celery, chopped
½ cup cucumber, peeled and chopped
½ cup cocktail peanuts, chopped
3 Tbsp onion, diced
½ cup mayonnaise
½ cup sour cream
¾ tsp prepared horseradish
¼ tsp honey mustard
Salt and pepper to taste

Combine cabbage, celery, cucumber, peanuts and onion in a large bowl. Set aside. Combine remaining ingredients and mix well. Add to cabbage mixture, then toss well. Cover and chill.

Makes 6 servings.

Source: www.freerecipe.org

▶ Peanuts also help prevent tooth decay. They can be eaten at the end of the meal, instead of right after each cavity-causing food.

▶ Tea is rich in fluoride, which resists tooth decay. Some Japanese tea drinkers believe it helps fight plaque. Take some tea and see. You may want to try Kukicha tea. It's tasty, relaxing, caffeine-free and available at health food stores or Asian markets. Incidentally, you can use the same Kukicha tea bag three or four times.

▶ Blackstrap molasses contains an ingredient that seems to inhibit tooth decay. Sunflower seeds are also supposed to inhibit tooth decay. Have a tablespoon of molasses in water and/or a handful of shelled, raw, unsalted sunflower seeds every day. Be sure to rinse thoroughly with water after consuming the molasses.

Clean Your Toothbrush

▶ Dissolve a tablespoon of baking soda in a glass of warm water and soak your toothbrush overnight. Rinse it in the morning and notice how clean it looks and feels.

Throw Away Your Toothbrush

▶ Bacteria from your mouth settle in the bristles of your toothbrush and can reinfect you with whatever you have—a cold sore, a cold, the flu or a sore throat.

As soon as symptoms appear, throw away your toothbrush. Use a new one for a few days, then throw that one away and use another new one. If you want to be super-cautious, use a new toothbrush as soon as you're all better.

Plaque Remover

▶ Dampen your dental floss and dip it in baking soda, then floss with it. It may help remove some of the plaque buildup.

Tartar Remover

▶ Mix equal parts of cream of tartar and salt. Brush your teeth and massage your gums with the mixture, then rinse very thoroughly.

Teeth Whitener

▶ Burn a piece of toast—really char it. (For some of us, that's part of our everyday routine.) Then pulverize the charred bread, mix it with about ½ teaspoon of honey and brush your teeth with it. Rinse thoroughly. Put on a pair of sunglasses, look in the mirror and smile!

> **WARNING:** Diabetics and people with honey allergies should not use honey.

Halitosis (Bad Breath)

Most people have bad breath at some point every day (like when you wake up—*yeeech!*). This is basically caused by tiny bits of food that decay in the mouth. Proper toothbrushing can tackle most cases of the stinkies, but chronic bad breath may be caused by an underlying illness.

> **NOTE:** It's important to find the cause of bad breath. Get checked for chronic sinusitis or indigestion, and see a dentist.

While no one ever dies from bad breath, it sure can kill a relationship. Here are some refreshing remedies that are worth a try.

▶ Suck on a piece of cinnamon bark to sweeten your breath. Cinnamon sticks come in jars or can be bought loose at some food specialty shops. They can also satisfy the craving for a sweet treat or cigarettes.

▶ Bad breath is sometimes due to food particles decaying between one's teeth. If that's the case, use dental floss and brush after every meal.

▶ Take a piece of 100% pure wool—preferably white and not dyed—put ½ teaspoon of raw honey on it and massage your upper gums. Put another ½ teaspoon of raw honey on the wool and massage the lower gums.

> **WARNING:** Diabetics and people with honey allergies should not use honey.

Did you say that sounds crazy? We can't argue with you there, but it's worth a try. Rinse your mouth thoroughly with water after using honey—it can contribute to tooth decay.

▶ If your tongue looks coated, it may need to be scraped, which will help combat bad breath. Use your toothbrush or a tongue scraper (available at health food stores-and pharmacies) to scrape your tongue after breakfast and at bedtime.

Herbal Rinse

▶ Stock up on mint, rosemary and fennel seeds (available at health food stores) and prepare an effective mouthwash for yourself.

For a daily portion, use ⅓ teaspoon of each of the three dried herbs. Pour 1 cup of just-boiled water over the mint, rosemary and fennel seeds, cover the cup, and let the mixture steep for 10 minutes. Then strain it.

At that point, it should be cool enough for you to rinse with. You might also want to swallow a little. It's wonderful for digestion (which may be causing the bad breath).

▶ At bedtime, take a piece of myrrh the size of a pea and let it dissolve in your mouth. Since myrrh is an antiseptic and can destroy the germs that may cause the problem, hopefully you can say "bye-bye" to dragon breath.

▶ When leaving an Indian restaurant, you may have noticed a bowl filled with seeds near the door. They are most likely anise. Suck on a few of those licorice-tasting seeds to help sweeten your breath.

You may want to have a bowl of anise at your next dinner party.

Garlic or Onion Breath

▶ Mix ½ teaspoon of baking soda into a cup of water, then swish it—one gulp at a time—around your mouth. Spit out. Be careful not to swallow this mouthwash. By the time you've rinsed your mouth with the entire cup, your breath should be fresh.

▶ Chew sprigs of parsley—yes, especially after eating garlic. Take your choice—garlic breath or little pieces of green stuff between your teeth.

▶ If you're a coffee drinker, drink a strong cup of coffee to remove all traces of onion from your breath.

Of course, then you have coffee breath, which, to some people, is just as objectionable as the onion breath. So eat an apple. That will get rid of the coffee breath. In fact, forget the coffee and just eat an apple.

▶ Chew a whole clove to sweeten your breath. People have been doing that for over 5,000 years to freshen their breath.

▶ Suck a lemon! It should make your onion or garlic breath disappear. Some people get better results when they add salt to the lemon, then suck it. (That's also a good remedy for getting rid of hiccups.)

⚡ **CAUTION:** Do not suck lemons often. Do this only in an emergency social situation. With repeated use, the strongly acidic lemon juice can wear away tooth enamel.

Mouthwash

▶ Prepare your own mouthwash by combining ¼ cup of apple cider vinegar with 2 cups of just-boiled water. Let it cool and store it in a jar in your medicine cabinet.

Swish a mouthful of this antiseptic solution as you would commercial mouthwash, for about one minute, and spit it out. Then, be sure to rinse with water to remove the acid stains.

Canker Sores

Canker sores are painful, annoying little sores that develop on the gums, cheeks and tongue, which can last for weeks. They are believed to be brought on by stress.

▶ Get an ear of corn, discard the kernels and burn a little piece of cob at a time. Apply the cob ashes to the canker sore three to five times a day. (Too bad this isn't a remedy for the toes—we'd have "cob on the corn.")

▶ Several times throughout the day, keep a glob of blackstrap molasses in your mouth on the canker sore. Molasses has extraordinary healing properties. Be sure to rinse thoroughly with water after using molasses.

▶ According to psychic healer Edgar Cayce, castor oil is soothing and promotes healing of canker sores. Dab the sore with it each time the pain reminds you it's there.

Bacterial Cure

▶ Yogurt with active cultures (make sure the container specifies "living" or "active" cultures) may ease the condition faster than you can say *Lactobacillus acidophilus*. In fact, lactobacillus tablets may be an effective treatment for canker sores.

Again, make sure the tablets have living organisms. Start by taking two tablets at each meal, then decrease the dosage as the condition clears up.

▶ Until you get the *Lactobacillus acidophilus*, dip one regular (nonherbal) tea bag in boiling water. Squeeze out most of the water. When it's cool to the touch, apply it to the canker sore for three minutes.

▶ Take a mouthful of sauerkraut juice (use fresh from the barrel or in a jar found at health food stores, rather than the cans found in supermarkets) and swish it over the canker sore for about a minute. Then either swallow the juice or spit it out.

Do this throughout the day, four to six times every day, until the sore is gone. It should disappear in a day or two.

If you're like us, you'll come to love the juice. You may even want to try making your own sauerkraut. (*See* "Preparation Guide" on page 252.)

ULCERS

There is a small percentage of people who develop ulcers (sores on the lining of the stomach or small intestine) from continual use of aspirin and other painkillers. If that doesn't apply to you, keep reading.

A recent incredible discovery was made about the main cause of ulcers. About 80% of all ulcers can be blamed on *Helicobacter pylori,* bacteria that are more commonly referred to as H. pylori. It is estimated that half of the American adult population has H. pylori present but dormant in their stomachs.

Why do some people develop ulcers and others don't? Our commonsense guess is that emotional upsets, fatigue, nervous anxiety, chronic tension and/or the inability to healthfully handle a high-pressure job or situation may devitalize the immune system, lowering one's resistance to the H. pylori.

If you're a member of this "fret set," we can suggest remedies for the ulcer, but you have to remedy the cause first. Change jobs, meditate, look into self-help seminars or do whatever is appropriate to transform your specific problem into something that is positive and manageable.

And now, we're asking you nicely—please don't try any of these remedies without your doctor's blessing, okay?

Dietary Remedies

▶ According to a report that was published in the medical journal *Practical Gastroenterology* (*www.practicalgastro.com*), "Aside from its failure to promote healing of gastric ulceration, the bland diet has other shortcomings—it is not palatable, and it is too high in fat and too low in roughage." So jazz up your food with some spices!

▶ We learned that milk may not be the cure-all we thought it was. It may neutralize stomach acid at first, but because of its calcium content, gastrin is secreted. Gastrin is a hormone that encourages the release of more acid. Steer clear of milk.

High-Fiber Healing

▶ A high-fiber diet is believed to be best for treatment of ulcers and prevention of relapses.

▶ If your doctor approves, take 1 tablespoon of extra-virgin, cold-pressed olive oil in the morning and 1 tablespoon in the evening. It may help to soothe and heal the mucous membrane that lines the stomach.

▶ Barley and barley water are soothing and help rebuild the stomach lining. Boil 2 ounces of pearled barley in 6 cups of water until there's about half the water—3 cups—left in the pot. Strain. If necessary, add honey and lemon to taste. Drink it throughout the day. Eat the barley in soup, stew or by itself.

See the "Barley Water" information on page 249 of "Preparation Guide."

▶ Recent research has substantiated the effectiveness of cabbage juice, a centuries-old folk remedy for relief of ulcers. While today's pressured lifestyle is quite conducive to developing ulcers, we, at least, have modern machinery to help with the cure—a juice extractor.

Juice a cabbage and drink a cup of the juice right before each meal, then another cup before bedtime. Make sure the cabbage is fresh, not wilted. Also, drink the juice as soon as you prepare it. In other words, don't prepare it ahead of time and refrigerate it. It loses a lot of value that way.

According to reports on test groups, pain, symptoms and ulcers disappeared within two to three weeks after starting the cabbage-juice regimen.

People often ask, "Why cabbage?" *We researched and found two reasons…*

◆ Cabbage is rich in the nonessential amino acid glutamine. Glutamine helps the healthy stomach cells regenerate and stimulates the production of mucin, a mucoprotein that protects the stomach lining.

◆ Cabbage contains gefarnate, a substance that helps strengthen the stomach lining and replace cells. (It's also used in anti-ulcer drugs.)

Gentlemen, start your juicers! Raw cabbage is also good in sauerkraut, cole slaw and the Korean dish *kim chee*.

▶ For the acute distress of ulcers (and gastritis), Ray C. Wunderlich, Jr., MD, PhD, director of the Wunderlich Center for Nutritional Medicine in St. Petersburg, Florida, recommends lecithin granules—1 heaping tablespoon as needed. Lecithin capsules will also suffice. Both are available at health food stores.

URINARY PROBLEMS

The urinary system includes the kidneys, ureters, bladder and urethra.

Many of the remedies in this section are helpful for more than one condition. Therefore, most of the bladder and kidney ailments (infections, stones, inflammation, etc.) are bunched together. We suggest you read them all in order to determine the most appropriate one(s) for your specific problem.

CAUTION: Urinary infections, kidney stones and inflammation of the bladder and kidneys are serious conditions that should be evaluated by a health professional.

Natural Remedies

With your doctor's approval, here are some worth-a-try remedies that may help to ease your condition.

▶ Drink plenty of fluids, including parsley tea—3 to 4 cups a day. If you have a juicer, one or two glasses of parsley juice drunk each day, should prove quite beneficial.

Also, sprinkle fresh parsley on the foods you eat. You may start to see improvements in a mere three days or up to three weeks.

▶ Onions are a diuretic and will help to cleanse your system. So eat fresh onions often. Also, for kidney stimulation, apply a poultice of grated or finely chopped onions externally to the kidney area—on your back, just under the rib cage.

▶ Pure cranberry juice (no sugar or preservatives added) has been known to help relieve kidney and bladder infections.

Dose: Drink 6 ounces of room-temperature cranberry juice three times a day.

It's the Tops!

▶ Carrot tops and celery tops are tops in strengthening the kidneys and bladder. In the morning, cover a bunch of scrubbed carrot tops with 12 ounces of boiled water and let them steep. Drink 4 ounces of the carrot-top water before each meal. After each meal, eat a handful of scrubbed celery tops.

Within five weeks, there should be a noticeable and positive difference in the kidneys and bladder.

▶ Pumpkin seeds are high in zinc and good for strengthening the bladder muscle.

Dose: Eat one palmful (about 1 ounce) of unprocessed (unsalted) shelled pumpkin seeds three times a day.

▶ According to some Native Americans, corn silk (the silky strands beneath the husk of corn) is a cure-all for urinary problems. The most desirable corn silk is from young corns, gathered before the silk turns brown.

Take a handful of corn silk and steep it in 3 cups of boiled water for five minutes. Strain and drink the 3 cups throughout the day. Corn silk can be stored in a glass jar, not refrigerated.

If you can't get corn silk, use corn silk extract, available at most health food stores. Add 10 to 15 drops of the extract to a cup of water.

Bed-Wetting and Nighttime Urination

Frequent nighttime urination, known as nocturia, is a common but often-overlooked medical problem. To most people, a mild case—waking a few times a night—is bothersome, but not a reason to see a doctor.

But ignoring even mild nocturia is a mistake. Our kidneys and bladder are designed to retain urine during an 8-hour sleep. If you wake to urinate more than twice a night, consider these suggestions…

WARNING: Hypertension, diabetes, prostate problems, stroke, kidney disease and, in some cases, a tumor in the bladder can cause nocturia. Get a thorough physical, including a urinalysis to check for a bladder infection.

▶ Cut back on beverages. Certain beverages have a diuretic effect that can lead to nighttime urination—coffee, black or green tea, alcohol, caffeinated soda and herbal teas containing dandelion, burdock, linden, nettle or parsley. Abstain from these beverages after 6 pm, and limit your total fluid intake after dinner to 12 ounces of water or a nondiuretic, non-caffeinated tea, such as chamomile or peppermint.

▶ In people with allergies or certain medical conditions, including benign prostatic hyperplasia and interstitial cystitis, inflammation is the cause of nocturia. Quercetin, a strong antioxidant, decreases inflammation and inhibits cell damage in the kidneys. Cranberries and other dark red or purple berries, such as blue-berries and raspberries, contain a good amount of quercetin. Eat one cup of fresh berries every day, or take a 500-mg quercetin supplement twice daily with meals.

▶ Get tested for food allergies. Food allergens act as irritants, so your body tries to eliminate them quickly through a variety of mechanisms, including urination.

▶ Just when you may have thought that nothing could help, heeeeeere's uva ursi! This herb is said to help strengthen the urinary tract and, taken in small doses, has been known to end bed-wetting.

Add 1 tablespoon of dried uva ursi leaves or one tea bag to 1 cup of just-boiled water and steep for five minutes. Strain into a jar.

Dose: Take 1 tablespoon before each meal every day for six weeks. (Uva ursi is available at health food stores.)

> **NOTE:** Arbutin, the main component of the herb uva ursi, may cause the urine to turn brownish in color. It's absolutely nothing to worry about.

> **WARNING:** We do not list this as a children's bed-wetting remedy because none of our sources mentioned it for use by children. Uva ursi may be too strong for their delicate systems.

Diuretics

To stimulate urination, try any of the following foods in moderation, using good common sense and listening to your body...

- *Celery:* Cooked in chicken soup or raw in salads.
- *Watercress:* Soup or salads.
- *Leek:* A mild diuretic in soup, it's much stronger when eaten raw, and a perfect opening for a cheap joke about urination.
- *Parsley:* Used in soups, salads, juices or as a tea.
- *Asparagus:* Raw or cooked, or as a tea.
- *Cucumber:* Raw.
- *Corn silk:* Tea.
- *Onions:* Raw in salads and/or sliced to rub on your loins (hips, groin and lower abdomen). (Yes, you read that correctly.)
- *Horseradish:* Grate ½ cup of horseradish and boil it with ½ cup of beer. Drink this concoction three times a day.
- *Watermelon:* Eat a piece first thing in the morning and do not eat any other foods for at least two hours.

Incontinence

Any problems with incontinence should be evaluated by a health professional. But, until you get treated, these remedies may help.

▶ Direct the stream of water from an ordinary garden hose onto the soles of the feet for up to two minutes. It has been known to reduce urinary incontinence, particularly in older people. It also helps circulation in the feet.

Bully for Buchu

▶ This remedy comes from the Hottentot tribe of South Africa, where buchu shrubs grow. Steep 1 tablespoon of buchu leaves (available at health food stores) in 1 cup of just-boiled water for a half-hour.

Dose: Take 3 to 4 tablespoons, three to four times a day. Buchu leaves are known to be helpful for many urinary problems, including inflammation of the bladder and painful urination, as well as incontinence.

Frequent Urination

▶ Cherry juice or cranberry juice (no sugar or preservatives added) has been said to help regulate the problem of constantly having to urinate.

Dose: Drink 3 to 4 glasses of cherry or cranberry juice throughout the day. Be sure it's room temperature, not chilled.

> ✎ **NOTE:** Persistent frequent urination may be a sign of a urinary tract infection or diabetes and should be checked by a health professional.

Kidney Problems

▶ Lots of folk remedies include the use of apple cider vinegar to help flush the kidneys and to provide a natural acid. Dosage varies from source to source.

We think it makes the most sense to take 1 teaspoon of apple cider vinegar for every 50 pounds you weigh, and add it to 6 ounces of drinking water.

In other words, if you weigh 150 pounds, the dosage would be 3 teaspoons of vinegar in 6 ounces of water. Drink this twice a day, before breakfast and before dinner. Keep it up for two days, then stop for four days. Continue this two-days-on/four-days-off cycle as long as you feel you need it.

Aduki Dukes It Out

▶ Aduki (or azuki) beans, which can be found in health food stores, are used in the Orient as food and medicine. They're excellent for treating kidney problems.

Rinse a cupful of aduki beans. Combine the cup of beans with 5 cups of water and boil them together for one hour. Strain the aduki-bean water into a jar. Drink ½ cup of aduki water at least a half-hour before meals. Do this for two days—six meals.

To prevent the aduki water from spoiling, keep the jar in the refrigerator, then warm the water before drinking.

▶ Our gem therapist friend recommends wearing jade against the skin to help heal kidney problems. If your mate reads this and surprises you with a piece of jade jewelry, chances are you'll start to feel better immediately.

Kidney Stones

▶ According to a good old medical book called *The Elements of Materia Medica* (edited in 1854), asparagus was a popular remedy for kidney stones. It is said that asparagus acts to increase cellular activity in the kidneys and helps break up oxalic acid crystals.

Dose: Eat ½ cup of cooked and blended or puréed asparagus before breakfast and before dinner, or boil 1 cup of asparagus in 2

quarts of water and drink a cup of the asparagus water four times a day.

> ✎ **NOTE:** After eating asparagus, you may
> notice that your urine has an unusual smell.
> There are a few scientific theories as to what
> causes that specific smell.
>
> In 1891, the experiments of Polish doc-
> tor and chemist Marceli Nencki led him to
> conclude that the scent is due to a metabo-
> lite called *methanethiol*. This odoriferous
> chemical is said to be produced as the body
> metabolizes asparagus. Some say that the
> smell is a sign of kidney-bladder cleans-
> ing—others believe it indicates faulty secre-
> tion of gastric hydrochloric acid (HCL).

▶ A respected French herbalist recommends
eating almost nothing but strawberries for
three to five days. This is believed to relieve the
pain of kidney stones.

▶ A high level of oxalate in the urine contributes to the formation of most (calcium)
kidney stones. If this problem runs in your
family, or if you've already gone through the
agony of a kidney stone, chances are you'll
need to take every precaution to help prevent it
from happening to you once...or again.

Completely eliminate, or at least limit,
your intake of the foods and beverages that
are high in oxalates or that can produce oxalic acid. These include caffeine—coffee, black
tea (including orange pekoe), cocoa, chocolate—spinach, sorrel, beets, Swiss chard,
parsley, dried figs, poppy seeds, rhubarb, lamb's-
quarters, purslane, nuts and pepper.

▶ Eat foods that are rich in vitamin A, the vitamin that can help discourage the formation of
stones. These include apricots, pumpkin, sweet
potatoes, squash, carrots and cantaloupe.

> ⚡ **CAUTION:** Any sudden or dramatic change
> of diet should be supervised by a health profes-
> sional. And always thoroughly wash produce to
> reduce the risk of food-borne illness.

▶ Start your day by drinking a glass of (distilled, if possible) water in which you squeezed
the juice of a lemon. The citric acid and magnesium in the lemon may also help prevent the
formation of kidney stones.

Most important is that you drink a lot
of water daily. Distilled water is ideal.

WARTS

No matter how you feel about warts, they seem to have a way of growing on you.

Verruca vulgaris is the medical term for the common wart. (Don't you think a wart looks like a *Verruca vulgaris*?)

Warts usually appear on the hands, feet and face, and are believed to be caused by some type of virus.

The "quantity" award for home remedies goes to warts. We got a million of 'em—remedies, that is...not warts.

We tried to get warts for research purposes. We kept touching frogs. But it's a fallacy. You do not get warts from touching frogs. (Incidentally, you do not get a prince from kissing them either.)

Natural Remedies

If you have a wart, there are a wide variety of remedies to try in order to find the one that works for you.

▶ Crush a fresh fig until it has a mushy consistency and put it on the wart for a half-hour each day. Continue doing that until the wart disappears.

▶ First thing each morning, dab some of your own spittle on the wart.

▶ Pick some dandelions. Break the stems and put the juice that oozes out of the stems directly on the wart—once in the morning and once in the evening, five days in a row.

▶ Apply a used tea bag to the wart for 15 minutes a day. Within a week to 10 days you should be wartless.

▶ Warts on the genitals? Gently rub the inside part of pineapple skin on the affected area. Repeat every morning and evening until the warts are gone or the pineapple's gone.

✎ **NOTE:** Genital warts are a serious sexually transmitted disease. They are highly contagious and should be treated by a medical professional as soon as possible.

Get the Lime Out

▶ If you have warts on your body, you may have too much lime in your system. One way to neutralize the excess lime is to drink a cup of chamomile tea two or three times a day.

▶ Grate carrots and combine them with a teaspoon of olive oil. Put the mixture on the wart for a half-hour twice a day.

▶ Dab lemon juice on the wart with a cotton swab or cotton ball, immediately followed by a raw chopped onion. Do that twice a day for 15 minutes each time.

Potato Popper

▶ Put a fresh slice of raw potato on the wart and keep it in place with a bandage. Leave it on overnight. Take it off in the morning. Then repeat the procedure again at night. If you don't get rid of the wart in a week, replace the potato with a clove of garlic.

▶ Every morning, squish out the contents of a vitamin E capsule and rub it vigorously on the wart. This remedy is slow (it may take more than a month), but what's the rush?

▶ Dab on (with a cotton swab or cotton ball) the healing juice of the aloe vera plant every day until the wart disappears.

▶ Every day, apply a poultice of blackstrap molasses (*see* "Preparation Guide" on page 252) and keep it on the wart as long as possible. You should also eat a tablespoon of molasses daily (be sure to rinse your mouth with water after eating molasses).

In about two weeks, the wart should drop off without leaving a trace.

Chalk It Up to Experience

▶ We heard about a young woman who used an old remedy. She applied regular white chalk to the wart every night. On the sixth night, the wart fell off.

▶ In the morning and in the evening, rub the wart with one of the following—a radish, juice of marigold, flowers, bacon rind, oil of cinnamon, wheat germ oil or a thick paste of buttermilk and baking soda.

Egg Water

▶ Boil eggs and save the water. As soon as the water is cool, soak your warted hand(s) for 10 minutes. Do this daily until the wart(s) disappear.

▶ If you don't have the patience to tend to the wart on a daily basis, consider finding a competent, professional hypnotist. Warts may actually be hypnotized away.

Plantar Warts

▶ Plantar warts are the kind you find on the soles of the feet, usually in clusters. The wart starts as a little black dot. Don't pick it—you'll only make it spread. Instead, rub castor oil on it every night until it's history.

▶ At bedtime, puncture one or two garlic pearles (soft gels) and squeeze out the oil onto the plantar warts. Massage the oil on the entire area for a few minutes. Put a clean white sock on each foot and leave it on while you sleep.

Do this every night for a week or two, until the little black roots come out and fall off.

WEIGHT PROBLEMS

This "weighty" subject is close to our heart—and our hips, thighs, midriff, stomach and every other place we can pinch an inch…or two…or 10.

As hundreds of books and articles tell us, losing weight is hard—keeping it off is harder.

Most people go on a diet, living for the moment they can go *off* the diet.

The answer, then, is *not* to go on a diet. If you're not on a diet to begin with, you can't go off it, right?

We found some remedies that may help you lose weight without a temporary, "I-can't-wait-to-go-off-it" diet.

So, put some motivational reminders on your refrigerator—*Nothing stretches slacks like snacks! To indulge is to bulge! Those who love rich food and cook it, look it!*—and start to practice "girth control."

> ✎ **NOTE:** As for diet pills, they can be very helpful. Twice a day, spill them on the floor and pick them up one at a time. It's great exercise, especially for the waistline.

Weight Control Tips

Whether you've spent years yo-yoing your way through one diet after another and are heavier than ever, or you just need to lose a few pounds to look better in that bathing suit, here are suggestions to healthfully help you shed those unwanted pounds.

Commonsense Reducing Principles

▶ Try eating your larger meals early rather than late in the day. This gives your body lots of time to digest and burn off the calories.

We've come across an appropriate saying—"Eat like a king in the morning, a prince at noon and a pauper in the evening." While it's not always practical to have a four-course breakfast, you may want to eat a big lunch and a small dinner whenever possible.

Ancient Slimming Herbs

Each of these herbs has several wonderful properties—but the one component they all have in common is the ability to help you to be a weight loser. However, please try the herbs one at a time—not all at once.

> ✎ **NOTE:** Using these herbs does not give you license to start eating as though there's no tomorrow. They are tools that may help decrease the appetite and/or metabolize fat quickly, but they should be used in conjunction with a well-balanced eating and exercise plan.
>
> Check with your doctor before taking any herbs or natural supplements as part of a weight-loss plan.

It probably took you a while to reach your current weight. And it will take you a while to lose it. Be patient with yourself and give the herbs time to do their stuff. You can help the process along by eliminating or at least cutting down on foods with sugar, salt and white flour.

Within a couple of months, you should be ready for the "Nobelly Prize"!

You may want to taste each herb before deciding on one to stick with for at least a month. All of the herbs mentioned here are available in tea bags or loose at most health food stores.

Herb Preparation

To prepare, add 1 teaspoon of the dried, loose herb (or one tea bag) to a cup of just-boiled water. Cover and let steep for 10 minutes. Strain and enjoy.

Drink 1 cup about a half-hour before each meal and 1 cup at bedtime. It may take a

month or two before you see results, especially if you hardly change your eating habits at all.

Fennel Seeds

The Greek name for fennel is *marathron*, from *mariano*, which means "to grow thin." Fennel is known to metabolize and throw off fatty substances through the urine. Fennel is rich in vitamin A and is wonderful for the eyes. It also aids digestion.

Cleavers

Like fennel seeds, cleavers is not known to lessen the appetite, but rather to somehow accelerate fat metabolism. It's also a natural diuretic and can help relieve constipation. You may want to combine cleavers with fennel seeds for your daily drink.

Raspberry Leaves

As well as having a reputation as a weight-loss aid, raspberry-leaf tea is said to help control diarrhea and nausea, help eliminate canker sores and make pregnancy, delivery and post-delivery easier for the mother.

Yerba Maté (Jungle Punch)

We've heard that South American medical authorities who have studied yerba maté concluded that this popular beverage can improve one's memory, nourish the smooth tissues of

■ Recipe ■

Mexican Eggplant with Fennel Seeds

> 2 large or 3 medium eggplants
> 2 Tbsp olive oil
> 1 tsp cumin seeds
> 1 tsp fennel seeds
> 1 lb fresh tomatoes, pared and chopped
> 1" fresh ginger, grated
> 4 cloves garlic, crushed
> 1 tsp ground coriander
> 1 cup water
> Salt and pepper
> 2 to 4 serrano or jalapeño peppers, thinly sliced
> Sprigs of fresh parsley

Wash eggplant, remove stalks and cut into bite-size pieces. Fry cubes in oil for approximately 5 minutes or until brown. Drain on paper towels.

Fry cumin and fennel seeds for about 2 minutes, stirring constantly, until they turn a shade darker. Mix in chopped tomatoes, grated ginger, crushed garlic, peppers, coriander and water. Simmer for about 20 minutes until the mixture becomes thick.

Add the fried eggplant cubes to the mixture and heat through. Garnish with the sprigs of parsley and serve.

Source: www.recipegoldmine.com

the intestines, increase respiratory power, help prevent infection and is a tonic to the brain, nerves and spine as well as an appetite depressant and a digestive aid. (*See* page 131 for more information on this powerful beverage.)

> ✎ **NOTE:** Yerba maté contains caffeine (although not as much as coffee). We were told that, while it may act as a stimulant, it should not interfere with sleep.

Horehound

This Old World herb is a diuretic and is used in cases of indigestion, colds, coughs and asthma. It is also reported to be an effective aid for weight reduction.

Spirulina

This blue-green algae is an ancient Aztec food that's user-friendly. It's easily digestible and is reported to enhance the immune system, help detoxify the body and boost one's energy. Spirulina, taken daily, can help lift your spirits because of its high L-tryptophan content.

As for helping you lose weight, take spirulina about 20 minutes before mealtime, and it may give you that full feeling, like you've already eaten a meal and hardly have room for more. Spirulina comes in several forms—powder, tablets, capsules and freeze-dried. Look for it at your health food store.

Other Slimming Remedies

▶ We have a friend who's a light eater—as soon as it gets light, she eats. We told her about the grape juice remedy recommended by psychic healer Edgar Cayce. Since starting this grape juice regimen, our friend's craving for desserts has almost disappeared, her eating patterns are gradually changing for the better and she's fitting into clothes she hasn't worn in years.

Drink 3 ounces of pure grape juice (no sugar, additives or preservatives) that is mixed with 1 ounce of water a half-hour before each meal and at bedtime. Drink the mixture slowly, taking from five to 10 minutes for each glass.

▶ This Chinese acupressure technique is said to diminish one's appetite. Whenever you're feeling hungry, squeeze your earlobes for one minute. If you can stand the pressure, clamp clothespins on your lobes and leave them there for 60 seconds.

We wonder if women who wear clip-on earrings are generally slimmer than women without them. *Hmmmmm...*

Apple Cider Solution

▶ A woman we know dieted religiously (that means she wouldn't eat anything when she was in church). Out of control, desperate and tired of all the fad diets, she came to us, looked in our "overweight" remedy file and decided to follow the apple cider vinegar plan.

First thing in the morning, drink 2 teaspoons of apple cider vinegar in a glass of water. Drink the same mixture before lunch and dinner, making it three glasses of apple cider vinegar and water a day.

Within three months, the woman was no longer out of control or desperate. She felt that her days of binges were over and, thanks to the apple cider vinegar, she had the strength and willpower to stick to a well-balanced eating plan as the pounds slowly came off.

Fat's Where It's At

An unlikely hero in the battle of the bulge is, in fact, classified as a fat," says Jade Beutler, RRT, RCP, San Diego–based CEO of Lignan Research LLC, a licensed health care practitioner and a foremost authority of the benefits of flaxseed oil. *According to Beutler's research findings, flaxseed oil can help...*

◆ Decrease cravings for fatty foods and sweets

◆ Stoke metabolic rate

◆ Create satiation (feeling of fullness and satisfaction following a meal)

◆ Regulate blood sugar levels

◆ Regulate insulin levels

◆ Increase oxygen consumption

The ideal method of taking flaxseed oil for purposes of weight loss or maintenance is 1 to 2 tablespoons daily, in divided doses taken with each meal.

Read more about flaxseed oil in the "Six Sensational Superfoods" section on page 262.

▶ Lecithin is said to help break up and burn fatty deposits from stubborn bulges. It can also give you a full feeling even when you've eaten less than usual. The recommended daily dosage is 1 to 2 tablespoons of lecithin granules.

Doggy Bags

▶ As soon as you're served food at a restaurant, separate half the meal and ask for a doggy bag. Explain that you're into "portion control," and don't want to tempt yourself to finish everything on the plate.

High-Protein Lunch

▶ If you eat a high-protein lunch—filled with fish, soy products, yogurt, meat or chicken—you may find yourself eating fewer calories for dinner. Protein—just 2 or 3 ounces—is said to trigger a hormone that cuts your appetite and leaves you feeling satisfied. Give it a try.

Avoid high-carbohydrate lunches—ones that are heavy in pasta, rice and potatoes—and see if a higher portion of protein (along with veggies or salad—the good stuff) helps reduce your calorie intake at dinner.

Filling Foods

▶ Plan on eating foods that have a high water content. Prepare meals with fruits and vegetables—soups, stews and smoothies. An apple is 84% water, which is almost 4 ounces of water. A ½ cup of cooked broccoli is 91% water, giving you 2.4 ounces of water. Look how much water it takes to make rice (spaghetti, too). High water-content foods will fill you up and hydrate you at the same time.

Soup's On!

▶ In a study of 147 men and women who ate a reduced-calorie diet for a year, those who consumed 10.5 fluid ounces of low-fat, low-calorie soup twice a day lost 50% more weight than those who ate healthful but carbohydrate-rich snacks, such as baked chips or pretzels.

Although the soup had the same calories as the other snacks, the soup's greater weight and volume made study participants feel full enough to eat less for the rest of the day.

Consume one large mugful of a broth-based, low-fat, low-calorie and low-sodium soup that's rich in vegetables and/or beans as a first course twice daily.

The Salad Trick

▶ Large salads help you consume fewer calories. A recent study found that diners who have a large low-calorie salad before the main course of their meal consume 12% fewer total calories at the meal than those who have nothing before the main course at all.

Salad takes the edge off your appetite and helps fill you up.

Laugh Away the Pounds

▶ A recent study of students who watched comedy clips found that laughing for 10 to 15 minutes can burn 10 to 40 calories.

This means that 10 to 15 minutes of laughing daily could result in weight loss of about 4 pounds a year.

Mirror, Mirror on the Kitchen Wall

▶ Studies were done with more than 1,000 people who were divided into two groups—those who ate in front of mirrors and those who ate without seeing themselves in mirrors. The subjects who watched themselves chow down ate considerably less fat than those who were mirrorless.

Hanging a mirror in your kitchen may be the reminder you need each time to help you decide what to eat.

Healthy Snacks

▶ Fruit is a great, easy-to-prepare, fibrous, health-giving, sweet treat. We could fill a book

naming each fruit, its nutritional value and ways to prepare it.

Instead, we suggest that you be adventurous and creative. Go to your greengrocer or any ethnic market and find exotic fruit to add to your repertoire.

NOTE: Be sure to wash produce thoroughly before you eat it in order to reduce the risk of food-borne illness.

Yam It Up!

▶ Ever think of having a sweet potato or a yam as a snack? "Yam" is from the Guinean word for "something to eat." And it's something *wonderful* to eat!

Yams are rich in potassium. Sweet potatoes are rich in vitamin A. Both are good sources of folate (the heart-protective vitamin B) and vitamin C. Both are filling, easy to prepare, fat-free and worth the 100 to 140 satisfying calories.

▶ When you crave something crunchy, get out the finger vegetables. Chomp on baby carrots,

Remove Pesticides and Wax From Fruits and Vegetables

In a bowl or a basin, mix 4 tablespoons of table salt, 4 teaspoons of lemon juice and 1 quart of cool water. Soak fruits and vegetables in this mixture for five to 10 minutes.

Exceptions: Soak leafy greens for two to three minutes…berries, one to two minutes.

After soaking, rinse produce in plain cold water and dry.

An alternative is Veggie Wash. Made of 100% natural ingredients, it is available at supermarkets, health food store and on-line at *www.veggie-wash.com* (800-451-7096).

jicama and fennel sticks, strips of yellow or red bell pepper and the old standby, celery.

On a weekend morning, prepare a bowl of cut-up vegetables. Keep them in ice water in your refrigerator, and reach for the bowl whenever you need to nibble.

The Diet "Blues"

▶ The Wagner Institute for Color Research claims that blue food is unappetizing. Put a blue lightbulb in the refrigerator and a blue light in your dining area. Restaurants know all about people's responses to the color blue when it comes to food. When serving food on blue plates, customers eat less, saving the restaurants money on their all-you-can-eat "Blue Plate" specials.

Slowly, but Surely

▶ Change your lifestyle habits gradually. The key word is "gradually." *Gradually,* day by day, replace a couple of fattening foods with healthier choices. In doing so, you become super-aware of what you're eating. That's a major step in improving your daily food intake.

▶ Also, *gradually* start exercising. Check with your doctor before starting an exercise program, and start walking briskly for 10 minutes the first few days, then 12 minutes, then 15. Keep going until you work your way up to doing a supervised exercise routine that's appropriate for you.

Be happy if you lose one or two pounds each week. In terms of keeping the weight off permanently, losing no more than two pounds a week makes sense. If you lose more, your body thinks you're going to starve and, in an effort to protect you from dying of hunger, it will slow down your metabolism.

A loss of just one or two pounds a week will add up to a big difference in a matter of months. And that's weight that will most likely *stay off.*

Calories Per Hour

▶ Calories burned per hour—for a 155-pound person...

- ◆ *281 calories:* Raking the lawn, sweeping the sidewalk, leisure walking.
- ◆ *387 calories:* Scrubbing floors on hands and knees, mowing the lawn, light stationary biking, dancing—such as jazz, ballet or tango.
- ◆ *422 calories:* Moving furniture, cross-country skiing, shoveling snow.
- ◆ *493 calories:* Jogging, carrying boxes.
- ◆ *598 calories:* Vigorous stationary biking, mountain biking.
- ◆ *705 calories:* Moderate jumping rope, swimming, judo or karate, kick-boxing, running six miles per hour.

Yoga May Minimize Midlife Weight Gain

▶ In a recent finding, people in their 50s who regularly practiced yoga lost about five pounds over 10 years, while those who did not practice yoga gained about 13 pounds.

Most yoga exercises do not burn enough calories to account for the weight loss, but some practitioners believe that yoga keeps people aware of their bodies and eating habits.

Cellulite Eliminator

▶ Former fashion model Maureen Klimt was determined to get rid of cellulite, so she started taking omega-3 fatty acids—in the form of flaxseed. Maureen grinds the seeds in a little coffee grinder, sprinkles 1 to 2 tablespoons on her oatmeal every morning and then adds a touch of maple syrup.

After eating the flaxseeded oatmeal daily for months, she reports that the cellulite is no longer there. Although Maureen eats healthfully and exercises, she credits the flaxseed for the loss of her cellulite.

Read more about flaxseed in the "Six Sensational Superfoods" section on page 262.

Firm Thighs

▶ The Fairmont Sonoma Mission Inn & Spa in Sonoma, California (*www.fairmont.com/sonoma*), shared with us its once-secret treatment for jiggly thighs.

Rosemary is the key ingredient. (No, that's not a physical trainer who gives you a tough workout!) Rosemary is an herb that stimulates circulation and drains impurities, leaving skin firmer and tighter.

Mix 1 tablespoon of crushed dried rosemary (available at herb and health food stores) with 2 tablespoons of extra-virgin olive oil. Smooth the mixture over thighs, wrap in plastic wrap and leave on for 10 minutes. Then rinse. Do this treatment at least once a week.

Leg Slimming

▶ Every night, while lying on the floor or in bed, rest your feet as high on a wall as is comfortable. Stay that way for about an hour. At most, your legs will slim down. At least, it will be good for your circulation.

Rev Up Your Metabolism

▶ Kelp is seaweed that's rich in minerals and vitamins, especially the B family. Its high iodine content can help activate a sluggish thyroid. Dried kelp can be eaten raw, or crumbled into soups and on salads. Powdered kelp can also be used in place of salt. It has a salty, fishy taste that may take getting used to. If you really don't like the taste, there are kelp pills. Follow the recommended dosage on the label.

One of the good side effects of kelp is that it may make your hair shinier. But if you eat too much kelp, it can have a laxative effect.

Hot Stuff

▶ One British study showed that adding 1 teaspoon of hot-pepper sauce (something with cayenne pepper, like Tabasco sauce) and 1 teaspoon of mustard to every meal raised one's metabolic rate by as much as 25%.

▶ Before you eat dinner, exercise for 20 to 30 minutes. Just brisk walking will do. Exercise boosts your metabolic rate and it lasts through dinner, helping you digest and burn off the evening meal. For many, that before-dinner walk seems to reduce the urge for late-night snacks.

▶ Do not eat within three hours of bedtime. The body seems to store fat more easily at night, when the metabolism slows down.

Vitamin C Helps You Burn More Fat

▶ *In a recent study,* people who took 500 mg of vitamin C daily burned 39% more fat while exercising than people who took less. Since it is difficult to get enough vitamin C just from fruits and vegetables, take a vitamin C supplement to be sure you get at least 500 mg per day.

Why Juice or Water?

▶ The results of a study that was reported in the *American Journal of Clinical Nutrition* (*www.ajcn.org*) shows that drinking water or juice before a meal—rather than beer, wine or a cocktail—goes a long way with weight control.

The imbibers consumed an average of 240 calories in their alcoholic beverage and wolfed down about 200 more calories in their meals. They also ate faster. It took them longer to feel full, but that didn't stop them. They continued eating *past* the point of feeling full. And

all because they had an alcoholic drink before their meal. Waiter, just water for me, please!

Why Not Soda?

▶ It's been reported that people who are frequent soda drinkers (either diet or regular) have higher hunger ratings than people who drink unsweetened or naturally sweet beverages. Experiment by going off soda for a week to see if your desire for food decreases.

Holiday Challenges

▶ Forget about losing weight during the holidays. Settle for not *gaining* weight. Fill up on sweet potatoes, fruits, vegetables, white-meat turkey, whole-grain bread and an *occasional, tiny* portion of an obscenely fattening dessert.

▶ Eat a portion of healthy, nonfattening food right before you go to a holiday party.

▶ At a holiday event, drink designer water or sparkling water with a twist of lemon. A little wine is okay, but stay away from mixed drinks and liqueurs.

▶ According to Alan Hirsch, MD, director of the Smell & Taste Treatment and Research Foundation in Chicago, "People who are exposed to smells of food during the day eat less at night."

Proof that this may be so is evident during Ramadan, the Muslim holiday during which daytime fasting is followed by nighttime feasting. Muslim women's hunger ratings dropped, but men's hunger stayed the same throughout the month-long holiday.

Why? The women prepared food all day and, by mealtime, their hunger had abated. The food simply wasn't as appealing to them.

Use Smell to Lose Weight

In a recent study, participants who sprinkled powders that smelled like cheddar cheese, banana and raspberry on their food lost an average of 5.6 pounds per month over a six-month period.

Added scents fool the brain into thinking you have eaten enough. Smell every food before you eat it.

The Great Outdoors

A day without sunshine is like a day without serotonin, a brain chemical that can allay hunger. Your body needs sunlight to make serotonin, so get out there every chance you get. While you're outdoors, you may as well get a little exercise, too. Walk. Play. Skip. Enjoy yourself! And don't forget the sunscreen.

Determining Your Weight/ Health Profile

Body Mass Index (BMI) is one of the most accurate ways to determine when extra pounds translate into health risks. BMI is a measure that takes into account a person's weight and height to gauge total body fat in adults.

According to guidelines set by the National Institutes of Health, the definition of a healthy weight is a BMI of 24 or less. For both men and women, a BMI of 25 to 29.9 is considered overweight. Individuals who fall into the BMI range of 25 to 34.9 and have a waist size of more than 40 inches (for men) or 35 inches (for women) are considered to be at especially high risk for health problems.

BMI is reliable for most people between 19 and 70 years of age except women who are pregnant or breastfeeding, and people who are competitive athletes, body builders or chronically ill.

To use the table on page 203, find the appropriate height in the column on the left. Move across to a given weight. The number at the top of the column is the BMI for that height and weight. Pounds have been rounded off. ■

BODY MASS INDEX CHART

HEIGHT (in inches)	19	20	21	22	23	24	25	26	27	28	29	30	31	32	33	34	35
							BODY WEIGHT (in pounds)										
58	91	96	100	105	110	115	119	124	129	134	138	143	148	153	158	162	167
59	94	99	104	109	114	119	124	128	133	138	143	148	153	158	163	168	173
60	97	102	107	112	118	123	128	133	138	143	148	153	158	163	168	174	179
61	100	106	111	116	122	127	132	137	143	148	153	158	164	169	174	180	185
62	104	109	115	120	126	131	136	142	147	153	158	164	169	175	180	186	191
63	107	113	118	124	130	135	141	146	152	158	163	169	175	180	186	191	197
64	110	116	122	128	134	140	145	151	157	163	169	174	180	186	192	197	204
65	114	120	126	132	138	144	150	156	162	168	174	180	186	192	198	204	210
66	118	124	130	136	142	148	155	161	167	173	179	186	192	198	204	210	216
67	121	127	134	140	146	153	159	166	172	178	185	191	198	204	211	217	223
68	125	131	138	144	151	158	164	171	177	184	190	197	203	210	216	223	230
69	128	135	142	149	155	162	169	176	182	189	196	203	209	216	223	230	236
70	132	139	146	153	160	167	174	181	188	195	202	209	216	222	229	236	243
71	136	143	150	157	165	172	179	186	193	200	208	215	222	229	236	243	250
72	140	147	154	162	169	177	184	191	199	206	213	221	228	235	242	250	258
73	144	151	159	166	174	182	189	197	204	212	219	227	235	242	250	257	265
74	148	155	163	171	179	186	194	202	210	218	225	233	241	249	256	264	272
75	152	160	168	176	184	192	200	208	216	224	232	240	248	256	264	272	279
76	156	164	172	180	189	197	205	213	221	230	238	246	254	263	271	279	287

Source: National Heart, Lung and Blood Institute. For more information, go to *www.nhlbisupport.com/bmi/bmicalc.htm.*

Healing Remedies
For Children

Healing Remedies For Children

Safety First

Every baby-care book tells you to "childproof" your home. Make a crawling tour of each room in order to see things from a child's-eye view. Once you recognize the danger zones, you can eliminate problems by covering wires, nailing down furniture, etc. Do this every four to six months as your child grows.

Still, no matter how childproof a place is, a mishap can happen. We suggest that parents have a first aid book handy and/or take a first aid course through a local chapter of the American Red Cross (*www.redcross.org*).

It's also very important to keep a list of emergency numbers near every telephone in the house. *The list should include…*

- ◆ Pediatrician
- ◆ Poison Help hotline (800-222-1222)
- ◆ Police
- ◆ Fire department
- ◆ Hospital
- ◆ Pharmacy
- ◆ Dentist
- ◆ Neighbors (with cars)

In terms of home remedies for common conditions, we caution you that children's systems are much more delicate than adults'. So, while many remedies in the book can be used for youngsters, common sense must be applied in estimating doses and strengths.

In all cases, check with your child's pediatrician first.

ONE MAJOR CAUTION: Never give raw honey to a child under one year of age! Spores found in honey have been linked to botulism in babies.

Here are natural remedies that are specifically meant for children's ailments. They should help you—as well as your child—get through those tough times.

Acne

▶ It's common to see infants with an outbreak of pimples. According to a folk remedy from the 17th century, gently dab the acne with some of the mother's milk (on a cotton swab or cotton ball).

If you're not nursing, use a few drops of whole milk (not skim milk).

Attention Deficit/ Hyperactivity Disorder (ADHD)

This common disorder is a neurobehavioral condition that affects many school-age children (and some adults). It is characterized by inappropriate and distracting impulsivity, inability to focus (pay attention) and, in some cases, hyperactivity.

If your child has been diagnosed with ADHD, chances are you are looking for an answer so that your child doesn't have to take Ritalin or another prescribed medication.

Before trying any natural remedies, you should rule out other things that could be contributing to your child's behavior. *For example...*

- ◆ Toxic-metal excess
- ◆ Pesticides in the home
- ◆ Behavioral issues in the home and at school
- ◆ Malnutrition
- ◆ Allergies (including those to sweets, milk and cheese)
- ◆ Gluten intolerance

Your child's diet may play a major part in causing and overcoming this condition. But you may not know that several studies point to a connection between children with ADHD and an omega-3 fatty acid deficiency.

According to a paper published in *Physiology & Behavior* (*www.ibnshomepage. org,* then click on "Other Links") by a research team from the Department of Foods and Nutrition at Purdue University in West Lafayette, Indiana, boys with lower levels of omega-3 fatty acids in their blood showed more problems with behavior, learning and health than those with higher total levels of omega-3 fatty acids.

You may want to find out more about this and then consider adding flaxseed oil—the richest source of omega-3 essential fatty acids—to your child's daily diet. For more flaxseed information, *see* the "Six Sensational Superfoods" section on page 262.

Bed-Wetting

Wetting the bed may happen frequently as a child learns to control his/her bladder overnight. Be patient during this time, but if your child doesn't show improvement, consult his pediatrician.

Cinnamon Solution

▶ Give the child a few pieces of cinnamon bark to chew on throughout the day. For some unknown reason, it seems to control bedwetting for some kids.

▶ Prepare a cup of corn silk tea by adding 10 to 15 drops of corn silk extract to a cup of boiled water. Stir, let cool and have the child slowly sip the tea right before bedtime.

The Back Is Best

▶ If all else fails, try this—at bedtime, tie a towel around the child's pelvis, making sure the knot is in front. This teaches the child to sleep on his/her back, which seems to lessen bedwetting urges.

✎ **NOTE:** Chronic bedwetters should be treated by a health professional.

▶ This exercise strengthens the muscles that control urination. Starting with the first urination of the day, have the child start and stop urinating as many times as possible until he/she has finished.

If you make it into a game, counting the number of starts and stops, the child might look forward to breaking his own record each time. It's important, however, not to make the child feel inadequate if he finds this exercise difficult.

Chicken Pox

When we were children, it seemed like everyone had chicken pox—and if someone had it, he was sure to give it to the rest of us. This virus is more uncommon now that kids receive vaccinations, but it's still extremely contagious and spreads through coughs and sneezes. A child with chicken pox should be in bed, kept warm and on a light diet, including pure fruit juices.

▶ According to herbalists, yarrow tea helps children's eruptive ailments. Add 1 tablespoon of dried yarrow (available at health food stores) to 2 cups of just-boiled water and let it steep for 10 minutes. Strain, then add 1 tablespoon of raw honey (if the child is older than one year). Give the child 1 tablespoon three or four times a day.

Eye Irritants

See adult "Eye Irritants" on pages 72–73.

▶ Irrigate eye with water.

▶ Peel an onion near the child so that his natural tears wash away the irritant.

> **WARNING:** If chemicals or another toxic substance have gotten into the child's eye, call 911 or the Poison Help hotline (800-222-1222) immediately.

Colds and Flu

▶ According to a study published by two doctors in a respected scientific journal, zinc gluconate lozenges can dramatically shorten the duration of a cold.

The lozenges (honey-flavored are the best…lemon are the pits) should not be taken on an empty stomach. Even if the child is not eating much because of the cold, have him/her eat half a fruit before sucking a lozenge.

Dose: If a child weighs less than 60 pounds, he/she should take one to three zinc lozenges—as tolerated—23 mg each, per day. For teenagers, the maximum dose is three to six lozenges—as tolerated—23 mg each, per day.

Important: Do not give a child zinc lozenges for more than two days in a row.

Coughs

▶ When a child has a bad, hacking cough, spray his/her pillow with wine vinegar. Both you and the child may sleep better for it.

▶ Add ½ teaspoon of anise seeds and ½ teaspoon of thyme to 1 cup of just-boiled water. Let it steep for 10 minutes. Stir it, strain and let cool. Then add a teaspoon of honey.

Dose: Give 1 tablespoon to the child every half-hour. This remedy is for children who are over two years of age.

Black Thread at Night

▶ A woman from Oklahoma told us that whenever her child gets a cough that acts up at night, she loosely ties a black cotton thread around the child's neck. *The thread must be black.* This woman said she tried other colors and nothing but the black works.

We were intrigued with the remedy and tested it on our friend's child. It worked like magic. We researched it and found a printed source that credited this remedy to shamans (spiritual practitioners) in ancient Egypt.

Croup

Oh, the barking! Oh, the hacking! If your child sounds like a seal from Sea World, he/she probably has the croup. Young children often develop this terrible cough when they have a cold.

▶ Scottish folk healers treat the croup by wrapping a piece of raw bacon around the child's neck, bundling him up in a blanket and taking him into a steamy bathroom for a few minutes.

☞ **WARNING:** Do not put raw meat on broken skin. It can cause an infection.

Diarrhea

▶ Give the baby pure blackberry juice, 2 or 3 tablespoons, four times a day.

Soupy Soother

▶ Carrot soup (*see* recipe at right) not only soothes the inflamed small bowel, it also replaces lost body fluids and minerals. Carrots also contain an antidiarrheal substance called pectin.

You can also prepare the soup by mixing a jar of strained-carrots baby food with a jar of water. Feed the child carrot soup until the diarrhea abates.

▶ Another way of treating diarrhea in infants is to give them barley water throughout the day.

■ Recipe ■

Carrot Soup

1 lb carrots
½ oz onions
1 oz butter
1 pint boiling water
½ oz flour
1 pint milk
Salt and pepper to taste

Cut the carrots and onions into small pieces, and cook them in the butter for five minutes. Add the water and cook until the vegetables are tender. Rub through a sieve. Return to the saucepan.

In a small bowl, mix the flour smoothly with a little bit of the milk. Set aside.

Add the remainder of the milk to the main mixture and bring to a boil. When boiling, add the flour mixture. Cook for 10 minutes. Season and serve.

Source: www.freerecipe.org

(*See* "Preparation Guide" on page 249 for the barley water recipe.)

Dutch Treat

▶ This children's remedy for diarrhea comes from the Pennsylvanian Dutch. In a warmed cup of milk, add ⅛ teaspoon of cinnamon. The child should drink as much as possible.

▶ Raspberry-leaf tea is excellent for treating diarrhea. Combine ½ ounce of dried raspberry leaves with 1 cup of water and simmer in an enamel or glass saucepan for 25 minutes. Strain and let the liquid cool to room temperature.

Dose: For a baby under one year of age, give ½ teaspoon four times a day...for a child over one year, give 1 teaspoon four times a day.

> ☞ **WARNING:** Seek medical attention if the child's digestive problem is painful, persistent or accompanied by repeated vomiting.

Fever

▶ To help bring down a child's fever, put sliced, raw potatoes on the soles of his/her feet and bandage in place. Let the novelty of this remedy provide a few laughs for you and your child. Isn't laughter the best medicine?

▶ Give your child a long, soothing bath in tepid water. Then, when you tuck your child in, be sure the blanket is not tucked in too tight. Leave it loose so that heat can escape.

> ☞ **WARNING:** If a fever persists for more than three days, seek medical attention.

Foreign Substance In the Nose

Lots of kids stick things up their noses. Lydia put a yankee bean in her nostril when she was three years old, and it began to take root. Luckily, our father noticed that she was sitting still for more than 30 seconds at a time, so he realized something was wrong.

▶ Before you take a child to the doctor to perform a yankee-beanectomy, hold the unclogged nostril closed, open the child's mouth (make sure it's empty), place your mouth over it and briskly blow once. Your gust of breath may dislodge the object from the child's nostril. If it doesn't, seek medical attention.

Head Lice

It's estimated that at any given time, 10 million Americans have head lice. Lice can be transmitted from child to child via a common headrest, like a mat in the school gymnasium or from a seat at the movies. Just about the only way you can prevent a child from ever being exposed to lice is by keeping that child in a bubble.

Since the bubble is not an option, if your child has lice, there are over-the-counter shampoos that are safe and effective, unlike the prescription shampoos that can be dangerous to young children, pregnant or nursing women and anyone with a cut on his hand or arm. A friend tried several over-the-counter shampoos and found that the safest one that also worked best was RID.

For the shampoo to be effective, leave it on the child's head for at least five minutes—10 minutes is even better.

Nit-Picking

▶ After you shampoo and kill the lice, make sure you get rid of any remaining nits (eggs or young lice) by thoroughly rinsing the child's scalp with equal parts of white vinegar and water. Or first you can comb tea tree oil (available at health food stores) through the hair, and then rinse with vinegar and water.

> ⚡ **CAUTION:** Do not use your fingers to hunt down these critters. They can burrow their way under your fingernails. Yuck!

211

Eyelash Nits

▶ If the nits move down to the eyelashes, DO NOT use tea tree oil. It's much too strong and dangerous near the eyes.

Instead, before breakfast and after supper, carefully put a thin layer of petroleum jelly on the lashes. Do this for eight days. By then, the jelly will have smothered the nits and you will be able to simply remove them.

Indigestion, Colic and Gas

If your child has indigestion or gas, he/she might get very cranky from the tummy ache. If your baby has colic, he might cry for hours without stopping—and you'd try anything in the world to make him feel better. Doctors aren't sure what causes colic (allergy, indigestion or just disposition), but these remedies are worth a try.

> ☞ **WARNING:** Seek medical attention if the child's digestive problem is painful, persistent or accompanied by repeated vomiting.

Indigestion

▶ If a baby can't seem to keep his food down, you may want to try putting a teaspoon of carob powder (available at most health food stores) in the baby's milk. In some cases, it may make a big difference.

▶ Mild chamomile tea will soothe an upset stomach and calm tummy troubles. That is, if you can calm the kid long enough to drink the chamomile tea.

▶ Give your infant mild ginger tea. It's wonderful for digestion and gas problems.

▶ If your child seems to have a minor digestion problem, try 2 teaspoons of apple juice concentrate in half a glass of water before meals. Make sure the liquid mixture is room temperature, not chilled.

Colic

▶ A popular European colic calmer is fennel tea. Add ½ teaspoon of fennel seeds to 1 cup of just-boiled water and let it steep for 10 minutes. Strain the liquid tea into a baby's bottle. When it's cool enough to drink, give it to the baby. If he/she is not thrilled with the taste of fennel, try dill seeds instead.

▶ For 15 minutes, boil a cup of water with ⅓ of a bay leaf. Let it cool, remove the bay leaf, then pour the water into the baby's bottle and let the baby drink it. This old Sicilian remedy has cured many colicky bambinos.

▶ Caraway seeds are said to bring relief to colicky kids (and parents and neighbors). Add 1 tablespoon of bruised caraway seeds to 1 cup of just-boiled water. Let it steep for 10 minutes. Strain and put 2 teaspoons of the tea into a baby's bottle. When it's cool enough to drink, give it to the baby.

Go Cow-Free

▶ If you are breast-feeding your baby and he/she is colicky, try eliminating cow's milk from your diet. There's a 50/50 chance that if you no longer drink milk, the baby will no longer have colic.

Be sure, however, that you eat more calcium-rich foods, such as canned salmon, canned sardines, sunflower and sesame seeds, almonds, whole grains, green leafy vegetables, soy products (including tofu) and molasses.

▶ Milk isn't the only thing to eliminate from your diet if you are breast-feeding. You should also avoid whatever may be hard for you and/or your baby to digest, including bell (green) peppers, beans, cucumbers, eggs, chocolate, onions, leeks, garlic, eggplant, lentils, zucchini, tomatoes, sugar, coffee and alcoholic beverages. Also, go easy on the amount of fruit you eat.

Remember, it's not forever—either the diet restrictions or the colic!

▶ When baby is teething or has mild colic—or is just irritable because of indigestion or disturbed sleep—steep a chamomile tea bag in a cup of hot water. If the problem is indigestion, throw in a small piece of fresh ginger.

After steeping for about 10 minutes, take out the tea bag and the ginger. Give the baby a teaspoon of the tea every 15 minutes until he/she seems better.

Just Peachy

▶ Warm up a little of the heavy syrup from a can of peaches and give the syrup to your baby to stop nausea.

Picky Eaters

▶ Prepare a cup of chamomile tea and add $\frac{1}{16}$ teaspoon of ground ginger. An herbalist recommends giving 1 teaspoon of the warm tea a half-hour before meals to help stimulate a child's appetite.

Rashes

▶ If the rash is minor (and not on the face), gently rub the afflicted area with the red side of a piece of watermelon rind. It should stop the itching and help dry out the rash.

Diaper Rash

▶ Let the baby's bottom be exposed to the air. If weather permits, the sun (10 to 15 minutes at a time) can do wonders for clearing up diaper rash. Be sure to apply sunscreen to all of the exposed skin first.

⚡ **CAUTION:** Babies six months of age or younger should not be exposed to the sun.

Splinters

▶ To pinpoint the exact location of a wood splinter, pat some iodine on the area and the sliver of wood will absorb it and turn dark. Wait until the area is dry before trying to remove the splinter.

▶ If the child has a glass splinter, numb the area with an ice cube or some teething lotion before you start squeezing and scraping. But don't dig! If a splinter does not come out easily, see a doctor for treatment.

Teething

▶ When teething children are being fed, they often cry as if they do not want the food. But they may be crying because of the pain caused by a metal spoon. Feed the teething tot with an ivory, wood or bone spoon and make sure the edges are nice and smooth.

▶ Rub sore little gums with olive oil to help relieve the pain.

Tonsillitis

Most cases of tonsillitis are caused by infection and should be treated with antibiotics. In some cases, however, swollen tonsils may occur because of an intolerance for cow's milk. That's easy enough to test. Simply eliminate milk from the child's diet and see if he/she improves within a day or two.

If the child does not assimilate and digest cow's milk properly, there are many other wonderful sources of calcium and it is no big deal for a child not to have milk. Sunflower seeds and sesame seeds are rich in calcium. So are almonds, green leafy vegetables, canned salmon, sardines, molasses and whole grains.

There are also supplements, such as bonemeal, dolomite and calcium lactate. Check with your child's pediatrician before changing your child's diet or giving him/her supplements. ■

Healing Remedies
For Men

Healing Remedies For Men

Prostate Enlargement

It is estimated that one out of every three men over the age of 60 has some kind of prostate problem, such as inflammation (prostatitis), enlargement (benign prostatic hyperplasia) or prostate cancer.

WARNING: Consult a physician before trying any of these prostate remedies. Some are not appropriate for men who have been diagnosed with prostate cancer.

▶ To ease prostate tension, stimulate circulation and generally soothe the male organs, massage the area behind the leg in back of the ankle, about one or two inches higher than the shoe line of each foot.

WARNING: If you are suffering with pain, burning urination, testicular or scrotal swelling, have your condition evaluated by a health professional.

▶ Bee pollen is said to be effective in reducing swelling of the prostate. Pollen contains the hormone testosterone and traces of other male hormones. It seems to give the prostate a boost so that it may heal itself.

Dose: Take a total of five pollen pills daily —two in the morning, two in the afternoon and one in the evening (or take the equivalent in bee pollen granules).

CAUTION: People who are allergic to bee stings or honey should consult a doctor before taking bee pollen.

For more information on bee pollen, *see* the "Six Sensational Superfoods" section on page 258.

▶ Drink 2 to 4 ounces of coconut milk every day to strengthen the prostate gland. The milk is pure and uncontaminated and loaded with minerals. It's also a soothing digestive aid. (*See* "Preparation Guide" on page 249 for instructions on milking a coconut.)

Circle Massage

▶ To relieve prostate pain, in a circular motion, massage the area above the heel and just below the inner ankle of each foot and/or the inside of the wrists, above the palm of each hand. Keep massaging until the pain and soreness disappear.

▶ Prepare parsley tea by steeping a handful of fresh parsley in a cup of hot water for 10 minutes. Drink a few cups of the parsley tea throughout the day.

Sitz on This

▶ Take hot sitz baths—two a day. Sit in six inches of comfortably hot water for about 15 minutes each time. Within a week, inflammation and swelling should be greatly reduced.

▶ Corn silk tea has been a popular folk remedy for prostate problems. Steep a handful of the silky strings that grow around ears of corn in a cup of hot water for 10 minutes. Drink a few cups throughout the day.

If it's not fresh corn season, buy corn silk extract from a health food store, then add 10 to 15 drops in 1 cup of water and drink.

▶ For an enlarged prostate, grate part of a yellow onion and squeeze it through cheesecloth —enough for 1 tablespoon of onion juice. Take 1 tablespoon of onion juice twice a day.

Slip-Sliding Away

▶ In extremely painful cases, get slippery-elm capsules at a health food or vitamin store. Take the capsules apart—enough for ½ teaspoon of the slippery-elm powder—and mix the powder with 6 ounces of (preferably distilled) water. Drink the mixture before breakfast and a couple of hours after dinner.

▶ Asparagine, a health-giving alkaloid found in fresh asparagus, is said to be a healing element for prostate conditions. Use a juicer and juice equal amounts of fresh asparagus, carrots and cucumber—enough for an 8-ounce glass of juice. Drink a glass of the juice daily.

> ✎ **NOTE:** Organic vegetables are always preferable. If they're not available, wash the asparagus thoroughly, scrub the carrots and peel the cucumber.

▶ A teaspoon of unrefined sesame oil taken every day for one month has been known to reduce an enlarged prostate back to normal.

▶ Lecithin (available at health food stores) comes highly recommended from many sources. Take one lecithin capsule—1,200 mg each—three times a day, after each meal, or 1 to 2 tablespoons of lecithin granules daily.

▶ If your doctor hasn't already told you, eliminating all coffee and alcoholic beverages from your diet can help prostate problems.

▶ And now for a self-help prostate massage— lie down on the floor on your back. Put the sole of one foot against the sole of the other foot so that you're at your bowlegged best. While keeping the soles of your feet together, extend your legs as far as possible and then bring them in as close as possible to your chest. Do this "extend and bring in" exercise 10 times in the morning and 10 times at night.

▶ Ray C. Wunderlich, Jr., MD, PhD, director of the Wunderlich Center for Nutritional Medicine in St. Petersburg, Florida, recommends that you empty the gland by having ejaculations as frequently as you can tolerate. It may improve your urinary stream.

Impotence (Erectile Dysfunction)

Most men at some time during their lives experience the dreaded inability to have an erection. That's the bad news. The good news is that it is usually a temporary condition commonly caused by prescription drugs or by some kind of psychological trauma and emotional tension. While the psyche is being treated with professional help, physical steps can be taken to improve one's sexual energy.

You might want to read through these health hints whether or not anything is bothering you. Chances are you'll find some information you can use to help you maintain your health and sexual potency.

> **WARNING:** Men who are experiencing erectile dysfunction should see a doctor for a complete physical evaluation.

Time for Love

▶ According to the teachings of the late Yogi Bhajan, PhD, counselor and yoga master, a man should never have sexual intercourse within 2½ hours after eating a meal, the length of time it takes to digest food.

The sex act is strenuous and requires your mind, your entire nervous system and all of the muscles needed for the digestion process. Yogi Bhajan felt that lovemaking right after eating could ruin your stomach and, if done often, could eventually result in premature ejaculation.

While the Yogi believed that four hours between eating and sex is adequate, he recommended that, for optimal sexual function, a man should have nothing but liquids and juices 24 hours before making love.

Giddyup with Garlic

▶ Garlic is said to stimulate sexual desire and the production of semen. Eat raw garlic in salads, use it in cooking and take two garlic pills

a day. Then find a companion who doesn't mind the smell of garlic.

By the way, we wonder if it is a coincidence that the French and Italians have a diet that includes lots of garlic and are said to be incredible lovers?

▶ Mint is supposed to restore sexual desire. Eat mint leaves and drink mint tea. It's also good for combating garlic breath.

"Stamp Out" Impotence—Is It Organic Or Psychological?

Most men have about five erections while they're asleep. No matter how uptight they might be—and no matter what trouble they might be having with erections while they're awake—men who suffer from psychological impotency will have firm erections every night in their sleep.

To test for these erections, get an old-fashioned roll of need-to-be-licked postage stamps (any denomination) and gently wrap it once around the shaft of the penis. Tear off the excess stamps, then tape the two ends (the first and the last stamps) around the penis, firmly but not too tight. Sweet dreams!

When a nighttime erection occurs, the increased diameter of the penis should break the stamps along the line of one of the perforations. If impotency is organically caused, you will not have nightly erections and the stamps will be intact in the morning.

The "stamp act" should be repeated every night for two to three weeks. If, each morning, the stamps are broken along a perforation, chances are that you have a normal capability for erections, and impotency is psychologically caused. Sometimes just knowing that everything is working well physiologically will give

■ Recipe ■

40-Clove Garlic Chicken

> 8 pieces of chicken, skinned
> 2 Tbsp extra-virgin olive oil
> 1 cup onion, minced
> 2 cups celery, diced
> 2 Tbsp fresh parsley, minced
> 1 tsp dried tarragon
> ½ cup dry white vermouth
> ½ tsp salt
> ½ tsp ground pepper
> ½ tsp nutmeg
> 40 cloves garlic, separated but not
>   peeled (about 3 bulbs)

Preheat the oven to 325° F. Brush chicken pieces on all sides with olive oil. In a Dutch oven or large casserole dish, combine the onion, celery, parsley and tarragon. Arrange the chicken pieces on top and pour the vermouth over the chicken. Sprinkle with salt, pepper and nutmeg. Distribute the unpeeled garlic cloves throughout the casserole, tucking them under and around the chicken.

Tightly cover the casserole or pan with aluminum foil, and bake for 1½ hours. When done, serve the chicken over rice, barley or millet, along with the garlic.

Source: Garlic: Nature's Super Healer

nervous system. It's been known to be an effective remedy for "performance anxiety."

Add a teaspoon of damiana leaves (available at health food stores) to a cup of just-boiled water. Let it steep for 10 minutes. Strain and drink before breakfast, on a daily basis.

▶ El Indio Amazonico, a Bogotá *botánico* (medicine man), advises his impotent patients to not even try to have sex for 30 days. During that time, he suggests they eat goat meat every day, in addition to bulls' testicles ("mountain oysters"). He also recommends drinking tea made of cinnamon sticks and cups of cocoa.

When the abstention period is over, El Indio instructs his patients to rub a small amount of petroleum jelly mixed with a bit of lemon juice around—but not on—the scrotum. Then the patients are on their own.

Lower Your Voice to Love Better

▶ It is said that the higher a man's voice, the lower his masculine vitality. The theory is based on the fact that the vortex at the base of the neck and the vortex in the sex center are directly connected and affected by each other. So lower your voice and you'll increase the speed of vibration in these vortexes, which, in turn, may increase your sexual energy.

you the confidence and assurance you need to help you "rise to the occasion."

The Fear of Failure

▶ In the Mexican pharmacopoeia, *damiana* is classified as an aphrodisiac and a tonic for the

Stay Out of Hot Water

▶ Fast cold showers do not cool or dampen one's sexual desire. *Au contraire!* Short applications of cold water, particularly on the nape of the neck, can be sexually stimulating.

■ Recipe ■

Sexual-Stamina Eggplant

Hindi records, circa 10th century, tell about men who went to view the famous Temple of Khajuraho in India to study its pornographic stone carvings, depicting every known position of love. In order to have the stamina to test the positions, they were fed this dish.

1 eggplant

Butter

Chives, minced

Curry sauce

Slice the eggplant and cover with butter and minced chives on both sides. Brown the slices and cover with a spicy curry sauce.

The recipe (unspecific as it is) has been passed down from generation to generation—along with its reputation for making old men young again.

Stronger Erection

▶ Most men get a stronger erection and feel more of a sensation when their bladder is full. However, some sexual positions may be uncomfortable if the bladder is very full.

WARNING: Men with prostate problems should not practice this full-bladder erection technique.

Premature Ejaculation

▶ According to sex therapists, premature ejaculation seems to be one of the easiest conditions to cure, simply by behavior modification.

The late William H. Masters, MD, and Virginia E. Johnson—the pioneering sex therapists and researchers—developed this conditioning treatment. First, enlist the assistance of your mate. Lie on your back with your partner straddling your legs. Have her stimulate your penis until you feel that orgasm is just around the corner. At that second, give her a prearranged signal.

In response to the signal, she should stop stimulating and start squeezing the penis just below the tip. She should squeeze it firmly enough to cause you to lose your erection, but not to cause you pain. When the feeling that you are about to ejaculate leaves you, have her stimulate you again.

As before, signal her when orgasm is imminent and, once again, she should stop stimulating and start squeezing the penis. The erection should go down and you will not ejaculate.

Keep this up (and down) for a while and soon you will be able to control ejaculation.

The next step is intercourse. As soon as you feel like you are about to climax, signal your partner, withdraw from her and have her squeeze your penis until you lose the erection.

Remember—practice makes perfect! Masters and Johnson reported that in just two weeks of using this behavior modification program, 98% of men with premature ejaculation were cured.

The Heart and the Heat of Passion

It's a myth that sex is dangerous to the heart, according to Richard A. Stein, MD, director of the Urban Community Cardiology Program at New York University Medical Center, New York City and spokesperson for the American Heart Association (*www.americanheart.org*).

The stress to the heart is really very mild. The average heart rate increases up to 115 to 120 beats per minute during intercourse—a muscle workload equal to walking up two flights of stairs.

☞ **WARNING:** If a man is cheating on his mate, the heart rate and risk tend to rise with the excitement and danger of being caught.

Healing Remedies
For Women

Healing Remedies
For Women

We've come a long way, baby!" That old sentiment has never been more appropriate than it is now.

Today, we talk openly about menstruation, pregnancy and menopause, not as sicknesses, but as natural stages of life. We also recognize and deal with premenstrual tension and menopausal irregularities.

We are finally learning to question the male-dominated medical profession after hearing countless stories about hysterectomies, radical mastectomies and other surgeries that are sometimes performed—whether or not a woman needs the procedure.

Knowledge is power. Daytime talk shows, bookstores, local libraries and the Internet are filled with women's health information. Take advantage of these sources so that you can take responsibility for your own body and good health by intelligently choosing the most appropriate medical care and caregivers.

Meanwhile, here are several natural remedies that are time-tested, whispered down from generation to generation...

▶ As a general remedy, gently but firmly massage the back of your leg, around the ankle. Massaging that area can relax tension, stimulate circulation and soothe the female organs.

Bladder Control

▶ The Kegel (or pubococcygeus) exercises can help you gain control over your bladder, strengthen your abdominal muscles and tighten muscles that can enhance sexual activity.

Each time you urinate, start and stop as many times as possible. While squeezing the muscle that stops the flow of urine, pull in on the muscles of the abdomen. You can also do this exercise when not urinating. Sit at your desk, in your car, at the movies—anyplace—and flex...release...flex...release.

Cystitis

This chronic pain disorder can make life complicated, with frequent trips to the bathroom and constant discomfort in the pelvic region. Some of these remedies may provide relief.

▶ Pour a small box of baking soda into a bath of warm water and soak in it for at least a half-hour. Afterward, rinse under the shower.

▶ Even some physicians suggest cranberry juice for cystitis. You can get juice that's sugarless with no added preservatives at most supermarkets, or you can buy cranberry concentrate (which needs to be diluted) at health food stores, or use cranberry capsules and follow the dosage on the label.

Juice dose: Drink one 8-ounce glass of juice in the morning, before breakfast, and one glass in the late afternoon. Make sure it's at room temperature, not chilled.

▶ Take two garlic capsules a day and, if you don't mind smelling like a salami, drink garlic tea throughout the day. Mash a couple of garlic cloves into hot water and let them steep for five minutes. You can also make garlic tea with 1 teaspoon of garlic powder in hot water.

✎ **NOTE:** Persistent cystitis may require antibiotics prescribed by a doctor. If that is the case, be sure to eat yogurt that contains live or active cultures, during and after taking the antibiotics.

Silky Solution

▶ According to Native Americans, corn silk (the silky strands beneath the husk of corn) can be a cure-all for urinary problems. The most desirable corn silk is from young corns, gathered before the silk turns brown. Take a handful of corn silk and steep it in 3 cups of boiled water for five minutes. Strain and drink the 3 cups throughout the day.

Corn silk should be stored in a glass jar, not refrigerated. If you can't get corn silk, use corn silk extract, available at health food stores.

Add 10 to 15 drops of the extract to a cup of hot water. Dried corn silk is also available.

Cystitis Prevention

▶ Women who frequently get cystitis should empty their bladders, if passion allows, *before* intercourse. It's also possible to lessen the number of attacks or stop them forever by urinating immediately *after* the act of intercourse. Forgo receiving oral sex.

▶ We've heard folk remedies requiring the cystitis sufferer to take baths. Recently, we were told by a research scientist that baths may cause the recurrence of the condition. If you are a bath-taker and have recurring cystitis, refrain from taking a bath for at least a month, and shower instead. You just may find you aren't troubled with cystitis anymore.

Lack of Desire

A lack of interest in sex (sometimes diagnosed as sexual arousal disorder or sexual dysfunction) often stems from poor communication between a woman and her partner. Sex counseling may be the only remedy that works.

Otherwise, here are some helpful natural remedies to try...

▶ As for the "Not tonight, honey" syndrome, eating a piece of halvah may awaken a woman's sexual desires. This Middle Eastern treat is made of sesame seeds and honey. The sesame seeds are high in magnesium and potassium. Honey contains aspartic acid. All three substances have been said to help women overcome lack of interest in sex.

▶ Licorice (the herb, not the candy) can do wonders for your love life. It is known to have a positive effect on one's libido. In France, it is not uncommon to see women drink licorice water, believing it may help to improve their love life.

Powdered licorice root is available at health food stores. Drink 1 teaspoon in a cup of water and get out the sexy lingerie. However, if you have high blood pressure, use the lingerie, but *NOT* the licorice.

CAUTION: Do not take licorice root if you have high blood pressure or kidney problems. It can cause renal failure.

A Bubbly Mix

▶ In ancient Greek mythology, Anaxarete was cold to her suitors. How cold was she? She was so cold that Aphrodite, the Goddess of Love, turned her into a marble statue. That's cold!

Here is an "antifreeze" that might work even for Anaxarete—boil 1 cup of finely minced chive leaves and roots (available at a greengrocer) with 2 cups of champagne. Then simmer until reduced to a thick cupful. Drink it unstrained.

It's no wonder this syrup may work. Centuries later, we learned it's rich in vitamin E (the love vitamin). Also, champagne has always been known to provoke passion. The legendary Italian lover Giacomo Casanova (1725–1798) used it continually in his erotic cookery.

Vaginitis (Vaginal Infections)

If you've got itching, swelling and burning "down there," you probably have this common infection, caused by bacteria or fungus.

▶ Wear cotton panties to absorb moisture, since moisture encourages the growth of fungus and bacteria. For that reason, stay away from moisture-inducing garments like pantyhose, girdles, leotards, tights, spandex, etc.

▶ Take showers instead of baths. Baths can add to your problems when the vaginal area is exposed to bathwater impurities.

▶ Do not use any chemical products, such as feminine hygiene sprays. Also, avoid tampons and colored or scented toilet tissue.

▶ Do not launder panties along with socks, stockings or other undergarments. Wash your panties separately with a mild soap or detergent, and rinse them thoroughly.

Menstruation

NOTE: None of these remedies will work if you are pregnant or have undergone a hysterectomy.

Bringing on Menstruation

▶ To help bring on and regulate menstruation, eat and drink fresh beets and beet juice. Have about 3 cups of beets and juice each day past your period-date until the flow begins.

▶ A footbath in hot water has been said to help start a late menstrual period.

▶ Add 1 tablespoon of basil to a cup of boiling water. Let it steep for five minutes. Strain and drink.

▶ In a circular motion, massage below the outer and inner ankle of each foot, as well as the outer and inner wrist of each hand. If there is tenderness when you rub those areas, you're in the right place. Keep massaging until the tenderness is gone. Chances are your problem will also soon be gone. Within a day or two, your period should start.

▶ Ginger tea can stimulate the onset of menstruation. Put four or five quarter-sized pieces of fresh ginger in a cup of boiling-hot water and let it steep for 10 minutes. Drink 3 or 4 cups of the tea throughout the day. It also helps ease menstrual cramps.

Excessive Menstrual Flow

If your menstrual flow is excessive, the following remedies have been said to help. We also suggest you have a medical checkup.

CAUTION: Hemorrhaging requires immediate medical attention! If you are not sure about the difference between hemorrhaging and excessive menstrual flow, do not take a chance—if you are bleeding profusely, call 911 and get medical attention quickly.

▶ Mix the juice of ½ lemon into a cup of warm water. Drink it down slowly an hour before breakfast and an hour before dinner.

▶ Throughout the day, sip cinnamon tea made with a piece of cinnamon stick steeped in hot water. Or put 4 drops of cinnamon bark tincture in a cup of warm water.

▶ When bleeding excessively, stay away from alcoholic beverages and hot, spicy foods—except for cayenne pepper because...

▶ Cayenne pepper is a powerful bleeding regulator. Add ⅛ of a teaspoon of cayenne pepper to a cup of warm water or your favorite herbal tea and drink it.

▶ To help control profuse menstrual flow, it's time for thyme tea. Steep 2 tablespoons of fresh thyme in 2 cups of hot water. Let it stand for 10 minutes. Strain out the thyme and drink 1 cup. Add an ice cube to the other cup of tea, then soak a washcloth in it and use it as a cold compress on the pelvic area.

▶ Drink yarrow tea—2 to 3 cups a day until the period is over. To prepare the tea, add 1 or 2 teaspoons of dried yarrow (depending on how strong you want the tea to be) to 1 cup of just-boiled water. Let it steep for 10 minutes. Strain and drink. You may not like the taste of the tea, but drink it as long as you get results.

Menstrual Cramps

▶ When it comes to menstrual cramps, how do naturalists spell relief? L-E-A-F-Y G-R-E-E-N-S. Eat lots of lettuce, cabbage and parsley before and during your period. To get the full benefit of all vegetables, eat them raw or steamed. Aside from helping reduce cramps, leafy greens are diuretics and will relieve you of some bloat.

NOTE: Be sure to thoroughly wash all raw produce to reduce the risk of food-borne illness.

Break Out the Tonic Water

▶ When your menstrual pains drive you to drink, head for the liquor cabinet and mix yourself a small gin and tonic. The quinine in the tonic will relax your muscles and believe us, the gin won't hurt either. Gin is prepared from a mash consisting of 85% corn, 12% malt and 3% rye, and is distilled in the presence of juniper berries, coriander seeds, etc. But go easy on it. You may get rid of the cramps, but you don't want to have to deal with a hangover.

✎ **NOTE:** Don't try the gin remedy if you have a problem or a past history of problems with alcohol. And if you do try this remedy, don't drive!

Menstrual Irregularities

▶ On a daily basis, thoroughly chew and then swallow 1 tablespoon of sesame seeds. Or you can grind flaxseed and sprinkle a tablespoon on your cereal, soup or salad. Both types of seed have been known to help regulate the menstrual cycle.

Premenstrual Relief

▶ Chamomile tea is a superb tension reliever and nerve relaxer. As soon as menstrual cramps start, prepare chamomile tea and sip it throughout the day.

▶ Premenstrual tension as well as menstrual cramps may be relieved by increasing calcium intake. Menopausal symptoms may also be prevented by adding calcium to the diet. On a daily basis, it is a good idea to eat at least one portion of two or three of these calcium-rich foods—leafy green vegetables (collard greens, dandelion greens, kale, mustard greens, broccoli, turnip greens, watercress, parsley, endive) as well as canned salmon, sardines and anchovies, figs and yogurt.

✎ **NOTE:** Be sure to thoroughly wash all raw produce to reduce the risk of foodborne illness.

▶ Minimize or completely eliminate caffeine and alcoholic beverages. Both increase the amount of calcium lost in the urine.

■ Recipe ■

Country Cole Slaw

½ large head green cabbage, shredded
1 cup red cabbage, shredded
2 medium carrots, shredded
1 large apple, chopped
½ cup raisins, plumped in hot water to cover
3 or 4 dates, chopped
½ cup of any chopped nuts

Dressing
½ cup soy mayonnaise
2 to 4 Tbsp lemon juice
1 Tbsp white miso
Freshly ground black pepper
1 tsp caraway seeds (optional)

Combine the cabbage, carrots, apple, raisins, dates and nuts in a large bowl and toss to distribute ingredients evenly.

Combine dressing ingredients in a small bowl, pour over the slaw and mix well. Makes about 4 to 6 servings.

Source: www.vegparadise.com

☞ **WARNING:** Check with a health professional before taking a calcium supplement. These supplements have been known to cause kidney stones in some people.

Peppermint Power

▶ Peppermint tea is soothing. It also helps digestion and rids you of that bloated feeling. Drink a cup of peppermint tea *after* (not during) your meal.

▶ For premenstrual relief for everything from the blues to breast tenderness, take two garlic supplements daily.

Pregnancy

Be sure to consult your obstetrician or midwife before trying any natural remedies or supplements.

During and After

Morning sickness: If you are troubled by morning sickness, check with your obstetrician about supplementing with 50 mg of vitamin B_6 and 50 mg of vitamin B_1 daily. Since garlic greatly increases the body's absorption of B_1, make an effort to eat garlic raw in salads and to cook with it.

CAUTION: Do not eat raw garlic or take garlic supplements if you have a bleeding disorder or ulcers, or are taking anticoagulants.

▶ A doctor at Brigham Young University in Provo, Utah, recommends taking 2 or 3 capsules of powdered ginger first thing in the morning to avoid morning sickness.

▶ Mix ⅓ cup of lime juice and ⅛ teaspoon of cinnamon in ½ cup of warm water. (Ugh—it sounds like it could bring on morning sickness!) Drink it as soon as you awaken. It's known to be quite effective.

Constipation during pregnancy: Keep a chair, stool or carton in the bathroom so that you can rest your feet on it when you're sitting on the toilet. Once your feet are on the same level as the seat, lean back and relax. To avoid hemorrhoids and varicose veins, do not strain and do not hold your breath and squeeze.

Increase milk production after pregnancy: Bring to a boil 1 teaspoon of caraway seeds in 8 ounces of water. Then simmer for five minutes. Let the tea cool and drink. Several cups of caraway seed tea each day may increase mother's milk supply.

▶ Brewer's yeast (available at health food stores) may also help to replenish milk.

Labor and Delivery

▶ Many sources agree on raspberry tea for the mother-to-be. What our sources don't agree on is the best time to start drinking the tea. Some say right after conception…others say three months before delivery…and still others say six weeks before your due date.

The consensus is that pregnant women should drink 2 to 3 cups of raspberry tea every day, starting at least six weeks before their due date. Ask your obstetrician or midwife about it.

To make the tea, add 1 teaspoon of dried raspberry leaves to 1 cup of just-boiled water. Let it steep for five minutes, strain and drink.

Breast-Feeding

▶ Add lentil soup to your diet. Lentils are very rich in calcium and other nutrients necessary for nursing mothers (*see* recipe on page 231).

▶ To stimulate milk secretion, drink a mixture of fennel seeds and barley water. Crush 2 tablespoons of fennel seeds and simmer them in a quart of barley water (*see* "Preparation Guide" on page 249) for 20 minutes. Let it cool and drink it throughout the day.

▶ Peppermint tea is said to increase the supply of mother's milk and it's also known to relieve nervous tension and improve digestion. Drink 2 to 3 cups a day.

Cracked and/or Sore Nipples

▶ When Las Vegas–based herbalist Angela Harris (*www.angelaharris.com*) was nursing each of her eight children, between nursings, she would moisten a black tea bag (usually Lipton's Orange Pekoe) and apply it to her cracked or sore nipple. It relieved the pain and helped heal the cracking.

Menopause

If you are getting hot flashes, it could mean one of two things—either the paparazzi are following you, or you're going through menopause. We have no remedy for the paparazzi, but we can provide recommendations that may relieve some of the menopausal chaos.

▶ A Viennese gynecologist has reported positive results among his female patients treated with bee pollen. Bee pollen contains a combination of male and female hormones. It has been known to help some women do away with or minimize hot flashes.

■ Recipe ■

Lentil Vegetable Soup

If you prefer thick soups, reduce the lentil cooking water to 6 cups and the vegetable cooking water to 1½ cups.

1 cup dried lentils
1 bay leaf
1 small onion, chopped
7 cups water
2 whole cloves
1 stick cinnamon
2 pinches fennel seeds
3 pods cardamom seeds, cracked
1 small onion, chopped
2 medium carrots, sliced
2 stalks celery, diced
1 large zucchini, cut into bite-sized
    pieces
1 yellow crookneck squash, cut into
    bite-sized pieces
1 small turnip, diced
2 cups water
Juice of one lemon
Salt and pepper to taste

Combine lentils, bay leaf, onion and 7 cups water in a large stock pot.

In a piece of cheesecloth, tie together the cloves, cinnamon stick, fennel seeds, and cardamom seeds and add to stockpot.

Bring to a boil, uncovered. Turn heat down to medium and simmer 45 minutes.

Combine onion, carrots, celery, squashes, turnip and water in a large wok or skillet, and cook over high heat just until tender, stirring frequently, about 6 to 8 minutes.

Add vegetables to cooked lentils and stir to distribute evenly.

Season to taste with lemon juice, salt and pepper. Makes 6 servings.

Dose: Take 3 bee pollen pills (500 mg) a day, or the granule equivalent.

For more information about bee pollen, *see* page 258 of the "Six Sensational Super-foods" section.

CAUTION: People who are allergic to bee stings or honey should consult a doctor before taking bee pollen.

▶ The estrogenic substances in black cohosh may relieve menopause symptoms, such as hot flashes and vaginal dryness. You'll find the herb in tincture form at health food stores. Follow the recommended dosage on the label.

Rummy Remedy

▶ If you have excessive menstrual flow during menopause, mix 1 ounce of grated nutmeg in 1 pint of Jamaican rum.

Dose: Take 1 teaspoon three times a day for the duration of your period.

WARNING: Do not take this remedy before driving or operating heavy machinery.

▶ Eat a cucumber every day. Cukes are said to contain beneficial hormones.

▶ Step into a tub that has six inches of cold water in it. Carefully walk back and forth for about three minutes. (Be sure to have nonslip stick-ons on the floor of the tub.)

Step out, dry your feet thoroughly and put on a pair of walking shoes (socks are optional). Then take a walk—even if it's just around your room—for another three minutes.

▶ Naturalists call pure licorice and sarsaparilla "hormone foods." These herbs are available at health food stores. Use each of them as teas and drink them often (*see* "Preparation Guide" on page 250).

WARNING: If you're on medication, do not take any herbs or supplements until you check with your health professional.

Remedies for
Natural Beauty

Remedies for Natural Beauty

SKIN CARE

Mirror, mirror on the wall...who's the fairest one of all?" Even Snow White had to take care of her complexion! Most people have skin problems at one time or another (*see* "Acne" starting on page 153), but one of the best ways to ensure you put your "best face" forward every day is to cleanse it properly, according to your skin type. Here are some good general cleansing recommendations.

Basic Skin Care

▶ Always use an upward and outward motion when doing anything to your face—whether you're washing it, doing a facial, applying makeup or removing makeup.

▶ When you wash your face, use tepid water. Either very hot or very cold water could break the small capillaries—those little red squiggly veins—in your face.

What's Your Type?

First, ask yourself, "What kind of skin do I have—dry, oily, combination or normal?" Once you know what kind of skin you have, you can learn how to take care of it. If you're not sure, Heloise (the helpful hints lady) developed a test you can take.

"Wash your face with [plain, non-gel] shaving cream. Rinse. Wait about three hours so that your skin can revert to its regular self. Then take cigarette papers or any other thin tissue paper and press pieces of it on your face.

"If it sticks, leaving an oily spot that's visible when you hold it up to the light, you've got oily skin. If it doesn't stick, your skin is dry. If it sticks, but doesn't leave oily spots, you've got normal skin. If the paper sticks on some areas, leaving oily spots, and doesn't stick on other areas, you have combination skin."

▶ It's important to wash your face twice a day. Washing removes dead skin, and keeps pores clean and skin texture good.

The morning cleansing is necessary because of metabolic activity during the night.

The night washup is necessary because of all the dirt that piles up during the day. Wash with a mild soap and a washcloth or cosmetic sponge, upward and outward. *Now, onward…*

> ✎ **NOTE:** We have included masks to treat oily, dry, normal and combination skin. But no matter what type of skin, the best time to apply a mask is before going to sleep, when you don't have to wear makeup for at least six to eight hours.
>
> Also, try to apply the mask after you've taken a bath or shower, or after you've gently steamed your face, so that the pores are open.

Firming Facial

▶ Chocolate is rich in copper, an essential nutrient for the skin-firming connective tissues.

Mix 1 heaping tablespoon of unsweetened cocoa powder with enough heavy cream to form a paste. Apply it to your clean, dry skin and leave it there for 15 minutes. Then lick it off…*just kidding*! Rinse it off with a washcloth and lukewarm water, then pat dry.

Make Your Own Beauty Mask

▶ In a blender, purée 1 cup of fresh pineapple and ½ cup of fresh (slightly green) papaya. Put the puréed fruit in a bowl and mix in 2 tablespoons of honey. Apply it to your just-washed face and neck, but NOT on the delicate area around your eyes. Leave it on for five minutes—not more—and rinse with cool water.

This once-a-week alpha hydroxy facial can boost the production of collagen (making your face firmer), slough off dead skin cells, even out skin tone and make tiny lines less noticeable. The enzymes in pineapple (brome-lain) and papaya (papain) do most of the work as the honey hydrates the skin.

Skin-Awakener Formula

One source described this treatment as "the cleansing acid that cuts through residue film and clears the way for a healthful complexion." Another source said, "This treatment will restore the acid covering your skin needs for protection." And still another said, "This formula is, by far, the simplest natural healer for tired skin. It gives you the glow of fresh-faced youth." With endorsements like that, what are you waiting for?

▶ Mix 1 tablespoon of apple cider vinegar with 1 tablespoon of just-boiled water. As soon as the liquid is cool enough, apply it to the face with cotton balls. Do NOT get it near the eyes.

Lydia tried this treatment. It made her skin feel smooth and tight. Her eyes were a little teary from the strong fumes of the diluted vinegar and, for about 10 minutes, she smelled like coleslaw.

Use this treatment to freshen you skin at least every other day—or whenever you have a craving for coleslaw.

▶ After a shower or bath, some people spray their bodies with a plastic plant mister filled with equal amounts of apple cider vinegar and water. It not only restores the acid mantle (pH balance) in the skin, it removes soap residue and hard water deposits, too.

Skin Toner

▶ In a blender, purée 4 medium-sized, well-washed strawberries, 2 dollops of plain yogurt and 1 tablespoon of fresh lemon juice.

Distribute the strawberry purée all over your face and neck, avoiding the delicate eye area. Leave it on for about 20 minutes, then rinse with tepid water.

Doing this skin-toning treatment twice a week is said to help prevent little age lines.

Caring for Oily Skin

The Basics

▶ Many folk healers suggest drinking a strong cup of yarrow tea, which is an astringent, to cut down on skin oiliness. Use 2 teaspoons of dried yarrow (available at health food stores) in a cup of just-boiled water. Let it steep for 10 minutes. Strain and drink every day.

▶ In a blender, blend ¼ of a small eggplant (skin and all) with 1 cup of plain yogurt. Smear the mush on your face and neck (but not on the delicate skin around your eyes) and leave it there for 20 minutes. Rinse with tepid water.

Finish this treatment with a toner—a nonalcoholic astringent like the yarrow tea (above) is ideal. Also, fill a plastic plant mister with a cup of the tea (chamomile is an astringent and can be used) and spray your face with it. Keep the mister in the refrigerator so you can use it to set your makeup or to freshen up.

Makeup Remover

▶ Cleansers seem to be a problem for oily skin because of the high alcohol content of most makeup-removing astringents. They're usually too harsh to be used on a regular basis.

Instead, use 1 teaspoon of powdered milk with enough warm water to give it a milky consistency. With cotton balls, apply the liquid to your face and neck (avoiding the delicate eye area), gently rubbing it on. Once you have

covered your entire face and neck, remove the makeup and dirt with a tissue…again, gently. Pat dry.

Mask

▶ Kitty litter has great absorbency and can be used for lots of things, including the *purr-fect* facial for oily skin. Be sure to get a natural litter that's 100% clay, no chemicals added.

Mash 2 tablespoons of the litter with enough water—about an ounce—to make a paste. Apply it to your just-washed face, but NOT to the delicate area around your eyes. Leave it on for about 15 minutes. Then rinse with tepid water.

Caring for Dry Skin

A leading cause of dry skin is towels. (Just checking to see if you're paying attention!)

The Basics

▶ Avocado is highly recommended for dry skin. Take the inside of an avocado skin and massage your just-washed face and neck with it.

Or, mix equal amounts of avocado (about ¼ cup) with sour cream. Gently rub it on the face and neck (but not on the delicate skin around the eyes) and leave it there for at least 15 minutes. Rinse with tepid water.

When you can no longer see a trace of the mixture, use your fingertips to work the invisible oil into your skin with an upward and outward sweep…again, gently.

Makeup Remover

▶ Instead of using soap and water, clean your face with whole milk. Warm 2 to 3 tablespoons of milk, add ½ teaspoon of castor oil and shake well. Dunk a cotton ball (not a tissue) into the mixture and start cleaning, using upward and outward strokes. Avoid the delicate eye area.

This combination of milk and oil is said to take off more makeup and city dirt than the most expensive professional cleansing products ever could. And it does it naturally, not chemically.

Complete the treatment by sealing in moisture with a thin layer of castor oil applied to the face.

Mask

▶ Scrub 2 to 3 medium-sized carrots, then cut each carrot into 1-inch pieces and put them in a pot with a few cups of water. Cook the carrots until they are slightly softened. Transfer the carrots to a blender or food processor and purée.

Massage the carrot purée all over your just-washed face and neck, avoiding the delicate eye area. Keep it there for about 20 minutes, then rinse with tepid water.

This mask is popular in European spas, where regular use is said to improve elasticity as well as smooth out wrinkles.

Caring for Combination Skin

Using different treatments for the dry and oily parts of your face can become a real nuisance. Instead, you may want to try these treatments, which are good for all types of skin.

The Basics

▶ This papaya facial helps remove dead skin cells and allows the new skin to breathe freely. Papaya accomplishes naturally what most commercial products do chemically.

In a blender, purée a ripe, peeled papaya. Spread the fruit on your face and neck and keep it there for 20 minutes. Rinse off with tepid water.

It would be most beneficial to have this facial once or twice a month, but since it's not always possible to get a ripe papaya, do it whenever you can.

Makeup Remover

▶ No makeup remover? Use whipped sweet butter or vegetable shortening instead. (Doesn't this sound like it's from a *Cosmopolitan* magazine list of "sleepover" suggestions?)

Whatever makeup remover you use, keep it on your eyelids and face for at least 30 seconds so that it has a chance to sink in and make it easier to gently rub off the makeup.

Mask

▶ This mask is for everyone, year-round. It's a honey of a honey mask. Folk practitioners claim that it helps rid the face of blemishes and blackheads…leaves a person feeling refreshed and invigorated…restores weather-beaten skin …slows down the skin's aging process by helping it maintain a normal proportion of moisture. The longer we go on, the more the skin is aging!

Here's how to apply the mask—start with a clean face and neck and pull your hair out of the way. Dip your fingertips in raw, unheated honey and gently spread it on your face and neck in an upward and outward motion. Make sure to avoid the eye area. Leave this on for 20 minutes, then rinse with tepid water. It's sweet and simple…and sticky.

Moisturizer

▶ Wet your clean face and rub on a glob of petroleum jelly. Keep adding water as you thin out the layer of jelly all over your face and neck until it's no longer greasy.

This inexpensive treatment is used at expensive spas because it's very effective.

Exfoliation Scrub

▶ Mix 1 teaspoon of sugar with a few drops of champagne—enough to form a paste. In circular motions, apply the mixture to your face and neck, then rinse it off with lukewarm water and pat dry.

The enzymes that are in champagne's tartaric acid, along with the abrasive quality of the sugar, should do a very thorough job of exfoliating your skin.

Make Your Own Body Scrub

▶ Create a paste by mixing together ¼ cup of freshly squeezed lemon juice and ¼ cup extra-virgin olive oil along with ½ cup of kosher (coarse) salt.

Massage the paste onto the parts of your body that need exfoliating. Then rinse off the mixture and feel how smooth it leaves your skin.

WARNING: Never use this scrub on your face. It's too strong and coarse for delicate facial skin.

GROOMING

Enrich Your Night Cream

▶ According to the legendary cosmetics expert Adrien Arpel, "To transform a skimpy night cream into an enriched vitamin skin treat, add ⅛ teaspoon of liquid vitamin C and the contents of a 100 IU vitamin E capsule to 4 ounces of ordinary night cream."

Magical Face Relaxer

Before applying your makeup for an evening out, take time to get the day's tension out of your face. *Here's how…*

▶ Lie down with your feet up. Take the cork from a wine bottle and put it between your teeth. Don't bite down on it—encircle it with your lips. Stay that way for 10 minutes—breathe easily and think lovely thoughts.

After the 10 minutes have flown by, your face should be smoother and more receptive to makeup. And you should be refreshed and more receptive to having a fun evening.

Double-Chin Prevention

▶ A simple yoga exercise called "the lion" firms the throat muscles under the chin.

The entire exercise consists of sticking your tongue out and down as far as it will go. Do this dozens of times throughout the day—in your car, watching TV, while doing the dishes or waiting for your computer to start up.

It's possible you'll see an improvement in your chin line within a few days.

Toweling Off

▶ Towels made of 100% cotton will dry you faster and more thoroughly than towels made of blended fibers.

Chapped Lips

▶ Apply a thin film of glycerin (available at drugstores) to soften and protect your lips.

Pleasing Tweezing

▶ If you can't stand the pain of tweezing your eyebrows, numb the area first by putting an ice cube on for a few seconds.

▶ If you don't need to go so far as to numb the area, but just want to have an easy time of it, tweeze right after a warm shower. The hairs come out more willingly then.

FINGERNAIL HOW-TO

Matchbook Method

▶ When you need an emery board and can't find one, look for a matchbook. File down a jagged-edged fingernail with the rough, striking part of the matchbook.

Polish Primer

▶ Wipe your unpolished fingernails with white vinegar to clean and prime the surfaces for nail polish. Once the vinegar dries, this treatment will help the polish stay on longer.

Manicure Protection

▶ Use a toothbrush and toothpaste to clean office-type stains (carbon, ink, etc.) off your fingertips without damaging your manicure.

GENERAL TIPS

Paint Remover for Skin

▶ If you've been painting walls or canvas, a little vegetable oil should clean off your paint-bespeckled face and arms—without torturing your skin.

Pain-Free Bandage Remover

▶ When you're wearing a bandage that's not "ouchless," saturate it with vegetable oil so that you can remove it painlessly.

Mirror, Mirror in the Bathroom

▶ Clean the bathroom mirror with plain, non-gel shaving cream, which will prevent it from fogging up for several weeks.

▶ After a shower or bath, use a hair dryer to unfog the steamed-up mirror.

Perfume Pick-Me-Up

▶ Douse a small natural sponge with your favorite perfume and put it in a plastic sandwich bag in your purse.

During or after a hard day at the office, moisten the sponge with some cold water and dab it behind your ears and knees, in your elbows and on your wrists to give you a refreshed feeling. ■

Remedies in a Class
By Themselves

Remedies in a Class By Themselves

Kiss of Life

There is a research center in Germany where scientists are studying the act of kissing. One of their findings is that the morning "Good-bye, dear" kiss is the most important one of the day. This particular kiss helps start the day with a positive attitude that leads to better work performance and an easier time coping with stress.

According to the researchers, that morning send-off kiss given on a daily basis can add up to earning more money and living a longer, healthier life.

Hey, what about us single people? We don't know about you, but we're going to make a deal with our doorman.

▶ According to a doctor quoted in a Roman newspaper, "Kissing is good for your health and will make you live longer." We certainly like that idea—tell us more!

The doctor explains, "Kissing stimulates the heart, which gives more oxygen to the body's cells, keeping the cells young and vibrant." He also found that kissing produces antibodies in the human body that, in the long run, can provide protection against certain infections.

Exercise Your Lung Power

▶ This remedy requires an investment of some money and time. But if you want to increase your lung power and breath control, try taking up a musical instrument—the harmonica. It's fun! Get the "Marine Band" style, made by Hohner. It's a good beginner's harmonica, and it's inexpensive.

Hohner also publishes books that teach you to play the harmonica while you strengthen your lungs. Playing the harmonica has even been known to alleviate symptoms of emphysema. Who knows—it may start you on a whole new career. Visit *www.hohnerusa.com* for more information.

Yawn All the Way

▶ Do not stifle a yawn. Yawning restores the equilibrium between the air pressure in the middle ear and that of the outside atmosphere, giving you a feeling of relief. (And you thought you were just bored!)

Confessions...Good for the Immune System

▶ We've all heard that "confession is good for the soul." According to James W. Pennebaker, PhD, professor of psychology at the University of Texas in Austin, "When we inhibit feelings and thoughts, our breathing and heartbeat speed up, putting an extra strain on our autonomic nervous system."

By writing about the stresses in your life, you release pent-up emotions, freeing the immune system to do its real job, that of guarding the body against unwanted invaders.

After following Dr. Pennebaker's formula exactly as directed, you should feel lighter, happier and may experience better health during the next six months.

Dr. Pennebaker's Process

- ◆ Find a quiet place where you can be alone for 20 minutes.

- ◆ Write down a confession of what's bothering you. Be as specific as you can.

- ◆ Don't worry about spelling or grammar. Just write continuously for the entire 20 minutes.

- ◆ Keep going, even if it feels awkward. Letting go takes practice. If you reach a mental block, repeat your words.

- ◆ For four days in a row, write for 20 minutes a day. After four days of writing, you should be ready to throw the paper away and enjoy your newly recharged immune system.

Feel free to repeat this exercise anytime something stressful comes up. Regular release will keep your immune system strong.

Success Through Napping

▶ It is said that a nap during the day can do wonders for balancing emotions and attitudes and, in general, harmonizing one's system without interference from the conscious mind.

US presidents Harry S Truman, John F. Kennedy and Lyndon B. Johnson were well-known nappers. Other prestigious, productive people who caught some shut-eye on a daily basis include inventor Thomas A. Edison, politician and statesman Winston Churchill and, appropriately, French general and emperor Napoleon Bonaparte.

Practice Preventive Medicine: Laugh!

▶ The late writer and magazine editor Norman Cousins turned to laughter as a medicine to help overcome his doctor-diagnosed "incurable" disease (tuberculosis), for which he was incorrectly hospitalized as a child.

According to Cousins, who referred to laughter as "inner jogging," there's scientific proof that it oxygenates the blood, improves respiration, stimulates the body's immune system and helps release substances described as "the body's anesthesia and a relaxant that helps human beings to sustain pain."

Log on to any Internet search engine, enter "jokes" or "humor," and laugh it up!

Have a Good Cry

▶ Emotional tears have a higher protein content than onion-produced tears. A researcher at the St. Paul-Ramsey Medical Center (now called Regions Hospital) in St. Paul, Minnesota, accounted for that difference as nature's way of releasing chemical substances (the protein) created during an emotional or stressful situation. In turn, the release of those chemical substances lets the negative feelings flow out, allowing a sense of well-being to return.

According to Margaret T. Crepeau, PhD, professor of nursing at Marquette University in Milwaukee, Wisconsin, people who suppress tears are more vulnerable to disease. In fact, suppressing any kind of feeling seems to take its toll on one's system. Face your feelings and let 'em out!

Calcium Concern

The mineral calcium helps your body build strong bones and teeth—and to keep them strong, you need to get adequate amounts of calcium in your diet.

We should all—particularly women—eat foods rich in calcium. These include canned sardines, canned salmon, soybean products (including tofu), dark-green leafy vegetables, asparagus, blackstrap molasses, sunflower seeds, sesame seeds, walnuts, almonds, peanuts, dried beans, corn tortillas and dairy products.

The body is depleted of calcium when there is a high consumption of caffeine, colas and other soft drinks. Also, calcium absorption is compromised in people who smoke, take antacids that are high in aluminum or are on a low-sodium and/or a high-protein diet.

Give Healing Orders

A survey conducted at Johns Hopkins Hospital in Baltimore concluded that three out of four ailments stemmed from emotional factors. It makes sense. Crises in our lives cause emotional reactions which cause biochemical changes that disrupt the body's harmony, weaken immunity and upset hormone production.

We do it to ourselves—therefore, we can undo it!

▶ Relax every part of your body (follow the visualization exercise in the "Tension and Anxiety" section—it's on page 177).

Once you're completely relaxed, order your body to heal itself. Actually give your body this command out loud. Be direct, clear and positive. Picture your specific problem. (There's no right or wrong—it's all up to your own imagination.)

Once you have a clear picture of your problem, see it healing. Envision pain flying out of your pores…picture the condition breaking up and disintegrating. Say and see whatever seems appropriate for your particular case.

End this daily session by looking in the mirror and repeating a dozen times, "Wellness is mine"—and mean it!

The Ultimate Remedy

According to retired professor emeritus Sidney B. Simon of the University of Massachusetts in Amherst, "Everyone needs at least three hugs a day in order to be healthy."

And the oft-quoted St. Aelred, abbot of Rievaulx (1110–1167), said, "No medicine is more valuable, none more efficacious, none better suited to the cure of all our temporal ills than a friend."

Keeping those thoughts in mind, we figured out The Ultimate Remedy—hug three friends once a day…or hug one friend three times a day! Either way, it will make you (and your friends) feel great. ■

Preparation Guide

Preparation Guide

Barley

Hippocrates, the Greek physician and father of medicine (460–377 BC), believed that everyone should drink barley water every day to maintain good health. Barley is rich in iron and vitamin B. It is said to help prevent tooth decay and hair loss, improve the strength of fingernails and toenails, and help heal ulcers, diarrhea and bronchial spasms.

Pearl or pearled barley has been milled. During the milling process, the double outer husk is removed—along with its nutrients. A less refined version is pot or Scotch barley. Once it's gone through a less severe milling process, part of the bran layer remains, along with some of the nutrients.

Hulled barley, with only the outer, inedible hull removed, is a rich source of dietary fiber, and has more iron, trace minerals and four times the amount of thiamine (vitamin B_1) of pearled barley. It's available at some health food stores, as is Scotch barley. If you can't get either, you should be able to find pearled barley at the supermarket.

Barley Water

Boil 2 ounces of barley in 6 cups of water (distilled water, if possible) until there's about half the water—3 cups—left in the pot. Strain. If necessary, add honey and lemon to taste.

Coconut Milk

To get the milk in the easiest way possible, you need an ice pick or a screwdriver (Phillips head, if possible) and a hammer. The coconut has three little, black, eye-like bald spots on it. Place the ice pick or screwdriver in the middle of one black spot, then hammer the end of it so that it pierces the coconut.

Repeat the procedure with the other two black spots and then pour out the coconut milk. The hammer alone should then do the trick on the rest of the coconut. Watch your fingers! (Also watch your figure. Coconut meat is high in saturated fat.)

Eyewash

You'll need an eye cup (available at drugstores). Carefully pour just-boiled water over the cup to sterilize it. Then, without contaminating the rim or inside surfaces of the cup, fill it half full with whichever eyewash you've selected (*see* "Eyewashes" on pages 79–80). Lean forward, apply the cup tightly to the eye to prevent spillage, then tilt your head back. Open your eye wide and rotate your eyeball to thoroughly wash the eye. Lean forward and discard the eyewash contents. Use the same procedure with the other eye, if necessary.

✎ **NOTE:** Always remove contact lenses before doing an eyewash.

Garlic Juice

When a remedy calls for garlic juice, peel a clove or two of garlic, mince it finely onto a piece of cheesecloth, then squeeze out the juice. A garlic press will make the job even easier.

Ginger Tea

Peel or scrub a nub of fresh ginger and cut it into three to five quarter-sized pieces. In a cup or mug, pour just-boiled water over the pieces and steep for five to 10 minutes.

If you want strong ginger tea, *grate* a piece of ginger, then steep it, strain it and drink it. Television personality and chef Ainsley Harriott told us that he freezes fresh ginger, which makes it easier to grate.

Herbal Bath

Besides offering a good relaxing time, an herbal bath can be extremely healing. The volatile oils of the herbs are activated by the heat of the water, which also opens your pores, allowing for absorption of the herbs.

As you enjoy the bath, you're inhaling the herbs (aromatherapy), which pass through the nervous system to the brain, benefiting both mind and body.

Herbal Bath Directions

Simply take a handful of one or a combination of dried or fresh herbs and place them in the center of a white handkerchief. Secure the herbs in the handkerchief by tying a knot and turning it into a little knapsack. Toss the herb-filled knapsack into the tub and let the hot water run until it reaches the level you want. When the water cools enough for you to sit comfortably, do so. Enjoy the scented soak.

After your bath, open the handkerchief and spread out the herbs to dry. You can use them a couple more times.

Instead of using dried or fresh herbs, you can also use herbal essential oils. Be careful—oils will cause the tub to be slippery. Take it easy getting out of the tub, and be sure to clean the tub thoroughly after you've drained the bath.

Herbal Tea

Place a teaspoon of the herb (or the herbal tea bag) in a glass or ceramic cup and pour just-boiled water over it.

✎ **NOTE:** The average water-to-herb ratio is 6 to 8 ounces of water to 1 round teaspoon of herb. There are exceptions, so be sure to read the directions on the tea package.

According to the herbal tea company Lion Cross, never use water that has already been boiled. The first boiling releases oxygen, so the second boiling results in "flat," lifeless tea.

Cover the cup and let the tea steep according to the package directions. The general rule of thumb is to steep approximately three minutes for flowers and soft leaves… about five minutes for seeds and leaves…and about 10 minutes for hard seeds, roots and barks. (Of course, the longer the tea steeps, the stronger it will get.)

Strain the tea or remove the tea bag. If you need to sweeten it, use a bit of raw honey (never use sugar because it is said to negate the value of most herbs), and when it's cool enough, drink the tea slowly.

Onions

The onion belongs to the same plant family (*Liliaceae*) as garlic—and is almost as versatile. The ancient Egyptians looked at the onion as the symbol of the universe. It has long been regarded as a universal healing food, used to treat earaches, colds, fever, wounds, diarrhea, insomnia, warts…and the list goes on.

It is believed that a cut onion in a sickroom disinfects the air, as it absorbs the germs in that room. And half an onion will help absorb the smell of a just-painted room. With that in mind, you may not want to use a cut piece of onion that has been in the kitchen for more than a day, unless you put it in plastic wrap and refrigerate it.

Onion Juice

When a remedy calls for onion juice, grate an onion, put the gratings in a piece of cheesecloth and squeeze out the juice. A garlic press should also work.

Pomanders

To make an orange-spice pomander, you will need…

    1 thin-skinned orange
    1 box of whole cloves
    1 oz orrisroot
    1 oz cinnamon
    ½ oz nutmeg
    2 ft of ¼"–½"-wide ribbon

Tie the ribbon around the orange and knot it, leaving two long ends of ribbon. Stick the cloves all over the orange, but not through the ribbon. Mix the three herbs together in a bowl, then place the orange in the bowl. Let it stay there for four or five days, turning the orange occasionally. When it's ready, hang the orange-spice pomander in a closet.

Potatoes

Raw, peeled, boiled, grated and mashed potatoes…potato water…and potato poultices all help heal, according to American, English and Irish folk medicine. In fact, a popular 19th-century Irish saying was, "Only two things in this world are too serious to be jested on—potatoes and matrimony."

The skin or peel of the potato is richer in fiber, iron, potassium, calcium, phosphorus, zinc and vitamins C and B than the inside of the potato. Always leave the skin on when preparing potato water, but scrub it well first.

Do not use potatoes that have a green tinge. The greenish coloring is a warning that there may be a high concentration of solanine, a toxic alkaloid that can affect nerve impulses and cause vomiting, cramps and diarrhea. The same goes for potatoes that have started to sprout. They're a no-no.

Potato Water

Scrub two medium-sized potatoes (use organic, if possible) and cut them in half. Put the four halves in a pot with 4 cups of water (filtered, spring or distilled, if possible) and bring to a boil. Lower the flame a little and let the potatoes cook for 30 minutes.

When they're done, take out the potatoes (eating them is optional) and save the water. Most remedies suggest that you drink 2 cups of potato water. Refrigerate the leftover water for the next time.

✎ **NOTE:** People with eczema should avoid touching raw potatoes with their bare hands. Persistent or chronic eczema is best treated by a health professional.

Poultices

Poultices are usually made with vegetables, fruit or herbs that are either minced, chopped, grated, crushed or mashed, and sometimes cooked. These ingredients are then wrapped in clean fabric—such as cheesecloth, white cotton or unbleached muslin—and applied externally to the affected area.

A poultice is most effective when moist. When the poultice dries out, it should be changed—the cloth as well as the ingredients.

Whenever possible, use fresh fruits, vegetables or herbs. If these are unavailable, use dried herbs. To soften dried herbs, pour hot water over them. Do not let herbs steep in water that's still boiling, unless the remedy specifies to do this. For the most part, boiling herbs will diminish their healing powers.

Let's use comfrey as an example of a typical poultice. Cut a piece of cloth twice the size of the area it needs to cover. If you're using a fresh leaf, wash it with cool water, then crush it in your hand. Place the leaf on one half of the cloth and fold over the other half.

If you are using dried comfrey root and leaves, pour hot water over the herb, then place the softened herb down the length of the cloth, about two inches from the edge.

Roll the cloth around the herb so that it won't spill out, and place it on the affected body part. Gently wrap an elastic bandage or another piece of cloth around the poultice to hold it in place and to keep in the moisture.

Sauerkraut

Sauerkraut, which is fermented cabbage, has been a popular folk medicine throughout the world for centuries. The lactic acid in sauerkraut is said to encourage the growth of friendly bacteria and help destroy enemy bacteria in the large intestine (where many people believe disease begins) and in other parts of the digestive tract.

Sauerkraut is rich in vitamin B_6, which is important for brain and nervous system functions, and high in calcium—for healthy teeth and bones. In fact, in the hills of western Germany, it is reported that sauerkraut is given to children as a snack to help prevent tooth decay and heal bad skin conditions.

The sauerkraut that comes in cans has been processed, and this may destroy its valuable health-giving properties. It is for that reason you should eat fresh sauerkraut cold (straight from the refrigerator), at room temperature or after it's been warmed over a low flame. Overheating sauerkraut may destroy the lactic acid and beneficial enzymes.

You can buy raw sauerkraut in jars at the health food market or out of barrels at some ethnic stores. You can also make your own sauerkraut, which is what we recommend. *Here's how to do it...*

Ingredients and Supplies

1 large head of white cabbage (about 8 cups when shredded)

8 tsp sea salt

1 Tbsp caraway seeds or fresh or dried dill (optional)

1 large container (earthenware crock, glass bowl or stainless steel cookware)

A cover or plate that fits snugly inside the above container

A brick, a few stones or any 10-lb weight that's clean

A cloth or towel that will fit over the container

Preparation

Remove the large, loose outer leaves of the cabbage, rinse them and set aside for later. Core and finely shred the rest of the cabbage. Spread a layer of shredded cabbage (about 1 cup) on the bottom of the container. Sprinkle the layer with a teaspoon of sea salt and a few caraway seeds or dill. Repeat layering with shredded cabbage, salt and seeds, ending with a layer of salt. Place those loose outer leaves of cabbage over the top layer of salt.

Then, press the cabbage down with the plate or cover and place the 10-pound weight on top of it. Cover the entire container with a cloth or towel and set it aside in a warm place for seven to 12 days, depending on how strong you like your sauerkraut.

When it's ready, remove the weight and the plate. Throw away the leaves on top and skim off the yucky-looking mold. Transfer the sauerkraut to smaller glass jars with tight lids, and refrigerate them. The sauerkraut should keep this way for about a month. ■

Six Sensational
Superfoods

Six Sensational Superfoods

H ippocrates, the famed Greek physician who is considered to be the father of medicine, said, "Let food be your medicine." Those wise words were considered revolutionary back in 400 BC. But today, those same words are being repeated by many health professionals.

After years of study and research, the scientific community now recognizes the great value of food that can be used for the prevention and treatment of just about every ailment. (Lots of examples are listed throughout the main "Remedies" section of this book.)

Supplement companies certainly realize the healing power of food—they've been extracting and processing beneficial food substances for years. These foods have been packaged as pills, pearles, capsules, powders, teas, tinctures, creams, gels and more.

With all due respect to the esteemed Dr. Hippocrates, we would like to paraphrase his timeless words of wisdom—to make them even more appropriate for the information contained in this section—"Let food help *prevent* your need for medicine."

Decisions, Decisions

We considered several criteria for choosing the Six Sensational Superfoods. First and foremost, we decided that each one had to be extremely health-giving in many ways, readily available and—very important—affordable.

Then we narrowed down our list by selecting foods that most people eat, or at least are familiar with, but might not know how very healthful they are. That's how garlic, ginger, nuts and yogurt made our list. Four down and two to go.

We then thought of including foods that may need an introduction. In other words, if not for reading about them here, you might not have known about the big difference they can make in the way you eat and feel. That's how we decided to include flaxseed and bee pollen, which round out our Six Sensational Superfoods.

Eating these superfoods regularly can go a long way toward alleviating certain health conditions, preventing others and, in general, helping you overcome the shortcomings of your gene pool.

Expand Your Healthy Horizons

Read about our Six Sensational Superfoods and consider working them into your daily diet. So as not to overwhelm yourself, add one or two of these foods each week, replacing one or two less health-giving foods. Try to be creative. Experiment with different ways to prepare the foods, try different brands and different varieties. Approach it as a rewarding adventure. It will be.

Hearty appetite!

1. Bee Pollen

The bee is awesome. Any engineer knows that, when you consider the size and shape of this creature, there is no way it should be able to fly. Honeybees are frequent flyers. Their flights from flower to flower are responsible for cross-pollination.

In case you don't remember learning about it in school, here's a quick refresher course—every flower produces pollen, which is the male reproductive element that is transferred by wind or insects (mostly bees) to fertilize the ovule of another flower. Each tiny grain of pollen (it takes tens of millions to fill a spoon) has the power to produce the seed that can eventually become a flower, a bush or a tree. The pollen that honeybees collect is called, appropriately, bee pollen.

Quality, Color, Taste and What-for

"The honeybee instinctively collects only the freshest and most potent pollen from what's available," says James Hagemeyer, a beekeeper who works with Health from the Hive in Madisonville, Tennessee. "There are numerous varieties of flowers in bloom at any given time, so the pollen collection varies with the season,

resulting in all colors of pollen (from white to black and every color in between) with differing and distinctive tastes—some sweet and some bitter. The overall taste of most pollen is slightly bitter."

Mr. Hagemeyer, or "Mr. Bee Pollen" as he is known in the beekeeping community, tells everyone who he encounters—"Although pollen is a food, not a drug, it shouldn't be eaten just because it tastes good—it should be eaten because it's good for you!"

Nature's Perfect Food

Referred to as the most complete food in nature, bee pollen has all of the necessary nutrients needed for human survival—at least 18 of the 22 amino acids…more than a dozen vitamins—it's especially rich in B-complex, A, C, D and E…almost all known minerals…trace elements…11 enzymes or co-enzymes…and 14 beneficial fatty acids. Bee pollen contains the essence of every plant the bees visit, combined with digestive enzymes from the bees.

It's 35% proteins, 55% carbohydrates, 2% fatty acids, and 3% vitamins and minerals. That leaves 5% unaccounted for. That 5%, which science has not yet been able to isolate and identify, may be what's alluded to in whispers—"the magic of the bee" that makes bee pollen so powerful. (Unfortunately, there are no recipes that use bee pollen. But we have included a few honey recipes instead.)

Pollen Power

According to Steve Schechter, ND, HHP, director of the Natural Healing Institute in Encinitas, California, more than 40 research studies document the therapeutic efficacy and safety of bee pollen. Clinical tests show that orally ingested bee pollen particles are rapidly and easily absorbed—they pass directly from the stomach into the blood stream.

Dr. Schechter's overview is that "Bee pollen rejuvenates your body, stimulates organs and glands, enhances vitality and brings about a longer life span."

CAUTION: People who have had an allergic reaction to bee stings or honey should consult their doctor before taking bee pollen.

Here are some specifics…

◆ *Bee pollen offers relief from allergies.* The pollen reduces the production of histamine, which can cause problems like hay fever. The pollen's protein can help the body build a natural defense against allergic reactions. To desensitize yourself, start taking bee pollen daily, a month or two before the start of hay fever season.

Do not confuse the pollen that the wind blows around, which is a cause of allergies, with bee pollen. The pollen collected by bees is heavier and stickier and, even though it will rarely cause allergy symptoms, it is best to begin taking it in very small amounts.

Start with just one or two granules the first day, and increase the amount daily until you reach your target dose.

◆ *If, at any time, you have an allergic reaction,* such as a rash, hives, wheezing or swollen lips, take ¼ to ½ teaspoon of baking soda in water along with an antihistamine, then seek medical attention immediately. Needless to say, discontinue taking bee pollen.

◆ *Bee pollen is used by many athletes to help increase their strength,* endurance, energy and speed. Pollen is said to help the body recover from exercise, bringing the breathing and heart rate back to normal more quickly.

◆ *Bee pollen can alleviate mental fatigue and improve alertness and concentration,* helping you remain focused for longer periods of time. It's reported that bee pollen improves the mental as well as the physical reactions of athletes.

◆ *Bee pollen has been known to promote fertility as well as sexual vitality.* Noel Johnson—a San Diego–based marathon runner who lived into his 90s—credited bee pollen as one of the reasons for writing his autobiography, *A Dud at 70…A Stud at 80!*

◆ *"The skin becomes younger-looking,* less vulnerable to wrinkles, smoother and healthier with the use of honeybee pollen," according to dermatologist Lars-Erik Essen, MD, of Halsingborg, Sweden, who pioneered the use of bee products in treating skin conditions.

◆ *Studies show that food consumption is decreased by 15% to 20%* when bee pollen is taken daily with a glass of water (about 15 to 30 minutes before meals). Bee pollen is said to help correct an imbalance in the body's metabolism that may contribute to weight gain. It is thought that the lecithin in pollen speeds up the burning of calories. It also may assist in the digestive process and the assimilation of nutrients.

■ Recipe ■

Honey Lemon Basil Chicken

½ cup honey

¼ cup lemon juice

4 boneless, skinless chicken breast
   halves

¼ cup diced basil leaves

1 tsp garlic powder

½ tsp salt

2 Tbsp lemon zest

Mix together all ingredients (except chicken) in a plastic bag. Add chicken and let marinate for at least two hours, refrigerated. Grill or bake at 350° F for 35 to 45 minutes or until juices run clear. Do not overcook. Makes 4 servings.

Source: Sue Bee Honey, a trademark of the Sioux Honey Association

◆ *Bee pollen protects against radiation's adverse effects,* and helps strengthen the immune system. In our environment, humans are exposed to radiation (radioactive toxins) and chemical pollutants, which are known to cumulatively stress our immune systems. According to Dr. Schechter's research, several nutrients in bee pollen—such as proteins, beneficial fats, vitamins B, C, D and E, as well as beta-carotene, calcium, magnesium, selenium, nucleic acids, lecithin and cysteine—have been scientifically proven to strengthen immunity, counteract the effects of radiation and chemical toxins and generate optimal health and vitality.

▶ In one research study, bee pollen significantly reduced the usual side effects of both radium and cobalt-60 radiotherapy in 25 women who had been treated for cancer. The women who took the pollen were considerably healthier, had stronger immune responses and reported feeling an improved sense of well-being. The dosage of bee pollen prescribed for these women was approximately 2 teaspoons taken three times per day.

☞ **WARNING:** This dosage should only be taken under the supervision of your health professional.

Forms and Dosage

Bee pollen is available in gelatin caps, tablets and granules. We suggest the granules. We feel that the body absorbs the granules more efficiently, and they're less processed.

We like to take 1 teaspoon with water before each meal. If we need an extra boost in energy, we take another teaspoon during the day.

▶ Dr. Schechter reports that, for preventive purposes, a common adult dosage of bee pollen granules is initially ⅛ to ½ teaspoon once per day. The dosage is gradually increased to 1 to 2 teaspoons, taken one to three times per day.

⚡ **CAUTION:** Adults suffering from allergies are best advised to start off with 1 to 3 granules daily, and then gradually increase to higher doses, usually over a period of one month or more.

▶ If you prefer to take bee pollen capsules for preventive purposes, the suggested amount is two 450 to 580 mg capsules, taken three to four times daily. A short-term, therapeutic amount of bee pollen is about three times the preventive amount and should be taken only under the supervision of your health professional.

✎ **NOTE:** Be sure to buy bee pollen that comes from the US. Foreign pollens may be fumigated and baked.

▶ Bee pollen should not be heated in any way. It's best to keep it in the refrigerator. If, for economical reasons, you buy a large quantity, you can keep what you're not using in the freezer. James Hagemeyer told us that viable bee pollen was found in 5,000-year-old Egyptian tombs. If it kept that long in tombs, it should keep at least 1,000 years in your freezer!

Bee Pollen for Animals

Have you noticed that some dogs seem to suffer from the same health challenges as humans? According to Janet Lipa, breeder of golden retrievers and owner of Golden Tails, a holistic food company for animals in Bowmanville, New York (*see* "Sources" on page 299), over-vaccinating pets, particularly purebred dogs, may be responsible for the animals' health problems. Those annual inoculations may cause a buildup of toxins in the liver, compromising the immune system and making the animal more susceptible to illness.

Bee pollen can help boost an animal's immune system and help your pet get rid of allergies. Be sure to check with your veterinarian before giving your animal bee pollen or any natural supplement.

▶ For a 1,000-pound horse, mix 1 heaping tablespoon of bee pollen into the morning feeding, and repeat with the afternoon feeding.

▪ Recipe ▪

Four-Bean Bake

1 can baked beans
1 can butter beans
1 can lima beans
1 can kidney beans
1 small onion, chopped
½ lb bacon, cooked and cut up
½ lb browned hamburger
½ cup brown sugar
1 cup honey
1 cup ketchup
2 Tbsp chili powder
1 tsp dry mustard

Mix all ingredients in large saucepan and bring to a boil. Simmer on the stovetop, about 30 minutes. The mixture can also be baked at 350° F for 1 hour in a 9" x 13" pan instead.

Source: Sue Bee Honey, a trademark of the Sioux Honey Association

▶ For other animals, use ⅛ teaspoon per 15 pounds of body weight. Mix the bee pollen in with their food in the morning, and repeat with the afternoon feeding. Allow approximately 30 to 60 days to see results.

Make a Beeline...

Your local beekeeper or health food store should sell bee pollen or have information on how you can obtain it. The "Sources" section on page 299 can also point you in the right direction, so that you can *bee all that you can bee*.

ASSOCIATIONS

American Apitherapy Society

This nonprofit association is committed to encouraging the use of bee products for healthy living and researching the various restorative benefits of bee products.

> 500 Arthur St.
> Centerport, NY 11721
> Phone: 631-470-9446
> Fax: 631-693-2528
> *www.apitherapy.org*

International Bee Research Association

Contact this non-profit organization to learn more about the vital roles bees play in our environment and in all our lives.

> 16 North Rd.
> Cardiff, Wales
> CF10 3DY United Kingdom
> Phone: +44-0-29-2037-2409
> Fax: +44-0-5601-135640
> *www.ibra.org.uk*

The Honey Association

This organization provides a multitude of information on the beneficial qualities and uses of honey. The information is enhanced with recipes, honey facts and includes beauty and health uses for this nourishing food.

> c/o Grayling Group
> 1 Bedford Ave.
> London, England
> WC1B 3AU United Kingdom
> Phone: +44-0-20-7255-1100
> Fax: +44-0-20-7255-5454
> *www.honeyassociation.com*

BOOKS

Bee Pollen, Royal Jelly, Propolis, and Honey: An Extraordinary Energy and Health Promoting Ensemble, by Rita Elkins. Woodland Publishing.

Bee Well, Bee Wise: With Bee Pollen, Propolis and Royal Jelly, by Bernard Jensen, PhD. Bernard Jensen Publishing.

Bee Pollen, by Jack Scagnetti, Lynda Lyngheim. Wilshire Book Company.

2. Flaxseed

People have been eating flaxseed for thousands of years. In the south—that is, southern Mesopotamia, circa 5,200 to 4,000 BC—records show that irrigation was used to grow flax. The Babylonians cultivated flaxseed as early as 3,000 BC and—wouldn't you know it—Hippocrates, the great Greek physician of the ancient world, used flaxseed for the relief of intestinal discomfort. He might have told his patients, "Take two tablespoons of flaxseed and call me in the morning."

Stephan Cunnane, PhD, a leading nutrition and brain-metabolism specialist at the Research Centre on Aging in Sherbrooke, Canada, said, "Flaxseed will be the nutraceutical food of the 21st century because of its multiple health benefits." *That makes sense to us, and here's why…*

What's So Great About Flax?

Flax oil, which is processed from flaxseed, contains the highest concentration of *essential* omega-3 fatty acids of any source on the planet. A deficiency of omega-3 has been positively correlated with more than 60 illnesses, including arthritis, atherosclerosis, cancer, diabetes, hypertension (high blood pressure), immune disorders, menopausal discomfort and stroke. And so, adding omega-3 to your daily diet may go a long way in helping to prevent, improve or reverse those unhealthy conditions.

■ Recipe ■

Pancake or Waffle Mix

1½ cups whole wheat flour, semolina grind

½ cup ground flaxseed

1½ cup pancake mix or all-purpose flour

¼ tsp baking powder (double if you use flour, not mix)

¼ tsp baking soda (double if you use flour, not mix)

1 Tbsp sugar

¼ tsp salt

2 Tbsp olive or canola oil

1 whole egg (or 2 egg whites)

3–4 cups (approx.) buttermilk to preferred consistency

Mix all ingredients. Pour pancakes on griddle or electric skillet at 375° F to 400° F, or cook waffles on waffle iron.

Source: Flax Institute of the United States

Flaxseed contains phytonutrients called lignans. Lignans are reported to have the following attributes—an estrogen-mimicking effect without the risks associated with estrogen therapy…powerful antioxidant capabilities…antiviral properties…antibacterial properties…and antifungal properties.

Studies suggest that lignans may help prevent many health problems, including breast and colon cancer, and can help lower cholesterol, regulate women's menstrual cycles and reduce or eliminate menopausal symptoms.

Forms and Dosage

If you're thinking that flaxseed, in some form, should be part of your daily diet, we think it's a wise decision.

To help you decide which form(s) to take, you should know…

▶ Flaxseeds have hard outer shells. You can eat them as is after you've soaked the seeds in water overnight. Or, the most popular way to eat flaxseeds is to grind them in a spice or coffee grinder. Then sprinkle a tablespoon of the ground flax on your cereal, add it to a smoothie or mix it into a portion of fat-free yogurt or fat-free cottage cheese. When baking, you can replace a few tablespoons of your regular flour with this ground-flax flour.

▶ To make sure we get our daily dose of the omega-3 oils and lignans, we find it most convenient to take flax oil. We were advised to start with 2 tablespoons a day—one in the morning and one either in the afternoon or evening. Then, after a couple of months, regulate the daily dosage to 1 tablespoon of flax oil per every 100 pounds of body weight.

Smooth Operator

▶ We also add the flax oil to a smoothie—it doesn't change the taste of the smoothie, it just keeps it from getting overly aerated, which is a good thing—or we mix flax oil into fat-free yogurt, along with a minced clove of garlic. It's delicious! We also use flax oil in a homemade salad dressing. There are lots of recipes using flax oil. (*See* the "Recommended Reading List" on page 319 for a flax oil cookbook.)

▶ When we first started looking for flax oil, we went to the refrigerated section of our local health food store and found Barlean's Flax Oil. (*See* "Natural Foods and More" listed in the "Sources" section on page 299.) It had all of the qualities we were looking for, including and especially "lignan rich." (Typically, lignans—the important phytoestrogens that may help prevent cancer—are not present in appreciable amounts in most flaxseed oils.)

Also, due to flaxseed oil's limited shelf life—it's an oil that can become rancid and should be kept refrigerated—we checked the "pressing date" and the "best before date," making sure they didn't exceed a four-month timespan.

Your Life in the Balance

For those of you who want more of the whole picture of essential fatty acids in our body, Jade Beutler, RRT, RCP, San Diego–based CEO of Lignan Research LLC, and a licensed health-care practitioner, agreed to share some information with us.

Health, life and longevity critically rely on a delicate balance of two *essential* nutrients. The imbalance of these two vital nutrients is credited as possibly the leading cause of death and disability in America today.

Both omega-3, found abundantly in flax oil, and omega-6, found in a plethora of processed oils (including corn, safflower and sunflower), have been deemed as essential nutrients by the World Health Organization, headquartered in Geneva, Switzerland. As *essential* nutrients, we must get these essential fatty acids (EFAs) directly in the foods we eat or through nutritional supplementation. The body cannot manufacture them from other nutrients.

According to Artemis P. Simopoulos, MD, president of the Center for Genetics, Nutrition and Health in Washington, DC, "Throughout human history, omega-3 and omega-6 fatty acids have been ingested in near-perfect proportion. That is to say, roughly a 50/50 concentration.

"For millions of years, the equal ingestion of these two EFAs has created a delicate check-and-balance system within the body that is in control of, literally, thousands of metabolic functions. That means everything including immune function, cellular communication, insulin sensitivity and inflammatory response to hormone and steroid production. It is impossible for optimal health to be attained with a tissue imbalance of omega-3 to omega-6 fatty acids."

Fooling Mother Nature?

"Within the last 100 years, coinciding with the industrial revolution, has come the processing of seeds that are dominant in omega-6 oils," explains Mr. Beutler.

These oils, once ingested moderately in the diet, are now ingested disproportionately as vegetable oil and in the fried and processed foods that contain them.

Removing natural omega-3 fatty acids from the food chain has compounded the problem. Food manufacturers were quick to find out that omega-3 fatty acids greatly diminished the desired shelf life of one to two years. Therefore, omega-3s are either removed from the food or avoided entirely.

Modern methods of animal husbandry call on the predominant use of omega-6 dominant seeds and oils to *fatten up* the livestock for slaughter. As a result, animal meats that once provided a concentrated source of omega-3 are

■ Recipe ■

Flax Cookies

1 cup buttermilk

½ cup applesauce

½ cup canola or olive oil

2 whole eggs (or 4 egg whites)

1 tsp vanilla extract

1 cup brown sugar

½ cup granulated sugar

½ tsp salt

1 tsp baking soda

1 tsp cinnamon

1 cup raisins and chocolate chips (combined)

1½ cups all-purpose flour

1 cup ground flaxseed

3 cups quick Quaker Oats

Preheat oven to 350° F. Mix and beat all wet ingredients with sugar, salt, soda and cinnamon. Add raisins and chips, then add flour, flaxseed and quick oats. If necessary, gradually add more milk or water to get a "flowing" dough. Drop by teaspoons onto a cookie sheet and bake for 15 to 18 minutes.

Source: Flax Institute of the United States

now nearly completely devoid of it, although they teem with omega-6.

Consequences and Conclusions

Beutler's research has led him to the realization that, "The mass ingestion of omega-6 at the expense of omega-3 has created a drastic shift in human biophysiology."

In addition, Japanese researchers, after reviewing more than 500 studies, concluded, "The evidence indicates that increased dietary linoleic acid (omega-6) and relative omega-3 deficiency are major risk factors for Western-type cancers, cardiovascular and cerebrovascular diseases, and also for allergic hyper-reactivity. We also raise the possibility that a relative omega-3 deficiency may be affecting the behavioral patterns of a proportion of the young generations in industrialized countries."

Getting Back to Balance

Dr. Simopoulos believes that it would take the human body one million years to adapt to the drastic shift in ingestion of omega-3 to omega-6 fatty acids that has occurred in only the last 100 years.

"The implication is clear," says Mr. Beutler. "And so is the solution. We must consciously shift the omega-3/omega-6 balance by supplementing our diet with omega-3 to avert otherwise certain degenerative disease."

As mentioned before—flax oil contains the highest concentration of essential omega-3 fatty acids of any source on the planet.

ASSOCIATIONS
AmeriFlax

This association promotes healthy living through flaxseed products. The site is a treasure trove of flaxseed information—it describes the benefits of flaxseed, offers recipes, gives locations where flaxseed products are available, provides nutrition information and more.

2718 Gateway Ave., Suite 301

Bismarck, ND 58503

Phone: 701-663-9799

Fax: 701-223-4130

www.ameriflax.com

Flax Institute of the United States

The Web site for the Institute offers contacts for obtaining flaxseed, recipes that use this nutritional food, information on the Institute's work and more.

> Department of Plant Sciences
> North Dakota State University
> Box 5051
> Fargo, ND 58105
> Phone: 701-231-7973
> *www.ndsu.nodak.edu/flaxinst/*

Flax Council of Canada

Provides fun flaxseed facts for consumers, as well as more specialized information for nutritionists, dietitians, food producers, manufacturers and flax growers.

> 465-167 Lombard Ave.
> Winnipeg, Manitoba
> Canada, R3B 0T6
> Phone: 204-982-2115
> Fax: 204-982-2128
> *www.flaxcouncil.ca*

BOOKS

Flaxseed Oil: The Premiere Source of Omega-3 Fatty Acids, by Rita Elkins, Kate Gilbert Udal. Woodland Publishing.

Flaxseed (Linseed) Oil and the Power of Omega-3, by Ingeborg Johnston, James R. Johnston. McGraw-Hill.

The Flax Cookbook: Recipes and Strategies for Getting the Most from the Most Powerful Plant on the Planet, by Elaine Magee. Marlowe & Company.

3. Garlic

When it comes to garlic, we wrote the book. No, we really did! This comprehensive tome is appropriately titled *Garlic: Nature's Super Healer* (Prentice Hall). In the book, we talk about how you can use the healing power of garlic for more than 90 ailments.

Garlic is a natural antibiotic with antiviral, antifungal, anticoagulant and antiseptic properties. It can act as an expectorant and decongestant, antioxidant, germicide, anti-inflammatory agent, diuretic and sedative, and it is believed to contain cancer-preventive chemicals. It's also said to be an aphrodisiac, but you must find a partner who likes garlic.

CAUTION: Do not eat raw garlic or take garlic supplements if you have a bleeding disorder or ulcers, or are taking anticoagulants.

Why the Smell?

Once a garlic clove is bruised in any way (cut, crushed, mashed, pressed, diced, sliced or minced), there is a highly complex conversion process that occurs in which allicin is formed and spontaneously decomposes into a group of odoriferous compounds. This is also what provides much of garlic's medicinal punch.

How to Eat Raw Garlic

Using garlic in cooking is fine, but when garlic is heated, it loses some of its health-giving power. Garlic gurus agree that *raw* garlic does the most good as an antibiotic and as preventive medicine.

CAUTION: Eating too much raw garlic can cause headaches, diarrhea, gas, fever and, in extreme cases, gastric bleeding. This garlic is strong stuff! Do not overdo it.

The Power of Two

▶ The most delicious and soothing way to eat raw garlic is to mix a minced clove into a dollop of plain, nonfat yogurt or fat-free cottage cheese. Yes, it tastes good!

After reading the information on flax, you may also want to mix in a tablespoon of flax oil, making it an extremely healthy snack.

Anna Maria Clement, co-director and chief health administrator of the Hippocrates Health Institute in West Palm Beach, Florida, recommends a variation. She says to put a tablespoon of ground flaxseed in a glass of water and leave it overnight. In the morning, the flaxseed water will have a viscous consistency. Stir it and drink up. It will protect your stomach so that you can eat a clove or two of raw garlic.

Raw Garlic Made Easy

▶ The more we research and write about the benefits of garlic, the more garlic we want to eat! And we found a way to eat it so that we

---

■ Recipe ■

Roasted Garlic

Peel outer skin layer from head of fresh garlic, leaving cloves and head intact. Place head on double thickness of aluminum foil. Top with 1 teaspoon butter and a sprig of fresh rosemary or oregano (or ¼ teaspoon dried). Fold up and seal. Bake in a 375° F oven for 55 to 60 minutes. Squeeze cloves from skins and discard skins. Spread the garlic on crusty bread.

Source: The Gutsy Gourmet

Shopping for Garlic

- Buy bulbs that are sold loose rather than packaged so that you can see and feel them.
- The papery, outer skin should be taut and unbroken.
- Beware of sprouting green shoots, discoloration, mold, rot (feel for soft spots) or shriveling. When garlic gets old, it dries out, its flavor dissipates and it becomes bitter.
- Look for garlic bulbs that are plump, solid and heavy for their size.
- A bulb has anywhere from eight to 40 cloves. The average is about 15 cloves. Look for bulbs that have large cloves so you can cut down on peeling time.

---

don't walk around with garlic breath. We mince the garlic cloves and drink them down in some water or orange juice. As long as we don't chew the little pieces of garlic, the smell doesn't linger on our breath. Chewing a sprig of fresh parsley also helps.

And you can put a minced clove of garlic in yogurt or sour cream. It's delicious that way, and no one will know that you just ate raw garlic.

▶ Brian Clement, director of the Hippocrates Health Institute in West Palm Beach, Florida, says to take a big bite of an apple (organic, of course). Make sure to chew it thoroughly, letting the apple's pectin get around your mouth before swallowing. Then pop a raw garlic clove. There shouldn't be any burning, thanks to the enzymes and pectin in the apple.

▶ Minced garlic in applesauce is a tasty, painless way to eat raw garlic.

■ Recipe ■

Mashed Sweet Potatoes with Garlic

5 lbs sweet potatoes/yams (about 8), roasted

2 heads garlic, roasted (*see* recipe, page 267)

1 tsp olive oil

1 cup soy margarine

1 cup milk

3 cups vegetarian chicken broth (available at health food stores)

Salt and pepper to taste

Cut the sweet potatoes in half and, into a bowl, scoop out the potato from the skins. Squeeze the roasted garlic pulp into the bowl and mash with olive oil. Add margarine, milk and enough broth to give the mixture a light consistency. Season with salt and pepper, and serve. Makes 6 servings.

Source: Garlic: Nature's Super Healer

▶ A fast and easy way to peel a clove of garlic is to pound the clove with a blunt object—the side of a heavy knife, a rolling pin or the bottom of a jar.

▶ You can also sprinkle raw, minced garlic on a salad, or prepare dressing with it.

Storing Garlic

Store garlic bulbs away from any heat source like a stove or the sun. A cool, dry, dark place is ideal, and in an open container, a crock with ventilation holes or a net bag that allows air to circulate around them.

■ Recipe ■

Pasta with Zucchini and Roasted Garlic

1 lb pasta (rotini, twists or spirals), uncooked

8 medium cloves of garlic, peeled

½ tsp dried thyme

½ tsp dried rosemary, crushed

2 Tbsp vegetable oil

3 medium zucchini, coarsely grated (about 5–6 cups)

Salt and ground pepper to taste

Preheat oven or toaster oven to 450° F. Lay a 12"-square piece of tinfoil on the counter, and put the garlic on it. Sprinkle the thyme and rosemary over the garlic. Then pour the vegetable oil over the garlic and herbs. Draw up the edges of the foil and make a sealed package, and bake for 20 minutes.

While the garlic is baking, cook the pasta according to package directions. Two minutes before the pasta is done, add the grated zucchini to the pasta's cooking water. Cook for 2 minutes, then drain the zucchini and pasta.

When the garlic is ready, open the foil package, and mash the garlic and herbs lightly with a spoon. Toss mixture into the pasta and zucchini, then season with salt and pepper to taste. Makes 4 servings.

Source: Garlic: Nature's Super Healer

Do not freeze uncooked garlic. Its consistency will break down and it will emit an awful, ungarlicky smell.

Homemade preparations containing garlic-in-oil must be refrigerated. Put a date on the label. Do not keep it longer than two weeks! Rancid oil can be dangerous.

Garlic Supplements

Commercial supplements should not be chosen by impressive advertising campaigns, and expensive pills are not necessarily better.

"Basically, it's a consumer-beware market for garlic supplements," believes Elizabeth Somer, MA, RD, a nationally recognized dietician and nutritionist. "Some garlic products have 33 times more of certain compounds than other garlic products. Unless the label lists specific amounts (per capsule or tablet) of the active ingredients, such as allicin, S-allyl-cysteine, ajoene, dialyl sulfides or at least total sulfur content, then assume the product is 'condiment grade' and no better or worse than garlic powder seasoning—just a lot more expensive." We think it's important that the label says "allicin" and lists one or more of the other active ingredients.

The late Varro E. Tyler, dean emeritus of the School of Pharmacy and professor of pharmacognosy (drugs made from natural sources) at Purdue University in West Lafayette, Indiana, told us that *enteric-coated* garlic supplements are recommended for the maximum absorption of allicin. A supplement that is enteric-coated resists the effects of stomach acid and allows the intestinal enzymes to dissolve it so that the full benefit of the supplement is obtained. Check labels for the words "enteric-coated" as well as "allicin."

■ Recipe ■

Garlic Soup

3 cups vegetable broth
1 head garlic, peeled
2 potatoes, cubed
1½ cups carrots, chopped
½ cup evaporated milk plus ½ cup
    water (combined)
Ground pepper and hot sauce to taste

Simmer the broth, garlic, potatoes and carrots in a covered pot for 20 minutes. Purée in a food processor when cool. Season with ground pepper and hot sauce, then add enough of the milk/water mixture to reach your idea of the perfect soup consistency. Heat and serve with croutons.

Source: Garlic: Nature's Super Healer

ASSOCIATIONS
The Garlic Seed Foundation
This is an association for people who love garlic—growing it, marketing it and testing its durability as a crop. The Foundation's Web site provides the dates and locations for garlic festivals around the country, publishes a newsletter for garlic fans and more.

    c/o Rose Valley Farm
    Rose, NY 14542-0149
    Phone: 315-587-9787
    www.garlicseedfoundation.info

Gilroy Garlic Festival Association, Inc.
Located in California, the leader of the garlic-growing states, the Gilroy Garlic Festival uses its annual celebratory garlic festival to benefit local charities.

Box 2311
Gilroy, CA 95021
Phone: 408-842-1625
www.gilroygarlicfestival.com

American Botanical Council

As a distinguished international research organization, the American Botanical Council uses education to promote the safe and beneficial use of herbal medicine. A great informational resource!

6200 Manor Rd.
Austin, TX 78723
Phone: 512-926-4900
Fax: 512-926-2345
www.herbalgram.org

Herb Research Foundation

The HRF is the world's first and foremost source of accurate, scientific data on the health benefits and safety of herbs—including garlic.

4140 15th St.
Boulder, CO 80304
Phone: 303-449-2265
Fax: 303-449-7849
www.herbs.org

Gourmet Garlic Gardens

For anyone interested in learning more about garlic, this site contains articles on everything from tips on growing garlic to how garlic works in the human body. There are several links where consumers can order different varieties of garlic as well as other garlic-related products.

12300 FM 1176
Bangs, TX 76823
Phone: 325-348-3049
www.gourmetgarlicgardens.com

BOOKS

The Garlic Cure, by James F. Scheer, Lynn Allison, Charlie Fox. McCleery and Sons Publishing.

Garlic, Garlic, Garlic: Exceptional Recipes for the World's Most Indispensable Ingredient, by Linda Griffith, Fred Griffith. Houghton Mifflin Co.

Honey, Garlic & Vinegar: Home Remedies & Recipes: The People's Guide to Nature's Wonder Medicines, by Patrick Quillin. Leader Company.

Garlic: Nature's Super Healer, by Joan Wilen, Lydia Wilen. Prentice Hall.

4. Ginger

What are friends for? To share their expertise with you and your readers—that is, if you're lucky enough to be friends with someone like Paul Schulick, master herbalist, founder and CEO of NewChapter (*www.new-chapter.com*) in Brattleboro, Vermont, and a leading authority on ginger, one of our Six Sensational Superfoods. *He told us the following story…*

"Doctor," said the imaginary patient, "I have a host of serious problems." The doctor listened very carefully and compassionately (remember, this is make-believe) as the patient recounted his ailments.

"Doctor, I think I have parasites, and they make me nauseated all the time. In addition, my family has a history of colon cancer, and I have some blood in my stool. And I suppose I could handle that, but I feel feverish, and my joints constantly ache. I started out this year at 5' 7", and I think I must be shrinking. Also, my cholesterol is elevated, and I was taking aspirin to avoid blood clotting, but it tore my stomach up. I think I now have ulcers! Doctor, what should I take? And don't prescribe too much, because my memory is not what it used to be."

■ Recipe ■

Ginger Cookies

1 tsp baking soda

½ cup boiling water

1 cup granulated sugar

1 cup melted butter

½ tsp salt

1 cup dark molasses

½ tsp ginger

½ tsp cloves

1 tsp cinnamon

1 egg

3 cups flour

Dissolve baking soda in the boiling water. Mix all other ingredients together. Roll thin. Cut dough with cookie cutter. Bake at 325° F until light brown. Watch carefully, though…these cookies brown very quickly.

Source: www.recipegoldmine.com

Did You Know?

Ginger *potentiates* or increases the power of other herbs, so it is valuable to use with green tea, echinacea, ginseng and kava.

Most recently, a new extract of ginger called a "Supercritical Extract" has become available, which allows you to take a powerful and pure concentrate (up to 250:1) of the healing, pungent compounds.

See page 274 for more information on forms and dosage.

The doctor listened to this patient and then told him about the medicinal power of one herb that might just be the answer for all his problems. The doctor told the story of *Zingiber officinale*, commonly known as "ginger." This common herb, really a rhizome (edible root), has some profound and scientifically well-documented healing properties. The doctor told the patient to listen, but not to worry about memorizing the features. *They are…*

- ◆ Antiparasitic (against schistosoma mansoni, anisakis and dirofilaria immitis).

- ◆ Antibacterial (against staph, E. coli, salmonella and strep) and antiviral.

- ◆ Anti-emetic (for relief from nausea) that is more effective than the prescription drug metoclopramide.

- ◆ Antimutagenic (cancer preventative) against COX-2 related cancers (such as colon, pancreas, skin, esophageal), leukemia and multiple tumor growth factors.

- ◆ Balances and modulates inflammatory hormones associated with arthritis.

- ◆ Balances and modulates the enzyme 5-lipoxygenase, which is associated with prostate and breast cancers, bone resorption (osteoporosis) and conditions of inflammation. (There are 22 identified 5-lipoxygenase inhibitors.)

- ◆ Inhibits the COX-2 enzyme associated with brain inflammation and with the neuronal death in Alzheimer's disease. (There are three known COX-2 inhibitors—melatonin, kaempferol and curcumin.)

■ Recipe ■

Ginger–Onion Vinaigrette

¼ cup extra-virgin olive oil

1 cup very fine strips of white leeks

1 small red onion, finely chopped

12 whole fresh green onions, thinly
  sliced

1 tsp finely chopped fresh garlic in oil

2 medium shallots, skinned and finely
  chopped

1 cup red wine vinegar

1 cup chicken stock or broth

1 tsp fresh ginger, peeled and finely
  grated

1 tsp finely chopped crystallized
  ginger

2 cups mayonnaise

Kosher salt to taste

Dash of cracked black pepper

Heat olive oil in a large sauté pan. When the oil is hot, sauté the leeks, red and green onion, garlic and shallots until they are about half done. Remove from the heat, then add the red wine vinegar. Return to the heat. This will help de-glaze the pan. Add chicken stock, fresh and crystallized ginger and bring the mixture to a boil. Cook until the liquid has been reduced by half. Remove from heat and let cool at room temperature for at least 15 minutes.

In a large bowl, combine cooked mixture and all other ingredients. Taste. If it is too vinegary, add just a touch of sugar. Additional salt and pepper may also be added to your taste.

Source: www.recipegoldmine.com

◆ Powerful antioxidant that enhances the potency of other antioxidants. Contains at least 12 known anti-aging constituents that deactivate destructive free radicals.

◆ Wound healing and anti-ulcerative. Contains more wound-healing compounds than any other botanical.

◆ Aphrodisiac.

◆ Antihistamine.

◆ Powerful digestive enzyme—ginger has 180 times the protein-digesting power of papaya.

◆ Supports the growth of beneficial bacteria in the large intestine, specifically Lactobacillus plantarum, by a factor of five.

◆ Modulates thromboxane, the hormone responsible for blood platelet aggregation and blood clotting, thus protecting against heart attack and stroke. More effective in this respect than garlic.

◆ Reverses the inflammation associated with rheumatoid arthritis more effectively than prescription drugs, according to international medical research.

◆ Increases bile secretion for better fat metabolism.

◆ Lowers serum cholesterol.

◆ Contains 11 sedative compounds, more than any other spice.

The patient listened with astonishment. "Do you mean to tell me that *one drug* can do all that?"

The doctor replied, "No, I am not talking about a drug. Remember, I am that rare MD who is open to the phytomedicinal power of

■ Recipe ■

Sautéed Tofu with Ginger Sauce

Ginger Sauce

6 Tbsp rice vinegar

6 Tbsp granulated sugar

¾ cup plus 1 Tbsp water

2 Tbsp soy sauce

1 tsp cornstarch

1 Tbsp finely minced gingerroot

In small saucepan, combine vinegar, sugar, ¾ cup water and soy sauce. Bring to a boil, reduce heat and simmer, stirring occasionally, for 5 minutes.

Meanwhile, in a small bowl, combine cornstarch and 1 tablespoon water—then stir into sauce. Cook mixture, stirring, until clear and thickened. Remove pan from heat, and stir in ginger. Makes 1 cup of sauce.

Tofu

½ lb firm tofu

½ cup unbleached flour

2 Tbsp toasted wheat germ

½ tsp thyme

¼ tsp dill weed

¼ tsp garlic powder

¼ tsp paprika

¼ tsp black pepper

1 whole egg (or 2 egg whites)

1 Tbsp milk

3 drops hot pepper sauce

2 Tbsp safflower oil

While ginger sauce is simmering, cut tofu into 1" squares about ¼" thick. Set aside. In a medium bowl, combine flour, wheat germ and seasonings.

In a separate bowl, lightly beat egg. Add milk and hot pepper sauce. In a large skillet, heat oil. Piece by piece, dip tofu in flour, then in egg mixture and again in flour. Sauté until lightly browned, about 3 minutes on each side.

Serve warm, arranged on a platter with cocktail forks and a bowl of ginger sauce. Surround platter with curly lettuce leaves or large sprigs of parsley. Makes 4 to 6 servings.

Source: www.recipegoldmine.com

healing botanicals. I am talking about 'ginger,' which is absolutely NOT a drug. A drug has one synthetic molecule, and ginger has at least 477 natural compounds, all working together to promote safe and balanced healing."

This conversation may never have occurred in any MD's office that you have visited, but people are talking about ginger. Its popularity is long overdue. For thousands of years, ginger has been known in Ayurvedic medicine as *vishwabhesaj*, the Universal Medicine. It is said that legendary Chinese sage and philosopher Confucius (551–479 BC) considered no meal complete without ginger…it was considered to be the Alka-Seltzer of the Roman Empire…and it was so valuable to Arab traders that purchasers were told that ginger came from the mythical kingdom of Xanadu so as to hide its true origins. And to top it all off, its invigorating taste has stimulated palates and calmed stomachs for thousands of years. High-quality ginger remains a prized commodity.

Forms and Dosage

There are several ways to enjoy the benefits of ginger. Fresh ginger is delightful, but it is important to use organic ginger, because *conventional* (often better described as *chemically grown*) ginger is often heavily fumigated.

▶ Ginger can be purchased both dried and ground, which is an excellent way to obtain the intestinal and protein-digesting benefits of this whole-fiber herb. Extracts are available of the fresh ginger juice, which can be used to make hot or cold teas or ginger ales.

But most important, organic ginger belongs in your daily life, for it is simply one of the finest (if not the finest) daily tonics available from the botanical world.

ASSOCIATIONS
American Botanical Council

As a distinguished international research organization, the American Botanical Council uses education to promote the safe and beneficial use of herbal medicine. A great informational resource!

> 6200 Manor Rd.
> Austin, TX 78723
> Phone: 512-926-4900
> Fax: 512-926-2345
> *www.herbalgram.org*

Herb Research Foundation

The HRF is the world's first and foremost source of accurate, scientific data on the health benefits and safety of herbs—including ginger.

> 4140 15th St.
> Boulder, CO 80304
> Phone: 303-449-2265
> Fax: 303-449-7849
> *www.herbs.org*

The Ginger People

This Web site was created by Royal Pacific, an innovative, quality-oriented and environmentally conscious ginger producer. Learn about all things ginger and get ginger-related information, recipes, products, tips and more.

> 215 Reindollar Ave.
> Marina, CA 93933
> Phone: 800-551-5284
> Fax: 831-582-2495
> *www.gingerpeople.com*

BOOKS

Ginger: Common Spice and Wonder Drug, by Paul Schulick. Hohm Press.

A Spoonful of Ginger: Irresistible Health-Giving Recipes from Asian Kitchens, by Nina Simonds. Knopf.

5. Nuts

Nuts! For years, neither of us ate nuts. We love nuts, but they're very high in fat. And then, one day in the mid-1990s, we read an article extolling the health-giving properties of nuts—fat and all. What a wonderful surprise! The article reported the findings of a research team at Loma Linda University's School of Public Health in Loma Linda, California. The research team was headed by Joan Sabaté, MD, DrPH, professor and chair of the School's department of nutrition.

We immediately called the university and got another surprise. Dr. Joan Sabaté is a man—"Joan" being a man's name in Spain and Portugal—and, lucky for us, one who was willing to share his research.

Results of the Studies

Starting in the mid-1970s, a team of epidemiologists at Loma Linda followed the eating habits of more than 25,000 Seventh Day Adventists. At the end of 10 years, the researchers found that there was only one common food linked to good health—nuts.

Dr. Sabaté said, "The results couldn't have been more striking. People who ate nuts often—five or more times a week—were half as likely to have a heart attack or die of heart disease as people who rarely or never ate them. Eating nuts just one to four times a week cuts the heart risk by 25%." The doctor said it did not matter if people were slim or fat, young or old, active or sedentary.

Dr. Sabaté conducted his own study with two groups of people. Both groups ate a typical cholesterol-lowering diet from the American Heart Association (*www.americanheart.org*)—the kind that doctors would recommend.

In addition to the food that was allowed on the diet, one group ate 2 to 3 ounces of walnuts daily and the other group ate no walnuts. The cholesterol levels went down in both groups, but more so among the walnut eaters. Their blood cholesterol levels dropped 22 points in just a few weeks.

Many studies of the effects of nuts have been done—an almond study at the Health Research and Studies Center in Los Altos, California…a walnut study at the University of California at San Francisco…a Harvard Nurses' Study conducted by the Harvard School of Public Health in Boston, Massachusetts, that tracked 86,000 nurses…a Harvard Physicians' Health study with 22,000 doctors…another study with 31,000 vegetarians…and still another with 40,000 postmenopausal women.

The results all point to the same conclusion—nuts are a health-giving superfood!

Health Benefits—in a Nutshell

All nuts contain flavonoids, which are potent antioxidants that help protect the body against cancer and heart disease.

Nuts are one of the best sources of vitamin E. They also have B vitamins—thiamine, niacin, folic acid and riboflavin. Most nuts are rich in potassium, which is needed to help regulate blood pressure and heart rate. Nuts are also a good source of the fatigue- and stress-fighting minerals iron, magnesium and zinc. (Almonds and pecans are particularly rich in magnesium …cashews and pecans are rich in zinc.)

Nuts are packed with the antioxidants selenium and copper. (Brazil nuts are particularly rich in selenium…cashews, filberts and walnuts are rich in copper.)

In the 16th and 17th centuries, it was thought that various foods helped heal the body parts that they resembled. And so, our ancestors believed that walnuts helped the head and brain. They may have been right. Copper, an essential mineral for maintenance of the nervous system *and* brain activity, is found in many types of nuts.

Most nuts also have some calcium, but almonds have more than any other nut. Brazil nuts and filberts also have substantial amounts of calcium.

One ounce of nuts gives you as much fiber as two slices of whole wheat bread. Almonds have the highest dietary fiber content of any nut.

Nut protein is loaded with the amino acid arginine, known to protect arteries from injury and to stop blood clots from forming.

■ Recipe ■

Walnut Macaroni Casserole

1 Tbsp salt

8 oz elbow macaroni

2 cups (one 16-oz can) canned
   tomatoes

½ tsp low-sodium baking soda

1 cup (one 8-oz can) tomato sauce

1¼ cups low-fat cottage cheese

¼ cup grated parmesan cheese

1 (10-oz) package frozen chopped
   spinach, thawed and squeezed dry

1½ cups frozen peas, thawed

1 tsp dried basil

½ tsp pepper

¾ cup toasted* walnuts, chopped

2 Tbsp parsley, chopped

Salt to taste

Preheat the oven to 350° F. Bring about 6 quarts of water to a boil with 1 tablespoon salt. Add the macaroni and cook, stirring occasionally, for about 8 minutes or until done.

While the macaroni is cooking, place the tomatoes and their juice into a large bowl. Add the baking soda and, with a fork or your fingers, break the tomatoes into small chunks. Stir in the tomato sauce. Add the cottage cheese, parmesan cheese, spinach, peas, basil and pepper, and toss to combine—set aside.

When the macaroni is done, drain well in a colander. Add to the cheese mixture, toss to mix thoroughly, then pour into an oiled 2¼-quart baking dish.

Cover the baking dish with aluminum foil and bake the casserole for 20 minutes. Then uncover and bake 10 minutes longer. Stir in the walnuts and sprinkle with parsley. Makes 6 servings.

*Toasting walnuts is optional

Source: Walnut Marketing Board

Nuts contain phytochemicals (plant sterols or phytosterols, which help lower cholesterol and are thought to protect against colon cancer)…antioxidants (which help to protect against heart disease and cancer)…saponins (which help lower cholesterol and also show evidence of having anticancer properties) …and phytic acid or phytate (which has been found to be protective against colon cancer).

Here are some nutty facts (in case you're ever on a TV game show)…

- ◆ The oldest food tree known to humankind is the walnut tree. It dates back to 7,000 BC.

- ◆ The nut with the highest fat content (over 70%) is the pecan.

- ◆ Cashew shells are thick, leathery and have a blackish-brown oil that causes human skin to blister in a way similar to poison ivy.

- ◆ You may know that filberts are also called hazelnuts, but do you know another name for them? Cobnuts.

- ◆ Brazil nuts have the hardest shell of all nuts. Before cracking them—or any hard-shell nut—put them in the freezer for six hours. The deep-freeze makes the shells much easier to crack.

■ Recipe ■

New West Crab Cakes

1 lb crabmeat, picked over

2 egg whites

1 egg yolk

¾ lb mashed potatoes (instant may be used)

⅓ cup chopped red onions or chives

Pinch of salt

½ cup walnuts, chopped

1 cup bread crumbs

Combine crabmeat, egg whites, egg yolk, potatoes, onions, salt, ¼ cup chopped walnuts and ½ cup bread crumbs in a bowl. Form mixture into 8 flat patties. Mix together remaining ½ cup of bread crumbs and finely chopped walnuts. Coat crab patties with bread crumb mixture. Cook over medium heat in skillet with brushed oil.

Serve with lemon wedges or fresh tomato relish made with chopped green and yellow peppers, red onion and diced, seeded tomatoes, seasoned to taste (or you may substitute already prepared salsa).

Source: Walnut Marketing Board

♦ Peanuts are really legumes (related to beans and peas), but are nutritionally similar to nuts.

♦ Nuts in their shells stay fresh twice as long as shelled nuts. If kept in a cool, dry place, raw, unshelled nuts can keep for six months to a year. But why would you want to keep them that long? Eat 'em now!

Dosage

Nuts have helped us change the way we think of fats. We now know that there are good fats—the unsaturated fats—which are found in flaxseed, cold-water fish, avocado and, of course, in nuts.

Dr. Sabaté told us that 1 to 2 ounces of either almonds, cashews, pistachios, walnuts or even peanuts five times a week is a heart-healthy amount to eat.

How to Eat Nuts

▶ Be sure the nuts are raw, except for peanuts. (Most of the recipes included here contain nuts that are cooked or roasted…these treats should be consumed in moderation.) Organically grown nuts are always preferred. Stay away from the red-dyed (how and why did *that* get started?) and salted pistachios.

If you want peanut butter, the best is the natural kind you grind yourself or that you can get from a health food store. Avoid commercially prepared peanut butter with all its additives and preservatives.

▶ For optimum health, don't just add nuts to your diet. Let nuts take the place of saturated, unhealthy fat. Cut back on meat, cheese and deep-fried foods. Keep working your way toward a predominantly plant-based diet.

▶ The late Gene Spiller, PhD, director of the Health Research and Studies Center in Los

■ **Recipe** ■

Pecan Four-Cheese Pizza

1 12" prepared pizza crust

1 Tbsp olive oil

2 large onions, sliced

3 Tbsp goat cheese, softened

3 Tbsp cream cheese, softened

½ cup feta cheese, crumbled

1 cup shredded mozzarella cheese

⅔ cup pecans, coarsely chopped

Chopped parsley for garnish

Preheat oven to 450° F. Place pizza crust on cookie sheet. In frying pan, heat oil. Add onions and cook slowly until caramelized, about 20 minutes. Cool slightly. Mix the goat cheese and cream cheese together and spread on crust, then spread the cooked onions over the cheese. Sprinkle the feta and mozzarella cheeses over the onions, and top with the pecan pieces. Bake for about 5 minutes or until cheeses melt.

Sprinkle parsley over top before serving. Cut into 6 wedges to serve. Makes 2 to 3 servings.

Source: National Pecan Shellers Association

■ **Recipe** ■

Hazelnut Corn Bran Muffins

1 cup milk

½ cup bran flakes

¼ cup (½ stick) butter

3 Tbsp brown sugar

1 egg, room temperature

1 tsp oil

1 cup white flour

½ cup cornmeal

½ cup hazelnuts, roasted and chopped

2 tsp baking powder

½ tsp salt

Combine milk and bran flakes in medium bowl and let stand at room temperature 8 hours or overnight. Preheat oven to 400° F. Grease 12 2½" muffin tins. Cream butter with sugar in large bowl. Stir in egg and oil, blending well. Fold in flour, cornmeal, hazelnuts, baking powder, salt and bran mixture until dry ingredients are just moist. Divide batter in muffin tins. Bake about 20 to 25 minutes or until tester comes out clean. Cool 7 minutes. Makes 12 muffins.

Source: Oregon Hazelnut Industry

Altos, California, believed that nuts are so nutrient-rich that they quell hunger pangs. It's possible that by eating a few nuts, you won't want to eat as much of everything else.

▶ A nutritionist/spokesperson for Weight Watchers (*www.weightwatchers.com*) said that the problem with nuts is that once you start eating them…too much of a good thing is no longer a good thing. So the bottom line is—try not to go nuts!

ASSOCIATIONS
Northern Nut Growers Association

The NNGA is a great resource for information on nut tree–growing. This national non-profit organization has a library that contains many articles and research papers on nuts and how

■ Recipe ■

Cashew Shrimp

1 lb medium shrimp
1 Tbsp plus 1 tsp cornstarch
¼ tsp granulated sugar
¼ tsp baking soda
¼ tsp salt
⅛ tsp pepper
½ cup vegetable oil
½ cup onions, chopped
¼ cup red peppers, chopped
1 clove garlic
1 cup unpeeled zucchini, chopped
3½ cups cooked rice
¾ cup cashews
Sweet red pepper rings

Cut shrimp in half lengthwise. Combine cornstarch, sugar, baking soda, salt and pepper. Mix well. Add shrimp and toss gently to coat. Let stand 15 minutes.

Heat oil in a large skillet over medium heat. Add shrimp. Cook, stirring constantly, 3 to 5 minutes. Remove shrimp and set aside. Drain off drippings, leaving 2 tablespoons in the skillet. Sauté onions, chopped red peppers and garlic until tender. Add zucchini and sauté 2 minutes. Stir in shrimp, rice and cashews. Cook over low heat, stirring constantly, until thoroughly heated.

Spoon into serving dish. Garnish with red pepper rings.

Source: www.recipegoldmine.com

Box 6216
Hamden, CT 06517
www.northernnutgrowers.org

Almond Board of California

Almonds are California's largest tree crop. The ABC devotes itself to expanding the market for almonds through public relations, advertising and nutrition research. The Board also tracks and publishes industry statistics on almonds in the *Almond Almanac.*

1150 Ninth St., Suite 1500
Modesto, CA 95354
Phone: 209-549-8262
Fax: 209-549-8267
www.almondboard.com

California Walnut Board

Representing the walnut growers and handlers of California, the California Walnut Board encourages the consumption of walnuts by publishing healthy recipes and facts.

101 Parkshore Dr., Suite 250
Folsom, CA 95630
Phone: 916-932-7070
Fax: 916-932-7071
www.walnuts.org

National Pecan Shellers Association

This trade association is committed to educating everyone about the nutritional benefits, various uses and great taste of pecans.

1100 Johnson Ferry Rd., Suite 300
Atlanta, GA 30342
Phone: 404-252-3663
www.ilovepecans.org

to cultivate them. The Web site provides links to other nut-growing associations as well as recipes and expert advice on nut growing.

■ Recipe ■

Peanut Ice Cream (circa 1925)

1 pint peanuts

2 cups sugar

2 quarts milk

1 pint cream

2 tsp vanilla

Roast, shell and roll the peanuts until they are quite fine. Brown one cup of sugar and add to the milk. Then add the remainder of the sugar, cream, vanilla and, lastly, the peanuts. Freeze.

Source: George Washington Carver (Tuskegee Institute National Historic Site)

National Peanut Board

This organization represents all US peanut farmers and their families. It works to increase peanut production while advancing the great taste, nutritional value and versatility of US-grown peanuts.

> 2839 Paces Ferry Rd., Suite 210
> Atlanta, GA 30339
> Phone: 866-825-7946
>   678-424-5750
> Fax: 678-424-5751
> *www.nationalpeanutboard.org*

BOOKS

Nuts: Sweet and Savory Recipes from Diamond California, by Tina Salter, Holly Stewart. Ten Speed Press.

The Totally Nuts Cookbook (Totally Cookbooks), by Helene Siegel, Caroline Vibbert. Celestial Arts.

■ Recipe ■

Tropical Fruit Salad with Ginger and Peanuts

2 Tbsp honey

2 Tbsp tangerine or juice concentrate

1 tsp fresh lime or lemon juice

5 cups mixed fresh fruit chunks, such as papaya, mango, Asian pear, pineapple, kiwi fruit and/or banana

½ cup dry-roasted peanuts

2 Tbsp crystallized ginger, chopped

In a small bowl, stir together honey, juice concentrate and the lime or lemon juice. Combine the fruit in 1½- to 2-quart bowl. Gently toss with juice mixture, peanuts and ginger. Serve promptly, or cover and chill for about an hour. If prepared more than 1 hour ahead, stir in peanuts and ginger just before serving. Makes 4 1-cup servings.

Source: National Peanut Board

6. Yogurt

In Egypt, it's called *benraid.* The Armenians call it *mayzoom.* The Persian word is *kast.* In Turkey, it's known as *yogurut,* from which our word "yogurt" is derived.

Although people have been making and eating yogurt for more than 4,000 years, it took the research of Nobel Prize–winning scientist Ilya Mechnikov in the beginning of the 20th century to stir up European interest in yogurt, which eventually made its way to America around 1940. In the 1950s, yogurt's reputation as a healthy, nutritional food started to spread across the country. Now, yogurt production is a major industry.

The Culture Club

Yogurt is most often made with the milk of cows. But it can also be made with milk from goats, sheep and buffalo, or with soymilk. Once the milk gets pasteurized, many commercial yogurt producers enrich it with powdered milk. So when ads say that the yogurt has more protein and calcium than dairy milk, it's true.

To meet the legal definition of yogurt, it is required that two cultures be added to the mixture. These cultures break down the lactose (milk sugar), producing lactic acid and giving yogurt its unique taste. The live, active cultures are primarily what make yogurt a health-giving superfood.

Health Benefits

Thanks to the live cultures, yogurt is a soothing and easily digested food, even for people who are lactose intolerant. In fact, yogurt helps digestion and, as a result, may clear up bad breath caused by stomach-acid imbalances.

As an added bonus, a daily dose of yogurt may completely eliminate gas problems.

▶ Yogurt is not only a good source of calcium, but the lactose helps improve calcium absorption. People at risk for osteoporosis should consider including a portion in their daily diet.

▶ Yogurt contains B_{12}, riboflavin, potassium, magnesium and zinc. It's also a wonderful source of protein. In fact, the US Department of Agriculture (*www.usda.gov*) recommends yogurt as a meat alternative in school lunches.

▶ Studies show that eating a daily 8-ounce serving of yogurt with active bacterial cultures restores and maintains a healthy bacterial environment that can help prevent both bladder infections and vaginal yeast infections.

▶ A daily serving of yogurt with "live cultures" seems to increase immune-enhancing chemicals, according to the results of experiments performed by George Halpern, MD, professor emeritus of the department of internal medicine at the University of California, Davis, School of Medicine. Dr. Halpern emphasizes the need for the yogurt to contain "live" or "active" cultures.

Friendly Acidophilus

Antibiotics have no discretion. They destroy the good as well as the bad bacteria found naturally in your digestive system. Replace the beneficial bacteria with *Lactobacillus acidophilus*. You can do that by eating yogurt—make sure the container says *Live* or *Active Culture with L. acidophilus*—or drinking acidophilus milk, or by taking an acidophilus supplement, available at health food stores.

▶ Whether you take a supplement, drink milk or eat yogurt (fat-free is fine as long as it says it contains *L. acidophilus*), do it two hours *after* taking an antibiotic, making sure that it's also at least two hours *before* you have to take another dose of the antibiotic. Allow that amount of time before and after the antibiotic so that the acidophilus doesn't interfere with the work of the antibiotic.

Keep consuming acidophilus in some form for at least a couple of weeks after you stop taking an antibiotic. It will help normalize the bacterial balance in the intestines, getting your digestive system working properly again.

■ **Recipe** ■

Eggplant–Yogurt Dip

3 large eggplants, whole with skin on
1 large head garlic, roasted (*see* recipe
     on page 267)
1 cup thick yogurt (plain)
2 Tbsp olive oil
1 medium Vidalia, red or other sweet
     onion, chopped
½ cup fresh Italian parsley, chopped
1 Tbsp fresh basil, chopped (optional)
¼ tsp Tabasco sauce (optional)
Salt and pepper to taste

On a gas or preferably charcoal barbecue, roast the whole eggplant evenly on all sides until the skin is charred or the eggplant is soft. Set aside and let cool. When cool, peel off the charred skin or scoop out the soft insides of the eggplant. Place in a large bowl.

Add garlic, yogurt, olive oil, onion, parsley, basil, Tabasco sauce, salt and pepper to taste. Mix well.

Serve along with Armenian cracker bread, as a vegetable dip or as a vegetable side dish. Can be served hot or cold.

Source: The Gutsy Gourmet

▶ After a bout of diarrhea, yogurt can help reestablish bacterial balance. Studies show that yogurt can decrease the duration of an attack of diarrhea in infants and children.

▶ Studies also indicate that *Lactobacillus acidophilus* in yogurt helps lower cholesterol levels by interfering with cholesterol reabsorption in the intestine.

▶ All of the live cultures of bacteria in yogurt can enhance immunity, kill off certain unwanted strains of unhealthy bacteria and increase production of antibodies (the natural killers of disease organisms) in your blood.

What's great is that those beneficial bacteria stay in your system and continue to help long after the yogurt is gone.

Whey to Go

You know that watery part that you spill off before spooning out a portion of yogurt? That's the whey, and it has B vitamins and minerals, and little, if any, fat. Stir the whey into the yogurt so that it's part of your portion.

What to Look For

First and foremost, whether you want regular, low-fat or fat-free yogurt, be sure that the label says it contains "live" or "active" cultures. Most yogurt manufacturers list their specific

■ **Recipe** ■

Curried Turkey

2 cups cooked turkey breast, diced
¼ cup raisins
1½ stalks celery, chopped
¼ cup peanuts, finely chopped
½ cup plain nonfat yogurt
2 Tbsp light mayonnaise
½ tsp curry powder
Fresh-ground black pepper to taste

Combine ingredients and serve. Makes 4 servings.

Source: National Yogurt Association

live cultures. Look for and expect to find at least one, maybe two or three (more is better) types of friendly and helpful bacteria. *Try to get…*

- ◆ Lactobacillus acidophilus
- ◆ Lactobacillus bulgaricus
- ◆ Lactobacillus casei
- ◆ Lactobacillus reuteri
- ◆ Streptococcus thermophilus
- ◆ Bifidobacteria

▶ If fruit is mixed through yogurt, there's not much chance of there being live or active cultures in it. Buy plain yogurt and add a banana, berries, peaches or pineapple—this can be one of your five daily cancer-risk-reducing servings of fresh fruit. Plain yogurt also tastes great with a little honey mixed in.

▶ See what other ingredients are listed on the label. You do not want yogurt to contain any additives or artificial sweeteners.

▶ Before buying yogurt, check the expiration date and be sure the container's contents have not exceeded that date—or even come close.

▶ If you really get into yogurt, you may want to try making your own (*see* recipe on page 284). Kits are available in some health food stores. You'll need to use yogurt as a starter to make more yogurt. And that's one way to test the store-bought product for active live cultures. If the cultures are alive and well, they will help produce more yogurt.

▶ Sorry, but none of the health benefits of yogurt apply to frozen yogurt. Freezing tends to destroy the good stuff.

There is also the unwanted presence of sugar or aspartame and lots more ingredients on the less-than-healthy list.

■ Recipe ■

Yogurt Cereal Bars

2 cups corn flakes
¾ cup flour
¼ cup firmly packed brown sugar
½ tsp ground cinnamon
½ cup margarine
1 cup lowfat vanilla yogurt
1 egg, slightly beaten
2 Tbsp flour

Preheat oven to 350° F. Combine cereal, ¾ cup flour, sugar and cinnamon in a small bowl. Cut in margarine until coarse crumbs form. In the bottom of a greased 8" square pan, press half the mixture firmly. Mix yogurt, egg and 2 tablespoons flour in another small bowl. Spread over cereal mixture in pan, and sprinkle with remaining cereal mixture. Bake 30 minutes or until golden brown. Cool in pan on wire rack. Cut into bars, and store in an airtight canister. Makes 16 servings.

Source: Stonyfield Farm Yogurt

The Last Word on Yogurt

In several ancient Middle Eastern languages, the word for yogurt was synonymous with *life*.

ASSOCIATIONS
National Yogurt Association
The NYA is the national trade association representing manufacturers of refrigerated cup and frozen yogurt products that contain live and active cultures. Products that meet the NYA's standards will have a "Live and Active

■ Recipe ■

Make Your Own Yogurt

½ gallon whole milk (you can also use low-fat or skim milk)

½ cup mahdzoon or yogurt starter (available at specialty and health food stores, or you may use plain yogurt from the supermarket)

Bring milk to just a boil and then set aside to cool—just cool enough not to bite the finger to touch (about 120° F). Pour warm milk into a glass or Pyrex bowl, and add the mahdzoon starter. Mix well by stirring in the starter slowly. Completely cover the bowl with towels top and bottom to maintain an even temperature. Keep covered at room temperature until mahdzoon has set, about 3 to 4 hours. Refrigerate for 8 hours before serving. Serves 6 to 8.

To store, keep in the refrigerator. This will keep well for a week or more.

Source: The Gutsy Gourmet

Cultures" seal on the side of the container. This will assure that the product has met standards for cultures used in production.

The NYA sponsors scientific research regarding the health benefits of eating yogurt, and serves as a source of information about these benefits. The NYA also acts as a resource for both the media and the general public on subjects related to yogurt that contains live and active cultures.

2000 Corporate Ridge, Suite 1000
McLean, VA 22102
Phone: 703-821-0770
www.aboutyogurt.com

The National Dairy Council

The NDC, a division of Dairy Management Inc., strives to provide timely scientific data on the amazing health benefits of dairy products. The Council is also involved in dairy nutrition research, education and communication.

10255 West Higgins Rd., Suite 900
Rosemont, IL 60018
Phone: 800-426-8271
        847-803-2000
Fax: 847-803-2077
www.nationaldairycouncil.org

BOOKS

Cooking with Yogurt: The Complete Cookbook for Indulging with the World's Healthiest Food, by Judith Choate. Atlantic Monthly Press.

The Book of Yogurt, by Sonia Uvezian. Ecco Publishing.

Yogurt, Yoghurt, Youghourt: An International Cookbook, by Linda K. Fuller. Food Products Printing. ■

Amazing, Super-Duper
Facts and Advice

Amazing, Super-Duper Facts and Advice

Think Positive, Live Longer

Having an optimistic outlook may actually prolong your life span, according to a study conducted at the Mayo Clinic in Rochester, Minnesota. Researchers studied patients for more than 30 years and concluded that the pessimistic participants ran a 19% greater risk of death compared with the more optimistic ones.

It's difficult to put much credence in this study since so many variables come into play. But we hope you can see that being optimistic is a happier way to go through life than being pessimistic—and it's certainly much more pleasant for everyone around you.

The Full Moon Boom

Research that was conducted at the University of Illinois Medical Center in Chicago concluded that some health problems may act up—and can possibly become more severe—when there's a full moon. (Are there any werewolves reading this?)

The "Rest" of the Story

Everyone—from your mother and mate to your doctor—at one time or another probably suggested or insisted on "bed rest" to recuperate from an illness.

A study done by researchers at Michigan State University in East Lansing said, "Rest, not bed rest." The difference between the two is important.

When you *rest*, you slow down but keep moving. *Bed rest* implies staying still (in bed) for a long period. This can lead to muscle fatigue and even overall weakness. The researchers based their findings on close to 6,000 patients with 17 different medical conditions.

Conclusion: It's good to get sick people out of bed as soon as possible. Although you may get out of bed, you may still need rest. It's important to find the proper balance. As your mother, mate or doctor will tell you, "Don't overdo it!"

NOTE: Equal time is demanded by one of our medical advisors, who reminds us that, in some cases, "Don't underdo it!"

287

Doctor's Fee

In ancient China, doctors were paid when they kept their patients well. Believing it was their job to prevent illness, the doctors often paid patients who got sick.

Those certainly were the good old days!

Fever: Friend or Foe?

Thomas Sydenham, a 17th-century English physician—who was one of the principal founders of epidemiology—once famously said, "Fever is Nature's engine which she brings into the field to remove her enemy."

It looks like research scientists agree with Dr. Sydenham when it comes to fevers that are below 104° F.

Matthew J. Kluger, PhD, is vice president of federal and corporate relations for George Mason University in Fairfax, Virginia. As one of the leading researchers of fever therapy, Dr. Kluger recommends that fever be allowed to run its course and believes that it may actually shorten the duration of an illness. Studies done at the University of Texas Southwestern Medical Center in Dallas showed that fever supports antibiotic therapy. And researchers at Yale University School of Medicine in New Haven, Connecticut, proved that patients with fever are less contagious than those with the same infection but who have suppressed their fever with medication.

Ray C. Wunderlich, Jr., MD, PhD, director of the Wunderlich Center for Nutritional Medicine in St. Petersburg, Florida, says, "Mothers whose babies get hot in the middle of the night know that high fever paralyzes the household and may create extreme stress. Be sure the baby is not excessively clothed and blanketed. A 20- to 30-minute tepid bath may help the baby feel better and even feel like ingesting fluids or food."

Freshen Up a Sickroom

▶ Dip a cotton ball into eucalyptus oil (available at health food stores), put it on a little dish and place it on a surface—not near an open window or a draft—in the room where someone is recovering. Eucalyptus oil is said to generate ozone. It's also a strong antiseptic. The oil has a powerful scent, so before you do this, be sure the sick person agrees to having it there.

Prescription Reading Made Easy

These are some of the Latin terms commonly used on prescription medication...

Term	Abbreviation	Meaning
ante cibum	ac	before food
bis in die	bid	twice a day
gutta	gt	drop
hora somni	hs	at bedtime
oculus dexter	od	right eye
oculus sinister	os	left eye
per os	po	by mouth
post cibum	pc	after food
pro re nata	prn	as needed
quaque 3 hora	q3h	every 3 hours
quaque die	qd	every day
quattuor in die	qid	4 times a day
ter in die	tid	3 times a day

How to Take Pills...Really

▶ Take pills standing up and keep standing for about two minutes afterward. Swallowing them with at least a half cup of water and while standing will give the pills a chance to move swiftly along, instead of staying in your esophagus where they may disintegrate and cause nausea or heartburn.

▶ According to Stephen H. Paul, PhD, professor of pharmaceutical economics and health care delivery at Temple University's School of Pharmacy in Philadelphia, a multivitamin and fat-soluble vitamins A, D and E should be taken with the largest meal of the day. That's when the most fat is present in the stomach to aid in the absorption of the vitamins.

▶ The water-soluble vitamins—C and B-complex—should be taken while eating a meal or a half-hour before the meal. The vitamins help start the biochemical process that breaks down food, making it available to use for energy and tissue building.

▶ If you take large doses of vitamin C, take it in small amounts throughout the day. Your body will use more of it that way, and you will help prevent urinary-tract irritation.

CAUTION: Never take megadoses of any vitamins, minerals or herbs unless you do so under the supervision of a health professional.

Coming to Your Senses

The average pair of eyes can distinguish nearly 8 million differences in color.

The average pair of ears can discriminate among more than 300,000 tones.

The average nose can recognize 10,000 different odors.

There are 1,300 nerve endings per square inch in each average fingertip. The only parts of the body more sensitive to touch are the lips, the tongue and the tip of the nose.

That covers four of our five senses. As for the fifth sense, well—everyone knows, there's no accounting for taste!

Dropper in a Pinch

▶ If you need a dropper *now* for any of your orifices and don't have one (a dropper, that is), you may be able to improvise with a drinking straw. A 3-inch piece of plastic straw will yield about 15 drops of liquid. Of course, that means you have to have a straw *now*.

Do-It-Yourself Hot-Water Bottle and Ice Pack

▶ Don't throw away empty plastic containers made for laundry detergent. The next time you need a hot-water bottle, fill one of those containers. Just be sure the cap is tight-fitting.

▶ You know the plastic bottle with the tight-fitting cap that you just used for a hot-water bottle? You can also fill it with ice and cold water for an instant ice pack.

▶ You can make a flexible ice pack with a towel. Dunk a towel in cold water, wring it out and place it on aluminum foil in the freezer. Before it freezes stiff, take it out and mold it around the bruised or injured body part.

A Fishy Story

Do you have any idea how the custom of serving a slice of lemon with fish first started? It wasn't to cut the fishy taste or to heighten the flavor.

A long time ago, lemon was thought to be more medicine than food. If someone swallowed a fish bone, the thinking was that the lemon juice was so strong that it would dissolve the bone.

Good Health, Italian-Style

It's unusual to find older Italians who have asthma, tuberculosis or gallbladder trouble, thanks to the garlic and olive oil they consume in two of their three daily meals.

Save Vitamins in the Microwave

Fewer vitamins are destroyed during the cooking process when you prepare food in a microwave. Prevent food from burning by adding water—just a little will help to retain as many of the food's nutrients as possible. Also, cover foods while microwaving them in order to reduce the zapping time and keep in more of the nutrients.

Lettuce: Choose Dark Green

The darkest-green salad greens are the best. Compared to iceberg lettuce, romaine lettuce has two times as much folic acid, six times as much vitamin C and eight times as much beta-carotene. Spinach? Dark green. Watercress? Dark green. Collard greens, mustard greens—both dark green.

While you're at it, you may want to include parsley as a salad green, not just as a garnish. Parsley is rich in beta-carotene and vitamin C. It tastes good, too.

CAUTION: Be sure to thoroughly wash raw produce to reduce the risk of food-borne illness. Also, use one of the pesticide-removal rinses below.

Moldy Food

Mold is not a good thing. While it probably won't kill you, it can make you sick. If you see mold on any kind of food, do not give it the "smell test" to see if it has gone bad. Just a whiff of the mold spores can trigger an allergic or respiratory reaction.

Get rid of any soft foods or drinks that have even a hint of mold. However, if certain hard foods, such as Swiss cheese, contain mold, you can chop off the moldy part (play it safe and discard an inch all around the moldy part) and salvage the rest.

Herb and Spice Storage

▶ Store fresh or dried herbs and spices in a cool, dry area. The refrigerator is ideal. When exposed to heat, such as from the kitchen stove, many spices and herbs lose their potency…and their colors fade, too.

Remove Pesticides from Fruits and Vegetables

Poisonous sprays and pesticides can be removed from raw produce using Jay "The Juiceman" Kordich's method.

▶ Fill the sink with cold water, then add 4 tablespoons of salt and the fresh juice from half a lemon. This will make a diluted form of hydrochloric acid.

Soak most fruits and vegetables for five to 10 minutes…soak leafy greens two to three minutes…soak strawberries, blueberries and all other berries one to two minutes. After soaking, rinse the produce thoroughly in plain cold water and enjoy.

▶ You can also soak produce in a sink or basin with ¼ cup of white vinegar. Then, with a vegetable brush, scrub the produce under cold water. Give it a final rinse, then it's ready to be eaten.

Sweet and Salty Substitutes

▶ When substituting honey for sugar in a recipe, use ½ cup of honey for every cup of sugar. Honey has about 65 calories per teaspoon—sugar has 45 calories per teaspoon. Since honey is twice as sweet as sugar, you need to use only half as much honey as sugar. You end up saving calories by using honey.

☞ **WARNING:** Diabetics and people who have honey allergies should not substitute with honey.

▶ If salt is a no-no, a spritz of lemon juice instead may help provide the kick that salt gives food.

Working with Onions Tearlessly…Almost

In her search for a method of working with onions tearlessly, Joan has worn sunglasses, chewed white bread, let cold water run, frozen the onion first and cut off the root end of the onion last. *And then…*

▶ Joan heard *Wheel of Fortune* letter-turner Vanna White thank the TV game show's host, Pat Sajak, for this hint—put a match, unlit, sulfur-side out, between your lips as though it were a cigarette. Keep it there while you peel, grate or cut onions, and you won't have to worry about your mascara running.

This hint is, by far, the best, but a really strong onion will still bring a tear to Joan's eye.

Unhand Those Garlic and Onion Odors

▶ This helpful hint works like magic. Take a piece of flatware (any metal spoon, knife or fork will do), pretend it's a bar of soap and wash your hands with it under cold water. The garlic or onion smell will vanish in seconds.

▶ Those pungent garlic and onion odors can also be removed by rubbing your hands with a slice of fresh tomato.

Hold on to Your Pantyhose

▶ Onions and potatoes will keep better and longer if you store them in a piece of clean hosiery in a cool place. The hose allows the air to move around them.

Natural Insect Repellents

▶ Ants steer clear of garlic. Rub a peeled clove of garlic on problem areas and they will be ant-free in no time. Also vampire-free.

▶ Make pomanders using oranges and cloves (*see* "Preparation Guide" on page 251). Put a pomander in each clothes closet and say bye-bye to moths.

▶ Flies are repelled by thyme tea. Fill a plant mister with a cup of thyme tea and spray around doors and windows to keep flies away.

▶ To keep insects out of bags of grain and flour, add a couple of bay leaves to the containers.

Natural Air Cleaners

Your tax dollars have paid for research conducted by the National Aeronautics and Space Administration (NASA), and now you should—and can—benefit from it.

NASA's scientists in Washington, DC, discovered that several common houseplants can dramatically reduce toxic chemical levels in homes and offices.

If you don't think your home or office is polluted, think again. There's benzene (found in inks, oils, paints, plastics, rubber, detergents, dyes and gasoline)...formaldehyde (found in foam insulation, particle board, pressed-wood products, most cleaning agents and paper products treated with resins, including facial tissues and paper towels)...and trichloroethylene (TCE), which is found in dry-cleaning processes, printing inks, paints, lacquers, varnishes and adhesives. And that's just to name a few.

Here are low-cost, attractive solutions in the form of hardy, easy-to-find, easy-to-grow household plants...

◆ Spider plant (*Chlorophytum comosum "Vittatum"*)—very easy to grow in indirect or bright, diffused light. Be sure to provide good drainage.

◆ Peace lily (*Spathiphyllum species*)—very easy to grow in low-light location. But can be toxic to pets.

◆ Chinese evergreen (*Aglaonema "Silver Queen"*)—very easy to grow in low-light location. Remove overgrown shoots to encourage new growth, and keep the plant bushy. Can be toxic to pets.

◆ Weeping fig (*Ficus benjamina*)—easy to grow, but requires a little special attention. Indirect or bright, diffused light is best.

◆ Golden Pothos or Devil's Claw (*Epipremnum aureum*)—very easy to grow in indirect or bright, diffused light. Can be toxic to pets.

Moderately moist soil is preferred for all of these plants.

NASA (*www.nasa.gov*) recommends placing 15 to 18 plants in an 1,800-sq. ft. home. In a small- to average-sized room, just one plant ought to be effective, especially if it's put where air circulates.

After the plants are in place, you, your colleagues and/or members of your household may notice that their sore throats, headaches, irritated eyes and stuffy noses have cleared up.

Deodorizing Food Jars

▶ In order to reuse a jar, you may want to remove the odors left by its original contents.

For a medium-sized jar, put 1 teaspoon of dry mustard in the jar and fill it to the rim with water.

Leave it that way for four to six hours, then rinse with hot water.

Salt Rub for Gas Odors

▶ To get the smell of gasoline off your hands, rub them with salt.

Stuffed Toys on Ice

▶ Beanie Babies® and other beloved stuffed toys are home to dust mites. Those dust mites can trigger allergic reactions and asthma attacks. To kill those mighty mites, simply put the stuffed critter in a plastic bag and leave it in the freezer for 24 hours, once a week.

Explain to your child that the stuffed toy joined the cast of *Holiday on Ice,* and it is "showtime" every Sunday or whenever.

Cradling Baby

▶ The Talmud (a book of ancient Hebrew writings) suggests that a woman who begins to nurse her child should start on the left side, as this is the source of all understanding.

The late Lee Salk, PhD, who was an expert in child and family psychology, found that 83% of right-handed and 78% of left-handed mothers held their babies on the left side.

Holding a baby on the left side frees up the baby's left ear to hear its mother's voice. Sounds that enter the left ear go to the right side of the brain, which processes tone, melody and emotion.

Bathing Made Easy

For those of you who can't stand long enough to take a shower, or who find it very hard to get up out of a bathtub once you've gotten into it, make the bathing/showering process easier by placing an aluminum beach chair in the tub. Turn on the shower and sit in the chair.

Also, be sure to have those nonslip stick-ons on the floor of the tub. ■

Sources

Sources

HERBAL PRODUCTS AND MORE

Atlantic Spice Company
2 Shore Rd., Box 205
North Truro, MA 02652
Phone: 800-316-7965
Fax: 508-487-2550
www.atlanticspice.com

Blessed Herbs
109 Barre Plains Rd.
Oakham, MA 01068
Phone: 800-489-4372
Fax: 508-882-3755
www.blessedherbs.com

Flower Power Herbs and Roots, Inc.
406 East Ninth St.
New York, NY 10009
Phone: 212-982-6664
www.flowerpower.net

Great American Natural Products
4121 16th St. North
St. Petersburg, FL 33703
Phone: 727-521-4372
Fax: 727-522-6457
www.greatamerican.biz

Herbs by Dial
60 N. Main St.
Manti, UT 84642
Phone: 800-288-4618 or 435-835-9476
www.herbsbydial.com

Indiana Botanic Gardens
3401 West 37th Ave.
Hobart, IN 46342
Phone: 800-644-8327
Fax: 219-947-4148
www.botanicchoice.com

NOW Foods
395 South Glen Ellyn Rd.
Bloomingdale, IL 60108
Phone: 888-669-3663
www.nowfoods.com

NewChapter, Inc.
90 Technology Dr.
Brattleboro, VT 05301
Phone: 800-543-7279
Fax: 800-470-0247
www.newchapter.com

Penn Herb Co. Ltd.
10601 Decatur Rd., Suite 2
Philadelphia, PA 19154
Phone: 800-523-9971 or 215-632-6100
Fax: 215-632-7945
www.pennherb.com

San Francisco Herb Company
250 14th St.
San Francisco, CA 94103
Phone: 800-227-4530 or 415-861-7174
Fax: 415-861-4440
www.sfherb.com

GEMS, NEW-AGE PRODUCTS AND GIFTS

Beyond the Rainbow
Box 110
Ruby, NY 12475
Phone: 845-336-4609
www.rainbowcrystal.com

Crystal Way
2335 Market St.
San Francisco, CA 94114
Phone: 415-861-6511
Fax: 415-861-4229
www.crystalway.com

Mystic Trader
1334 Pacific Ave.
Forest Grove, OR 97116
Phone: 800-634-9057
Fax: 503-357-1669
www.mystictrader.com

VITAMINS, NUTRITIONAL SUPPLEMENTS AND MORE

Bionatures
16508 East Laser Dr., Suite 104
Scottsdale, AZ 85268
Phone: 800-624-7114
Fax: 480-837-8420
www.bionatures.com

Freeda Vitamins
47-25 34th St., Third Floor
Long Island City, NY 11101

Phone: 800-777-3737 or 718-433-4337
Fax: 718-433-4373
www.freedavitamins.com

NutriCology Inc.
2300 North Loop Rd.
Alameda, CA 94502
Phone: 800-545-9960
Fax: 800-688-7426
www.nutricology.com

Nutrition Coalition, Inc.
Box 3001
Fargo, ND 58108
Phone: 800-447-4793 or 218-236-9783
Fax: 218-236-6753
www.willardswater.com

Puritan's Pride/Vitamins.com
1233 Montauk Hwy.
Box 9001
Oakdale, NY 11769
Phone: 800-645-1030
Fax: 631-471-5693
www.puritan.com or *www.vitamins.com*

Superior Nutritionals Inc.
8813 Dr. Martin Luther King, Jr. St. North
St. Petersburg, FL 33702
Phone: 727-577-4344
Fax: 727-577-3166

TriMedica International, Inc.
1895 South Los Feliz Dr.
Tempe, AZ 85281
Phone: 800-800-8849 or 480-998-1041
www.trimedica.com

The Vitamin Shoppe
2101 91st St.
North Bergen, NJ 07047
Phone: 866-293-3367
Fax: 800-852-7153
www.vitaminshoppe.com

NATURAL FOODS AND MORE

Barlean's Organic Oils LLC
4936 Lake Terrell Rd.
Ferndale, WA 98248
Phone: 800-445-3529
www.barleans.com

Gold Mine Natural Food Co.
7805 Arjons Dr.
San Diego, CA 92126
Phone: 800-475-FOOD (3663)
Fax: 858-695-0811
www.goldminenaturalfood.com

Jaffe Bros. Natural Foods, Inc.
28560 Lilac Rd.
Valley Center, CA 92082
Phone: 760-749-1133 or 877-975-2333
Fax: 760-749-1282
www.organicfruitsandnuts.com

BEE PRODUCTS AND MORE

C.C. Pollen Co.
3627 East Indian School Rd., Suite 209
Phoenix, AZ 85018
Phone: 800-875-0096 or 602-957-0096
Fax: 602-381-3130
www.ccpollen.com

Nutraceutical Corporation
1400 Kearns Blvd.
Park City, UT 84060
Phone: 800-669-8877
Fax: 800-767-8877
www.nutraceutical.com

PET FOOD AND PRODUCTS

All the Best Pet Care
8050 Lake City Way
Seattle, WA 98115
Phone: 206-524-0199
www.allthebestpetcare.com

American Holistic Veterinary Medical Association
2218 Old Emmorton Rd.
Bel Air, MD 21015
Phone: 410-569-0795
www.ahvma.org

Golden Tails
6511 Transit Rd., Building A
Bowmansville, NY 14026
Phone: 716-681-6986
www.goldentails.com

Halo Purely for Pets
12400 Race Track Road
Tampa, FL 33626
Phone: 800-426-4256
www.halopets.com

Harbingers of a New Age
717 East Missoula Ave.
Troy, MT 59935
Phone: 406-295-4944
Fax: 406-295-7603
www.vegepet.com

HEALTH-RELATED PRODUCTS

Gaiam—A Lifestyle Company
833 W. South Border Rd.
Box 3095
Boulder, CO 80307
Phone: 877-989-6321
www.gaiam.com

HEALTH-RELATED TRAVEL PRODUCTS AND MORE

Magellan's (Essentials for the Traveler)
110 West Sola St.

Santa Barbara, CA 93101
Phone: 800-962-4943
Fax: 800-962-4940
www.magellans.com

WHOLESALE/RETAIL HEALTH APPLIANCES

Acme Equipment
1032 Concert Ave.
Spring Hill, FL 34609
Phone: 800-882-0157
www.acmeequipment.com

AROMATHERAPY, FLOWER ESSENCES AND MORE

Aromaland
1326 Rufina Circle
Santa Fe, NM 87507
Phone: 800-933-5267
Fax: 505-438-7223
www.aromaland.com

Flower Essence Services
Box 1769
Nevada City, CA 95959
Phone: 800-548-0075
Fax: 530-265-6467
www.fesflowers.com

SERVICES

World Research Foundation (WRF)
For a nominal fee, cofounders LaVerne and Steve Ross will do a search (which includes 5,000 international medical journals) and provide the newest holistic and conventional treatments and diagnostic techniques on almost any condition. The Foundation's library of more than 10,000 books, periodicals and research reports is available to the public free of charge.

41 Bell Rock Plaza
Sedona, AZ 86351
Phone: 928-284-3300
Fax: 928-284-3530
www.wrf.org

US Consumer Product Safety Commission
This government agency, located near Washington, DC, has a toll-free, 24-hour hotline where consumers can obtain product safety and other agency information as well as report unsafe products.

4330 East-West Hwy.
Bethesda, MD 20814
Hotline: 800-638-2772
For hearing impaired: 800-638-8270
Fax: 301-504-0124 or 301-504-0025
www.cpsc.gov

American Board of Medical Specialties
The ABMS is an organization of 24 approved medical specialty boards. It offers a toll-free number where you can confirm that a "specialist" is exactly that. Just provide the doctor's name, and the ABMS will verify whether the doctor is listed in a specialty and his/her year of certification.

222 North LaSalle Street, Suite 1500
Chicago, IL 60601
Phone Verification:
866-ASK-ABMS (275-2267)
Phone: 312-436-2600
www.abms.org

Consumer Information Catalog
The CIC lists more than 200 free and low-cost publications from Uncle Sam—on everything from saving money, staying healthy and getting federal benefits to buying a home and handling consumer complaints. *To get your free copy of the catalog…*

◆ Call toll-free: 888-8-PUEBLO (878-3256).

◆ Send your name and address to:
Consumer Information Catalog
Pueblo, CO 81009

◆ Go to the Internet site *www.pueblo.gsa.gov* to order the catalog. You can also read, print out or download any CIC publication for free.

DISCLAIMER: Addresses, telephone numbers, Web sites and other contact information listed in this book are accurate at the time of publication. However, they are subject to frequent change. ■

Health Resources

Health Resources

Before we begin www-ing through the pages, there is something you should know (but then, you probably already know this)—you can't always trust the information you get on the Internet.

Since we're talking about your health, it can be mighty dangerous to accept and use the wrong advice. We recommend you take whatever information you get online, and show it to and/or discuss it with your health professional.

And there's something else you may already know—and, if not, you should. There's an organization called the Health On the Net (HON) Foundation, which is associated with the University Hospital of Geneva in Switzerland. HON is like the Better Business Bureau for medical Web sites. Its prestigious governing body certifies sites that must abide by eight user-protecting principles. So, if HON gives a site its stamp of approval, you will see it on the site.

Health On the Net Foundation (HON)
Medical Informatics Service
University Hospital of Geneva
24, rue Micheli-du-Crest

1211 Geneva 14
Switzerland
Phone: +41 22 372 62 50
Fax: +41 22 372 88 85
www.hon.ch

Healthcare.com is a site that connects consumers and healthcare professionals with information, enabling tools and online communities. It strives to promote a model of patient-driven healthcare.

HealthCare.com, Inc.
3301 NE 1st Ave., Suite L307
Miami, FL 33137
Phone: 786-472-2966
Fax: 786-472-2969
www.healthcare.com

At these Web sites, you'll find direct links to established (and certified, of course) medical and health resources. Although you may be able to trust the integrity of the information you find on the Web a bit more, it's still important to check out any and all advice with your health professional.

Organizations, Associations and Journals

Administration on Aging
Washington, DC 20201
Phone: 202-619-0724
www.aoa.gov

Alzheimer's Association
225 North Michigan Ave., Floor 17
Chicago, IL 60601
Phone: 800-272-3900
312-335-8700
www.alz.org

American Academy of Allergy, Asthma & Immunology
555 East Wells St.
Milwaukee, WI 53202
Phone: 800-822-2762
414-272-6071
www.aaaai.org

American Academy of Dermatology
Box 4014
Schaumburg, IL 60618
Phone: 866-503-7546
www.aad.org

American Academy of Medical Acupuncture
1970 E. Grand Ave., Suite 330
El Segunda, CA 90245
Phone: 310-364-0193
www.medicalacupuncture.org

American Academy of Neurology
1080 Montreal Ave.
Saint Paul, MN 55116
Phone: 800-879-1960
Fax: 651-695-2791
www.aan.com

American Academy of Orthopaedic Surgeons
6300 North River Rd.
Rosemont, IL 60018
Phone: 800-346-AAOS (2267)
847-823-7186
Fax: 847-823-8125
www.aaos.org

American Academy of Otolaryngology—Head and Neck Surgery
1650 Diagonal Rd.
Alexandria, VA 22314
Phone: 703-836-4444
www.entnet.org

American Association of Naturopathic Physicians
4435 Wisconsin Ave. NW
Suite 403
Washington, DC 20016
Phone: 866-538-2267
202-237-8150
Fax: 202-237-8152
www.naturopathic.org

American Association of Poison Control Centers
515 King St.
Suite 510
Alexandria, VA 22314
Phone: 703-894-1858
Emergency hotline: 800-222-1222
www.aapcc.org

American Board of Medical Specialties
1007 Church St., Suite 404
Evanston, IL 60201-5913
Phone: 847-491-9091
Board Certification Verification:
866-ASK-ABMS (275-2267)
www.abms.org

American Botanical Council
6200 Manor Rd.
Austin, TX 78723

Phone: 512-926-4900
Fax: 512-926-2345
www.herbalgram.org

American Cancer Society
1599 Clifton Rd. NE
Atlanta, GA 30329
Phone: 800-ACS-2345 (227-2345)
www.cancer.org

American Chiropractic Association
1701 Clarendon Blvd.
Arlington, VA 22209
Phone: 800-986-4636
www.acatoday.org

American Chronic Pain Association
Box 850
Rocklin, CA 95677
Phone: 800-533-3231
www.theacpa.org

American College of Obstetricians and Gynecologists
409 12th St. SW
Box 96920
Washington, DC 20090
Phone: 800-673-8444
202-638-5577
www.acog.org

American College of Rheumatology
1800 Century Place
Suite 250
Atlanta, GA 30345
Phone: 404-633-3777
www.rheumatology.org

American Headache Society
19 Mantua Rd.
Mt. Royal, NJ 08061
Phone: 856-423-0043
www.achenet.org

American Council on Exercise
4851 Paramount Dr.
San Diego, CA 92123
Phone: 888-825-3636
858-279-8227
www.acefitness.org

American Dental Association
211 E. Chicago Ave.
Chicago, IL 60611
Phone: 312-440-2500
www.ada.org

American Diabetes Association
National Call Center
1701 North Beauregard St.
Alexandria, VA 22311
Phone: 800-DIABETES (342-2383)
www.diabetes.org

American Dietetic Association
120 South Riverside Plaza
Suite 2000
Chicago, IL 60606
Phone: 800-877-1600
www.eatright.org

American Gastroenterological Association
4930 Del Ray Ave.
Bethesda, MD 20814
Phone: 301-654-2055
www.gastro.org

American Geriatrics Society
350 Fifth Ave., Suite 801
New York, NY 10118
Phone: 212-308-1414
www.americangeriatrics.org

American Heart Association
7272 Greenville Ave.
Dallas, TX 75231
Phone: 800-AHA-USA-1 (242-8721)
www.americanheart.org

American Holistic Medical Association
23366 Commerce Park, Suite 101B
Beechwood, OH 44122
Phone: 216-292-6644
www.holisticmedicine.org

American Journal of Clinical Nutrition
9650 Rockville Pike
Bethesda, MD 20814
Phone: 301-634-7038
Fax: 301-634-7351
www.ajcn.org

American Liver Foundation
75 Maiden Lane, Suite 603
New York, NY 10038
Phone: 800-GO-LIVER (465-4837)
212-668-1000
www.liverfoundation.org

American Lung Association
1301 Pennsylvania Ave. NW
Washington, DC 20004
Phone: 800-586-4872
212-315-8700
www.lungusa.org

American Lyme Disease Foundation, Inc.
Box 466
Lyme, CT 06371
www.aldf.com

American Macular Degeneration Foundation
Box 515
Northampton, MA 01061
Phone: 413-268-7660
www.macular.org

American Pain Foundation
201 North Charles St.
Suite 710
Baltimore, MD 21201
Phone: 888-615-PAIN (7246)
www.painfoundation.org

American Physical Therapy Association
1111 North Fairfax St.
Alexandria, VA 22314
Phone: 800-999-APTA (2782)
703-684-APTA (2782)
For hearing impaired: 703-683-6748
www.apta.org

American Psychological Association
750 First St. NE
Washington, DC 20002
Phone: 800-374-2721
202-336-5500
www.apa.org

American Red Cross
National Headquarters
2025 E St. NW
Washington, DC 20006
Phone: 800-733-2767
www.redcross.org

American Running Association
4405 East-West Hwy., Suite 405
Bethesda, MD 20814
Phone: 800-776-2732
301-913-9517
www.americanrunning.org

American Sleep Apnea Association
6856 Eastern Ave. NW, Suite 203
Washington, DC 20012
Phone: 202-293-3650
www.sleepapnea.org

American Society for Nutrition
9650 Rockville Pike
Bethesda, MD 20814
Phone: 301-634-7050
Fax: 301-634-7892
www.nutrition.org

American Society of Hypertension
148 Madison Ave., Fifth Floor
New York, NY 10016

Phone: 212-696-9099
www.ash-us.org

American Society of Plastic Surgeons
444 East Algonquin Rd.
Arlington Heights, IL 60005
Phone: 888-4-PLASTIC (475-2784)
www.plasticsurgery.org

American Speech–Language–Hearing Association
2200 Research Blvd.
Rockville, MD 20850
Phone: 800-638-8255
www.asha.org

American Stroke Association
7272 Greenville Ave.
Dallas, TX 75231
Phone: 888-4-STROKE (478-7653)
www.strokeassociation.org

American Tinnitus Association
Box 5
Portland, OR 97207
Phone: 800-634-8978
        503-248-9985
www.ata.org

American Urological Association
1000 Corporate Blvd.
Linthicum, MD 21090
800-828-7866 (Urology Health
        Hotline)
Phone: 866-746-4282
        410-689-3700
www.urologyhealth.org

Anxiety Disorders Association of America
8730 Georgia Ave., Suite 600
Silver Spring, MD 20910
Phone: 240-485-1001
www.adaa.org

Arthritis Foundation
Box 7669
Atlanta, GA 30357

Phone: 800-283-7800
www.arthritis.org

Asthma and Allergy Foundation of America
8201 Corporate Drive, Suite 1000
Landover, MD 20785
Phone: 800-7-ASTHMA (727-8462)
Fax: 202-466-8940
www.aafa.org

Center for Science in the Public Interest
1875 Connecticut Ave. NW
Suite 300
Washington, DC 20009
Phone: 202-332-9110
Fax: 202-265-4954
www.cspinet.org

Council for Responsible Nutrition
1828 L St. NW, Suite 510
Washington, DC 20036
Phone: 202-204-7700
www.crnusa.org

Crohn's & Colitis Foundation of America
386 Park Ave. South
17th Floor
New York, NY 10016
Phone: 800-932-2423
www.ccfa.org

Deafness Research Foundation
641 Lexington Ave.
New York, NY 10022
Phone: 866-454-3924
        212-328-9480
For hearing impaired: 888-435-6104
www.drf.org

Endocrine Society
8401 Connecticut Ave.
Suite 900
Chevy Chase, MD 20815
Phone: 301-941-0200
www.endo-society.org

Food and Nutrition Information Center

National Agricultural Library
Room 105
10301 Baltimore Ave.
Beltsville, MD 20705
Phone: 301-504-5755
For hearing impaired: 301-504-6856
Fax: 301-504-6409
www.nal.usda.gov/fnic/

Glaucoma Research Foundation

251 Post St., Suite 600
San Francisco, CA 94108
Phone: 800-826-6693
     415-986-3162
Fax: 415-986-3763
www.glaucoma.org

Healthfinder

National Health Information Center
Box 1133
Washington, DC 20013
www.healthfinder.gov

Herb Research Foundation

4140 15th St.
Boulder, CO 80304
Phone: 303-449-2265
www.herbs.org

Hippocrates Health Institute

1443 Palmdale Court
West Palm Beach, FL 33411
Phone: 800-842-2125
     561-471-8876
Fax: 561-471-9464
www.hippocratesinst.org

International Chiropractors Association

1110 North Glebe Rd., Suite 650
Arlington, VA 22201
Phone: 800-423-4690
     703-528-5000
Fax: 703-528-5023
www.chiropractic.org

International Food Information Council

1100 Connecticut Ave. NW
Suite 430
Washington, DC 20036
Phone: 202-296-6540
Fax: 202-296-6547
www.foodinsight.org

Interstitial Cystitis Association

100 Park Ave., Suite 108A
Rockville, MD 20850
Phone: 800-HELP-ICA (435-7422)
     301-610-5300
Fax: 301-610-5308
www.ichelp.com

Journal of the American Medical Association

P.O. Box 10946
Chicago, IL 60610
Phone: 800-262-2350
     312-464-4444
www.jama.ama-assn.org

Kushi Institute

198 Leland Rd.
Becket, MA 01223
Phone: 800-975-8744
     413-623-5741, x101
Fax: 413-623-8827
www.kushiinstitute.org

The Lancet

Customer Services
Elsevier Ltd.
The Boulevard, Langford Lane
Kidlington, Oxford
OX5 1GB, United Kingdom
Phone: 800-462-6198
     +1-407-345-4082
Toll-free Fax: 800-327-9021
www.thelancet.com

Leukemia & Lymphoma Society

1311 Mamaroneck Ave.
White Plains, NY 10605

Phone: 800-955-4572
914-949-5213
www.leukemia-lymphoma.org

Melanoma International Foundation
250 Mapleflower Rd.
Glenmoore, PA 19343
Phone: 866-INFO-NMF (463-6663)
610-942-3432
www.melanomainternational.org

Merck Manuals Medical Library
Merck Publishing Group
Merck & Co., Inc.
P.O. Box 2000 RY84-15
Rahway, NJ 07065
Phone: 732-594-4600
www.merck.com/mmhe/index.html

National Cancer Institute
6116 Executive Blvd.
Bethesda, MD 20892
Phone: 800-4-CANCER (422-6237)
For hearing impaired: 800-332-8615
www.cancer.gov

National Capital Poison Center
3201 New Mexico Ave. NW
Suite 310
Washington, DC 20016
Phone: 202-362-3867
Emergency line: 800-222-1222
www.poison.org

National Center for Complementary and Alternative Medicine
NCCAM Clearinghouse
Box 7923
Gaithersburg, MD 20898
Phone: 888-644-6226
301-519-3153
For hearing impaired: 866-464-3615
Fax: 866-464-3616
www.nccam.nih.gov

National Center for Homeopathy
801 North Fairfax St.
Suite 306
Alexandria, VA 22314
Phone: 703-548-7790
Fax: 703-548-7792
www.homeopathic.org

National Eye Institute
2020 Vision Place
Bethesda, MD 20892
Phone: 301-496-5248
www.nei.nih.gov

National Headache Foundation
820 North Orleans, Suite 217
Chicago, IL 60610
Phone: 888-NHF-5552 (643-5552)
www.headaches.org

National Heart, Lung and Blood Institute
Building 31, Room 5A52
31 Center Dr., MSC 2486
Bethesda, MD 20892
Phone: 301-592-8573
For hearing impaired: 240-629-3255
Fax: 240-629-3246
www.nhlbi.nih.gov

National Institute for Occupational Safety and Health
395 E. Street SW, Suite 9200
Washington, DC 20201
Phone: 800-232-4636
513-533-8328
www.cdc.gov/niosh

National Institute of Allergy and Infectious Diseases
6610 Rockledge Dr.
MSC 6612
Bethesda, MD 20892
Phone: 866-284-4107
301-496-5717
www3.niaid.nih.gov

National Institute of Arthritis and Musculoskeletal and Skin Diseases

One AMS Circle
Bethesda, MD 20892
Phone: 877-22-NIAMS (226-4267)
301-495-4484
For hearing impaired: 301-565-2966
www.niams.nih.gov

National Institute of Dental and Craniofacial Research

National Institutes of Health
Bethesda, MD 20892-2190
Phone: 301-402-7364
www.nidcr.nih.gov

National Institute of Diabetes and Digestive and Kidney Diseases

Building 31, Room 9A06
31 Center Dr., MSC 2560
Bethesda, MD 20892-2560
Phone: 301-496-3583
www.niddk.nih.gov

National Institutes of Health

9000 Rockville Pike
Bethesda, MD 20892
Phone: 301-496-4000
www.nih.gov
(other toll-free NIH telephone
numbers can be found at *www.nih.
gov/health/infoline.htm*)

National Institute of Mental Health

6001 Executive Blvd.
MSC 9663, Room 8184
Bethesda, MD 20892
Phone: 866-615-NIMH (6464)
301-443-4513
For hearing impaired: 301-443-8431
www.nimh.nih.gov

National Institute of Neurological Disorders and Stroke

Box 5801
Bethesda, MD 20824

Phone: 800-352-9424
301-496-5751
For hearing impaired: 301-468-5981
www.ninds.nih.gov

National Institute on Aging

Building 31, Room 5C27
31 Center Dr., MSC 2292
Bethesda, MD 20892
Phone: 301-496-1752
www.nia.nih.gov

National Institute on Alcohol Abuse and Alcoholism

5635 Fishers Ln., MSC 9304
Bethesda, MD 20892
Phone: 301-443-3860
www.niaaa.nih.gov

National Kidney Foundation

30 East 33rd St.
New York, NY 10016
Phone: 800-622-9010
www.kidney.org

National Multiple Sclerosis Society

733 Third Ave.
New York, NY 10017
Phone: 800-FIGHT-MS (344-4867)
www.nmss.org

National Osteoporosis Foundation

1232 22nd St. NW
Washington, DC 20037
Phone: 800-231-4222
202-223-2226
www.nof.org

National Prostate Cancer Coalition

1154 15th St. NW
Washington, DC 20005
Phone: 888-245-9455
202-463-9455
www.zerocancer.org

National Psoriasis Foundation
6600 SW 92nd Ave.
Suite 300
Portland, OR 97223
Phone: 800-723-9166
503-244-7404
www.psoriasis.org

National Safety Council
1121 Spring Lake Dr.
Itasca, IL 60143
Phone: 630-285-1121
www.nsc.org

National Sleep Foundation
1522 K St. NW, Suite 500
Washington, DC 20005
Phone: 202-347-3471
www.sleepfoundation.org

National Spinal Cord Injury Association
1 Church St. #600
Rockville, MD 20850
Phone: 800-962-9629
www.spinalcord.org

National Stroke Association
9707 East Easter Ln.
Centennial, CO 80112
Phone: 800-STROKES (787-6537)
Fax: 303-649-1328
www.stroke.org

National Women's Health Information Center
8270 Willow Oaks Corporate Dr.
Fairfax, VA 22031
Phone: 800-994-WOMAN (9662)
www.4women.gov

New England Journal of Medicine
10 Shattuck St.
Boston, MA 02115
Phone: 800-445-8080
617-734-9800
Fax: 617-739-9864
www.nejm.org

Parkinson's Disease Foundation
1359 Broadway, Suite 1509
New York, NY 10018
Phone: 800-457-6676
www.pdf.org

Practical Gastroenterology
c/o Shugar Publishing, Inc.
99B Main St.
Westhampton Beach, NY 11978
Phone: 631-288-4404
Fax: 631-288-4435
www.practicalgastro.com

School of Natural Healing (and Christopher Publications)
Box 412
Springville, UT 84663
Phone: 800-372-8255
801-489-4254
Fax: 801-489-8341
www.schoolofnaturalhealing.com

SeekWellness.com
75 South Main St.
PMB #162
Concord, NH 03301
Phone: 800-840-9301
www.seekwellness.com

Skin Cancer Foundation
149 Madison Ave.
Suite 901
New York, NY 10016
Phone: 800-SKIN-490 (754-6490)
www.skincancer.org

Susan G. Komen Breast Cancer Foundation
5005 LBJ Freeway
Suite 250
Dallas, TX 75244
Phone: 877-465-6636
Toll-Free Breast Care Helpline:
800-IM-AWARE (462-9273)
ww5.komen.org

US Centers for Disease Control and Prevention

1600 Clifton Rd.
Atlanta, GA 30333
Phone: 800-232-4636
www.cdc.gov

US Department of Agriculture

1400 Independence Ave. SW
Washington, DC 20250
Phone: 877-677-2369
www.usda.gov

US Department of Health and Human Services

200 Independence Ave. SW
Washington, DC 20201
Phone: 877-696-6775
www.hhs.gov

US Food and Drug Administration

5600 Fishers Ln.
Rockville, MD 20857
Phone: 888-INFO-FDA (463-6332)
www.fda.gov

US National Library of Medicine

8600 Rockville Pike
Bethesda, MD 20894
Phone: 888-FIND-NLM (346-3656)
301-594-5983
www.nlm.nih.gov

US Soyfoods Directory

c/o Physicians Laboratories
1031 E. Mountain St., Building 302
Kernersville, NC 27284
Phone: 800-738-4825
www.soyfoods.com

Weight-Control Information Network (WIN)

One WIN Way
Bethesda, MD 20892
Phone: 877-946-4627
Fax: 202-828-1028
http://win.niddk.nih.gov

Wunderlich Center for Nutritional Medicine

8821 Dr. Martin Luther King, Jr.
St. North
St. Petersburg, FL 33702
Phone: 727-822-3612
Fax: 727-578-1370
www.wunderlichcenter.com

Online-Only Resources

www.acupuncture.com

Information and resources on alternative medicine. It has a provider directory, provides answers to frequently asked questions, and allows you to call on its experts to answer more specific questions.

www.kidshealth.org

KidsHealth is the largest site on the Web providing doctor-approved health information about children from before birth through adolescence. The site was created by pediatric medical experts at the Nemours Foundation.

www.mealsforyou.com

Thousands of recipes, meal plans and complete nutritional information. Look up recipes by name, ingredient or nutritional content.

www.medlineplus.gov

Health information selected by the US National Library of Medicine and the National Institutes of Health (NIH) from a database of more than 4,000 medical journals.

www.mothernature.com

In addition to its main commerce area, this site provides a wealth of health information, an encyclopedia of natural health topics, expert advice and an archive of articles on a range of subjects.

www.pain.com

This site offers comprehensive resources about pain studies, links to other pain-control sites and more.

www.pitt.edu/~cbw/altm.html

The Alternative Medicine Homepage is a jump-station for sources of information on unconventional, unorthodox, unproven or alternative, complementary, innovative and integrative therapies.

www.webmd.com

This comprehensive site includes information on a variety of illnesses and diseases as well as herbs, alternative medicine and more. ■

Recommended
Reading List

Recommended Reading List

Body Power/Brain Power

Body for Life, by Bill Phillips with Michael D'Orso. HarperCollins.

The Healing Power of the Mind, by Rolf Alexander, MD. Healing Arts Press.

Your Miracle Brain, by Jean Carper. HarperCollins.

Food, Healthful Eating and Weight Programs

Flax for Life!, by Jade Beutler, RRT, RCP. Apple Publishing.

Food Enzymes—The Missing Link to Radiant Health, by Humbert Santillo, MH, ND. Lotus Press.

40-30-30 Fat-Burning Nutrition, by Joyce and Gene Daoust. Wharton Publishing.

Garlic—Nature's Super Healer, by Joan Wilen and Lydia Wilen. Prentice Hall.

Healthy Nuts, by Gene Spiller, PhD. Avery Publishing Group.

The Omega Diet, by Artemis P. Simopoulos, MD, and Jo Robinson. HarperCollins.

Seaweed—A Cook's Guide, by Lesley Ellis. Fisher Books.

7-Day Detox Miracle, by Peter Bennett, ND, and Stephen Barrie, ND, with Sara Faye. Prima Lifestyles.

Understanding Fats & Oils, by Michael T. Murray, ND, and Jade Beutler, RRT, RCP. Apple Publishing.

Herbs

The Green Pharmacy, by James A. Duke, PhD. St. Martin's Press.

The Herbal Home Spa, by Greta Breedlove. Storey Books.

Herbal Remedy Gardens, by Dorie Byers. Storey Books.

Natural Healing with Herbs, by Humbert Santillo, MH, ND. Hohm Press.

10 Essential Herbs, by Lalitha Thomas. Hohm Press.

Just for Men

The Viagra Alternative, by Marc Bonnard, MD. Healing Arts Press.

Just for Women

The Estrogen Alternative, by Raquel Martin with Judi Gerstung, DC. Inner Traditions International.

Your Pregnancy—Every Woman's Guide, by Glade B. Curtis, MD, OB/GYN. DaCapo Lifelong.

Just for Pets

Natural Pet Cures, by John Heinerman, PhD. Prentice Hall.

New-Age and Age-Old (Mostly Alternative) Therapies

Alternative Medicine: The Definitive Guide, compiled by The Burton Goldberg Group. Ten Speed Press.

Ayurvedic Secrets to Longevity and Total Health, by Peter Anselmo with James S. Brooks, MD. Prentice Hall.

Common Scents, by Lorrie Hargis. Woodland Publishing.

Creative Healing, by Michael Samuels, MD, and Mary Rockwood Lane, RN. John Wiley & Sons.

The Healing Power of Color, by Betty Wood. Destiny Books.

Healing Visualizations, by Gerald Epstein, MD. Bantam Books.

Laffirmations—1,001 Ways to Add Humor to Your Life and Work, by Joel Goodman. Health Communications, Inc.

The Power of Touch, by Phyllis K. Davis, PhD. Hay House, Inc.

Prayer, Faith and Healing—Cure Your Body, Heal Your Mind and Restore Your Soul, by Kenneth Winston Caine and Brian Paul Kaufman. Rodale Books.

Qigong—Essence of the Healing Dance, by Garri Garripoli and Friends. Health Communications, Inc.

The Ultimate Healing System, by Donald Lepore, ND. Woodland Publishing.

Your Own Perfect Medicine, by Martha M. Christy. Wishland Publishing.

Specific Health Challenges

An Alternative Medicine Definitive Guide to Cancer, by W. John Diamond, MD, and W. Lee Cowden, MD, with Burton Goldberg. Alternativemedicine.com Books.

Asthma-Free in 21 Days, by Kathryn Shafer, PhD, with Fran Greenfield, MA. HarperCollins.

Beyond Aspirin, by Thomas Newmark and Paul Schulick. Hohm Press.

Enhancing Fertility Naturally, by Nicky Wesson. Healing Arts Press.

Naturally Healthy Skin, by Stephanie Tourles. Storey Books.

The Pain Cure, by Dharma Singh Khalsa, MD, with Cameron Stauth. Warner Books.

The Prozac Alternative, by Ran Knishinsky. Healing Arts Press.

Depression-Free, Naturally, by Joan Mathews Larson, PhD. Ballantine Books.

Vitamins and Other Supplements

Dr. Heinerman's Encyclopedia of Nature's Vitamins and Minerals, by John Heinerman, PhD. Prentice Hall.

The Natural Pharmacist: Natural Health Bible, edited by Steven Bratman, MD, and David Kroll, PhD. Crown Publishing. ■

Recipe Index

Breakfast Fare
The Amazing Gin-Soaked Raisin
 Remedy, 13
Banana Bread Oatmeal, 22
Hazelnut Corn Bran Muffins, 278
Pancake Mix, 263
Three-Cherry Jam, 93
Waffle Mix, 263
Yogurt Cereal Bars, 283

Beverages
The Koch Family Guggle-Muggle, 41
Love Elixir, 148
Papaya Shake, 123

Appetizers
Apple Salsa with Cinnamon Tortilla
 Chips, 108
Cinnamon-Roasted Almonds, 132
New West Crab Cakes, 277
Sunrise Salsa, 34

Salads
Papaya Salad with String Beans, 11
Organic Garden Salad with Fresh
 Herbs, 26
Tropical Fruit Salad with Ginger and
 Peanuts, 280
Yogurt Fruit Salad with Sunflower
 Seeds, 75

Soups
Carrot Soup, 210
Chicken Soup with Okra, 48
Chilled Czech Blueberry Soup, 76
Dr. Ziment's Chicken Soup, 36
Garlic Soup, 269
Lentil Vegetable Soup, 231
Lillian Wilen's Essential Chicken
 Soup, 35

Entrées
Cashew Shrimp, 279
Champagne-Poached Salmon, 73
Curried Turkey, 282
40-Clove Garlic Chicken, 220
Four-Bean Bake, 261
Honey Lemon Basil Chicken, 260
Pasta with Zucchini and Roasted
 Garlic, 268
Pecan Four-Cheese Pizza, 278
Sautéed Tofu with Ginger Sauce, 273
Walnut Macaroni Casserole, 276

Side Dishes
Beets in Orange Sauce, 70
Broccoli Slaw, 90
Country Cole Slaw, 229
Cucumbers in Sour Cream, 120
Garlicky Greens, 141
Jade Green Broccoli, 39
Lemony–Parsley Carrots, 78

Mashed Sweet Potatoes with Garlic,
 268
Mexican Eggplant with Fennel Seeds,
 195
Peanut Slaw, 182
Roasted Garlic, 267
Sauerkraut, 253
Sexual-Stamina Eggplant, 221
Sweet Pickled Jerusalem Artichokes,
 18

Dips/Sauces
Eggplant–Yogurt Dip, 282
Emerald Sauce, 25
Ginger–Onion Vinaigrette, 272

Desserts
African Banana Fritters, 54
Apricot Snowballs, 168
Elderberry Pie, 163
Flax Cookies, 265
Ginger Cookies, 271
Make Your Own Yogurt, 284
Peanut Ice Cream, 280
Sweet and Spicy Pumpkin Seeds, 143

Index

A

Acid burns, 30
Acne, 153–154
  in children, 207
  scars from, 155
Acorns for sexual problems, 149
Acupressure
  for appetite management,
    196
  for colds and flu, 38
  for constipation, 47
  for coughs, 50
  for depression, 55
  for diarrhea, 58
  for headaches, 105
  for hiccups, 117
  hoku point, 181
  for insomnia, 165
  for muscle cramps, 136
  for tension and anxiety, 175
  for toothache, 179
Acupuncture
  for colds and flu, 38
  eyes and, 79
Aduki beans for kidney problems,
    190
Aerobic exercise, hearing and, 68
Age spots, 28
Alcoholic beverages. *See also*
  Drinking
    calcium and, 229
    dehydration and, 129
    prostate problems and, 218
    weight control and, 201
Alcoholism, 59

Allergies. *See also* Asthma; Hayfever
  bee pollen for, 259
  to bee stings, 4
  hangovers and, 61
  to honey, 4, 49
  prevention of, 3
  honeycomb for, 4
  relief from, 3
Allicin, 37
Allspice for indigestion, 126
Almonds. *See also* Nuts
  allergy to, 4
  for dead skin, 155
  for headaches, 103–104
  for heartburn, 127
  for hemorrhoids, 113
  intoxication, preventing, with,
    63
  for memory problems, 132
Aloe vera
  for arthritis, 16
  for burns, 30
  for headaches, 105
  for shingles, 115
  for warts, 193
Alopecia, 94
Amber
  for nosebleeds, 140
  for sore throats, 43
Amethyst
  for memory problems, 132
  for preventing intoxication,
    63
Ammonia for insect stings, 7
Anemia, 5–6

Animals
  bee pollen for, 261
  bites, 6
Anise remedies
  for coughs, 209
  for halitosis, 184
  for indigestion, 122, 126
  for nightmares, 166
  for sore throats, 45
Anisette liqueur for flatulence, 125
Antibiotics, yogurt and, 281–282
Anticoagulants with garlic, 24
Anti-Jet Lag Diet, 129
Anxiety. *See* Tension and anxiety
Aphrodisiacs, 150–152, 272
Apple butter for burns, 30
Apple cider vinegar
  for aching feet, 84
  for arthritis, 13
  for colds and flu, 37–38
  for cold sores, 115
  for coughs, 48
  for fatigue, 82
  for hair problems, 96
  for headaches, 106
  for heartburn, 127
  for hiccups, 117
  for hoarseness/laryngitis, 44
  for indigestion, 123
  for kidney problems, 190
  for leg cramps, 135
  for memory problems, 132
  for pruritis, 143
  for rectal itching, 144
  for shingles, 116

in skin-awakener, 236
  for sore throats, 42
  for sprains, 171
  for varicose veins, 88–89
  for weight management, 196
Apples/apple juice remedies
  cholesterol and, 20
  for coffee breath, 184
  for colds and flu, 39
  for conjunctivitis, 71
  for constipation, 46
  for diarrhea, 58
  for eye inflammation, 73
  for high blood pressure, 119
  for hoarseness/laryngitis, 44
  for indigestion, 212
Apricot products
  for anemia, 5
  for asthma, 18
  for constipation, 46
  in stopping smoking, 169–170
Arginine
  for herpes, 114
  in nuts, 275
Arrhythmia, 110
Arrowroot for indigestion, 124
Arthritis
  natural remedies for, 10–12
  topical treatments for, 12–16
Artificial tears, 72
Ascorbic acid for hemorrhoids, 113
Asparagine for prostate enlargement, 218
Asparagus
  as diuretic, 189
  for kidney stones, 190
Aspirin
  for hair problems, 98
  for heart attacks, 109
Asthma, 16–19. *See also* Allergies; Hayfever
    wild cherry-bark tea for, 17
Atherosclerosis
  cholesterol and, 20–22
  natural remedies for, 19–20
Athletes, bee pollen for, 259
Athlete's foot, 87
Attention deficit/hyperactivity disorder (ADHD), 208
Autohypnotic suggestions for constipation, 47
Avocados
  cholesterol and, 20–21

for dry elbows and knees, 158
  for dry skin, 237
Ayurvedic medicine, 273

B
Back pain, 23–25
  ginger for, 271
Baking soda
  for animal bites or insect stings, 6
  for corns and calluses, 85
  for halitosis, 184
  as hand cleanser, 101
  for hives, 143
  for pyorrhea, 181
  for shingles, 116
Baldness, 94–95
Banana remedies
  allergies and, 3
  for bruises, 27
  for cuts, 159
  for depression, 53
  for diarrhea, 58
  for leg cramps, 134
  for poison ivy, 147
  for splinter removal, 159
  in wrinkle prevention, 160
Bancha leaves for sties, 77
Bandage remover, pain-free, 240
Barley/barley water, 249
  for coughs, 49
  for diarrhea, 57–58, 210
  for ulcers, 186
Basil
  for indigestion, 124
  menstruation, for bringing on, 227
  in pain relief, 14
Bathing made easy, 293
Bay leaves
  for colic, 212
  for flatulence, 125
B-complex vitamins, when to take, 289
Beans. *See also* Black beans; Garbanzo beans
  for coughs, 50
  in stabilizing blood sugars, 22
Beauty mask, making your own, 236
Bed rest, disadvantages of, 287
Bed-wetting, 188–189
  in children, 208–209
Bee pollen, 258–262
  for enlarged prostate, 217

for fatigue, 81–82
  for menopause, 231
Bee stings, allergies to, 4
Beet remedies
  for constipation, 46
  for coughs, 49
  for dandruff, 95
  for low blood pressure, 121
Ben Wa Balls for sexual problems, 149
Bioflavonoids
  for atherosclerosis, 20
  for hay fever, 4
  for nosebleed, 141
  for spider bites, 9
Bites and stings, 6–9
Black beans
  for back pain, 23–24
  for hoarseness/laryngitis, 44
Blackberries for diarrhea, 58, 210
Black cohosh for menopause, 231–232
Black eyes, 28–29
Black radish for gallbladder problems, 92
Blackstrap molasses
  for bruises, 27
  for canker sores, 185
  for constipation, 48
  in preventing tooth decay, 182–183
  for warts, 193
Black thread as cough remedy, 209–210
Black widow spider bites, 9
Bladder control in women, 225
Bleeding disorders and garlic, 5
Bleeding gums, 180, 182
Blisters, fever, 115
Blood clots, rocking chair to prevent, 135
Blood pressure. *See* Hypertension; Low blood pressure
Blood-related conditions
  anemia, 5–6
Bloodshot eyes, 69
Blue
  in attracting mosquitoes, 8
  effect of, on suicide rate, 133
  food consumption and, 199
Blueberries for night vision, 76
Body Mass Index (BMI), 202, 203
Body odor, 25–26

Boils, 156–158
Brain fog. *See* Jungle Punch
Bran
 for earaches, 65
 for indigestion, 125, 126
Brazil nuts, 275–276
Breast-feeding, 230–231
 colic and, 212–213
Brewer's yeast
 for acne, 154
 for cataracts, 70
 cholesterol and, 21–22
 for constipation, 47
 for corns and calluses, 86
 for eczema, 142
 for nursing mother, 230
 for wrinkles, 160
Broccoli remedies
 for colds and flu, 39
 for heart problems, 111
Bromelain for carpal tunnel
 syndrome, 34
Bronchial coughs, 51
Brown recluse spider bites, 9
Brown rice for acne, 154
Brown spots, 28
Bruises and skin discoloration,
 27–29
Burdock for carpal tunnel syndrome,
 34
Burning feet, 31
Burns, 29–31
Burnt throat, 31
Burnt tongue, 31
Bursitis, 10
Butcher's broom for phlebitis,
 142
Buttermilk. *See also* Dairy products
 for diarrhea, 58
 for enlarged pores, 155
 for freckles, 158
 for genital itching, 144
 in wrinkle prevention, 161
B vitamins, 6. *See also* specific
 vitamin
 for fingernail problems, 102
 for hangovers, 62

C
Cabbage remedies
 for alcohol consumption, 62
 for migraine headaches, 107
 for ulcers, 186–187

Caffeine. *See also* Coffee
 calcium and, 229
 depression and, 53
Calcium, 6, 281
 for leg cramps, 134, 135
 need for, 245
 nervous tics and, 55
 for premenstrual relief, 229
Calendula for hair problems, 97
Calluses, 85–86
Calories burned per hour, 199
Cancer therapy, bee pollen and, 260
Candida/yeast problems and carrot
 juice, 78
Canker sores, 185
Capsaicin for carpal tunnel syndrome,
 34
Caraway seed remedies
 for colic, 212
 for earaches, 65
 for indigestion, 122, 126
Carbonated drinks for nausea and
 vomiting, 137
Cardamom seeds for indigestion,
 122
Carob
 as caffeine substitute, 175
 for indigestion, 212
Carotenoids and stopping smoking,
 169
Carpal tunnel syndrome, 32–34
Carrots/carrot juice
 as blood fortifier, 6
 cholesterol and, 21
 for diarrhea, 210
 for dry skin, 238
 for eye problems, 78, 80
 for heartburn, 127
 for memory problems, 131
 for pruritis, 143
 in stopping smoking, 169
 for urinary problems, 188
 for vision, 76, 78
 for warts, 192
 for weeping sores, 156
Cashews, 275, 276, 277
Castor oil
 for canker sores, 185
 for corns and calluses, 85
 for earaches/ear infections, 65
 for freckles, 158
 for plantar warts, 193
 for rough hands, 101

 for tinnitus, 67–68
 for wrinkles, 160
Cataracts, 69–71
 sun blindness and, 77
Catnip for sprains, 172
Cavity prevention, 182–183
Cayenne pepper remedies
 for arthritis, 15–16
 for carpal tunnel syndrome, 34
 diarrhea and, 57
 for excessive menstrual flow, 228
 as fever reducer, 42
 for hangovers, 60
 for heart problems, 112
 for high blood pressure, 120
 for indigestion, 124
 for motion sickness, 138
 for nosebleeds, 140
 for sprains, 171
 for tension and anxiety, 175
 for toothache, 179
 for wounds, 156
Celery/celery juice
 for arthritis, 11
 for depression, 55
 as diuretic, 189
 for sciatica, 24
Cellulite, eliminating, 200
Chalk for warts, 193
Chamomile
 for carpal tunnel syndrome, 34
 for earaches, 65
 for eye problems, 71, 74, 76, 79
 for hair problems, 97, 99
 for heart palpitations, 110
 for indigestion, 123, 212
 for insomnia, 162, 164
 as mood lifter, 53–54
 for motion sickness, 138
 for nausea and vomiting, 137
 for oily skin, 237
 for picky eaters, 213
 for premenstrual relief, 229
 for sore throats, 43
 for toothache, 178
 for warts, 192
Champagne
 for exfoliation scrub, 239
Chapped hands, 101–102
Chapped lips, 239
Charcoal
 activated, for diarrhea, 57
 for flatulence, 125

Charley horse, 133
Chemical burns, 30
Chemicals as eye irritants, 72
Cherries/cherry juice
    for arthritis, 10–11
    for gout, 92
Cherry-bark tea for asthma, 17
Chia seeds
    as energy booster, 83
    for tension and anxiety, 176
Chicken pox
    in children, 209
    virus causing, and relation to
        shingles, 115
Chicken soup
    for colds, 35–37
    for hangovers, 62
Chickpeas for brown spots, 28
Chihuahuas, asthma and, 16
Children's health
    acne, 207
    attention deficit/hyperactivity
        disorder, 208
    bed-wetting, 208–209
    chicken pox, 209
    colds and flu, 209
    colic, 212–213
    coughs, 209–210
    croup, 210
    diarrhea, 210–211
    eye irritants, 209
    fever, 211
    foreign substance in the nose, 211
    head lice, 211–212
    indigestion, 212–213
    picky eaters, 213
    rashes, 213
    splinters, 213
    teething, 214
    tonsillitis, 214
Chinese balls for carpal tunnel
    syndrome, 33
Chives
    for hair problems, 96
    iron in, 5
Chocolate
    craving for, 175
    for firming facial treatment, 236
Cholesterol
    high, 20–22
    nuts to lower, 276
Choline for memory problems, 131
Chromium, cholesterol and, 21–22

Cinnamon remedies
    for bed-wetting, 208
    for diarrhea, 57, 210
    for excessive menstrual flow, 228
    for flu, 41
    for halitosis, 183
Citrus essential oils as mood lifter, 54
Clams for sexual problems, 150
Cleavers for weight control, 195
Clove remedies
    for halitosis, 184
    for memory problems, 131
    for nausea and vomiting, 137
    for paper cuts, 159
    in stopping smoking, 169
    for toothache, 180
Cobnuts, 276
Cob webs for wounds, 156
Coconut macaroons for diarrhea,
    58–59
Coconut milk, 249
    for enlarged prostate, 217
Coconut oil for type 2
    diabetes, 56
Cod-liver oil
    for arthritis, 12
    for boils, 157
Coenzyme Q-10 for pyorrhea, 181
Coffee. *See also* Caffeine
    for arthritis, 14–15
    elimination from diet, for prostate
        problems, 218
Coffee breath, 184
Cola syrup for nausea and vomiting,
    138
Cold feet, 86–87
Colds and flu, 35–45
    in children, 209
Cold showers in stimulating sexual
    desire, 221
Cold sores, 115
Colic in children, 212–213
Color as mood lifter, 55. *See also*
    Blue; Yellow
Combination skin, 238–239
Comfrey remedies
    for gout, 92–93
    for phlebitis, 89–90
    for sprains, 172
Computers, carpal tunnel syndrome
    and use of, 33
Confucius, 273
Conjunctivitis, 3, 71

Constipation, 46–48
    prunes for, 131
    during pregnancy, 230
Contact lens, removal of, before
    doing eyewash, 80
Copper, 5, 275
Coriander seeds for sexual problems,
    151
Corn for canker sores, 185
Cornmeal
    in dry shampoo, 97
    for stomach cramps, 128
Corn oil
    as source of polyunsaturated
        fats, 22
    for dandruff, 96
Corns and calluses, 85–86
Corn silk/corn silk tea
    for arthritis, 14
    for bed-wetting, 208
    for cystitis, 226
    as diuretic, 189
    for enlarged prostate, 218
    for urinary problems, 188
Cornstarch
    for bruises, 27
    in dry shampoo, 97
    for genital itching, 144
    for hives, 144
    for shaving rash, 145
Cortisone
    garlic therapy as substitute
        for, 17
    yucca as substitute for, 15
Coughs, 48–52
    in children, 209–210
Cox-2 inhibitors, 271
Crab for poison ivy, 147
Cracked heels, 88
Cramp bark for leg cramps, 135
Cranberries/cranberry juice
    for asthma, 19
    for cystitis, 226
    for hemorrhoids, 113
    for urinary problems, 188
Cream of tartar
    for hives, 144
    for sore throats, 42
Crohn's disease, 58–59
Croup in children, 210
Cucumber remedies
    for acne, 154
    for drinking problems, 60

for eye inflammation, 74
for high blood pressure, 119
for menopause, 232
Cuts and scrapes, 158–159
Cystitis, 225–226

D

Daikon
for bruises, 27
for indigestion, 122
Dairy products and asthma, 17
Damiana for impotence, 220
Dandelion remedies
for corns and calluses, 86
for freckles, 158
for warts, 192
Dandruff, 95–96
Dates for constipation, 47
Deep breathing, low blood pressure
and, 121
Dental floss, bad breath and, 183
Dental work, preparing for, 180
Depression and stress, 53–55
Dermatitis, 3
Detoxification, 169
Devil's claw, 292
for carpal tunnel syndrome, 34
Diabetes, 56
coconut oil for, 56
infected sores and, 156
Diamonds for insomnia, 162
Diaper rash, 213
Diarrhea, 56–59
cherries as cause of, 11
in children, 210–211
yogurt for, 59, 282
Dill seeds for indigestion, 126
Diuretics, 188–189
potassium loss and, 134–135
Double-chin prevention, 239
Dried beans, soaking, in preventing
gas, 126
Drinking, 59–63. *See also* Alcoholic
beverages
Drug allergies, 3
Dry cough, 51
Dry eyes, 71–72
Dry shampoo, 97
Dry skin, 237–238
Dysentery, 59

E

Earaches, 64–65
Ear pressure, 66

Ears
infections in, 65–66
insects in, 66
wax build-up in, 67
Echinacea for colds and flu, 38–39
Eczema, 3, 142
Egg/egg white
for asthma, 17–18
for boils, 157
Eggplant
for impotence, 221
for oily skin, 237
Elbows, dry, 158
Elderberry
for insomnia, 162
for sciatica, 24
Emphysema, 69
Energy boosters, 82–84
Epsom salts
for aching feet, 84
for charley horse, 133
for depression, 55
for shingles, 116
for tooth extractions, 180–181
Escarole for constipation, 47
Essential fatty acids (EFAs), 262–266
Eucalyptus oil
for arthritis, 16
as mosquito repellent, 8
Exercise
for constipation, 47
hearing and, 68
Kegel, 149, 225
in preventing carpal tunnel
syndrome, 32–33
weight management and, 199–200,
201, 202
Exfoliant, making your own, 239
Eyebright
for eye problems, 71, 76, 79
for memory problems, 132
Eyebrows, tweezing, 240
Eye irritants, 72–73
in children, 209
Eyelash nits, 211–212
Eyes
bloodshot eyes, 69
cataracts, 69–71
conjunctivitis, 71
dry eyes, 71–73
eye inflammation, 73–74
eye irritants, 72–73, 209
eyestrain, 74–75

eye strengtheners, 78–79
eye twitch, 75
glaucoma, 75–76
night vision, 76
puffiness, 74
sties, 76–77
sun blindness, 77
sunburn, 173
Eye wrinkles, 160

F

Face relaxer, tip for, 239
Facial masks, 236
for combination skin, 238
for dry skin, 238
for oily skin, 237
Fainting, 81
Fatigue, 81–84
Feet and legs. *See* Foot and leg
problems
Fennel seed remedies
for colic, 212
for eye problems, 74, 76, 79
for milk production when breast
feeding, 230
for sexual problems, 151
for weight control, 195
Fenugreek/fenugreek tea
for boils, 157
cholesterol and, 21
for hay fever, 4
for indigestion, 123
for sexual problems, 149–150
Fertility, bee pollen for, 259
Fever blisters, 115
Fevers, 288
in children, 211
relievers, 41–42
Fig remedies
for boils, 157
as energy booster, 83
for toothache, 180
for undereye circles, 28
for warts, 192
Filberts, 275, 276
Fingernail polish for cold sores,
115
Fingernails, 102–103
buffing, 94
manicure protection, 240
Finger sores, 103
Flatulence, 125–126
Flavonoids, 275

Flaxseed, 262–266
    blood-thinning medications and, 72
    cholesterol and, 21
    for constipation, 46
    for insomnia, 162–163
    for menopausal symptoms, 263
    for psoriasis, 142
Flu. *See* Colds and flu
Fluoride in preventing tooth decay, 182
Folic acid, 275
Food allergies, indigestion and, 122
Foot and leg problems, 84–90
Foreign substance in the nose in children, 211
Freckles, 158
Frostbite, 91
Frozen vegetables for black eye, 29

G
Gallbladder problems, 92
Garbanzo beans for brown spots, 28
Garlic, 266–270. *See also* Garlic remedies
    breath, 184–185
    odor on hands, 291
    supplements, 5, 269
Garlic remedies
    for acne, 154
    for arthritis, 12
    for asthma, 17
    for atherosclerosis, 19–20
    for athlete's foot, 87
    as blood fortifier, 5
    for boils, 157
    cholesterol and, 21
    for colds and flu, 37
    for cold sores, 115
    for constipation, 47
    for cystitis, 226
    for diarrhea, 58
    for flu, 40–41
    for gout, 93
    for hair problems, 95
    for headaches, 106
    for heart problems, 111
    for high blood pressure, 119
    for hoarseness/laryngitis, 44
    for impotence, 219
    for indigestion, 124
    as mosquito repellent, 8
    for plantar warts, 193
    for poison ivy, 147

for premenstrual relief, 230
for psoriasis, 142
for pyorrhea, 181
for ringworm, 145
for sciatica, 24
for sinus problems, 152
for tinnitus, 68
for toothache, 180
Gas, 125–126
Gem therapy
    amber, 43, 140
    amethyst, 63, 132
    diamonds for insomnia, 162
    jade for kidney problems, 190
    topaz for colds and flu, 40
    turquoise for sexual problems, 152
Genital herpes, 114–115
Genital itching, 144
Genital warts, 192
Geranium
    as mosquito repellent, 8
    for shingles, 116
    for wounds, 156
Gin for menstrual cramps, 228–229
Gin-soaked raisins, 13–14
Ginger, 270–274
    as anti-inflammatory, 271
Ginger remedies
    for arthritis, 16
    in bringing on menstruation, 228
    for carpal tunnel syndrome, 34
    for colds and flu, 39–40
    for coughs, 49
    for diarrhea, 57
    for earaches, 64
    for flatulence, 126
    for hair problems, 96
    for hangovers, 61
    for heart problems, 112
    for indigestion, 122
    for insomnia, 162
    for memory problems, 131
    for motion sickness, 138–139
    for muscle aches, 133
    for sprains, 171
Ginseng as aphrodisiac, 150
Glaucoma, 75–76
Glutamine for hangovers, 62
Goldenseal
    for colds and flu, 38–39
    for high blood pressure, 120
Gomasio
    for headache, 104

for heartburn, 127
for seasickness, 139
Gout, 10, 92–93
Grapefruit/grapefruit juice
    for dry elbows and knees, 158
    as energy booster, 83
    for insomnia, 162
    for muscle aches, 133
    reaction with medications, 47
    for swimmer's ear, 66
Grapes/grape juice
    for arthritis, 14
    as energy booster, 83
    as fever reducer, 42
    as source of iron, 5
Grooming, 239–240
Gum problems, 181–182
Gum remover, 100

H
Hair. *See* Hair problems
Hair dryer for migraine headaches, 107–108
Hair problems
    dandruff, 95–96
    dry hair, 96
    frizziness, 96
    gray hair, preventing, from yellowing, 100
    green tinge from chlorine, 98
    natural coloring, 99–100
    promoting growth, 94–95
    revitalizers for, 97–98
    setting lotions, 100
    stopping loss, 94–95
Hair spray remover, 100
Halitosis, 122, 183–185
Hand problems, 101–102. *See also* Fingernails
Hangovers, 60–62
Hawthorn
    for heart problems, 111
    for vein health, 90
Hay fever, 3–4. *See also* Allergies; Asthma
Hazelnuts, 276, 278
Headaches, 103–109
    lemon rind to relieve, 106
    sinus, 153
Head lice in children, 211–212
Hearing loss, 68
Heart, sex and, 221
Heart attack, 109

Heartburn, 127–128
Heart helpers, 110–112
Heart palpitations, 110
Heating pad, for tinnitus, 67
Heat rash, 145
Hemorrhoids, 112–114
Herbal bath, 250
Herbal tea, 250–251
Herbs, storage of, 290
Herpes, 114–116
Hiccups, 116–118
High blood pressure. *See* Hypertension
Hives, 143–144
Hoarseness, 44–45
Hobo spider, 9
Holidays, weight loss during, 201–202
Homeopathic eye drops, 71–72
Homeopathic theory, 60
Honey
    for acne, 154, 155
    allergies to, 4, 49
    for arthritis, 13
    for asthma, 19
    for athlete's foot, 87
    bad breath and, 183–184
    in beauty mask, 236
    for boils, 157
    for burns, 30
    for cold sores, 115
    for colds and flu, 37–38
    for coughs, 49, 50
    for cuts, 158–159
    for diarrhea, 58
    for drinking problems, 60
    for dry mouth, 177–178
    for emphysema, 69
    in hair restoration, 95
    for hangovers, 61
    for headaches, 106, 107
    for heart problems, 110
    for heartburn, 127
    for hoarseness/laryngitis, 44
    for indigestion, 123
    for insect stings, 7
    for insomnia, 162
    for leg cramps, 135
    for low sex drive, 226
    for migraine headaches, 107
    as mood lifter, 54–55
    for rough hands, 101
    for sinus problems, 152–153
    for sore throats, 43

    for weeping sores, 156
    for wrinkles, 160
Honeycomb for managing allergies
    and hay fever, 4
Hop pillow
    for insomnia, 162
    for tension and anxiety, 175
Horehound for weight control, 196
Horse chestnut remedies
    for phlebitis, 90
    for varicose veins, 89
Horseradish remedies
    for acne, 153
    for arthritis, 12
    for asthma, 19
    for coughs, 49
    as diuretic, 189
    for insect stings, 6
    for sciatica, 24
    for sinus problems, 152
    for sore throats, 43
    for toothache, 179
Horsetail for eye inflammation, 74
Hot water compress for flatulence,
    125
Hypertension, 118–121
    licorice root and, 3
Hypnosis, auto-, for constipation, 47

I
Ice
    for earaches, 65
    for spider bites, 9
    for sprains, 171
    for tooth extractions, 181
Ice packs, 289
    for bruises, 27
    for fainting, 81
Immune system, confessions and, 244
Impotence, 218–222
Incontinence, 189–190
Indigestion, 122–125
    bad breath and, 183
    belching and, 126
    in children, 212
    gas/flatulence and, 125–126
    heartburn and, 127–128
    stomach cramps and, 128
Ingrown toenails, 87–88
Insect repellents, natural, 291–292
Insect stings, 6–8
Insomnia, 161–165
    onion chunks for, 162

Intoxication prevention, 62–63
Iron, 5
    barley as source of, 249
Iron-deficiency anemia, 5

J
Jade for kidney problems, 190
Jerusalem artichokes
    for asthma, 18
    in insulin production, 56
Jet lag, 129–130
Jogger's leg cramps, 136
Jungle Punch for brain fog, 131

K
Kegel exercises, 149, 225
Kelp in boosting metabolism, 200
Kidney problems, 190–191
    licorice root and, 3
Kidney stones, 190–191, 229
Kiwi, to lower cholesterol, 21
Knees, dry, 158
Kosher salt
    for arthritis, 13
    in body scrub, 239
    in dry shampoo, 97
    for sore throats, 42–43

L
Lactic acid in yogurt, 281
Lactobacillus acidophilus, 185, 281,
    282
Lactose in yogurt, digestibility of, 281
Lactucarium in lettuce, as sleep
    inducer, 163
Lanolin in sheep's wool, 102
Laryngitis, 44–45
Laughter for weight loss, 198
Lavender oil for weeping sores, 156
Laxatives. *See* Constipation
Lecithin
    for acne, 154
    cholesterol, to lower, 21
    for colds and flu, 40
    for phlebitis, 90
    for prostate enlargement, 218
    for seborrhea, 146
    for ulcers, 187
    in weight management, 197
Leek remedies
    as diuretic, 189
    iron in, 5
    for sprains, 172
Leg cramps, 134–136

Legumes, 277
Lemon/honey/water fast, as blood
    fortifier, 5
Lemon remedies
    for aching feet, 84
    for bad breath, 184–185
    for blackheads, 155
    in body scrub, 239
    for boils, 157, 157–158
    for charley horse, 133
    for colds and flu, 37
    for constipation, 46
    for corns and calluses, 85
    for coughs, 49
    for cuts, 159
    for dandruff, 95
    for dry elbows and knees, 158
    for eye irritants, 73
    for finger sores, 103
    for freckles, 158
    for gallbladder problems, 92
    for hair coloring, 99
    for headaches, 106
    for heartburn, 127
    for hiccups, 118
    for insect stings, 7
    for itching, 143
    for kidney stones, 190–191
    for mosquito bites, 7
    for motion sickness, 138
    for paper cuts, 159
    for poison ivy, 147
    for rough hands, 101
    for sinus congestion, 152
    in skin toner, 236–237
    for stiff neck, 134
    for warts, 192
    for wounds, 156
Lentils for breast feeding, 230
Lesions, 156
Lettuce, 290
    for insomnia, 163
    for nightmares, 166
Lice in children, 211–212
Licorice
    as antiallergen, 3
    for asthma, 17
    for coughs, 50
    for lack of sexual interest,
        226–227
    for menopause, 232
Lignans, 263, 264
Lip line, prevention of, 161

Lips, chapped, 239
Liver spots, 28
Low blood pressure, 121
Lysine for herpes, 114–115

M
Macaroons, coconut, for diarrhea,
    58–59
Magnesium, 281
    for asthma, 18
    leg cramps and, 134
    nervous tics and, 55
Magnolia-bark tea in stopping
    smoking, 169
Makeup removers for different skin
    types, 237–238
Manicure, protecting, 240
Marjoram/marjoram tea
    for nervous stomach, 123
    for seasickness, 139
    in stopping smoking, 169
Massage
    in bringing on menstruation,
        227–228
    for indigestion, 123
    for prostate enlargement, 217,
        218
Mayonnaise for hair problems,
    96
Melanin in infants' skin,
    172–173
Memory problems, 131–133
Men
    healing remedies for, 217–222
    sexual problems in, 218–222,
        148–152
Menopause, 231–232
    flaxseed for, 263
Menstruation, 227–230
Metabolism, boosting, 200–201
Migraine headaches, 107–109
Milk. *See also* Buttermilk; Coconut
    milk
        and asthma, 17
        for boils, 157
        colic and, 212–213
        diarrhea and, 57
        for dry skin, 237–238
        for eye irritants, 73
        goat's, for insomnia, 163
        for oily skin, 237
        for poison ivy, 147
        for sunburns, 173
        and ulcers, 186

Mint
    for headaches, 104
    for impotence, 219
Mirror, shaving cream in cleaning,
    240
Moisturizers
    for combination skin, 238–239
    for rough hands, 101–102
Mold, 290
Monounsaturated fatty acids, 20, 22,
    47, 277
Mood lifters, 53–54
Morning sickness, 230
Mosquito bites, 7–8
Motion sickness, 138–139
Mouthwash, making own, 184, 185
Mud
    for insect stings, 6–7
    for poison ivy, 147
Muscle aches
    charley horse, 133
    leg cramps, 134–136
    neck tension, 133–134
    stiff neck, 134
    whiplash, 134
Mustard seed remedies
    for flatulence, 125
    for indigestion, 124
    for memory problems, 132
Myrrh
    for gum problems, 181
    for halitosis, 184

N
Napping, 244
Nausea and vomiting, 137–139
Neck tension, 133–134
Nervous cough, 52
Nervous stomach, 123
Nervous tics, 55
Neuralgia, 139–140
Niacin. *See* Vitamin B$_3$ (niacin)
Nicotine nails, 103
Night cream, enriched, 239
Nightmares, 165–166
Nightshade foods, 10, 12
Nighttime cough, 51–52
Night vision, 76
Nipples, cracked and/or sore,
    231
Norepinephrine, 53
Nosebleeds, 140–141
Numb toes, 88

Nutmeg
    for acne scars, 155
    for insomnia, 161
    for neutralizing alcohol, 59
Nutrients, absorption of, 288–289
Nuts, 274–280

O

Oats/oatmeal
    for acne, 153–154
    cholesterol and, 22
    for coughs, 50
    as hand cleanser, 101
    for heartburn, 127
    for indigestion, 122, 125, 126
    for poison ivy, 147
    for pruritis, 143
    for sexual problems, 151–152
    for splinter removal, 159
    in wrinkle prevention, 160–161
Oily skin, 237
Okra, for constipation, 48
Olive oil
    for acne, 153
    for back pain, 24
    in body scrub, 239
    for burnt throat, 31
    for calluses, 85
    for cholesterol reduction, 22
    constipation and, 47
    for coughs, 48
    for earaches, 64
    for ear infections, 65
    for eye irritants, 73
    for frostbite, 91
    for hair problems, 94, 95, 97
    for hearing loss, 68
    for indigestion, 124
    for jellyfish stings, 7
    for rough hands, 101
    for scars, 159
    for sciatica, 24
    for sun-abused skin, 174
    for swimmer's ear, 66
    for teething, 214
    for ulcers, 186
    for warts, 192
    for weak fingernails, 102
    for wrinkles, 160
Omega-3 fatty acids
    artificial tears and, 72
    attention deficit/hyperactivity
        disorder and, 208

cholesterol and, 22
flaxseed and, 262–266
for heart problems, 111
hypertension and, 119
Omega-6 fatty acids, flaxseed and,
    264–265
Onion breath, 184–185
Onion remedies, 251
    for acne, 154
    for asthma, 19
    for athlete's foot, 87
    for brown spots, 27–28
    for bruises, 27
    for burns, 29
    for colds and flu, 40
    for corns and calluses, 85
    for coughs, 49
    for diarrhea, 57
    as diuretic, 187
    for dysentery, 59
    for earaches, 65
    for eye irritants, 73
    for fever, 41–42
    for flatulence, 125
    for hair loss, 95
    in hair restoration, 95
    for heart problems, 112
    for insect stings, 7
    for insomnia, 162, 165
    iron in, 5
    for itching, 143
    for laryngitis, 44
    for migraine headaches, 107
    as mood lifter, 53–54
    for nausea and vomiting, 137
    for nervousness, 175
    odor on hands, 291
    for pimples, 154
    for prostate enlargement, 218
    for pruritis, 143
    for sinus headaches, 153
    for splinter removal, 159
    for stomach cramps, 128
    for stress, 54–55
    for tension and anxiety, 175
    for toothache, 180
    for urinary problems, 187
    for warts, 192
    working with, tearlessly, 291
Optimism, 12–13, 287
Orange remedies
    for colds and flu, 39

for indigestion, 124
for muscle aches, 133
to quit smoking, 168
for sprains, 171
Orange-spice pomander, 251
Oregano
    depression and, 53
    for nervous stomach, 123
Osteoporosis, 281

P

Pain-free bandage remover, 240
Papaya remedies
    in beauty mask, 236
    for black eyes, 29
    for carpal tunnel syndrome, 34
    for combination skin, 238
    for corns and calluses, 86
    for dead skin, 155
    for heartburn, 127
    for hemorrhoids, 114
    for indigestion, 123–124
    for weeping sores, 156
Paper cuts, 159
Parsley/parsley water
    for arthritis, 11
    beta-carotene and vitamin C in,
        290
    for bruises, 27
    for colds and flu, 39
    as diuretic, 189
    for hair problems, 97
    for halitosis, 184
    as mosquito repellent, 8
    for prostate enlargement, 218
    for sciatica, 24
    for sinus problems, 152
    for sties, 76
    for stomach cramps, 128
    for urinary problems, 187
Passion fruit for sexual problems, 151
Peaches
    as blood fortifier, 5
    nausea and, 213
Peanut butter for preventing
    intoxication, 63
Peanut oil, 22
    for arthritis, 12
Peanuts, 277
    in preventing tooth decay, 182
Pearl barley, 249
Pecans, 275, 276

Peppermint tea
　for breast feeding, 230
　for depression, 55
　for flatulence, 125
　for gallbladder problems, 92
　for heart attack/palpitations, 109,
　　110
　for hoarseness/laryngitis, 44
　for indigestion, 123
　for motion sickness, 138
　for premenstrual relief, 229
Persimmon remedies
　for constipation, 47
　for hangovers, 61
Pesticides, removing, from produce,
　198, 290–291
Petroleum jelly, for combination skin,
　238–239
Phlebitis, 89–90
Phytochemicals, 276
Picky eaters, children as, 213
Pigeon toes, 88
Pills, secrets to taking, 288–289
Pineapple remedies
　in beauty mask, 236
　for black eyes, 29
　for corns and calluses, 86
　in preparing for dental work, 180
　for sore throats, 42
Pinkeye, 71
Pistachios, 277
Plantar warts, 193
Plaque remover, 183
Plums for motion sickness, 139
Poison ivy, 146–147
Pollen, 3, 258–262
Pomanders, 251
Portuguese man-of-war bite, 7
Potassium, 198, 275, 281
　leg cramps and, 134
Potato remedies, 251–252
　for arthritis, 12
　for black eyes, 29
　for burning feet, 31
　for burns, 30
　for conjunctivitis, 71
　for eczema, 142
　for eyestrain, 75
　for freckles, 158
　for frostbite, 91
　for headaches, 105
　for heartburn, 127

　for high blood pressure, 120
　for indigestion, 122
　for insect stings, 6
　for sciatica, 24
　for warts, 192
Poultices, 252
　apple, 173
　for black eyes, 29
　blackstrap molasses, 193
　for boils, 157
　cabbage, 159
　carrot, 44, 156
　chamomile, 65
　comfrey, 90, 172
　for corns and calluses, 85–86
　for earaches, 65
　for eye inflammation, 74
　garlic, 157
　for headaches, 105, 107, 153
　honey, 156
　horseradish, 153, 179
　for infections, 156, 157
　kosher salt, 13, 42–43
　onion, 107, 153, 175
　for phlebitis, 90
　potato, 29, 74, 105
　sauerkraut, 30
　for sores, 156
　for sore throats, 44
　for splinters, 159
　for sprains and strains, 172
　for sunburn, 173
　for tension, 175
　for toothache, 179
　vinegar, 85–86
　for warts, 193
　yogurt, 71
Pregnancy, 230–231
Premature ejaculation, 221
Premenstrual relief, 229–230
Prescription reading, 288
Prostate cancer, zinc and, 26
Prostate enlargement, 217–218
Prune remedies
　for constipation, 46, 48
　for memory problems, 131
Pruritis, 143–144
Psoriasis, 142–143
Pumpkin
　as blood fortifier, 5
　for boils, 157
　for burns, 30

Pumpkin seeds
　for rectal itching, 144
　for urinary problems, 188
Pyorrhea, 181

Q
Quinine for leg cramps, 135

R
Radish remedies
　for hoarseness/laryngitis, 44
　for indigestion, 123
　iron in, 5
Raisins
　gin-soaked for arthritis, 13–14
　for hoarseness/laryngitis, 44
　in managing anemia, 5
Rashes, 142–147
　in children, 213
Raspberries/raspberry tea
　for diarrhea, 57, 210–211
　for labor and delivery, 230
　for leg cramps, 135
　for weight control, 195
Rectal itching, 144
Red clover, in stopping smoking,
　169
Red eyes, 69, 79, 80
Red wine, for heart problems, 111
Reflexology, 61, 64, 98, 134
Retinal damage, sun blindness and,
　77
Rheumatism, 10
Riboflavin. *See* Vitamin B$_2$
Rice
　brown, for acne, 154
　for diarrhea, 58
Ringworm, 145
Rocking chair, therapeutic value of,
　135
Rope burns, 31
Rosemary
　in cellulite elimination, 200
　for eyestrain, 75
　for hair problems, 97
　for headaches, 104
　in pain relief, 14
Rose petals
　for arthritis, 12–13
　as eye strengthener, 77–78
　for the heart, 112
Rum for pruritis, 144
Runny ear infection, 65–66

Rutabaga for coughs, 49
Rutin
    for atherosclerosis, 20

S

Saffron tea, as mood lifter, 54
Sage/sage tea
    for body odor, 26
    for depression, 55
    for frostbite, 91
    for hair problems, 97, 98
    for insomnia, 162
    for memory problems, 131
    in pain relief, 14
    for toothache, 179
Salad for weight loss, 197
Saliva, heartburn and, 127
Salt. *See also* Epsom salts; Kosher salt
    for black eyes, 29
    eye puffiness and, 74
    for insect stings, 6
    in managing snake bites, 9
Salt substitutes, 291
Sandalwood oil for sexual problems, 151
Sandbaths for arthritis, 15
Saponins, 50, 276
Sarsaparilla root
    for menopause, 232
    for psoriasis, 142–143
    for sexual problems, 148–149
Sauerkraut, 252–253
    for burns, 30
    for canker sores, 185
    for constipation, 46
    for diarrhea, 58
    for flu, 41
    in fortifying blood, 5
    for hangovers, 62
    preparing own, 252–253
    for sciatica, 24
Scars, 155, 159
    honey and nutmeg for, 155
Sciatica, 24–25
Scotch barley, 249
Scrapes, 158–159
Sea salt for psoriasis, 142
Seasickness, 139
Seborrhea, 145–146
Selenium, 275
Serotonin in bananas, for depression, 53

Sesame remedies
    for arthritis, 16
    for hair problems, 95, 98–99
    for menstrual irregularities, 229
    for stretch marks, 159
Setting lotions, 100
Sexual problems, 148–152
Sexual vitality, bee pollen for, 259
Shaving cream for cleaning mirror, 240
Shaving rash, 145
Shingles, 115–116
Silva method for insomnia, 162
Sinus headaches, 153
Sinusitis, 152–153
Sitz bath for prostate pain, 218
Skin care, 235–239. *See also* Skin problems
        bee pollen for, 259
        paint remover for, 240
        for sun-abused skin, 174
Skin discoloration, 27–29
Skin problems
    acne, 154–155
    blackheads, 155
    boils, 156–158
    cuts and scrapes as, 158–159
    dead skin and enlarged pores, 155
    dry elbow and knees, 158
    freckles, 158
    scars, 155, 159
    splinters as, 159
    stretch marks, 159
    wounds and sores, 156
    wrinkles, 160–161
Skin type, identifying, 235
Skunk spray, 9
Sleep apnea, 166–167
Sleeping
    with carpal tunnel syndrome, 32
    problems with, 161–167
Sleepwalking, 166
Slippery-elm for prostate enlargement, 218
Smell, use of, to lose weight, 202
Smoker's cough, 51
Smoking, 166–171. *See also* Tobacco
Snacks, healthy, 198–199
Snake bites, 8–9
Snoring, 166–167
Soda, appetite and, 201

Sores, 156
    canker, 185
    finger, 103
Sore throats, 42–44
Soup for weight loss, 197
Sour cream for sunburn, 173
Spices, storage of, 290
Spider bites, 9
Spinach
    for anemia, 5
    for constipation, 47
Spirulina for weight control, 196
Splinters, 159
    in children, 213
Sprains and strains, 171–172
Squash as blood fortifier, 5
Stage fright, 177–178
Stained nails, 102
Steak for black eyes, 28
Sties, 76–77
Stings, insect, 6–7
St. John's wort for shingles, 115
Stomach cramps, 128
Stool softeners, 48
Strawberry remedies
    for acne, 154
    for cleaning teeth and gums, 182
    for depression, 55
    for gout, 93
    for hangovers, 62
    for headaches, 106
    for kidney stones, 190
    in skin toner, 236–237
Strep throat, 45
Stress. *See* Depression and stress
Stretch marks, 159
Sugar for hiccups, 117–118
Sun blindness, 77
Sunburn, 172–174
Sunchokes, 18, 56
Sunflower remedies
    for asthma, 18
    cholesterol, to lower, 21–22
    for colds and flu, 38
    for constipation, 46
    for coughs, 50
    for eyestrain, 74
    as eye strengthener, 78
    in inhibiting tooth decay, 182
    for memory problems, 132
    in stopping smoking, 170

Sunscreen, use of, on infants, 172–173
Superfoods
  bee pollen, 258–262
  flaxseed, 262–266
  garlic, 266–270
  ginger, 270–274
  nuts, 274–280
  yogurt, 280–284
Sweaty feet, 88
Sweet potatoes, 198
Sweet substitutes, 291
Swimmer's ear, 66
Systolic pressure, 119

T
Tangerine juice for belching, 126
Tartar remover, 183
Tea bags
  for corns and calluses, 86
  for eye inflammation, 74
  for sties, 77
  for sunburn, 173
  for tooth extractions, 180
Teas. *See* specific type of tea
Teething in children, 214
Teeth whitener, 183
Tennis elbow, 172
Tension and anxiety, 175–178
Tension headaches, 103–107
Testicles, touching, 148
Testosterone, 149
Thiamine. *See* Vitamin B$_1$
Thyme
  for excessive menstrual flow, 228
  for nightmares, 166
  for pruritis, 143
Tick bites, 9
Tinnitus, 67–68
Tobacco. *See also* Smoking
  for hemorrhoids, 113
  for insect stings, 7
  for snake bites, 8
  for wounds, 156
Toenails, ingrown, 87–88
Tofu for poison ivy, 147
Tomatoes/tomato juice
  for skunk spray, 9
  for splinter removal, 159
Tongue
  burnt, 31
  scraping, 184

Tonsillitis, 45
  in children, 214
Tonsils, removal of, 45
Toothache, 178–180
Toothbrush
  cleaning, 183
  throwing away, 183
Tooth extractions, 180–181
Toothpaste for insect stings, 6
Tooth problems, 178–185
Tryptophan for insomnia, 165
Turmeric in preventing heartburn, 128
Turnip greens and anticlotting drugs, 111
Turnip remedies
  for aching feet, 85
  for body odor, 25
  for bruises, 27
  for coughs, 50
Tweezing, pain-free, 240
Tyramine for asthma, 17

U
Ulcers, 186–187
  and garlic, 5
Undereye circles, 28
Uric acid
  gout and, 92
  neutralizing, 11
Urinary problems, 187–191
Urticaria, 143
US Army, research on allergies, 4

V
Vaginitis, 227
Valerian root, 176
Valium, 176
Varicose veins, 88–90
  rocking chair to prevent, 135
Vegetable juices
  for arthritis, 16
  for asthma, 17
  depression and, 53
  for enlarged prostate, 218
Vinegar, white. *See also* Apple cider vinegar
  for athlete's foot, 87
  for brown spots, 28
  for corns and calluses, 85–86
  for coughs, 49
  for headaches, 106

for hives, 144
for insect stings, 7
for nosebleeds, 141
for pimples, 154
for poison ivy, 146
prior to polishing nails, 240
for sore throats, 43
for swimmer's ear, 66
for toothache, 179–180
Visualization, 245
  for asthma, 18
  for tension and anxiety, 177
Vitamin A, 6, 289
  kidney stones and, 191
Vitamin B$_1$ (thiamine), 6, 21, 275
  barley as source of, 249
  as mosquito repellent, 8
  for sciatica, 24
  for toothache, 180
Vitamin B$_2$ (riboflavin), 6, 21, 275, 281
  in bloodshot eyes, 69
  deficiency in, as cause of cataracts, 70
  in glaucoma, 75–76
Vitamin B$_3$ (niacin), 21, 275
Vitamin B$_6$
  for carpal tunnel syndrome, 32
  for leg cramps, 135
  nervous tics and, 55
  for numb toes, 88
  in sauerkraut, 252
Vitamin B$_{12}$, 281
Vitamin C, 6, 289
  for atherosclerosis, 20
  for bleeding gums, 182
  to burn fat, 201
  cataracts, to prevent, 70
  cholesterol and, 21
  for headaches, 105
  for heat rash, 145
  for hemorrhoids, 113–114
  in night cream, 239
  in preventing nosebleed, 141
  for pruritis, 143
  rutin and, 20
  smoking and, 168
  for spider bites, 9
  for sunburned eyes, 173
Vitamin D, 289
Vitamin E, 275, 289
  for brown spots, 28

for burns, 29
for healthy heart, 111
for leg cramps, 134
in night cream, 239
for shaving rash, 145
for warts, 192
Vitamin K
anticlotting medications and, 111
in preventing nosebleed, 141
Vitamins, retention of, by
microwaving, 290
Vomiting. *See* Nausea and vomiting

W
Walking
for heart problems, 110–111
for hemorrhoids, 114
for memory problems, 132
varicose veins and, 89
for weight loss, 201
Walnuts, 275, 276, 277
for cold sores, 115
Warts, 193–194
Water
for hiccups, 116–117
for stomach cramps, 128
weight control and, 201
Watercress remedies
as antiallergen, 3
as diuretic, 189
iron in, 5
for night vision, 76
for sciatica, 24
Watermelon remedies
as diuretic, 189
for heat rash, 145
for high blood pressure, 120
for rashes in children, 213
Wax and pesticides, removing, from
produce, 198
Weak ankles, 90
Weeping sores, 156
Weight control
Body Mass Index (BMI), 202, 203
calories burned per hour, 199

cellulite, 200
healthy snacks, 198–199
herbs for, 194–196
holiday challenges, 201
hot-pepper sauce for, 200
metabolism, raising, 200–201
mustard for, 200
slimming remedies, 196–198
smell, using, to lose weight, 202
tips for, 194–203
vitamin C for, 201
water or soda, 201
yoga for, 199–200
Wheat germ/wheat germ oil
for animal bites/stings, 6
for dry, frizzy hair, 96
for heart health, 111
for rectal itching, 144
Wheat grass for body odor, 26
Whey, 282
Whiplash, 134
White wine for indigestion, 124
Whitlows, 103
Wild cherry-bark tea. *See* Cherry-
bark tea for asthma
Willow bark for carpal tunnel
syndrome, 33–34
Witch hazel remedies
for black eyes, 29
for hemorrhoids, 113
for shingles, 116
for varicose veins, 89
Women's health
bladder control, 225
carpal tunnel syndrome, 33
cystitis, 225–226
heart attack risk, 111
intoxication, 63
menopause, 231–232
menstruation, 227–230
pregnancy, 230–231
vaginitis, 227
Wounds, 156. *See also* Bites and stings
healing of, 245

Wrinkles, 160–161
prevention of, 259

Y
Yams, 198
Yarrow/yarrow tea
for chicken pox, 209
for excessive menstrual flow, 228
for hair problems, 97
for nausea and vomiting, 137
for oily skin, 237
Yawning, 243
Yellow
for indigestion, 123
for memory problems, 133
stress, contribution to, of, 175
Yellow sac spider, 9
Yerba maté. *See also* Jungle Punch
for memory problems, 131
for weight control, 195
Ylang-ylang oil for sexual problems,
151
Yoga
alternate-nostril breathing in, 176
for hemorrhoids, 114
"lion" exercise in, 239
to slow midlife weight gain,
199–200
Yogurt, 280–284
for canker sores, 185
for diarrhea, 58, 282
frozen, 283
goat milk, 71
for oily skin, 237
in skin toner, 236–237

Z
Zinc, 281
for body odor, 26
for colds and flu, 38, 209
prostate cancer and, 38
Zinc sulfate for fingernail problems,
102
Zucchini for indigestion, 124

Away
from
Home

Anita Lobel

Away
from
Home

Greenwillow Books ▣ *New York*

Watercolor and gouache paints were used for
the full-color art. The text type is Leawood.
Copyright © 1994 by Anita Lobel
All rights reserved. No part of this book may
be reproduced or utilized in any form or by
any means, electronic or mechanical, including
photocopying, recording, or by any information
storage and retrieval system, without permission
in writing from the Publisher, Greenwillow Books,
a division of William Morrow & Company, Inc.,
1350 Avenue of the Americas, New York, NY 10019.
Printed in Singapore by Tien Wah Press
First Edition 10 9 8 7 6 5 4 3 2 1

Library of Congress Cataloging-in-Publication Data

Lobel, Anita.
Away from home / by Anita Lobel.
  p.   cm.
Summary: Proceeds through the alphabet
using boys' names and the names of exotic
places in alliterative fashion.
ISBN 0-688-10354-5 (trade).
ISBN 0-688-10355-3 (lib. bdg.)
[1. Travel—Fiction.   2. Alphabet.]
I. Title.   PZ7.L7794Aw   1994   [E]—dc20
93-36521   CIP   AC

With love for Adam,
who likes nothing better than to be at home with his family

Adam arrived in Amsterdam.

Bernard ballooned in Barcelona.

Craig crawled in Cracow.

David danced in Detroit.

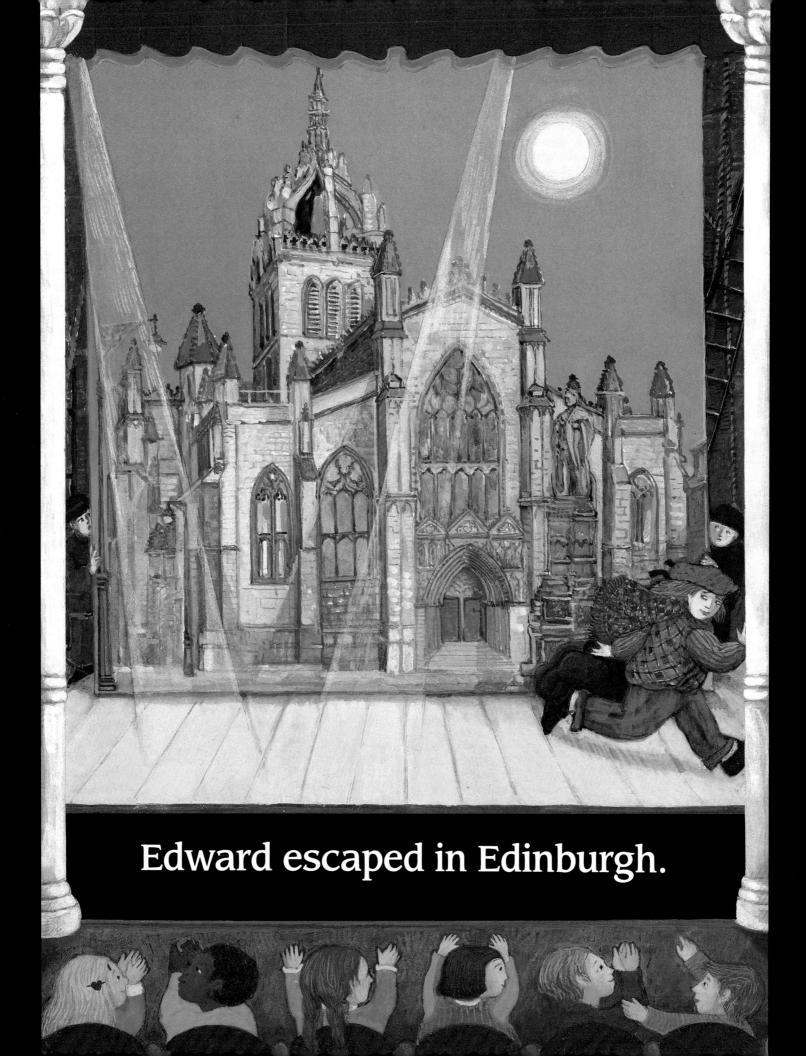

Edward escaped in Edinburgh.

Frederick fiddled in Florence.

Garrett gazed in Giza.

Henry hoped in Hollywood.

Isaac idled in Innsbruck.

John juggled in Jerusalem.

Kevin knelt in Kyoto.

Lloyd limped in London.

Michael moped in Moscow.

Nathan nibbled in New York.

Oliver oscillated in Odense.

Paul painted in Paris.

Quincy quivered in Quebec.

Richard rolled in Rio.

Shaun sailed in Stockholm.

Thomas trumpeted in Tulsa.

Upton unpacked in Uxmal.

Vincent vacationed in Venice.

William waited in Washington.

Xavier xylophoned in Xian.

Yale yawned in Yakutsk.

Zachary zigzagged in Zaandam.

WHERE THEY WENT

AMSTERDAM is a city in the Netherlands famous for its canals, art treasures, and houses that look like these.

BARCELONA is an elegant city in Spain. These towers crown the Templo de la Sagrada Familia, a cathedral designed by Antonio Gaudi.

CRACOW is the city in Poland where I was born. This is its central square.

DETROIT, Michigan, U.S.A., is the home of motor cars and Motown music. These are the buildings of its new Renaissance Center.

EDINBURGH is the capital of Scotland. This is the Cathedral of Saint Giles.

FLORENCE, Italy, is known for its art and architecture. This building, called the Baptistery, was built in the eleventh century.

GIZA is in Egypt. These ancient pyramids stand in the desert nearby.

HOLLYWOOD, California, U.S.A., is famous for its motion picture industry. Many actors come here hoping to be movie stars.

INNSBRUCK, Austria, has colorful houses along the Inn River. People from all over the world come to ski in the tall mountains nearby.

JERUSALEM is an ancient and holy city in Israel. This is the section known as the Old City.

KYOTO was once the capital of Japan. It has many temples and palaces like these.

LONDON is the capital of England. This is the Tower Bridge, which crosses the Thames River near the Tower of London.

MOSCOW is the capital of Russia. The great Cathedral of Saint Basil stands in Red Square.

NEW YORK, New York, U.S.A., is celebrated for many things, among them the Statue of Liberty and hot dogs from Nathan's Famous.

ODENSE, Denmark, is the birthplace of Hans Christian Andersen. This is the house in which he lived.

PARIS, the capital of France, has always been the home of celebrated authors and artists. This is the Cathedral of Notre Dame, one of the most famous churches in the world.

QUEBEC is the capital of the French-speaking Canadian province of the same name. This hotel, the Chateau Frontenac, stands on a hill above the St. Lawrence River.

RIO DE JANEIRO in Brazil is famous for this 120-foot-high statue of Christ the Redeemer, which looks down on the city from Corcovado Mountain.

STOCKHOLM, the capital of Sweden, is a city built on water. This is the City Hall.

TULSA, Oklahoma, where this statue of an oilman stands, is a center of the oil industry in the United States.

UXMAL, Mexico, is the site of this ruined temple that was built by the Mayas more than 1,000 years ago.

VENICE, Italy, is known for its canals, gondolas, art, and architecture. This church, the San Giorgio Maggiore, was designed by Palladio in the sixteenth century.

WASHINGTON, D.C., is the capital of the United States. This is the statue of Abraham Lincoln in the Lincoln Memorial.

XIAN is the city in China where more than 8,000 life-size soldiers made of clay were buried 2,000 years ago. They were not discovered until 1974.

YAKUTSK, Russia, lies in the cold, snowy region of Siberia. This log tower is part of an old fort.

ZAANDAM is a small city in the Netherlands. This modern building is an art gallery designed by Aldo Rossi.

HAPPY ABC JOURNEY TO ALL!

Anita Lobel 1994